The ART *of* SEEING

THIRD EDITION

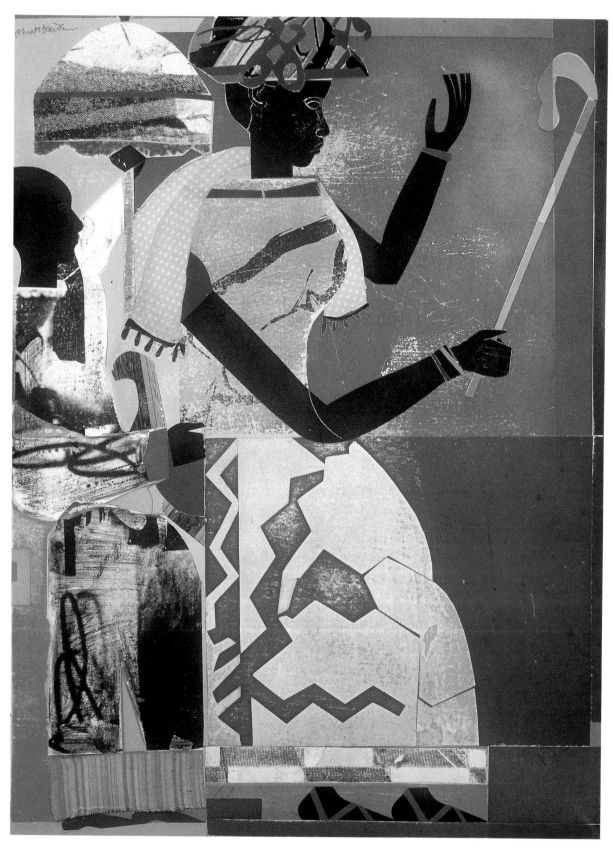

Romare Bearden, *She-Ba*, 1970. Collage on composition board, 48 × 36 ins (122 × 91 cm).
Wadsworth Atheneum, Hartford. The Ella Gallup Summer and Mary Caitlin Summer Collection.

The ART *of* SEEING
THIRD EDITION

PAUL ZELANSKI
University of Connecticut

MARY PAT FISHER

Prentice Hall Inc., Upper Saddle River, N.J. 07458

Prentice Hall, Inc.
A Division of Simon & Schuster
Upper Saddle River, NJ 07458

10 9 8 7 6 5 4 3 2

ISBN 0-13-059916-6

This book was designed and produced by
CALMANN & KING LTD, LONDON

Designer: Karen Osborne
Picture researcher (3rd edition): Donna Thynne
Maps: Eugene Fleury
Typeset by Fakenham Photosetting Ltd, Norfolk
Printed in Hong Kong

Cover: (*front*) Pablo Picasso, *Portrait of Marie-Thérèse Walter,* 1937.
Oil on canvas, 39¼ x 33¾ ins (100 x 86 cm).
Musée Picasso, Paris. Photo RMN.
© DACS 1993.

(*back*) Roy Lichtenstein, *Big Painting No. 6,* 1965.
Collection of Robert Scull, New York.
Photo Bridgeman Art Library, London.
© The Equitable Life Assurance Society of the United States/
© Roy Lichtenstein/DACS 1993.

CONTENTS

PART 2
TWO-DIMENSIONAL MEDIA AND METHODS 209

PART 3
THREE-DIMENSIONAL MEDIA AND METHODS 317

CREDITS

The authors, publishers, and Calmann & King Ltd. wish to thank the artists, museums, galleries, collectors, and other owners who have kindly allowed works to be reproduced in this book. In general, museums have supplied their own photographs, other sources, photographers, and copyright holders are listed here.

PREFACE

This third edition constitutes a major revision and expansion of *The Art of Seeing*. We have strengthened those features that already made it very popular and have developed new ways of bringing the reader closer to an informed, awakened appreciation of the art of all cultures and all media. Even more than in previous editions, we present art from the artist's point of view.

Artists' own words about their work are a treasure mine for the student of art appreciation. We have therefore woven many more such statements by artists into the text. In addition, we have created 22 feature boxes in which artists speak at length about some facet of their work that is related to the subject under discussion. Some of these are developed from our personal interviews with these artists, some from historical documents.

To acknowledge major new areas of excitement in the art world, we have greatly increased our illustration and discussion of multicultural art and of art by women. In addition to doing so throughout the text, we have also added to the history chapter new sections on the growing critical appreciation of the richness of such previously ignored sources of art. In the same vein, we have also developed a new section on the "discovery" of outsider art.

Similarly, to help broaden previously Euro-centric Western tastes in art, we have added a new section to Chapter 15, which examines a few works in great detail, incorporating all the forms of appreciation discussed in the book. This new section looks at the use of a craft medium—beadwork—as complex sculpture by a contemporary African-American woman, Joyce Scott, who is also a performance artist. Her observations about how she is working can be applied not only to the understanding of political and emotional statements made in the art of oppressed cultures but also to recognizing the human complexities with which many artists are dealing.

We are also excited to introduce six maps in Chapter 14. These show the regions where major trends in Western art were developed, and indicate key artistic centers and the location of important buildings and monuments. Each of the maps is accompanied by a timeline giving a global historical context to the evolution of Western art.

Throughout the book, coverage of many topics—both traditional and contemporary—has been expanded, including creativity, encaustic, fresco, wood engraving, computer art, graphic design, photography, xerox and FAX art, video art, conceptual art, performance art, earthworks, installation pieces, folk art, and outsider art.

THE NATURE OF THIS BOOK

As before, we have made considerable effort in *The Art of Seeing* to make art come to life. The language we use is vigorous and down-to-earth, with numerous quotations from the artists themselves to help explain, in their own words, what they were trying to do. Unfamiliar words are carefully defined when they are first used and also in an extensive illustrated glossary at the end of the book.

Perhaps even more important than the writing in *The Art of Seeing* is the art. The illustrations for each concept are clearly related to the text and conscientiously described. There are some 605 illustrations, 260 of them in color, and many of these are reproduced at full-page size. They are taken from all the visual arts, from painting and sculpture to clothing and industrial design. Many cultures are represented, as is the work of many women artists. As well as being good reference for the explanations in the text, the illustrations provide a stimulating, exciting visual gallery.

ITS ORGANIZATION

Part 1 of *The Art of Seeing* lays the foundation for truly seeing the aesthetic aspects of a work of art. In the first chapter of Part 1 we develop an initial vocabulary and an intellectual framework for considering artworks: the basic forms of art, the functions of art for the artist and the viewer, and the ways in which art can be appreciated. Chapter 2 is devoted to extensive analysis of the visual elements with which the artist works: line, shapes, form, space, texture, light, color, and time. Chapter 3 covers the subtle organizing principles by which these elements are used in a work of art.

The next two parts of the book approach art through the materials and techniques used by artists. By revealing the difficulties associated with each method, we hope to enhance appreciation of the artists' accomplishments in the face of the intractibilities of their media. Part 2 covers two-dimensional techniques and media: drawing, painting, printmaking, graphic design, photography, photocopy, fax, film, television, video, and computer graphics. Part 3 covers three-dimensional media: sculpture, crafts, industrial design, clothing design, architecture, interior design, environmental design, and the performing arts.

Part 4 approaches art as it exists in time. We first offer a succinct and intelligible approach to historical styles in Western Art. Some 45 major movements, from prehistoric to contemporary, are concisely covered, with an illustrated timeline on pages 416 and 417 as an aid to understanding how the distinctively different aesthetic movements are related in time. In addition, six maps show close-ups of particular periods so that one can see where the major artists of the time were working, in the context of major world events of the time.

The final chapter is a unique in-depth examination of specific works of art, including their evolution in time. It approximates the actual experience of encountering a work of art, drawing on all levels of appreciation developed in the book in order to analyze and respond to five special works: a round stone barn built by a Utopian community, Picasso's *Guernica*, Rodin's *The Gates of Hell*, Michelangelo's *Sistine Chapel ceiling*, and the bead sculpture of Joyce Scott.

ACKNOWLEDGEMENTS

In revising *The Art of Seeing*, we have been helped by many people, including Sal Scalora, Katherine Ferina, Richard Swibold, Peter and Jan Good, The Schomburg Society for the Preservation of Black Culture, the National Museum of African Art, Jamison-Thomas Gallery. We would also like to thank the following reviewers for their helpful comments on the text: Professor Elizabeth C. Nuell of Middle Tennessee State University, Professor Kevin Harris of Northern Kentucky University, Professor Pamela A. Lee of the University of Washington, Professor LeRoy D. McDermott of Central Missouri State University, and Professor Frederick J. Zimmerman of SUNY Cortland. As always, Bud Therien of Prentice Hall, Rosemary Bradley, Melanie White, and Karen Osborne of Calmann and King, and Annette Zelanski have offered great support.

We feel that these improvements will be very helpful to all those who seek an educated, sharpened sense of art appreciation. We ourselves grow in appreciation each time we approach this book.

Paul Zelanski
Mary Pat Fisher

PART

1

LEARNING TO SEE

Art is life intensely experienced. For those with eyes to see, an encounter with a work of art can be deeply satisfying. With training, we can begin to recognize the elements and principles of design which are the artist's aesthetic tools. We may also learn to perceive the artist's intentions for the work.

ART APPRECIATION

Art appreciation is a skill that has to be learned. But it begins with simply looking with full awareness. We usually screen out most of the impressions our senses bring us, to avoid over-stimulation by the complexities of modern life. When we are reading a book, we don't notice the refrigerator humming or cars passing; when we walk through a room, we don't notice most of its furnishings; when we are driving a car, our attention may be so focused on the road and the other cars, or on some problem with which we are struggling, that we are unable to pay attention to the beauty of the sunset. Psychologists call this screening of sensations a DEFENSIVE GRID. Although it is a useful survival tool in our industrialized, cluttered existence, we must learn to abandon it when looking

1.1 Ruth Bernhard, *Bone and Passion Flower*, not dated. Photograph.

at art. If we want to really see a work of art, we must open ourselves to all the sensations it evokes.

To begin this journey into the great richness of the visual arts, take several minutes simply to look at Ruth Bernhard's photograph *Bone and Passion Flower* (**1.1**). Allow it to fill your awareness; explore its textures and forms, and the play of light and shadow. Bernhard herself experiences life intensely. She said in 1979:

> Living is a matter of passion. I feel intensely about every single day. Here I am, seventy-three years old, and still possessed with the curiosity of my childhood. . . . If we are aware that everything around us is constantly changing, then we can't ever become bored or lose our zest for living.[1]

We can participate in Bernhard's rich experience of life and bring to it something of ourselves by exploring what we see and feel in her photograph, if we give it our complete attentiveness and the curiosity we all had as children.

In addition to curiosity, we must be willing to be touched. Art is very difficult to define, and its definitions and varieties are expanding rapidly in contemporary society. But perhaps it is safe to say that something is effective as art if it is a human-created visual experience that touches us. The experience may or may not be pleasant.

While "I like it" and "I don't like it" are basic and valid reactions to any work of art, we can expand our personal tastes by exploring unfamiliar styles and forms of art. Indifference and even hostility may have been our first reaction to something we come to understand and appreciate. Today's communication technologies give us the unprecedented opportunity to expose ourselves to an enormous range of artworks. Art of all times, all places, all disciplines is now available in photographic reproduction as well as in museum shows. In this chapter, we will begin by sampling this diversity while exploring the general forms of art, their functions, and the levels of appreciation that we can cultivate, broadening and deepening the "I like it" reaction.

Our seeing is also informed by our knowledge. Throughout this book, we will be building up a body of knowledge about what specific artists have tried to do, the AESTHETIC and mechanical means they have used to achieve their goals, and their relationship to the historical progression of art movements. In many cases, knowing about the artists as individuals will further enrich our appreciation of their works.

FORMS OF ART

To many Westerners, the word "art" usually suggests paintings hanging in a museum, but of course paintings are just one of the many types of art. The world of art includes three-dimensional as well as two-dimensional pieces; both applied and fine arts; and works not just for public, but also for private display.

TWO- AND THREE-DIMENSIONAL ART

There is a major conventional distinction between two- and three-dimensional artworks. THREE-DIMENSIONAL works have spatial depth as well as height and width. TWO-DIMENSIONAL works, by contrast, are developed on a flat PLANE without depth (though the surface may be somewhat built up with gobs of paint or gesso). Many two-dimensional pieces are nevertheless representations of the three-dimensional world.

1.2 Jan Vermeer, *The Allegory of Painting*, c. 1665–70. Oil on canvas, 3 ft 11¼ ins × 3 ft 3⅜ ins (1.2 × 1 m). Kunsthistorisches Museum, Vienna.

Jan Vermeer makes us very aware of this process in his *The Allegory of Painting* (**1.2**). We see the artist— perhaps Vermeer himself, although this is debatable—observing a three-dimensional model and translating her form into a two-dimensional painting. In this very unusual picture, the apparent drawing aside of a curtain gives us what appears to be an intimate view into this process, looking over the artist's shoulder. We peek into the scene to puzzle over its historical references—such as the painter's courtly costume from the century prior to Vermeer's time, the map of the Netherlands (which carries Vermeer's signature just above the model's shoulders), and the symbols that the model is using to represent Clio, the Greek muse of history. Despite the mystery of what kind of statement is intended, the scene appears to have realistic spatial depth, with the curtain very close to us, the artist somewhat farther, and the model farther still, against the wall. Everything appears to have three-dimensional form.

1.3 Duane Hanson, *Woman with Suitcases*, 1973. Polyester resin and Fiberglas, life size. Courtesy of the artist.

1.4 House Post from the Moon House, Port Mulgrave, Yakutat, c. 1916–17. Wood with red, black, and green pigment and nails. Museum of the American Indian, Heye Foundation, New York.

But all of these effects are illusions, for the painting consists of marks on a flat surface, like the painting being started on the artist's easel.

Since two-dimensional works are often framed and hung on a wall or shown on a television screen or in the pages of a book or magazine, they exist on a plane other than the three-dimensional world of our experience. To assign meaning to them requires a sophisticated act of perception. Not so with three-dimensional works: if nothing else, they are barriers that we have to walk around. They exist in the same three-dimensional space that we ourselves occupy. Duane Hanson's sculptures, such as *Woman with Suitcases* (**1.3**), are often mistaken for, and responded to, as real people. Life-sized Fiberglas and polyester casts of actual human models, dressed in real clothing and equipped with the familiar trappings of our lives, they directly evoke the same kind of response we would have if we encountered their living prototype. In this case, depending on our personality, we may feel empathy for the woman's fatigue, curiosity about her story, depression over her unhappiness, or distaste at her lack of physical beauty. Then there comes the strangely unsettling recognition that the figure is not alive, but is instead a highly realistic work of art.

Within the category of three-dimensional art there are many degrees of three-dimensionality. The flattest works approach two-dimensionality. These are called RELIEFS: works in which an image is developed outward or inward from a two-dimensional ground. Such pieces are often categorized by the degree to which figures project from the background. In a LOW RELIEF (or "bas relief"), figures exist on nearly the same plane as the background, almost as in a drawing, but are sufficiently carved that shadows appear on surfaces where the light is blocked. Coins are familiar examples of low-relief pieces. In the low-relief Moon House post used to support a roof beam by the Kwashkan Tlingit of the north-west coast of North America (**1.4**), the shadows enhance the drama of the piece, drawing attention to the moon and wolf symbols of the family's membership in the wolf clan. Nevertheless, no area is entirely detached from the ground.

Technically, a work is considered a HIGH RELIEF only if at least half of the figures' natural spatial depth projects forward from the background. The fact that far more of the substrate is carved away than in a low relief creates a greater range of light and dark shadows that help to define the forms.

In the sculptured exterior of the Roman sarcophagus, or coffin (**1.5**), some limbs are completely undercut, lifting them away from the background entirely, while other more shallowly

1.5 Sculptured sarcophagus representing Dionysos, the Seasons, and other figures, c. AD 220–30. Marble, 35½ × 87¾ ×36¾ ins (90.2 × 222.9 × 93.3 cm). The Metropolitan Museum of Art, New York. Purchase 1955 Joseph Pulitzer Bequest.

1.6 René Lalique, *Suzanne au Bain*, c. 1925. Opalescent glass, 9¼ ins (23.5 cm) high. Courtesy of the Galerie Moderne Ltd, London

carved figures merge with the background. These variations in depth create a dynamic flow of values (modulations of darks and lights) and of projections toward and recesses from the viewer.

Some relief works, however, are not the result of carving into a block of wood or stone; rather, they are created by attaching materials to a closed backplane so that they project outward. Nevertheless, the basic orientation of a relief of any sort is the association of three-dimensional figures with a backing. Reliefs are principally designed to be seen straight-on; the farther to the side the viewer gets, the less sense the images make. The figures on the left of the sarcophagus in the photograph are hard to grasp because we see them at an extreme angle as the piece curves away from us; those on the right "work" because they are oriented in our direction.

Another form of three-dimensional art that is designed principally to be seen straight-on is called FRONTAL work. Although it is totally freestanding, allowing the viewer to walk all around it or turn it over if it is small, it does not invite viewing from more than one side. Necklaces are typically designed as frontal pieces; the interesting, worked side faces outward, while the back is often minimally worked and not designed to be seen. The decorative glass piece *Suzanne au Bain* (**1.6**) is not meant to be examined from the back or ends; its beauty lies totally in its frontal aspect. As one moves one's head ever so slightly from side to side, the opalescent glass seems to change color along its surface contours depending on the shifting relationship between the light source, the piece, and the angle of one's vision. It was designed in the late nineteenth-century flowing

Art Nouveau style by René Lalique, whose creations included jewelry as well as glassware. We tend to "read" the piece as if it were a piece of jewelry, enjoying the sensual play of forms and colors across the front.

Three-dimensional art in the FULL ROUND is freestanding and designed to be seen from all sides. When a full-round piece is effective, it often makes people want to walk all the way around it or turn it around in their hands to discover how it changes. A common lure artists use is to pique our curiosity to see what happens out of sight. If a leg disappears around a curve in the piece, we are likely to follow it to find the foot.

In the Akua'ba wood figure from the Akan people of Ghana, if we are curious enough to walk around it, we discover that the female image on one side (**1.7**) has a smaller male image behind it (**1.8**). Even though both are conceived rather frontally, it is interesting to look at the piece from the side (**1.9**) to see how they fit

1.7–1.9 Akua'ba figure from Ghana, Africa. Wood, double-figure of seated male and female. National Museum of African Art, Smithsonian Institution.

1.7 Female side.

1.8 Male side.

1.9 Side view.

together, back-to-back on a stool, and thus compare their relative sizes. Most of these pieces, used for fertility and for blessing a pregnancy, have only the female image; the addition of the male figure in this matrilineal society adds intriguing sociological as well as aesthetic puzzles.

The ever-changing quality of three-dimensional works in the full round can only be guessed at in the single two-dimensional photographs used to represent them. To fully appreciate a full-round piece, one must explore the real thing, from as many angles as possible, for each step and each movement of the head reveal new facets and new relationships among the parts of the piece.

An even fuller degree of three-dimensionality occurs in WALK-THROUGH works, which become part of the environment through which we move. Landscape

artists have long planned gardens as walk-through aesthetic experiences for us. A contemporary version of this experience is available to visitors to the Smithsonian Institution's central court, in Elyn Zimmerman's *Marabar* (**1.10**). We are invited to walk among the granite boulders, sensing and perhaps feeling their rough, organic strength and discovering the contrasting extremely smooth textures of the faces of those boulders that Zimmerman has cut and polished. These cut faces can be seen only from certain angles, so to experience the totality of the work we must walk varying paths through it, exploring what can be seen from many points.

All effective three-dimensional work subtly defines a certain area as "belonging" to it and to a certain extent influences our movements within this space. Work that surrounds the viewer—such as

1.10 Elyn Zimmerman, *Marabar*, 1984. Plaza and garden sculpture, National Geographic Society, Washington D.C. Five natural cleft and polished carnelian granite boulders, 36 to 120 ins (91.4 to 305 cm) high, surrounding a pool of polished carnelian granite.

1.11 Philip Johnson and John Burgee, Garden Grove Community Church (Crystal Cathedral), Garden Grove, California, 1980.

architecture—is the final step in this control, not only becoming an encompassing structure that we enter but also perhaps surrounding us with a certain psychological atmosphere. Architects Philip Johnson and John Burgee's Garden Grove Community Church (**1.11**), better known as the Crystal Cathedral, is designed to uplift local worshippers and television viewers with a multi-faceted experience of light, drawn in through myriad panes of reflective glass and re-reflected off shiny interior surfaces. The 128-foot-high (39 m) glass building is the setting for services by television evangelist Dr. Robert Schuller,

designed to emphasize the drama of his presentations with its vastness as well as its glittering lights, dancing fountains, marble pulpit, and energetic traceries of metal trusses holding the 10,900 panes of glass. Nearly 3000 people can be seated within its stretched four-pointed-star form, with the longer dimension reaching 415 feet (127 m) from point to point. Within this immense theatrical setting, one cannot maintain an everyday, humdrum attitude; whether or not one likes the theatrical approach to religion, one is inevitably touched by the drama of the architecture.

FINE AND APPLIED ARTS

Another kind of distinction that can be made among works of art is whether they were originally intended as objects purely to be looked at, or as objects to be used. The FINE ARTS, such as drawing, painting, printmaking, and sculpture, involve the production of works to be seen and experienced primarily on an abstract rather than practical level. Pieces of fine art may evoke emotional, intellectual, sensual, or spiritual responses in us. Those who love the fine arts feel that these responses are very valuable, and perhaps especially so in the midst of a highly materialistic world, for they expand our awareness of the great richness of life itself. The nineteenth-century sculptor Auguste Rodin, whose work *The Gates of Hell* (15.12–15.18) we explore in Chapter 15, offered a passionate challenge to artists—and to those who are touched by their works: "The main thing is to be moved, to love, to hope, to tremble, to live."[2]

Constantin Brancusi's elegant *Bird in Space* (**1.12**) has no utilitarian function whatsoever. It is solely "art for art's sake," a highly refined suggestion of that ephemeral moment when a bird in flight catches the light. When it is displayed with lighting that brings out its highly polished surface, the impression is stunning. Indeed, it captured Brancusi's imagination, and between 1910 and the early 1950s he created a series of 28 similar birds in bronze and marble, explaining that "The Bird has fascinated me and will not release me."[3] It is based on the Rumanian legend of Maiastra, a magical golden bird whose feathers shone like the sun, illuminating the darkness. When struck by light, Brancusi's bronze birds become radiant light-giving sources, formless points of light in the immensity of space. Brancusi said:

> As a child, I used to dream that I was flying among trees and up into the sky. I have always remembered this dream and for 45 years I have made birds. It is not the bird that I want to express but the gift, the taking off, the *élan*.... God is everywhere. One is God when one forgets oneself and if one is humble and makes the gift of oneself, there is God in your work.... One lady in New York felt that and, kneeling, wept before one of my Birds.[4]

In contrast to the nonfunctional appeals of the fine arts, the first purpose of the APPLIED ARTS is to serve some useful function. Lucy Lewis, a traditional potter from Acoma Pueblo in New Mexico, has applied a visually exciting surface decoration to her

1.12 Constantin Brancusi, *Bird in Space*, 1928. Bronze (unique cast), 54 × 8½ × 6½ ins (137.2 × 21.6 × 16.5 cm). Collection, The Museum of Modern Art, New York. Given anonymously.

1.13 Lucy Lewis, *Water jar*, 1979. Ceramic, 6 ins (15 cm) high.

water jar (**1.13**), using the chewed end of a yucca spine to paint the fine lines. But the jar's main reason for being however is to hold water. Some of the people of Acoma, which may be the oldest continually inhabited city in the United States, still follow the old ways, carrying water for drinking, cooking, and washing up to their adobe homes from natural rock cisterns on the cliff walls below. The forms of their water jars are therefore designed to prevent spilling and to balance readily on one's head. The pots must also be light in weight, so Acoma ware is some of the world's thinnest-walled pottery. Interestingly, the languages of most Native American peoples do not include a word that means "fine art." While they have traditionally created pottery, basketry, and weaving with a highly sophisticated sense of design, these pieces were part of their everyday lives.

The applied art of pottery-making, or CERAMICS, is one of the CRAFTS, the making of useful objects by hand. Other applied art disciplines are similarly functional. GRAPHIC DESIGNERS create advertisements, fabrics, layouts for books and magazines, logos for corporate identification, and so on; INDUSTRIAL DESIGNERS shape the mass-produced objects used by high-tech societies, from cars, telephones, and teapots, to one of the most famous visual images in the world: the Coca-Cola bottle (**1.14**). Other applied arts include clothing design, interior design, and environmental design.

Having made this traditional distinction between the fine and applied arts, we must note that the boundary between them is blurred. For one thing, certain works had functions when they were created that are now overlooked by those who consider them fine arts. The sculptures and stained-glass windows of Gothic cathedrals were functional, designed to teach and inspire people of the Christian faith. Furthermore, many functional pieces have been made with the accent on their visual appeal rather than their functional qualities. The fine porcelain stemcup shown in Figure **1.15** is so beautifully designed that we cannot consider it simply a functional piece. It is equally a work of fine art, created for those who could afford to surround themselves with costly beauty, even in the functional furnishings of their homes. Another reason for the blurring of the distinction between fine and applied arts is our culture's increasing appreciation of the artistic sophistication of many functional pieces and for the time and skill involved in handmade crafts. Pueblo potters' works, along with all other kinds of applied design, are now included in the collections of many major museums, solely to be looked at.

1.15 Stemcup, Ch'ing dynasty, Ch'ien Lung reign, 1736–9. Porcelain, 3⅞ ins (9.8 cm) high. Yale University Art Gallery, Connecticut. Gift of Dr. Yale Kneeland, Jr., B.A. 1922.

1.14 Alex Samuelson, Coca-Cola bottle, designed 1913, patented (with minor modifications) 1915, 1923, 1937.

PUBLIC AND PRIVATE ART

An even less obvious distinction can be made between works designed to be displayed to the public at large and those intended chiefly for private use or enjoyment. Governments and public institutions have long commissioned art on a grand scale as public statements. Rome's Arch of Constantine (**1.16**) was designed to glorify Constantine's victory over his greatest rival, a victory that made him absolute ruler of the Roman Empire. Its surface is decorated with a series of reliefs used to honor the emperor (though some were actually plundered from monuments to earlier rulers); the massiveness of the arch is a symbol of the emperor's public stature.

In all cultures, religious institutions have been major patrons of artists, commissioning paintings and sculptures to help tell the story of their tradition to the masses and inspire the people with the same beliefs. Much of our greatest architecture has been created in the service of centralized governments and religious bodies, who had the power or commanded the devotion to raise the large sums of money needed for monumental projects. A dazzling contemporary display of this power was Japan's Science Expo 85, a high-tech world's fair in the newly created city of Tsukuba, with such showpieces as the neon cube that appeared to float through what was actually a solid building, a dramatic illusion created by mirrored reflections (**1.17**).

1.16 Arch of Constantine, Rome, AD 312–15.

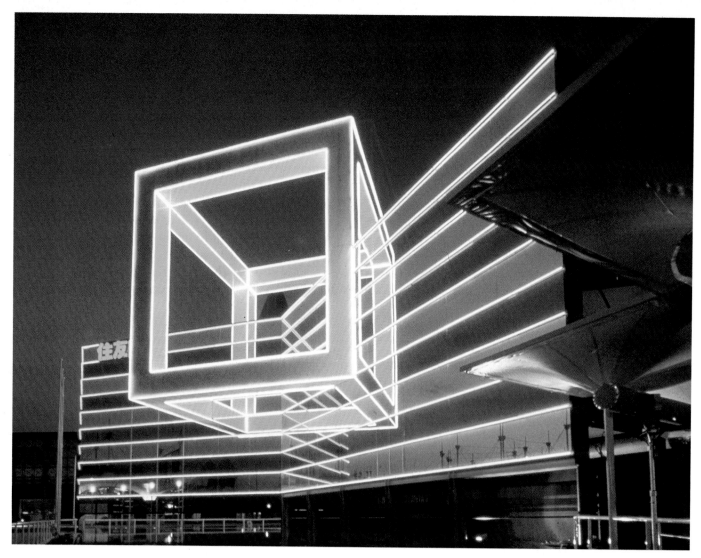

1.17 Sumitomo Building at Expo 85, Tsukuba Science City, Japan.

A relatively new form of concentration of wealth and power, business corporations and conglomerates, are increasingly becoming patrons of the arts as well. They buy and display large paintings and sculptures, partly to impress their clients and partly as good investments, for the commercial gallery and auction-house system has fostered a vigorous market in art as a financial commodity.

By contrast, some works of art are of a scale and character that invite more intimate participation, though they may end up on display at museums. Some Western paintings are "just the right size" to be hung over a sofa or mantel in a private home; magic fetishes may be intended for the use of only one person or family. In the traditional Japanese home, the *tokonoma* alcove, like the one shown in Figure **1.18**, is a quiet spot for private contemplation, usually decorated only by a single scroll painting and a vase with flowers, whose natural beauty is thought to humble anything created by humans. Originally set aside for the worship of ancestors, the alcove still invites contemplation of the sacred in the midst of life.

FUNCTIONS OF ART

In a sense, all art serves some purpose, whether it is strictly defined as fine or applied art. In fact, many pieces serve several purposes, both for the artist and for the viewer. In the following pages we will explore a number of the reasons why art is created, after first noting that the impulse for art may lie partly beyond our ability to explain our motives.

1.18 *Tokonoma alcove in a private home, Japan.*

Rick Bartow

on

THE INPUTS INTO CREATIVITY

The work and words of Rick Bartow (b. 1946) illustrate the rich variety of inputs behind artists' creations. Bartow lives near the Oregon coast on land that has belonged to his Yurok family for four generations. Trained as an artist, he had brutal experiences while serving in the Vietnam War and afterward became a psychologically wounded alcoholic. Pivotal in his own healing and prized by collectors, his artworks are the products of a very rich creative stew: formal design considerations, inner psychological struggles, difficult experiences of his friends that have touched him deeply, practicalities of what materials are at hand, Native American mythology, archetypal symbols, everyday happenings, observations of the natural world. The following are insightful extracts from his commentaries about his art:

"Being a recovering alcoholic, all of a sudden, forty-something years old, I'm feeling for the first time,

'Whoo, this is neat. I can appreciate this.' I used to think that the world owed me everything, and I didn't get it, so I was always angry. It doesn't owe you anything; it doesn't have to be nice. Lots of good happened, but nothing good happened in my eyes that was sustaining enough. So a lot of anger came and blew me out through these images of screaming out.

I just take everything that comes along. The past couple of weeks we've been aware of breast cancer ordeals people are going through, because it's happening to our friend. A kind of down piece like that (of a woman with breast cancer) is kind of a clearing house for me. The *Man in the Water* series comes from another friend's experience of being trapped in an upside-down fishing vessel.

I didn't know if I wanted to draw because I knew all this stuff was in there. But probably the worst alcoholic period in my life was when I was cut off from a studio situation

and couldn't work at all. In alcoholism, there's anger. I suppose some people know where that anger comes from, but it still flashes and I don't know where it comes from with such intensity. Making art helps me to deal with that, to modify that behavior and to maintain a positive behavior. Then I might wad it up and throw it away.

An Australian aborigine said it might take two months for him to do a bark painting, and then when he is done he could start a fire with it and it wouldn't matter. The old guy said that his praying while he was working was the spiritual happening of that piece, and what was done was a by-product of his spirituality. So he could sell it or give it away or throw it away, or just get up and leave it. The value of it was in the doing. It's like that for me.

Coyote (who appears in human-animal transformations in many of his drawings, as in *Coyote and Leda* (**1.19**), is the potential crazy man in any situation. One art critic saw

1.19 Rick Bartow, *Coyote and Leda*, 1991.
Pastel on paper, 60 × 36 ins (152 × 91.4 cm).
Photograph courtesy of the artist and the Jamison–Thomas Gallery, Portland, Oregon.

Coyote as being less a personage than a world condition. They call him Raven up north. Someone up there suggested that he was the shortcomings of all of mankind, not necessarily bad—just a confirmation of that. Coyote had a fall from grace, and was blown all over the ground, and he had to reassemble himself over a period of time.''

''I've run into people who think I'm into devil worship because I've got these strange images. For a while I always drew the hands coming out of the forehead because if I tried to show a man praying, it looked like he was vomiting. So I got into putting the hand coming out of the head, as the brain reaching for help.

Working in this contemporary manner allows me to honor that portion of me that is Native American, without being phony, without getting involved in things that are not mine and maybe are no longer, or that belong more to people who still live in the tribal situation, which I haven't since my grandfather came to this ground when I was three years old.

The fellow who takes the photos was commenting on the new colors in my work. I said, 'Yeah, about this time of year you run down on colors and you have these boxes of bizarre colors you haven't used and no money to buy new ones so you just start innovating.'

I hope that forty years from now somebody who bought one of my drawings could still be looking at little areas of line and color and design techniques for contrast and balance. That's what becomes important: all those little things that go in to make the whole. In my normal style of working, there will be a lot of pigmentation in some areas, and then a lot of negative unworked areas, with just frames of shapes. It relaxes out, and then gets heavy again. It's a constant in and out kind of feeling.''[5]

1.20 Saddle-cover from Pazyryk, Altai region, Russia, 5th century BC. Felt, leather, fur, hair, and gold, 3 ft 10⅞ ins (1.19 m) long. State Museum, Hermitage, St. Petersburg.

THE CREATIVE IMPULSE

The impulse to create art is so strong that artworks have appeared in all cultures, from the earliest days of our species. Perhaps as early as 70,000 years ago, our Paleolithic ancestors were apparently painting with red ocher, shaping ritual objects, and fashioning simple necklaces out of animal bones and teeth. Even weapons and sewing needles had decorations scratched onto them.

Artworks have been created and prized even by nomadic peoples whose belongings are limited to what they can physically carry as they follow the herds. Witness the beautifully detailed felt saddle-cover (**1.20**) preserved in the permafrost of Siberia from the fifth-century BC Scythians, horse-riding nomads. The deep-frozen body of a Scythian reveals that the arts of these people included intricate body-tattooing, as well as sophisticated animal figures of gold, bronze, wood, and leather.

Many artists have a very hard time defining why they make art, but they cannot imagine life without making art. It is like a spiritual calling. Whether or not the work sells, they are compelled to do it. When Rembrandt van Rijn, the great seventeenth century Dutch painter, fell out of favor, was forced to give up his fine things, declare bankruptcy, and live a life of poverty, he continued painting nonetheless and produced some of his very best work, such as the self-portrait on page 66. Auguste Renoir, the great French Impressionist painter of happy moments (see page 196), developed arthritis so painful that he could not hold a brush; it had to be strapped to his hand. But he continued painting. Perhaps part of what unconsciously touches us in their work is the passionate commitment from which it is born. Those who make art for more calculating reasons—such as making money—often fail to touch observers on a deep level.

The question is not so much why people make art but why some people don't. As children, we humans begin trying to shape materials in our environment into artistic creations as soon as our hands are able. This effort usually continues unless it is stifled by those who try to teach us the "right" way to make art or those who insist that we color within the lines of somebody else's drawing. We ourselves may compare our creations unfavorably with more skillful works and give up our attempts at making art.

On the other hand, training and practice are essential in the effort to make the hands create what the mind can imagine. Even the most seemingly uninhibited of modern artworks are created by highly trained artists who know very well what they are doing and struggle continually to perfect their skills.

Psychiatrist Oliver Sacks finds that some of his patients who cannot reach out to the world through any other means may communicate through artistic creations. He describes the case

1.21 José, *Dandelion*. From *The Man who Mistook his Wife for a Hat* by Oliver Sacks.

1.22 William Beckman, *Power Lines*, 1982. Pastel on paper, 24⅜ × 33 ins (61.9 × 83.8 cm). San Francisco Museum of Art. The Glenn C. Janss Collection.

of José, a young man diagnosed as autistic and hopelessly retarded. Invited to draw, José responded with great concentration and joyful appreciation for his subjects, such as a dandelion (**1.21**). Sacks speculates that José has a direct link with reality, undistorted by socially learned ideas.

When artists are working at their best, they too may be in intense communion with life. Their concentration can be such that they can work for hours without noticing the passage of time or the stiffness of their body. In this meditation-like altered state of consciousness, visual ideas may evolve without intellectual struggle, once one has developed a foundation of skills and design sensitivities. The chance of experiencing this direct communion with a deeper level of reality is at least part of what calls some to create—and us to share in the experience.

REPRESENTATION OF EXTERNAL REALITIES

The drive to create is manifested in many ways. One is the effort to represent what we see in the world around us. Such art is called REPRESENTATIONAL or FIGURATIVE work. Within this category there are many degrees of realism.

William Beckman's *Power Lines* (**1.22**) illustrates the highest degree of realism. Rather than painting only the conventionally "pretty" aspects of this rural scene, he included what might be considered blots on the landscape—the road and power lines. Such work is often termed PHOTOREALISM, for it records external reality almost as accurately as a camera. Nevertheless, the artist carefully chooses what slice of life to represent, just as a photographer carefully

1.23 Peter Paul Rubens, *Landscape with Rainbow*, c. 1635.
Panel, 37¼ × 48½ ins (94.6 × 123.2 cm).
Alte Pinakothek, Munich.

selects views that work well aesthetically. In *Power Lines*, the road and power lines curve in flowing relationship and opposition to each other, creating a harmony of movement that is balanced by the staid quietness of the rural scene.

A step removed from photorealism is IDEALIZATION—transforming the real world into one that approximates one's ideas of perfection. Idealized paintings of the human form may be more beautiful than any of the flesh-and-blood models actually used. Peter Paul Rubens' *Landscape with Rainbow* (**1.23**) paints a glowing picture of country life. Everyone seems healthy and happy, even the animals, and the sun's appearance after a shower of rain floods the scene with light from over our shoulder to the left, bringing out a double rainbow in the sky. The pastoral idyll expresses Rubens' own apparent pleasure with life. The most celebrated artist of his time in Europe, he had recently married a woman much younger than himself and started fathering a second family, and had bought an estate in the Flanders countryside which inspired paintings such as this one.

Another kind of shift from absolute realism is STYLIZATION—emphasizing principles or elements of design rather than exact representation when working with natural forms. Diego Rivera's *Flower Day* (**1.24**) stylizes human figures into massive forms. The simplified outlines turn arms and

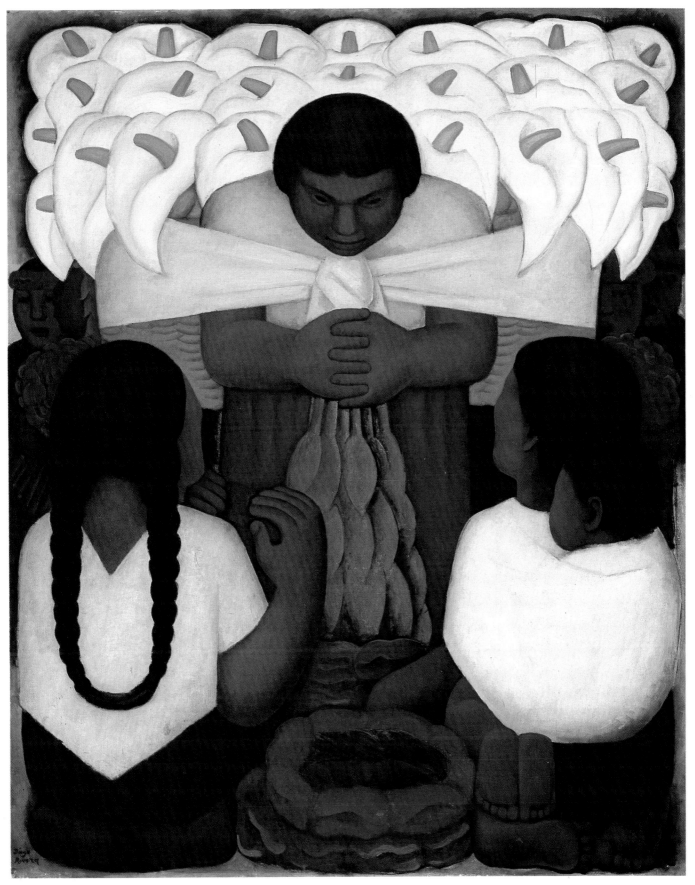

1.24 Diego Rivera. *Flower Day*, 1925. Encaustic on canvas, 4 ft 10 ins × 3 ft 11½ ins (1.47 × 1.20 m). Los Angeles County Museum of Art, L.A. County Funds.

garments into interlocking blocks of color, shaded at the edges for a monumental three-dimensional effect. The seated indigenous women and the flower-carrier are thus transformed into sacred statues honoring the abundance of the earth.

A somewhat different approach to figurative art is called ABSTRACTION: extracting the essence of real objects rather than representing their surface appearance faithfully. A series of trees by Dutch artist

Piet Mondrian illustrates the process of increasing abstraction. The first one shown (**1.25**) is a fairly representational depiction of what appears to be an old apple tree, with riotous interplay among the lines of the main branches and the secondary suckers that shoot upward from them. In the second (**1.26**) Mondrian has in effect pruned away the suckers, leaving only the branches that form a rhythmic series of arcs, echoing and counterbalancing the strong leftward arc of the main trunk. Mondrian also develops interest in the shapes of the spaces between the branches by painting them as if they had textures of their own. In the third, most abstract, tree image (**1.27**), the thickness of trunk and branches is also pared away, leaving only the interaction of arcing lines and the spaces between them. Here Mondrian has reduced the visual essence of a tree as lines in space to its bare bones.

1.25 Piet Mondrian, *Tree II*, 1912.
Black crayon on paper, 22¼ × 33¼ ins (57 × 85 cm).
Haags Gemeente Museum, The Hague.

1.26 Piet Mondrian, *The Gray Tree*, 1912.
Oil on canvas, 30½ × 42 ins (78 × 107 cm).
Haags Gemeente Museum, The Hague, on loan from S. B. Slijpen.

1.27 Piet Mondrian, *Flowering Apple Tree*, 1912.
Oil on canvas, 27½ × 41¾ ins (69.9 × 106 cm).
Haags Gemeente Museum, The Hague.

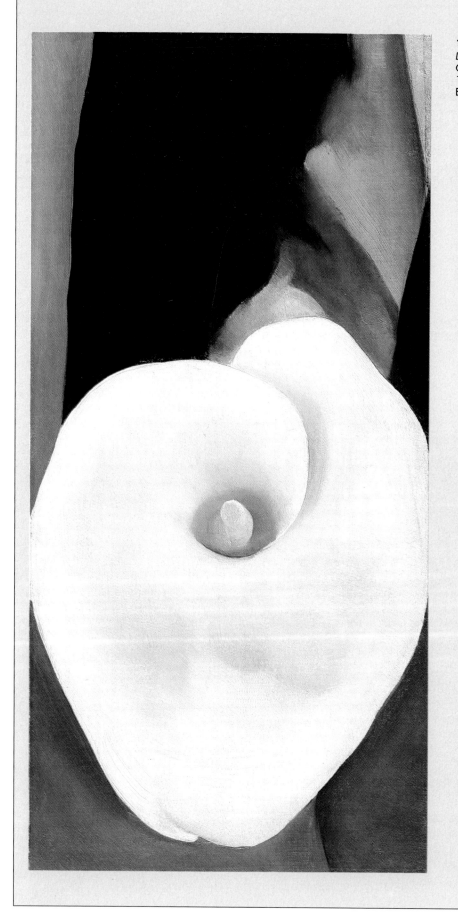

1.28 Georgia O'Keeffe,
Lily—White with Black, 1927.
Oil on board,
12 × 6 ins (30.5 × 15.2 cm).
Estate of Georgia O'Keeffe.

Georgia O'Keeffe

on

ABSTRACTION

Georgia O'Keeffe (1887-1986), an austere, strong-minded woman who painted until her death at the age of ninety-nine, is considered one of the greatest American artists of the twentieth century. She is particularly famous for her large abstractions of flowers (**1.28**), animal bones, mysterious organic forms, and landscapes of the New Mexico desert, where she spent her later years as a near-recluse. For her, painting was a way of communicating about her experiences and sensations that could not be expressed in any other way. Among her letters are these comments:

"The large White Flower with the golden heart is something I have to say about White—quite different from what White has been meaning to me. Whether the flower or the color is the focus I do not know. I do know that the flower is painted large to convey to you my experience of the flower—and what is my experience of the flower if it is not color.

I know I can not paint a flower. I can not paint the sun on the desert on a bright summer morning but maybe in terms of paint color I can convey to you my experience of the flower or the experience that makes the flower significant to me at that particular time.

Color is one of the great things in the world that makes life worth living to me and as I have come to think of painting it is my effort to create an equivalent with paint color for the world—life as I see it." *November 1, 1930*

"From experiences of one kind or another shapes and colors come to me very clearly—Sometimes I start in very realistic fashion and as I go on from one painting after another of the same thing it becomes simplified till it can be nothing but abstract—but for me it is my reason for painting it I suppose.

At the moment I am very annoyed—I have the shapes—on yellow scratch paper—in my mind for over a year—and I cannot see the color for them—I've drawn them again—and again—it is from something I have heard again and again till I hear it in the wind—but I can not get the color for it—only shapes." *April 22, 1957*

"I think [walking in the desert] almost the best thing to do that I know of out here—it is so bare—with a sort of ages old feeling of death on it—still it is warm and soft and I love it with my skin.... " *Early 1940s*

"I liked it that you liked the blue and the red of the bone series. It is a kind of thing that I do that makes me feel I am going off into space—in a way that I like—and that frightens me a little because it is so unlike what anyone else is doing. I always feel that sometime I may fall off the edge—It is something I like so much to do that I don't care if I do fall off the edge—No sense in it but it is my way...." *December 24, 1945*[6]

1.29 Richard Diebenkorn, *Ocean Park #115*, 1979. Oil on canvas, 8 ft 4 ins × 6 ft 9 ins (2.54 × 2.056 m). Collection, The Museum of Modern Art, New York. Mrs. Charles G. Stachelberg Fund.

The opposite extreme from photorealism is NONOBJECTIVE or NONREPRESENTATIONAL work—that which makes no reference at all to objects from the physical world. Richard Diebenkorn's *Ocean Park* series, of which #115 is shown in Figure **1.29**, is clearly nonobjective. The title of the series refers to the area of Santa Monica, California, where he has his studio, rather than to any physical imagery. He seems to be working instead with the pure elements and principles of design, particularly a counterplay between rigidly geometrical lines and shapes and a more organic sense of weathered, light-and-color-filled spaciousness created by repeated SCUMBLING (dry-brush applications of thin layers of paint) and scraping of paint pigments. To strain to find figurative imagery in these paintings is to mistake the artist's intentions.

The less representational a work is, the more we must bring to it to appreciate it. In Mondrian's more abstract trees, we have to use our memories of trees to interpret the images. We are also asked to become intellectually involved in discovering relationships between lines and spaces. When all figurative imagery is deleted, as in Diebenkorn's work, our response no longer has any base in our experiences of the physical world. Instead, we can explore the work as one would explore virgin territory, with no familiar landmarks. Indeed, nonobjective art has historically been used in many cultures to suggest spiritual realities that lie beyond form. The Yoruba divination bag shown in Figure **1.30** incorporates many common motifs for the intangible dimensions of life, including swirling circles within circles, the four directions of the universe, and intertwined lines. Very specific symbolic meanings are suggested by every element in such a design, but they may be known only to the initiated. We can admire them superficially as geometric patterns, but to have some sense of their sacred meaningfulness greatly enriches appreciation of such a piece.

1.30 Yoruba diviner's bag.

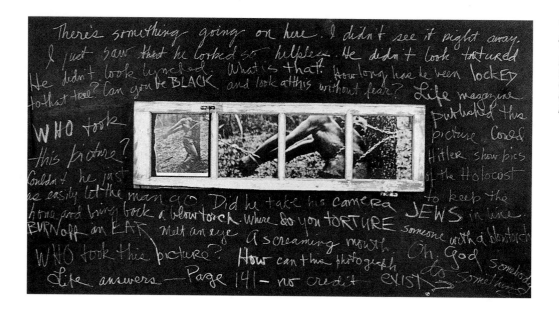

There's something going on here. I didn't see it right away. I just saw that he looked so helpless. He didn't look tortured. He didn't look lynched. What is that? How long has he been locked to that tree? Can you be BLACK and look at this without fear? Life magazine published this picture. Could Hitler show pics of the Holocaust to keep the JEWS in line. WHO took this picture? Couldn't he just as easily let the man go? Did he take his camera home and bring back a blowtorch. Where do you TORTURE someone with a blowtorch. BURN off an EAR. Melt an eye. A screaming mouth. Oh, God somebody do something. WHO took this picture? How can this photograph EXIST. Life answers—Page 141 - no credit.

1.31 Pat Ward Williams, *Accused/Blowtorch/Padlock*, 1986.
Mixed media and photograph, 5 ft × 8 ft 4 ins (1.52 × 2.54 m).
Collection of the artist.
Courtesy Williams College Museum of Art.

RECORDING ONE'S TIMES

Another outlet for the creative impulse is the creation of works intended to record something in the political or social rather than physical environment, to inform the public or to preserve an event for history. Some art historians look at all art from a sociopolitical point of view. They see it as giving information about the cultural and social background of when the artworks were produced.

Art may be used to provoke a reaction to political or cultural situations, not just to inform the viewer or record events for posterity. One cannot be unaffected by Pat Ward Williams' *Accused/Blowtorch/Padlock* (**1.31**). Any photograph carries a sense of immediacy and truth. Beyond that, by taking apart this photograph, presenting it in broken close-ups, Williams brings us into its horror; she says, "Come in closer; notice this!" Handwritten text surrounding the construction adds the agony of an observer's voice to more fully engage our emotions. As the handwriting leads us to notice, this man seems still to be alive. How could anyone take his picture and not do something to stop his torture? Then, by implication, how can anyone be indifferent to racial violence? Williams comments:

> A single, documentary shot is usually too little to express a broader idea about racism. That's why I started to make photographic constructions. . . . My constructions promote discussion. People can talk about the provocative or controversial images. Someone's curiosity might be sparked to look further into a situation or issue.[7]

This is not pretty art to adorn a wall—that is not its function. For the viewer, to appreciate this art is to be touched by it.

INNER EXPERIENCES

Rather than taking images or events outside themselves as their subjects, many artists have explored their own interior worlds. One aspect of this inner world is the capacity for FANTASY—for imagining things that have never been seen, such as Paul Klee's *Twittering Machine* (**1.32**). Despite the delicate playfulness of this painting, Klee spoke about the act of artistic creation very seriously, as having spiritual connotations. In his *Creative Credo* he asserted that "visible reality is merely an isolated phenomenon latently outnumbered by other realities." The method he used to gain access to other realms of possibility was to approach his materials with no preconceived subject matter, allowing unconscious understandings to guide his hand. "My hand is entirely the implement of a distant sphere,"[8] he explained. "What artist does not yearn to dwell near the mind, or heart, of creation itself, that prime mover of events in time and space?"[9]

Another artist who dove into the unconscious to bring forth fantasy images was Henri Rousseau. A retired Parisian customs collector, he painted exotic landscapes and creatures that he had never see, such as *The Dream* (**1.33**). The NARRATIVE, or "story," within the painting suggests the illogical happenings and inventive landscapes we experience in our dreams. Rousseau was a NAIVE ARTIST, one who had never been trained in the principles and techniques of art. For instance, the lighting in *The Dream* does not seem to come from the direction of the moon; Rousseau placed highlights and shadows where he wanted them, rather than where they would logically fall. Unencumbered by ideas of how things "should"

1.32 Paul Klee, *Twittering Machine*, 1922. Watercolor and pen and ink on oil transfer drawing paper, mounted on cardboard, 25¼ × 19 ins (63.8 × 48.1 cm). Collection, The Museum of Modern Art, New York. Purchase.

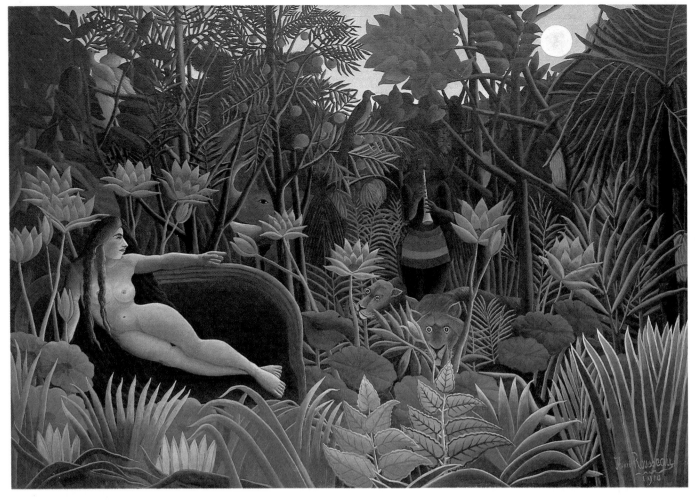

1.33 Henri Rousseau, *The Dream*, 1910. Oil on canvas, 6 ft 8½ ins × 9 ft 9½ ins (2.045 × 2.985 m). Collection, The Museum of Modern Art, New York. Gift of Nelson A. Rockefeller.

look or be represented, he was highly successful at tapping into a world of archetypal images that we respond to on some level beyond thought. His natural sense of design gives a haunting power to these landscapes of the soul.

Inner experiences may also be depicted directly, as it were, without any imagery from the outer world. Sometimes their subject matter is sheer emotion, beyond form. Such is the case in the work of Mark Rothko, whose own emotions led him to commit suicide in 1970. His sublime nonobjective paintings, such as *Green on Blue* (**1.34**), offer large, hovering, soft-edged fields of color for quiet contemplation. People often respond to them with powerful emotion, and this was Rothko's intention. He said:

> I am interested only in expressing the basic human emotions—tragedy, ecstasy, doom and so on—and the fact that lots of people break down and cry when confronted with my pictures shows that I *communicate* with those basic human emotions. The people who weep before my

pictures are having the same religious experience I had when I painted them. And if you ... are moved only by their color relationships, then you miss the point.[10]

In some cases, artists draw their imagery from external realities but project their own state of mind onto them. Some quality inside the artist communicates with that quality in the outer world, revealing inner truths: intangibles within the tangible. One who worked this way was Vincent van Gogh. His *The Starry Night* (**1.35**) reflects a dynamic vision of nature as everchanging, in continuous motion. The sky boils with swirling energy patterns; the hills roll like waves; the trees writhe upward like flames. The houses in the village seem dwarfed by the cosmic drama, with the possible exception of the church spire. One senses that to see this pastoral landscape thus, van Gogh must have been highly sensitive and seething with inner energy. Indeed, he was subject to attacks of madness, during one of which he cut off his ear.

1.34 Mark Rothko, *Green on Blue*, 1956. Oil on canvas, 7 ft 5¾ ins × 5 ft 3¼ ins (2.28 × 1.61 m). University of Arizona Museum of Art. Gift of Edward J. Gallagher, Jr.

Vincent van Gogh
on
COMBINING EMOTION AND INTELLECT

The great Dutch Post-Impressionist painter Vincent van Gogh (1853–90) did not consider himself an artist at first. He initially wanted to help people by being a clergyman like his father. When that and other odd jobs did not work, he discovered a love for painting. He spent all the money his supportive brother Theo sent him on paints and canvases, totally neglecting his physical health. At length he had to place himself in an asylum for protection during his periodic mental disorders. In July 1890 he tried to end his life, and died from the effects two days later. Although van Gogh is commonly associated with his mental imbalances and his intensity, he approached painting in a calculated, deliberate, albeit passionate, way, as he reveals in his letters to the faithful Theo:

"The cypresses are always occupying my thoughts, I should like to make something of them like the canvases of the sunflowers, because it astonishes me that they have not yet been done as I see them.

[The clump of cypresses, which rise in the left foreground of *The Starry Night* (**1.35**) but occurred in other van Gogh paintings as well] ... is as beautiful of line and proportion as an Egyptian obelisk.

And the green has a quality of such distinction.

It is a splash of black in a sunny landscape, but it is one of the most interesting black notes, and the most difficult to hit off exactly that I can imagine.

But then you must see them against the blue, *in* the blue rather. To paint nature here, as everywhere, you must be in it a long time."

Letter 596, June 25, 1889

"I am quite sure that *color*, that *chiaroscuro*, that *perspective*, that *tone* and that *drawing*, in short, everything has fixed laws which one must and can study, like chemistry or algebra. This is *far from being* the easiest view of things, and one who says, 'Oh, one must know it all instinctively,' takes it very easy indeed.

I do not at all intend to think and live less passionately than I do. By no means—I may meet with rebuffs, I may often be mistaken—often be wrong—but that only as far as it goes—basically I am not wrong."

Letter 381, October 1884

"I must warn you that everyone will think I work too fast.

Don't you believe a word of it.

Is it not emotion, the sincerity of one's feeling for nature, that draws us, and if the emotions are sometimes so strong that one works without knowing one works, when sometimes the strokes come with a sequence and a coherence like words in a speech or a letter, then one must remember that it has not always been so.... So one must strike while the iron is hot, and put the forged bars on one side."

Letter 504, Summer 1888

1.35 Vincent van Gogh, *The Starry Night*, 1889.
Oil on canvas, 29 × 36¼ ins (73.7 × 92.1 cm).
Collection, The Museum of Modern Art, New York.
Acquired through the Lillie P. Bliss Bequest.

"When I come back myself from the mental labor of balancing the six essential colors...sheer work and calculation, with one's mind utterly on the stretch, like an actor on the stage in a difficult part, with a hundred things at once to think of in a single half-hour.

Don't think that I would artificially keep up a feverish condition, but do understand that I am in the midst of a complicated calculation which results in quick succession in canvases quickly executed, but calculated long *beforehand*. So now, when anyone says that such and such is done too quickly, you can reply that they have looked at it too quickly."

Letter 507, Summer 1888[11]

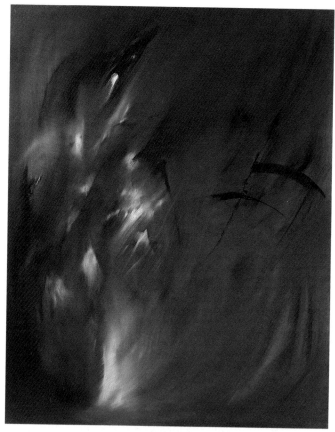

SPIRITUAL EXPRESSIONS

As may already be apparent in the words of the artists quoted, much art is highly spiritual in its inspiration and its intentions. Spirituality is different things to different people. It ranges from interest in the mysteries of one's own psyche, to interest in the supernatural, to worship of the divine within the framework of one of the organized religions.

A tremendous amount of the world's art has been created as objects for devotion and inspiration. *The Ecstasy of St. Teresa* (**1.36**) is the altarpiece of an entire chapel created by the great Baroque sculptor and architect Gianlorenzo Bernini. Its spiritual intent is to inflame the worshipper with the same sensuous ecstasy as Teresa of Avila experienced when in a vision she was speared by an angel, leaving her "completely afire with love of God."

Many works of contemporary abstract Western art refer to personal mystical experiences that are difficult to articulate in words, for our language is limited largely to experiences of the five senses. Lisa Bradley says of her luminous paintings (**1.37**):

> In them you can see movement and stillness at the same time, things coming in and out of focus. The light seems to be from behind. There is a sense of something like a permeable membrane, of things coming from one dimension to another. But even that doesn't describe it well.
>
> How do you describe truth in words? That's what I want to reach—that nonverbal level of truth. These are things that go beyond our ability to communicate verbally, but perhaps we can suggest them visually. At a certain point in the process of the painting, every stroke is in perfect accord; there is a sense of the rightness in every stroke, a resonance with what is true.[12]

Much of the sacred art of the world is produced by people who may not have been formally trained in the elements and principles of design, as systematized by Western art historians and art critics, but who are recognized as having a deep inner calling for the work. Their art gives a certain tangible reality to the unseen. In Australia, it is only the oldest members of the aboriginal society who may be privileged initiates into the symbols and mysteries of the Dreaming, the basis of existence, replete with powerful ancestral beings. It is they who are privileged to interpret certain Dreamings in art forms. Their exuberant acrylic paintings (as in **1.38**, products of new artistic traditions that began in the 1970s when acrylics were introduced to the aboriginals) are on one level aerial views of their sacred landscapes, as visited by the Dreamings. Other layers of meaning are known only to the initiated.

1.36 (far left) Gianlorenzo Bernini, *The Ecstasy of St. Teresa*, 1645–52. Marble, stucco, and gilt bronze, life size. Cornaro Chapel, Church of Santa Maria della Vittoria, Rome.

1.37 (left) Lisa Bradley, *The Moon Cannot be Stolen*. Oil on convas, 4 ft 2 ins × 3 ft 4 ins (1.27 × 1.02 m). Courtesy of the artist.

1.38 Darby Jampijimpa, *Burrowing Skink Dreaming at Parikirlangu*, 1986. Acrylic on canvas, 57¼ × 37 ins (145.3 × 94.2 cm). © The Asia Society Galleries and the South Australia Museum.

45

POWER AND PROPAGANDA

Another way in which artists' talents and creativity have been engaged is in the creation of works that allow the person or group who paid for them to gain prestige. In addition to the spiritual intentions of the Cornaro Chapel which houses *The Ecstasy of St. Teresa* (1.36), it was intended as a place to celebrate the future remains of Cardinal Cornaro, who commissioned it, and to honor his family. The intimate chapel is ornamented with such splendor that it must have served as a statement not only about the Cardinal's devotion to St. Teresa but also about his wealth. Certainly this was an intention behind the commissioning of many secular monumental pieces, such as Louis XIV's colossal palace at Versailles (**1.39**). A huge corps of architects, interior designers, sculptors, painters, and landscape artists worked for almost half a century to create not only the largest and grandest palace the world had ever seen, surrounded by an immense and elaborate park, but also an entire city for government officials, courtiers, servants, and the military. Their buildings radiate along avenues that intersect in the king's bedroom, symbolizing the vast wealth and power of the absolute monarch.

Mingled with a show of wealth is the desire to impress the public with one's good taste in art. Today corporations often choose for this purpose large nonobjective paintings and sculptures. These can suggest a sophisticated, contemporary corporate image and have no subject matter that would offend anyone. But it takes wealth and a certain daring to commission monumental modern sculpture to occupy expensive urban real estate. The point of using valuable Manhattan ground-level space for a

1.39 Louis le Vau and Jules Hardouin-Mansart, Palace of Versailles, France, 1669–85.

1.40 Isamu Noguchi, *Red Cube*, 1968. Marine Midland Plaza, New York.

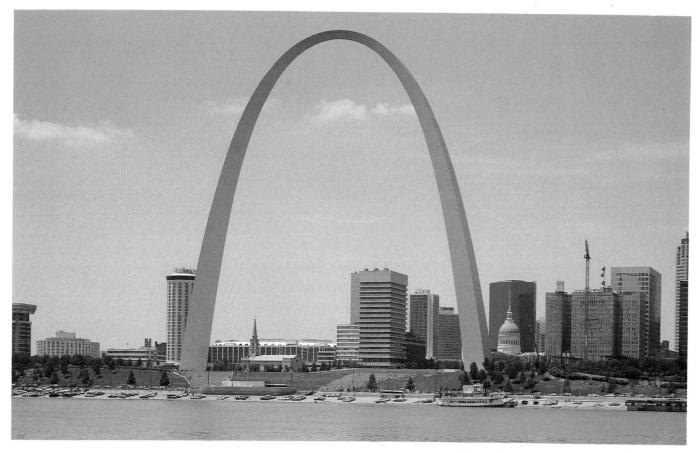

1.41 Eero Saarinen, Jefferson National Expansion Memorial (*The Gateway to the West*), St. Louis, Missouri, 1966.

1.42 Ludwig Hohlwein, Poster, c. 1943. Library of Congress, Washington D.C., Poster Collection.

huge cube resting precariously on one corner (**1.40**) may escape the uninitiated, but this sculpture by Isamu Noguchi is a signal to those who know something about art that its owner, the Marine Midland Bank, is imaginative, forward-looking, and prestigious.

Governments like to project positive self-concepts, presenting a proud image for local citizens and visitors. Such a monument to civic pride is the Jefferson National Expansion Memorial, magnificently engineered by architect Eero Saarinen (**1.41**). Built in 1966, it is part of a federal project originally funded under Franklin D. Roosevelt to glorify the territorial expansion of the United States. The great arch presents a visible symbol of St. Louis as "The Gateway to the West." From a distance, it appears as a line thrown against the sky. Up close, its girth becomes apparent: its triangular form is 54 feet (16.2 m) along each side at its bases, carrying stairways and elevators up to an observation room at the top. This soaring structure can be seen not only from the city but also from miles around.

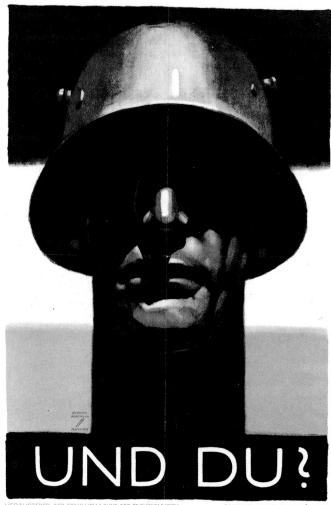

UND DU?

HERAUSGEBER: DER STAHLHELM, BUND DER FRONTSOLDATEN   DRUCK·HERM·SONNTAG&CO·MÜNCHEN

The same artistic skills that can express civic pride can also be used coercively. Graphic designers are skillful at using consumers' interest in self-pride to convince them to buy products. Advertisements for expensive cars often speak to people's aspirations to wealth and good taste; ads for clothing often manipulate people by their desire for sex appeal. Tragically, Adolf Hitler had a clear sense of the tremendous impact of media propaganda and used it extensively to build popular support for his regime. Nazi propagandist Ludwig Hohlwein's poster (**1.42**) presents such a powerful visual image that the mere words *"Und du?"* ("And you?") convey the aggressive challenge to the civilian to become part of the war machine. We are shown only the storm trooper's masculine features, nothing of his individuality, making him an abstraction for the idea of The German Soldier: a superhumanly strong man with the power of the group and the group's history behind him. The angle from which he is shown makes us look up at him, and the deliberate mingling of hero-worship, intimidation, and brooding power is characteristic of the totalitarian values of the regime that commissioned the image.

ENTERTAINMENT

In a lighter vein, many works of art are intended at least partially as entertainment and to be unambiguously playful. Institutions such as banks and corporations have often sought to express a serious or elegant image of financial success through the architecture of their buildings, but not so the Walt Disney Company. Its Chief Executive Officer, Michael D. Eisner, feels that even a great movie made by his company is rather transitory. By comparison, a building is a lasting statement, but still not exempt from gaiety: "The stakes are much higher, the risks are much greater, but it's much more fun."[13] He encourages a playful attitude among the architects of Disney buildings, such as the Walt Disney World headquarters officially nicknamed as "the Team Disney Building" (**1.43**). Architect Arata Isozaki conceived it as a three-dimensional cartoon of surprising colors, using surface decorations that contradict the building forms and even Mickey Mouse's ears as the entrance. Everything seems slightly out of kilter, but one knows implicitly that this is a light-hearted tune, not a frightening journey into entropy.

1.43 Arata Isozaki, Team Disney Building, near Orlando, Florida. Courtesy the Walt Disney Company.

1.44 Ventura Fabian, *Two Dancing Chickens*. Wood.
Photo by Vicki Ragan.

Folk art—exuberant, individualistic works created by aesthetically untrained people who are working in a community tradition—often strikes viewers as being funny, whether or not the folk artists intended that reaction. Two hundred families in the Oaxaca area of Mexico are now using the all-purpose machetes of their peasant culture and brushes of human hair to shape and paint copal wood as colorful animals, monsters, and angels. These creations grow out of their reality—the secular and sacred material of their lives—but those coming from other cultures may find them purely whimsical. To Ventura Fabian, his dancing chickens (**1.44**) are actually Nahuals, peasants who turn into animals by the light of the full moon. Collectors who find them humorous have paid up to US$3500 for such pieces in North American galleries.

THE SEARCH FOR BEAUTY

Although not all art is meant to be beautiful, satisfying the desire for beauty is one of the major functions of many works of art. Confronted by a physical world that often jars the senses, sensitive individuals have long sought refuge in beauty, both natural and manufactured. To surround ourselves with beautiful things soothes our spirits and brings a sense of the sublime into everyday life. Many artists have responded to this quest for the beautiful, but there are no absolute guidelines for them to follow.

Consider the changing ideas about the human figure, for example. To the ancient Greeks, the Warrior from Riace (**1.45**) represented the epitome of physical beauty in a male. Unadorned and highly toned, the figure is presented in a stance that accentuates the pleasing swell of buttocks and upraised arm to bring out the biceps. The bronze body is convincingly realistic and yet idealized to probably greater physical beauty than any Greek actually possessed. The nude human body—when in good shape—was contemplated as a beautiful image, perfect, with no connotations of shame.

Sandro Botticelli's *The Birth of Venus* (**1.46**) juxtaposes two different cultural ideals of female beauty: The nude Venus was modeled on a classical statue of Venus, suggesting in a mythological context the Roman and Greek appreciation for the natural body. To her right, the Early Renaissance ideal of clothed beauty is represented by the attendant nymph. She is dressed in contemporary fashion, with the high-waisted style that exaggerates the length of the legs. The flying figures at upper left are similarly elongated, reflecting current tastes in ideal physique.

1.45 (left) Warrior from Riace, 5th century BC.
Bronze with bone, glass-paste, silver and copper inlaid, 6 ft 7 ins (2 m) high. Museo Nazionale, Reggio Calabria.

1.46 Sandro Botticelli, *The Birth of Venus*, c. 1482.
Tempera on canvas, 5 ft 8 ins × 9 ft 1 in (1.75 × 2.78 m). Galleria degli Uffizi, Florence.

1.47 Hyacinthe Rigaud, *Louis XIV*, 1701. Oil on canvas, 9 ft ¼ ins × 6 ft ½ ins (2.75 × 1.84 m). Louvre, Paris.

To some, the ideal in human beauty is entirely a matter of artifice. An extreme example was Louis XIV, whose attention to dress set the style for high fashion in late seventeenth-century Europe. In Rigaud's portrait of the Sun King (**1.47**) everything considered beautiful is artificial. Surely his face is not particularly handsome by any standards. But the high-heeled shoes make the king appear taller and bring out his calf muscles for more shapely legs. The great bulk of the fine garments adds to the impressiveness of his appearance. The walking stick helps him stand straight and visually emphasizes the vertical in his carriage. And the immense wig gives his head a much larger-than-life importance, helping to balance the mass of his clothing. It was Louis who encouraged the elevation of the wig to an art form; his attendants at Versailles included 40 wigmakers.

DESIGNING THE UTILITARIAN

A final function of some artistic creativity is to create aesthetically pleasing forms for the objects of our everyday existence. In many cultures, no distinction is made between functional objects and art; everything is created with an eye for aesthetics. In the

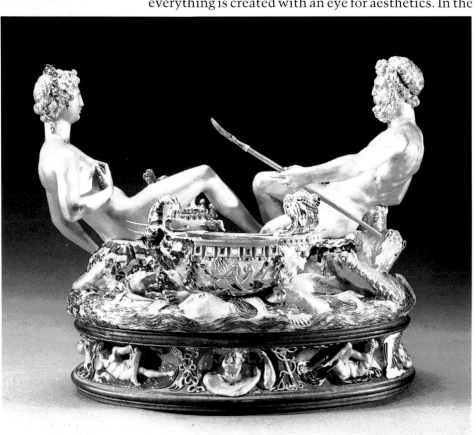

1.48 Benvenuto Cellini, *The Saltcellar of Francis I*, 1539–42. Gold and enamel, 10¼ × 13⅛ ins (26 × 33 cm). Kunsthistorisches Museum, Vienna.

West, art became the province of specialists whose offerings were available only to those with enough money to trade. Modern tastes in functional pieces often tend toward clean, uncluttered lines that reveal the elegance of the material. But in some times and places, highly ornamented works have been the aesthetic standard. Consider the saltcellar made for the sixteenth-century French king Francis I (**1.48**). Intricately modeled in gold, featuring the gods Neptune and Ceres (symbolizing the Sea and the Earth), it is worlds apart from the humble salt shakers found on most of our tables. At the time, salt was a sufficiently valuable commodity to deserve an expensive showcase—the masterpiece of the celebrated goldsmith and bronze sculptor Benvenuto Cellini.

Early in the twentieth century, a group of industrial designers, architects, and craftsmen tried to merge their talents with those of sculptors and painters in a German school of applied art called the *Bauhaus*. Their aim was to bring aesthetics to mass production. One of the products of their intended marriage between form and function was the classic chair designed by Mies van der Rohe (**1.49**). Also executed in white kid leather as a modern throne for

1.50 Nineteenth-century corkscrews.

the king and queen of Spain, it is commonly known as the "Barcelona chair" because it was displayed at the innovative German Pavilion, which Mies also designed, at an international exhibition in Barcelona. Long after its 1929 debut, the chair is still in production and used in settings from hotel reception areas to private living rooms. It is highly esteemed for its elegant form and the high quality of its workmanship. In contrast to Cellini's ornamental approach, the Bauhaus designers worked with the demanding principle "less is more."

The requirements of functionality place some restrictions on design. For all its visual elegance, the Barcelona chair would not be so popular if it were not also comfortable to sit on. However, there are many possible aesthetic solutions to the same utilitarian function. Take the issue of removing a cork from a bottle of wine. So many types of corkscrew have been devised that they have become collectors' items and museum pieces, complete with a corkscrew collectors' society and a magazine about corkscrew collecting. Those shown in Figure **1.50** are only a sample of the variety, ingenuity, and visual elegance evoked by attempts to create a cork-pulling tool that is at once useful and beautiful.

1.49 Ludwig Mies van der Rohe, *Barcelona Chair*, 1929. Steel and leather.

1.51 W. Eugene Smith, *Tomoko in a Bath*, 1972. Photograph. © 1972 Aileen & W. Eugene Smith.

LEVELS OF APPRECIATION

It has often been said that there are two aspects one can appreciate in a work of art: its form and its content. In this context, FORM refers to the physical qualities of a work—its elements and principles of design, techniques, and materials. CONTENT refers to the work's subject matter (what it is or represents), and the emotions, ideas, symbols, narratives, or spiritual connotations it suggests. Instead of making this traditional distinction here, however, we will focus instead on the realities of our personal reactions to a work. From this perspective, in encountering a work we may respond to it on several levels: how it affects our feelings; what the current critical opinion of the artist is; how well designed and crafted it is; what idea it suggests; and what we know of the history of its period and the artist.

FEELING

Many works engage our emotions on a subtle level that we may not even notice. Others, such as W. Eugene Smith's photograph *Tomoko in a Bath* (**1.51**), appeal quite directly to our feelings. The work is part of a series illustrating industrial pollution in Minimata, Japan. Tomoko is a victim of mercury poisoning; her mother is giving her a bath. The scene—dramatized by composition and lighting—is one of the most powerful photographs ever taken. It may evoke a strange mixture of feelings, from horror at Tomoko's deformed body and the effects of pollution, to compassion for the tenderness with which her mother is holding and looking at her. The pose and expression of great love in the midst of tragedy may remind some of Michelangelo's *Pietà* (14.21).

Sacred architecture has often been designed with consideration for its emotional impact on worshippers. The great Gothic cathedrals of Europe were intended to uplift people's emotions from the pettiness of the everyday to the heights of sublime adoration. They did so through their soaring vertical dimensions, making the devout feel individually insignificant in contrast with the grandeur of the divine. This attempt aspired to an unattainable peak at Beauvais, France, in what was to be the highest enclosed space ever—a stone structure rising 157 feet (48 m) above the floor (**1.52**). But the choir vault collapsed during construction, leaving only the APSE (the domed altar projection) intact. The structure was eventually redesigned and gradually rebuilt, but then a tower collapsed and there was not enough money to continue the impossible project. What survives is only a portion of the original grand dream, but it still has the intended self-transcending emotional effect.

Even humorous works may be intended to alter our habitual emotional patterns. Meret Oppenheim's *Object* (**1.53**) contradicts our usual reactions to both fur and cups. She provokes us visually into feeling what it would be like to drink from such an object, with the fur deliberately arranged thrusting toward where our mouth would go. Depending on our own psychological makeup, we may be amused by the expected sensation or filled with disgust at the Freudian associations.

1.52 (left) Choir of Beauvais Cathedral, France, c. 1225.

1.53 Meret Oppenheim, *Object*, 1936. Fur-covered cup, saucer, and spoon; cup 4⅜ ins (10.9 cm) diameter; saucer 9⅜ ins (23.7 cm) diameter; spoon 8 ins (20.2 cm) long; overall height, 2⅞ ins (7.3 cm). Collection, The Museum of Modern Art, New York. Purchase.

1.54 Norman Rockwell, cover illustration for *The Saturday Evening Post*, 1962.

CRITICAL OPINION

In addition to our personal emotional response, the opinions of art critics—and the mood of our times—may have considerable impact on how we respond to works of art. There are no absolute guidelines for judging quality in art. People tend to respond negatively to anything unfamiliar, but, over time, what was originally shocking and unprecedented may become quite familiar and acceptable. In the early 1960s, the average person thought Jackson Pollock was a fraud or a trickster, pretending to present works done with flung paint as serious art. Norman Rockwell's version of a Pollock (**1.54**), painted for the cover of the mainstream family magazine *Saturday Evening Post*, places us looking over the shoulder of an apparently traditional, dignified gentleman who is trying to decide what to make of this seemingly chaotic new stuff. Rockwell doesn't show us his face; what we read into his opinion is largely based on how we ourselves view Pollock, which in turn is now heavily influenced by the fact that the critics have declared Pollock a serious artist, worthy of being studied and collected. Nonobjective art is now "in," highly respectable and also highly priced.

Critical tastes have changed dramatically over time. When the French Impressionists such as Monet, Renoir, and Seurat began their experiments in seeing and in new ways of representing what they actually perceived, they were utterly rejected by the reigning French Academy. At one point, a bankrupt dealer tried to sell van Gogh's canvases in bundles of ten for 50 centimes to one franc per bundle. Today the works of the Impressionists are considered so valuable that only the very wealthiest can afford them. In 1990, van Gogh's *Portrait of Dr. Gachet* was sold for US$82.5 million, the most ever paid for any painting.

While the Impressionists were struggling to survive, a member of the French Academy named William Bouguereau was the favorite of the critics. His romantic paintings, such as *Nymphs and Satyr* (**1.55**), achieved flowing groupings of figures through

1.55 William Bouguereau, *Nymphs and Satyr*, 1873. Oil on canvas, 8 ft 6 ins × 5 ft 11 ins (2.59 × 1.8 m). Sterling and Francine Clark Art Institute, Williamstown, Massachusetts.

the application of traditional formulas for composition. But as Impressionism and later contemporary movements gradually took hold, accustoming viewers to more offbeat and abstract effects, Bouguereau's work lost favor. For a long time, it was considered too contrived and romanticized to be taken seriously. In recent years, however, some critics have reassessed this opinion; Bouguereau's work is being shown again at certain museums, and realistic figurative work is coming back into vogue.

CRAFTSMANSHIP AND DESIGN

Another level on which we can appreciate what we see is to admire the skill with which it was crafted or composed. When Kampuchea (Cambodia) is not devastated by war, one can marvel over the ruins of Angkor, a 75-acre complex of carved stone temples built by rulers from the ninth to the fifteenth century. Visitors to *Angkor Wat*, the most famous of these treasuries of South Asian art, are overwhelmed by the craftsmanship evident on every surface of this huge twelfth-century temple complex built by King Suryavarman II of the powerful Khmer dynasty. It took thousands of workers and hundreds of engineers and architects thirty years to quarry and transport massive stones to the site by canals, elephants, and oxcarts, cut them to fit, and then carve them into sculptures and low-relief panels of sacred mythology. The central tower thus constructed is over 200 feet (60.96 m) high (**1.56**). To increase appreciation of such technical triumphs, Parts 2 and 3 of this book will explore artists' media and methods, revealing the difficulties as well as the potential of each medium.

We can appreciate not only the way artists have handled their media but also their sense of design.

This level of appreciation encompasses the ELEMENTS OF DESIGN, which are the visible characteristics of matter: line, shape and form, space, texture, lighting, color, and movement or change through time. Artists study these characteristics and use them quite consciously to achieve their ends, as we will see in Chapter 2. It also involves an awareness of artists' use of the PRINCIPLES OF DESIGN—how a work is organized for a unified effect. The principles of design we will be studying in Chapter 3 include repetition, variety and contrast, rhythm, balance, compositional unity, emphasis, economy, proportion, and relationship to the environment. After studying these elements and principles of design, we might see in the black buck shown in Figure **1.57**, a page in an animal album created for the son of the emperor of Moslem India, the beautiful simplicity of the form of the buck, the sophisticated use of dark and light areas to complement the form, the use of calligraphy as a textural device, and the repetition and variety expressed in the floral border. Even without a formal awareness of the elements and principles at work, we may respond intuitively to their effects by recognizing the pleasing, aesthetically satisfying nature of the work.

1.56 Angkor Wat, Cambodia, 12th century. Stone, central tower 213 ft (64.9 m) high.

1.57 Mansur, *A Black Buck*, Mughal, period of Jahangir 1605–28.
Colors and gilt on paper, 15⅜ × 10¼ ins (39 × 26 cm). The Metropolitan Museum of Art, New York.

1.58 Vera Mukhina, *Machine Tractor Driver and Collective Farm Girl*, undated. Moscow.

IDEA

Another aspect of our appreciation is our understanding of the idea behind a work. The idea of a work is not what it *is* but what it is *about*. Within the subject category of heroic monuments, for instance, there may be variations in the ideas being expressed visually. Heroic monuments often express a larger-than-life ideal. Vera Mukhina's huge *Machine Tractor Driver and Collective Farm Girl* (**1.58**) was intended to inspire people of what was the Soviet Union with the ideals of their country—men and women of all classes working together with great vigor to build the new society. These muscular figures bespeak Youth, Strength, Optimism. They appear to be moving forward so powerfully into the future that their clothing is blown back by the wind. In them is no hint of the weaknesses which caused the dream to collapse less than three-quarters of a century after the Russian Revolution.

By contrast, Maya Lin's *Vietnam Veterans' Memorial* in Washington, D.C. (**1.59**) is a very quiet but nonetheless profoundly moving statement about the deaths of Americans in the Vietnam War. Elegantly and starkly simple, it consists of an angled wall of polished black granite, incised with the names of all the Americans who died in the Vietnam War, and then tapering down to disappear into the earth. In the face of the bitter divisions that once existed between proponents and opponents of American involvement in the war, Lin intentionally avoided presenting a blatant political idea. The meaning of the wall is to be discovered individually by each viewer. Lin explains:

> Many earlier war memorials were propagandized statements about the victor, the issues, the politics, and not about the people who served and died. I felt a memorial should be honest about the reality of war and be for the people who gave their lives. . . . I didn't want a static object that people would just look at, but something they could relate to as on a journey, or passage, that would bring each to his own conclusions. . . . I didn't visualize heavy physical objects implanted in the earth; instead it was as if the black-brown earth were polished and made into an interface between the sunny world and the quiet, dark world beyond, that we can't enter.[14]

The objects shown in a work of art are not necessarily what the work is "about". The subject of Paul Cézanne's *Still-Life with Apples* (shown in Figure 14.36) has far more to do with relationships of objects in space than with apples, bowl, vase, and draped fabric. This distinction between *object matter* and *subject matter* is a particularly important clue to understanding what is going on in nonobjective modern art. But unless the artist has made statements about his or her intentions, we have only our own experience and awareness of similarities with other work to draw on in understanding the subject matter of nonobjective works such as Mark Rothko's *Green on Blue* (1.34). All interpretations of the subject matter of such works must be accepted as speculative and personal.

Ideas are often expressed in visual symbols that will probably be understood by a particular audience. In Mexico, the Day of the Dead is an all-night vigil celebrated at graveyards the night of November 1. Families gather to welcome dead relatives to a feast on the one night they are allowed to return to earth.

1.59 Maya Ying Lin, Vietnam Veterans' Memorial, Washington D.C., 1984.

1.60 Pedro Linares, *Country Skull for the Day of the Dead*. Papier-mâché, 14 ins (35.6 cm) high. Collection of Sal Scalora. Photograph by Beverly Dickinson.

1.61 Hieronymus Bosch, *The Garden of Earthly Delights* (left panel), c. 1500. Museo del Prado, Madrid.

Joyful representations of the dead abound. The most common symbol is the skull, the part of the body least vulnerable to decay. In addition to small candy skulls decorated with flowers, family altars may bear larger papier-mâché skulls. The one shown in Figure **1.60** is a "country skull" by Pedro Linares, so-called because it represents the rejuvenation of life from death. A veritable landscape is sprouting from the material of the smiling, flower-eyed skull—grass, cactus, snake, and even a hill with a raven perched on it.

When a series of symbols is used to tell a familiar story, the imagery is called ICONOGRAPHY. In Judeo-Christian cultures, the most common subjects for iconography are stories from the Bible. The Flemish visionary painter Hieronymus Bosch knew that his contemporaries would recognize Figure **1.61**—the first panel of *The Garden of Earthly Delights*—as a depiction of the Biblical Garden of Eden. The naked humans are to be understood as Adam and Eve, the originally innocent first humans. The pink-robed male figure presenting Eve to Adam is a representation of God, imagined in the Judeo-Christian tradition as an old man. Flora and fauna are lavishly distributed throughout this earthly paradise. Trees laden with fruits are everywhere, but those who know Judeo-Christian iconography will recognize that the fruit hanging from the palm tree in the middle distance with a serpent coiled about it is forbidden, for it gives knowledge of good and evil. The tree behind Adam is apparently the Tree of Life, representing the immortality which the First Couple will forfeit when they eat the forbidden fruit. To this familiar iconography, Bosch adds lush details from his own imagination.

HISTORY

Finally, our appreciation of a work of art may be greatly enhanced through knowing something of the historical or personal context of the work. Some pieces are best understood within the framework of an established tradition; others are best understood as pioneering works that may have lost something of their original impact because the way they showed later became a familiar one.

Roger van der Weyden's *Portrait of a Lady* (**1.62**) fits well into today's spare aesthetic. But at the time, his minimization of detail in search of essence and expression was a departure from tradition. He and the other great Flemish masters of the fifteenth century were experimenting with the newly developing medium of oil and finding that it could be used to create fine details and subtle gradations of light and shadow that had been impossible with tempera. In van der Weyden's hands, oils also had a translucent quality, as though light were radiating outward through the model's fine skin. To help appreciate artists within their historical artistic context, in Chapter 14 we will review the major movements in Western art.

In some cases, it is also helpful to know something about artists' personal lives and inner motivations, as a framework for understanding what they were trying to do. As sensitive, imaginative individuals, artists have often lived unconventional lives, not always by their own choosing. Paul Gauguin, for instance, was

1.62 Roger van der Weyden, *Portrait of a Lady*, c. 1455. Oil on panel, 14½ × 10¾ ins (36.8 × 27.3 cm). The National Gallery of Art, Washington D.C., Mellon Collection.

led by events and his own inner search to abandon the life of a wealthy stockbroker in Paris (partly because business was failing), leaving behind a wife (who may have forced him out) and five children, and taking refuge finally in Tahiti. There his painting became more primitive, exploring the mysterious depths of the unconscious, as in *The Spirit of the Dead Watching* (**1.63**). This spiritual sensitivity, Gauguin felt, was being subverted by materialism in Western civilization. His life in the tropics was hardly idyllic, however. Deserted by his wife, heartbroken over the death of his daughter, impoverished, and physically tormented by syphilis, he tried to poison himself with arsenic but took so much that he threw it up and survived for a few more tortured years. His work can therefore be seen in the context of a determined search for truth in the face of physical and psychological torment.

Paul Gauguin
on
CROSS CULTURAL
BORROWINGS

The French Post-Impressionist painter, Paul Gauguin (1848–1903), had what he called "a terrible itching for the unknown which causes me to commit follies."[15] Leaving the security of his job as a stockbroker, he traveled widely, living as an impoverished artist. His journals and letters are full of disdain for European culture and idealistic impressions of the materially simpler Oceanic cultures in which he eventually tried to realize his dreams—to "escape to the woods of a South Sea Island and live there in ecstasy and peace."[16] But even in Tahiti and the Marquesas, he did not find inner peace, and he openly acknowledged that while his paintings seemed to be about Oceanic subjects, they were his own inventions. "My artistic center is in my head; I am not a painter who works from nature," he wrote in 1892. "With me, everything happens in my wild imagination."[17] The ideas behind his *The Spirit of the Dead Watching* (**1.63**) are those of a European wondering about something he does not fully understand. The paintings thus evoke in the viewer as well a sense of mystery:

"A young native girl lies on her belly, showing a portion of her frightened face. She lies on a bed covered with a blue *pareo* and a light chrome-yellow sheet. As it stands, it is a slightly indecent study of a nude, and yet I wish to make a chaste picture of it, and imbue it with the native feeling, character, and tradition.

The pareo being closely linked with the life of a Tahitian, I use it as a bedspread. The sheet, of bark-cloth, must be yellow, because, in this color, it arouses something unexpected for the spectator, and because it suggests lamplight. I need a background of terror, purple is clearly indicated.

I see only fear. What kind of fear? The *tupapau* (Spirit of the Dead) is clearly indicated. For the natives it is a constant dread. Once I have found my tupapau I attach myself completely to it, and make it the motif of my picture. The nude takes second place.

What can a spirit be, for a Maori? She knows neither theater or novels, and when she thinks of someone dead, she thinks necessarily of someone she has seen. My spirit can only be an ordinary little woman.

The title has two meanings, either she thinks of the spirit; or, the spirit thinks of her. The Soul of a living person linked to the spirit of the dead. Night and Day."[18]

As well as being intrigued by the Oceanic people and landscapes, Gauguin had great admiration for their design traditions. His own increasing use of large areas of relatively flat colors and abstracted shapes is probably influenced by the traditional approaches to design in the cultures he adopted. He wrote:

"We do not seem to suspect in Europe that there exists, both among the Maoris of New Zealand and the Marquesans, a very

1.63 Paul Gauguin, *The Spirit of the Dead Watching*, 1892. Oil on canvas, 38¾ × 36¼ ins (98.4 × 92 cm). Albright-Knox Art Gallery, Buffalo. A. Conger Goodyear Collection.

advanced decorative art. In the Marquesan especially there is an unparalleled sense of decoration. Give him a subject even of the most ungainly geometrical forms and he will succeed in keeping the whole harmonious and in leaving no displeasing or incongruous empty spaces.

Today, even for gold, you can no longer find any of those beautiful objects in bone, rock, iron-wood which they used to make. The police have stolen it all and sold it to amateur collectors; yet the Administration has never for an instant dreamed of establishing a museum in Tahiti, as it could so easily do, for all this Oceanic art.

None of these people who consider themselves learned has ever for an instant suspected the value of the Marquesan artists. Dowdy from head to foot, with their superannuated finery, vulgar hips, tumble-down corsets, imitation jewelry, elbows that threaten you or look like sausages, they are enough to spoil any holiday in this country. But they are white—and their stomachs stick out!

The Marquesan art has disappeared, thanks to the missionaries. The missionaries have considered that sculpture and decoration were fetishism and offensive to the God of the Christians.

That is the whole story, and the unhappy people have yielded."[19]

1.64 Rembrant van Rijn, *Self-Portrait*, c. 1660. Oil on canvas, 33 × 26 ins (84 × 66 cm). The National Gallery of Art, Washington D.C., Mellon Collection.

Some works are so strong that we can respond to them directly, without knowing anything of the artist's personal life or of the historical context. We don't think of Rembrandt as a period artist; we know him as one of the greatest artists of all times. Hundreds of years after the painting of his 1660 self-portrait (**1.64**), that face looks out at us from the darkness with such compelling truth, such strength in design, and such technical skill that its appeal seems timeless. Ultimately, time is the most telling test of quality in art. If a piece is so good that after hundreds of years people will still value it enough to keep and prize it, whether the artist is currently in favor or not, it is probably worthy of being considered great.

2

VISUAL ELEMENTS

The elements of design with which artists work are the observable properties of matter: line, shape and form, space, texture, value (lights and darks) and lighting, color, and time. Although these elements are unified in effective works of art, we will isolate and deal with one at a time to train our eye to see them and to understand how artists use them.

LINE

A mark or area that is significantly longer than it is wide may be perceived as a line. There are lines all around us in the natural world. A tree bare of its leaves, for instance, can be perceived as a medley of lines, as Mondrian noted in his tree abstractions (1.25–1.27). The sections that follow will develop the ability to discern lines in artworks and to understand the aesthetic functions they serve.

SEEING LINES

It is easiest to see lines in works that are primarily linear and two-dimensional, such as the lovely piece of calligraphy shown in Figure 2.1. CALLIGRAPHY is the art of fine writing, so highly developed in Arabic cultures, Japan, and China that some pieces are meant first as art and only secondarily as figures to be read. (Most non-Arabs will see the lines in this piece as purely abstract anyway, because they don't know how to read them as words.) Arabic characters are usually set down in straight lines, but the master calligrapher Sami Efendi worked the strokes into a flowing circular pattern to enhance their beauty and the unity of the design. When lines are made with a flat-pointed instrument, such as the reed pen used here, their thickness grows and diminishes as the lines swing through curves. Note the careful attention paid to the ends of each stroke.

2.1 Sami Efendi,
Levha in Celi Sülüs, 1872.
Private collection, London.

67

2.2 John Alcorn, *The Scarlet Letter*, 1980. Exxon Corporation, for Public Broadcasting Great Performances.

Lines may be seen in unworked as well as worked areas of a design. In John Alcorn's drawing to represent Hawthorne's novel *The Scarlet Letter* for television audiences (**2.2**) we can see not only black lines on white but also white lines defined by black-inked areas. Notice how gracefully Alcorn handles the rapid transitions from the white of the background to the white lines defining the hair, leading us to see the former as NEGATIVE, or unfilled, space, and the latter as POSITIVE, or filled space.

Even more subtly, we perceive lines along EDGES where two areas treated differently meet. Along the left side of Hester Prynne's face, as we see it, there is a strong white line belonging to and describing her profile; the black of her hair shadows is pushed behind it in space. On the right side of her face there is a strong edge belonging to the black of her hair, with her face appearing to be behind it in space.

In three-dimensional works, we may find lines that are incised, raised, or applied to forms. On the Maori ancestor figure (**2.3**) rows of small lines are used to create textured effects and slow the eye. These occur within larger patterns of curving lines that define the figure in a highly stylized, dynamic fashion. This symphony of lines is set off and brought to our attention by contrast with the large unworked club in the center.

Edges may be "read," or interpreted, as lines in three-dimensional work as well as in two-dimensional works. Part of the effectiveness of Barnett Newman's *Broken Obelisk* (**2.4**) lies in the sharp edges where flat planes meet, creating visual lines that emphasize the form and define its three-dimensionality (**2.5**). If the top and bottom segments were rounded, without the lines of the edges, the effect would be quite different.

2.3 Ancestor Figure, c. 1842.
Wood, 55 × 25¼ ins (140 × 64 cm) high.
National Museum of New Zealand.

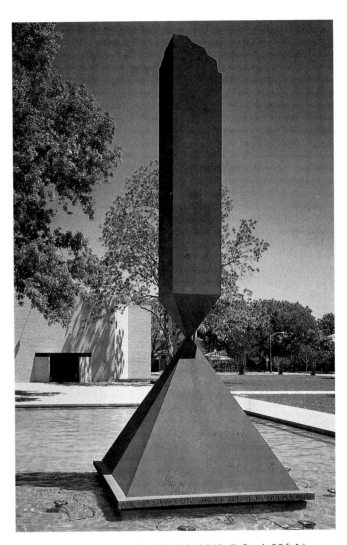

2.4 Barnett Newman, *Broken Obelisk*, 1963–7. Steel, 25 ft 1 in (7.65 m) high. Institute of Religion and Human Development, Houston, Texas.

2.5 Lines formed by the edges of *Broken Obelisk*.

2.7 Christo, *Running Fence, Sonoma and Marin Counties, California, 1972–76*, erected 1976. Nylon fabric, steel poles, cable, 18 ft × 24½ miles (5.5 m × 40 km). © Christo 1976. Photograph © Jeanne-Claude Christo 1993.

In some three-dimensional pieces, entire areas are so thin in relation to their length that they are seen as lines. The human figure is sometimes handled as abstract lines in space, a perception that is carried to an extreme in the attenuated figures of Alberto Giacometti, such as *Walking Man* (**2.6**). This reduction of a human to something less than a skeleton can be seen as a statement about the isolation and loneliness of the individual in modern civilization. Giacometti himself insisted that his focus lay not so much on the gaunt figure as on the vast, empty space that surrounds and presses in on it. It is hard to grasp this perspective when looking at a photograph, but in actuality, the small scale of the battered figure—only 27 inches (69 cm) high—does make the space surrounding it seem even greater.

EARTHWORKS—large-scale environment-altering projects in which the surface of the earth becomes the artist's canvas—sometimes create immense lines that can best be seen from a distance. Up close, Christo's *Running Fence* (**2.7**) appeared as a great fabric curtain, 18 feet (5.5 m) high. Its even more memorable aspect was the beautiful line it created over 24½ miles (40 km) of northern California countryside, ultimately disappearing into the Pacific Ocean. To erect this temporary structure for only

2.6 Alberto Giacometti, *Walking Man*, c. 1947–9. Bronze, 27 ins (69 cm) high. Hirshhorn Museum and Sculpture Garden, Smithsonian Institution, Washington D.C. Gift of Joseph H. Hirshhorn, 1966.

two weeks in 1976, Christo and a large crew of engineers and lawyers spent three years threading their way through public hearings and legal battles, including a 265-page environmental impact statement they were required to produce. These struggles with a disbelieving society are part of Christo's art form; the temporary end product is not the only goal. Neither was the line of the fence the only visual element in the design; its existence also called attention to the contours and features of the land. Speaking of the ranchers who gave their support to Christo in obtaining the permits and who were sorry when, as intended, it was taken down and all traces of it removed, Christo was pleased that "they can find that a part of *Running Fence* is their cows, and the sky, and the hills and the barns and the people."[1]

IMPLIED LINE

Some lines are not physically created; they are merely suggested by the artist. Our mind, with its penchant for trying to read order into the messages from the senses, does the rest, perceiving lines where there are none. Part of the visual excitement of the ad for *Harper's Magazine* (**2.8**) by The Beggarstaffs (a farsighted but short-lived British design studio around the turn of the century) is the filling in of lines that have been left out. Just enough information is given for us to see the famous figure of a beefeater in his distinctive uniform. The illusion works particularly well along the right side of his lower tunic, where an edge is suggested by very slight upward swings of the dark bands.

2.8 William Nicholson and James Pryde, called The Beggarstaff Brothers, Poster for *Harper's Magazine*, 1895. Victoria and Albert Museum.

2.9 Piet Mondrian, *Fox Trot A*, 1930.
Canvas, diagonal 3 ft 7¾ ins (1.09 m).
Yale University Art Gallery,
New Haven, CT. Gift of the
Société Anonyme.

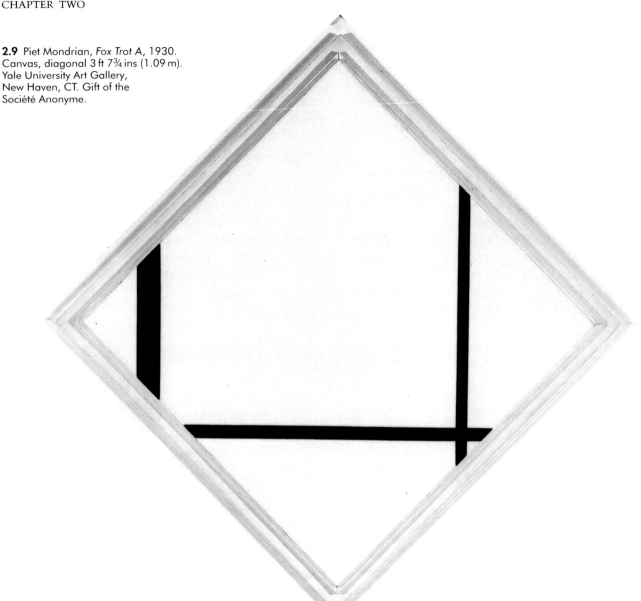

In many two-dimensional works the artist asks us to make assumptions about what "happens" beyond the edges of the picture. To do so, we need to be given enough information for us to draw inferences based on our experiences of the physical world. Geometric figures are perhaps easiest to predict. Shown part of a square or a circle, we may automatically fill in the rest with our imagination. In *Fox Trot A* (**2.9**), Piet Mondrian shows us a cropped segment of a linear image that by implication extends beyond the picture area. The challenge he sets for us is to determine how much larger the uncropped "original" would be. We automatically assume that the left vertical and the horizontal will continue as straight lines and intersect just beyond the picture. But what about the two verticals? Will they be joined by a crosspiece above the top? The only clue that the cropped segment shown may be part of a hypothetical series of rectangles—like a multi-paned window—is the crossing of the two lines at lower right. The suggestion that the figure doesn't end here leads the mind outward to imagine a much larger series of lines that it cannot see at all.

In addition to drawing the viewer into participating in a work, implied lines are often used for compositional ends. Eyelines—the implied lines

2.10 Thorn Puller (*Spinario*), 1st century BC.
Bronze, 28¾ ins (73 cm) high.
Capitoline Museums, Rome.

along which a subject's eyes appear to be looking—are a common device for directing the viewer's eye or pulling a composition together. Usually eyelines occur between figures, as in Bouguereau's *Nymphs and Satyr* (1.55), in which each person in the circle is looking at someone who is looking at someone else, so tying them all together. But in the Hellenistic bronze *Thorn Puller* (2.10), we follow the "line" between the youth's eyes and his own foot, for his concentration is so clearly fixed on his foot that our eyes go in the same direction. His limbs are also arranged to form lines that lead our eye toward the foot. Our attention is often drawn to points where many lines intersect. If our eye then strays to examining the figure as a whole, the lines of the body carry us around in a circle to arrive back at the same point.

DESCRIPTIVE LINE

Line that is DESCRIPTIVE tells us the physical nature of the object we are seeing and how it exists in space. By contrast, DECORATIVE line is that which provides surface embellishments, such as the A on Hester Prynne's dress (2.2).

In *Narcissus* (**2.11**), the spare inked line is purely descriptive. Although the paper has the same tone everywhere, the line tells us to read certain unfilled areas as positive leaves and flowers and the rest as negative unfilled space. Not only do the outlines allow us to "see" the narcissus plant; they also describe the space around it. The plant has been carefully placed on the page in such a way that the negative areas become satisfying in themselves as a series of shapes that alternately curve softly outward (such as the large unfilled space at lower left) and plunge in pointed tips into the heart of the stem. The lines also describe two enclosed pointed spaces below the flowers.

2.11 after Chu Ta, *Narcissus*, 1625–1705.
Ink on paper, 12⅛ × 10½ ins (30.8 × 26.5 cm).
British Museum, London.

2.12 Albrecht Dürer, *Head of an Apostle*, 1508. Brush on paper, 12½ × 8⅓ ins (31.7 × 21.2 cm).
Graphische Sammlung Albertina, Vienna.

2.13 Arnold Bittleman, *Martyred Flowers*, c. 1957.
Pen and ink, 26 × 38¾ ins (66 × 98 cm).
Fogg Art Museum, Harvard University, Cambridge MA.

Whereas the narcissus drawing is quite flat in space, lines are often used to describe three-dimensional form. *Head of an Apostle* by the great German artist Albrecht Dürer (**2.12**) appears to have continually varying contours and to be fully rounded in space. Dürer achieved this extremely detailed depiction of a venerable, beetle-browed head largely by highly skillful use of line. Drawn close together, dark parallel lines (HATCHING) and crossed parallel lines (CROSS-HATCHING) suggest shadows where contours curve away from the light. Where the lines seem to loop in visually incompleted ovals around an axis, a technique known as BRACELET MODELING, they imply the contours of the unseen back side of the form.

Many small lines placed close together may also be used to suggest texture. In Arnold Bittleman's *Martyred Flowers* (**2.13**) we readily perceive textural effects even though we cannot be sure what forms are being described. The title refers to flowers; yet in places the textures appear feathery, wing-like. These are not hastily scribbled strokes; each line was placed with great care. Where many are juxtaposed, dark areas develop that create a mysterious undulation in and out in space. Note that variations in thickness and spacing of the lines creates a range of degrees of darkness, or value, with many shades of gray.

EXPRESSIVE QUALITIES OF LINE

By its character—its size, movement, and the way it is laid down—line may express certain emotional qualities. Sharply angled lines may suggest excitement, anger, danger, or chaos; a relatively flat line suggests calmness; a wide, fast line suggests bold strength, directness; a gently curving line may suggest unhurried pleasure (2.14). Such expressive qualities may set the tone for works of art.

The reclining rocking chair by the Austrian firm of Thonet (2.15) suggests, by its long, flowing lines, the restful feeling that one expects to experience when lying in the chair. As the lines flow through lengthened curves, it is difficult to follow a single line; rather, we are visually drawn into the abstract expressive quality of the lines: the sense of languid movement. In the mid-nineteenth century, Michael Thonet had perfected a process of steaming and bending wood that allowed the creation of these plant-like lines and greatly reduced the need for structural joints in furniture. The graceful bentwood furniture designs became so popular that many have continued in production to this day.

2.14 Lines with varying expressive qualities.

2.15 Gebrüder Thonet, *Reclining rocking chair with adjustable back*, c. 1880. Steam-bent beechwood and cane, 30½ × 27½ × 68½ ins (77.5 × 70 × 174 cm). Collection, The Museum of Modern Art, New York. Phyllis B. Lambert fund and gift of the four seasons.

2.16 Eliza Schulte, *Alphabet*,
Gouache on paper, 11½ × 7½ ins (29.2 × 19 cm).
Courtesy of the artist.

Expressive lines in two-dimensional art often have a GESTURAL quality. That is, they directly reveal the artist's arm at work, transferring expressive gestures into marks on a surface. In Eliza Schulte's *Alphabet* (**2.16**) two very different kinds of calligraphic gestures are contrasted. The wide lines spelling ALPHABET have a powerful, graved-in-stone-forever feeling; we can picture the artist with feet firmly planted, making exaggerated vertical strokes with her brush. The thin letters seem to dance lightly and gracefully around them; one imagines their being made with large, flowing gestures with no breaks in the arm movement.

For another example of the expressive possibilities of pure line, consider John Crocker's album cover for Schubert's violin music (**2.17**). A blank set of staves goes through a gradual, comically plausible metamorphosis into a visual equivalent of Schubert's romantic music, with flourishes and embellishments. Such lines can quite literally be called *lyrical*, a term used in describing art that is the visual equivalent of melodies that express intimate emotions.

2.17 John Crocker, CBS album cover, 1968.

2.18 A. M. Cassandre, Poster, 1927. Colored lithograph, 41½ × 29½ ins (105 × 75 cm). Victoria and Albert Museum, London.

DIRECTIONAL LINE

Lines may be used in art to tell us which way to look. In the poster for a luxury train by the great French poster designer A. M. Cassandre (**2.18**), we are placed squarely on top of the rail that is perpendicular to the bottom edge of the poster. Our eye races along the rail to the point where all the rails converge and disappear on the horizon. The immediate impression is that of speed and elegance in covering great distances. These directional lines lead us effortlessly to our destination—and beyond, to a star.

SHAPE AND FORM

Throughout this book we will be using the word SHAPE to refer to defined two-dimensional areas. As we use the term, a shape is flat. We will reserve the word FORM for three-dimensional areas, also called "volume" or "mass." But flat shapes may appear on the surface of three-dimensional forms, and two-dimensional works may create on a flat surface the illusion of forms.

ACTUAL THREE-DIMENSIONAL FORMS

To understand the many ways in which three-dimensional forms work aesthetically, we can set up some overlapping categories of features. These include exterior and interior contours, open versus closed forms, and static versus dynamic forms. The surfaces of a three-dimensional work are sometimes called its CONTOURS. They may project outward (convex) or inward (concave) relative to the general body of the form.

Some three-dimensional works have both EXTERIOR and INTERIOR CONTOURS that can be examined. In architecture, the exterior form of a building gives quite a different impression from its interior structure. In some works, we are invited to look at both exterior and interior contours simultaneously. The lovely flask shown in Figure **2.19** is made of clear crystal, revealing the concave pear-shaped contour within a similar but convex exterior contour. The interior contour is emphasized and elaborated by the bubbles surrounding it.

2.19 Maurice Mainot, Flask, 1931.
Clear crystal glass with bubbles, 4⅞ ins (12.4 cm) high.
Victoria and Albert Museum, London.

A more subtle kind of interior form can only be sensed, rather than seen. Barbara Hepworth, whose work is shown in Figure 2.23, had a highly refined awareness of unseen interior forms. In her autobiography, published in 1970, she wrote:

There is an inside and an outside to every form. When they are in special accord, as for instance a nut in its shell or a child in the womb, or in the structure of shells or crystals, or when one senses the architecture of bones in the human figure, then I am most drawn to the effect of light. Every shadow cast by the sun from an ever-varying angle reveals the harmony of the inside and the outside.[2]

Many early Western sculptures were CLOSED FORMS that reflected the block from which they had been carved. The block of stone from which the early Egyptian sculpture of *Senmut with Princess Nefrua* (**2.20**) has been carved is drawn in only slightly at the

2.20 *Senmut with Princess Nefrua*, Thebes, Egypt, c. 1450 BC.
Black stone, 3 ft 4 ins (1.02 m) high.
Egyptian Museum, Berlin.

2.21 after Polyclitus, *Spear Bearer (Doryphorus)*,
Roman copy after a Greek bronze original of c. 450–400 BC.
Marble, 6 ft 6 ins (1.98 m) high. National Museum, Naples.

base. To create the heads—particularly that of the child—far more of the original block has been removed, yet the overall impression is that of a solid mass. As stone carving evolved, sculptors learned how to open the forms without losing their structural strength. In the *Spear Bearer* (**2.21**), the legs are placed apart and the arms are lifted slightly away from the body. Yet to keep the limbs from breaking off— as they often did—several props have been maintained.

The development of bronze casting allowed fully OPEN FORMS, such as the equestrian statue of Marcus Aurelius (**2.22**). This piece almost seems to show off the ability to support long projections from a central mass, with the horse's leg raised and the emperor's arm outstretched. The space around the horse and between its legs is so opened that it invites walking all the way around to see how the form changes. The tensile strength of bronze allows it to be cast into elongated forms without bending or breaking.

In the twentieth century, a number of sculptors have gone even farther, opening voids through the center of their works. In Barbara Hepworth's *Pendour* (2.23) the holes piercing the center of the form draw the focus of attention. These ambiguous voids are accentuated by contrast with the solidity and simplicity of the outer form. Defined by wood painted white, in contrast with the darker exterior, they suggest a quality of tender, hidden purity protected from the outside world. They lure us into looking through the sculpture, exploring what can be seen in and through it instead of just walking around its periphery.

2.22 Equestrian statue of Marcus Aurelius, c. AD 165. Bronze, over life size. Capitoline Hill, Rome.

2.23 Barbara Hepworth, *Pendour*, 1947. Painted wood, 10⅜ × 27¼ × 9 ins (26 × 69 × 23 cm). Hirshhorn Museum and Sculpture Garden, Smithsonian Institution, Washington D.C. Gift of Joseph H. Hirshhorn.

2.24 Henry Moore, *Sheep Piece*, 1971–2, at Hoglands, Hertfordshire, England.
Bronze, 19 ft (5.8 m) long.
Courtesy the Henry Moore Foundation, Herts.

Henry Moore
on
FORM AND SPACE

When Henry Moore (1898–1986) was a student at The Royal College of Art in London, he visited the British Museum twice a week to explore the riches of the world's sculptural traditions. The one that spoke to him the most was the sculpture of ancient Mexico, with its powerful closed forms. He also had a lifetime interest in organic forms, such as weather-worn bones and water-smoothed pebbles. From these and other elements, he evolved a distinctive personal sculptural style characterized by abstract rounded contours interwoven with shapely voids, as in his *Sheep Piece* around which sheep cluster at his homestead (**2.24**). Whether he was working in stone, wood, or bronze castings, Moore was consistently interested in the interplay between positive form and negative space, and in how a piece looks from all sides:

"Appreciation of sculpture depends upon the ability to respond to form in three dimensions. That is perhaps why sculpture has been described as the most difficult of all arts.... Many more people are 'form-blind' than colour-blind. The child learning to see, first distinguishes only two-dimensional shape; it cannot judge distances, depths. Later, for its personal safety and practical needs, it has to develop (partly by means of touch) the ability to judge roughly three-dimensional distances. But having satisfied the requirements of practical necessity, most people go no farther.... They do not make the further intellectual and emotional effort needed to comprehend form in its full spatial existence.

This is what the sculptor must do. He must strive continually to think of, and use, form in its full spatial completeness. He gets the solid shape, as it were, inside his head—he thinks of it, whatever its size, as if he were holding it completely enclosed in the hollow of his hand. He mentally visualises a complex form from all round itself; he knows while he looks at one side what the other side is like; he identifies himself with its centre of gravity, its mass, its weight."[3]

"At one time the holes in my sculpture were made for their own sakes. Because I was trying to become conscious of spaces in the sculpture—I made the hole have a shape in its own right, the solid body was encroached upon, eaten into, and sometimes the form was only the shell holding the hole. Recently I have attempted to make the forms and the spaces (not holes) inseparable, neither being more important than the other...."[4]

"If you hold your hand as I am doing now, the shape that those fingers could enclose if I were holding an apple would be different from the shape if I were holding a pear. If you can tell what that is, then you know what space is. That is space and form. You can't understand space without being able to understand form and to understand form you must be able to understand space. If I can really grasp in my mind the shape of your head, I must know what distance there is from your forehead to the back of your head, and I must know what shape the air is between your eyebrows and your nostrils, or down to the cheeks. The idea that space is something new in sculpture is only spoken of by people who can't know what space and form are."[5]

Finally, we can draw a distinction between static and dynamic forms. STATIC forms appear to be still, unchanging. The pyramid is a supremely static form, for its broad base seems to guarantee an immovable stability. Michael Heizer's *City Complex One* (**2.25**) has an enduring, monumental effect. Like the surrounding mountains, it looks set to remain standing a very long time. Indeed, in contrast to the more temporary nature of many earthworks, this structure was built to last, with concrete and steel reinforcing packed earth. The sense of historical permanence that Heizer's structure evokes is increased by its reference to ancient structures: the mastabas of ancient Egypt, which were tombs with rectangular base and sloped sides; the framing derived from a ball court at the ancient Mayan city Chichén-Itzá.

DYNAMIC forms are those that appear lively, moving, and changing, even if they are really standing still. The Art Nouveau movement in applied art often worked with dynamic forms, such as Louis Comfort Tiffany's exquisite *Flower-form Vase* (**2.26**). From chairs to vases to stair railings, Art Nouveau designs appear to be growing as though they are organic forms. Tiffany's vase exposes the dynamic process by which the glass was blown, pulled, and shaped when in a molten state. Although the end result is hard and fixed, it appears still to be in fluid motion, like a bud in the process of reaching upward and growing outward.

2.25 Michael Heizer, *City Complex One*, 1972–6, Garden Valley, Nevada. Cement, steel, and earth, 23½ × 140 × 110 ft (7 × 43 × 34 m). Collection: the artist and Virginia Dwan.

2.26 Louis Comfort Tiffany, Flower-form vase, c. 1900. Iridescent glass with internal decoration, 12¾ ins (32.3 cm) high. The Corning Museum of Glass, New York.

TWO-DIMENSIONAL ILLUSION OF FORM

Through the ages, artists of many cultures have developed ways of creating the illusion of three-dimensional form on a two-dimensional surface. One of the earliest devices is the use of OVERLAPPING: From our experience in a three-dimensional world, we know that if one thing covers another from our view, it must exist in front of it in space.

In the Persian miniature painting (**2.27**), the hands and sleeves of Moses (the figure on the left) and the archangel Gabriel obscure part of their garments,

2.27 *The Prophet Mohammad with the archangel Gabriel meeting Moses in Heaven.* Persian miniature painting from Mustafa Zarir's *The Book of the Life of the Prophet*, c. 1594. 12¼ × 8 ins (31.1 × 20.3 cm). Museum for Islamische Kunst, Berlin-Dahlem.

2.28 Jean Auguste Dominique Ingres, *Two Nudes*, study for *The Golden Age*, 1842.
Graphite on paper, 16⅜ × 12⅜ ins (41.6 × 31.4 cm). Fogg Art Museum, Harvard University, Cambridge MA.

telling us that the arms are closer to us than the rest of their bodies. Likewise, Gabriel's crown slightly overlaps his wings, placing crown ahead of wings spatially. Nevertheless, the figures are painted in solid colors, giving them a slightly flat appearance, like paper dolls.

Another set of devices—SHADING and MODELING of contours—brings out a sense of spatial depth. In the elegantly understated Ingres figure study (**2.28**) just the slightest indication of shading within the primary contours develops a full-bodied illusion of form, for we interpret shaded areas as existing behind contours that block the light. Curving lines of bracelet modeling, such as those on the woman's left leg, suggest that the form is also fully rounded on the side we cannot see. In areas such as the heads, where bracelet modeling is not added, the figures read more like reliefs than like full-round forms.

Another device for giving a two-dimensional surface the appearance of three-dimensional forms is to show more than one side of a form, indicating how it recedes into the distance. If we see only the front wall of a building, we have no idea of the building's depth in space. But if an artist depicts the building

from an angle that allows us to see one of the sides as well as the front, we immediately grasp the idea of its form. Paul Cézanne studied nature—and human perceptions of natural objects—with great care to determine how we see them and therefore how a painter might truthfully represent the optical sensations. In *Mont Sainte-Victoire seen from Les Lauves* (**2.29**), a complex array of buildings, trees, and facets of the mountain he so often painted are reduced to abstract geometric structures. Some are painted in clear linear perspective, with sides angling back toward the horizon. (The topic of linear perspective is covered in depth later in this chapter in the discussion of Space.) Others are brush-stroked suggestions of geometric form. In letters to an art student, Cézanne advised:

> To achieve progress nature alone counts, and the eye is trained through contact with her. . . . In an orange, an apple, a bowl, a head, there is a culminating point; and this point is always—in spite of the tremendous effect of light and shade and colorful sensations—the closest to our eye; the edges of the objects recede to a center on our horizon. . . . Treat nature by the cylinder, the sphere, the cone, everything in proper perspective so that each side of an object or a plane is directed toward a central point.[6]

2.29 Paul Cézanne, *Mont Sainte-Victoire seen from Les Lauves*, 1902–4. Oil on canvas, 27½ × 35¼ ins (69.8 × 89.5 cm). Philadelphia Museum of Art, George W. Elkins Collection.

SHAPES

In the terminology we are using, SHAPES are relatively flat areas. In *The Snail* (**2.30**), for instance, Henri Matisse was working primarily with large shapes that had been painted and then cut and organized into a dynamic composition in which each painted shape touches and is related to the sequence forming the whole. Shapes are particularly noticeable here because they have been physically cut out with clearly defined edges and then glued down. Note that the white shapes created between the colored shapes are active and interesting in themselves, and more varied in configuration than the colored patches.

There are a number of general kinds of shapes with which artists have worked. One is the distinctive result of tearing or cutting paper, as in the Matisse. Another is the flattening of objects from the three-dimensional world into two-dimensional shapes.

In his *Hiroshima Series: Boy with Kite* (**2.31**), Jacob Lawrence depicts the horror of the atomic bombing by reducing human figures into a series of disjointed, flattened shapes. The deformed shapes of skull-like heads and agonized hands stand out as disembodied parts of a whole that is no longer unified, that no longer works, as flat and broken as the torn shapes of the kite. We read such a composition from shape to shape across a relatively flat surface in which the only indication of any depth is the continual overlapping of one shape by another.

2.30 Henri Matisse, *The Snail*, 1953.
Painted, cut, and pasted paper, 9 ft 4¾ ins × 9 ft 5 ins (2.86 × 2.87 m). The Tate Gallery, London.

2.31 Jacob Lawrence, *Hiroshima Series*, 1983, No. 7: *Boy with Kite*. Gouache on paper, 23 × 17½ ins (58.4 × 44.5 cm). Seattle Art Museum. Collection of Gwendolyn and Jacob Lawrence.

Arshile Gorky

on

THE INTENSITY OF ART

At first glance, Arshile Gorky's shapes may seem fanciful, spontaneous, playful, but his own life and words correct this impression. Born in Armenia in 1904 as Vosdanik Adoian, Gorky experienced both the joys of life in a well-to-do family in the Armenian countryside and the terrible sufferings of the Armenian people. His father left for America when Gorky was four years old, to avoid being drafted by the Turks to fight other Armenians. The Turks killed all his grandparents, six uncles, and three aunts, in some cases before his eyes. His family residence was shelled, and his people were forced to undertake a 150-mile death march. That year, 1915, two million Armenians were massacred by the Turks. Gorky and his younger sister worked to bring home what food they could in the face of a Turkish blockade, but when he was fifteen his beloved mother died of starvation in his arms while dictating a letter to his father.

In 1920 Gorky emigrated to America, where he faced hunger and poverty but gradually achieved recognition and considerable influence as an artist, only to see some of his best works destroyed in a barn fire. In 1948, his father died. The same year Gorky's neck was broken and his painting arm paralyzed in an automobile crash. His wife also left him, taking their two children with her. He ended this life of suffering that year by hanging himself. Gorky's words about art therefore ring with the intensity of his personal experience:

"My Armenian experiences have quickened my consciousness to a greater sensitivity of feeling and a higher level of discrimination. In revealing myself, it is my purpose to reveal people to themselves. An artist must see and feel and understand as opposed to those who merely glimpse but do not really see.

The camera has rendered impotent any attempt to compete with it. What reason, therefore, remains to sit in the stagnation of realism? Art is more than mere chronicle. It must mirror the intellect and the emotion, for anyone can portray realism. The mind's eye in its infinity of radia-tions. It is left for the artist to forge the new metal, to resurrect his ancient role as the uncoverer and interpreter, but never the recorder, of life's secrets.

When I speak of the great influence of Armenia on my art, some here mistakenly call it chauvinism. It is decidedly not chauvinism at all and they do not understand; for good or bad I believe that I have experienced more than most of my fellow artists. This does not automatically enable me to know more. But it does enable me to respond necessarily to more experiences than they have had the ability to observe directly. As Armenians of Van, we were forced to experience with greater intensity and in a short-er time what others can only read about while sitting in comfort. We lived and experienced it. The blood of our people at the hands of the Turks, the massacres and genocide. Our death march, our relatives and dearest friends dying in battle before our eyes. The loss of our homes, the destruction of our country by the Turks, Mother's starvation in my arms.

2.32 Arshile Gorky, *Making the Calendar*, 1947. Oil on canvas. The Munson-William-Proctor Institute, Utica, New York. Edward W. Root Bequest.

We have been made privy to mankind's evil secrets as well as its glorious achievements. And the living, sensitive, thinking man cannot help but respond with greater than normal intensity. And the remembrance of Armenia's beauty prior to the bloodshed. The art and accomplishments of our unfortunate people. Great art's problem, that is to say my goal, is to enable those who have not experienced certain elements of reality to experience them through the power of my work on their mind and eyes and imagination. To enable them to come as close to realization of reality as possible, simply through my work.

To be alive is to feel, to be sensitive, and above all to be aware. Art must always remain earnest. Great art contains great topics. What do I mean by great? Not kings, rich men, and clerics, not publicized political scoundrels. I mean love of man, love of nature, love of beauty, love of progress in the well-being of man. Sarcasm has no place in art because it verges on cynicism, which is weakness and the inability to face reality, to master reality.

The history of our Armenian people has shown us the secret of creativity. The secret is to throw yourself into the water of life again and again, not to hang back, no reservations, risk everything, but, above all, strike out boldly with all you have."[7]

Abstracted shapes may be so extensively reworked that they begin to lose their representational identity, for everyone except the artist. Arshile Gorky's shapes in *Making the Calendar* (**2.32**) may appear purely imaginative inventions, but they are derived from a family scene: One of his daughters sits on the left before a window onto the Connecticut countryside, below a calendar. In the center of the painting, there is a dog on the floor in front of a fireplace. To the right, Gorky stands reading a magazine with one hand on the shoulder of his wife, who is rocking their baby in a cradle. Gorky says of such work, "Though the various forms all had specific meaning to me, it is the spectator's privilege to find his own meaning."[8]

Geometric shapes have long been used as a design element in many cultures. The water jar by the pueblo potter Lucy Lewis (1.13) is decorated with black and white triangles within squares, alternating with diamond-like shapes created by lines, woven into squares of the same size. A Liberian gown (**2.33**) is composed largely of geometric shapes—circles, squares, rectangles, and triangles—whose symmetry is a striking counterpoint to the asymmetrical style of the gown. Although the shapes are worked flat on the cloth, when the gown is worn they will become more three-dimensional as the cloth drapes over the contours of the body.

Shapes can be created in unfilled as well as filled areas of a design. We perceived unworked white shapes in Matisse's *The Snail* (2.30), but they were not the focus of the work. In Helen Frankenthaler's *Mauve District* (**2.34**), an unpainted white area appears as a POSITIVE shape that is as important as the painted areas. We are meant to perceive the unworked space as "filled" rather than "empty." Frankenthaler explains:

That area not painted on didn't need paint because it had paint next to it. So it operated as forcefully, and the thing was to decide where to leave it and where to show it and where to say, "This doesn't need another line or another

2.33 Gown, made by the Mandingo of Liberia. Dyed and woven cotton cloth, decorated wilth embroidery and appliqué, 36½ ins (93 cm) high. British Museum, London.

2.34 Helen Frankenthaler, *Mauve District*, 1966.
Synthetic polymer on unprimed canvas, 8 ft 7 ins × 7 ft 11 ins (2.616 ×2.43 m).
Collection, The Museum of Modern Art, New York. Mrs. Donald B. Strauss Fund.

pail of color." In other words, the very ground was part of the medium. Red, blue, against the white of cotton duck or the beige of linen has the same play in space as the duck. Every square inch of that surface is equally important in depth, shallowness, space, so that it isn't as if background meant the background is a curtain or a drape in front of which there is a table, on which there is a plate, on which there are apples. The apples are as important as the drape, and the drape is as important as the legs of the table.[9]

The shapes shown thus far are HARD-EDGED. That is, their boundaries are clearly distinguished from surrounding areas by contrasts in color along the edges where they meet. The fact that Jacob Lawrence turns body parts into hard-edged shapes in his Hiroshima painting (2.31) forces the eye to focus on the frighteningly erratic outlines of those shapes.

Some artists work instead with SOFT-EDGED shapes. When edges are not precisely delineated, it may be hard to pinpoint where one shape stops and another begins, but we may still get a sense of the presence of shapes. Odilon Redon, one of the foremost of the Symbolist painters of the late nineteenth century, created a dream-like atmosphere for *Orpheus* (2.35) through softly diffused lights and shadows and a barely defined outline for the severed head of Orpheus. The blue cloth is an even more soft-edged shape. Redon, who sought visible expression of the products of the unconscious, saw the mythical still-singing head of the dead Orpheus as a symbol of art's immortality.

Shapes may also be created to express a certain

93

2.35 Odilon Redon, *Orpheus*, after 1903.
Pastel, 27½ × 22¼ ins (70 × 56.5 cm).
Cleveland Museum of Art.

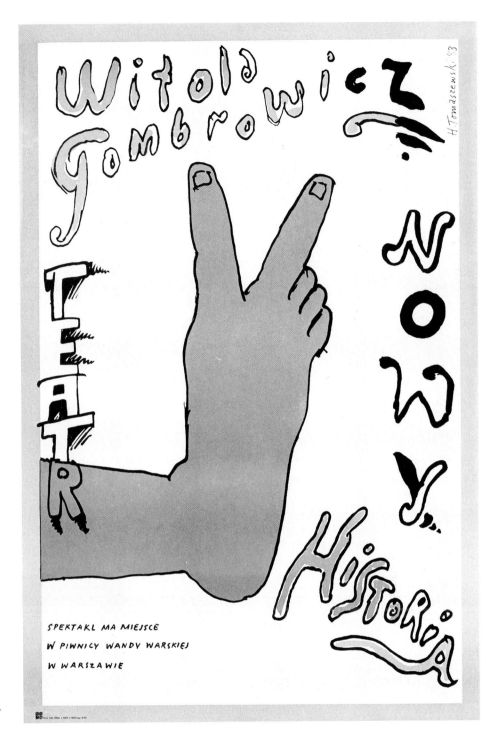

2.36 Henryk Tomaszewski,
Poster for the work of Witold Gombrowicz,
1983. Stedelijk Museum, Amsterdam.

emotion. In the context of martial law in Poland in 1983, there was no ambiguity about the emotion being expressed by the great Polish poster artist, Henryk Tomaszewski, in his poster advertising an art show (**2.36**). Prohibited by censorship from showing a "V for victory" hand signal, Tomaszewski presented a foot that clearly bespeaks a defiant, playful freedom. With its slightly bumpy, hairy edges, this shape immediately suggests a down-to-earth populace who will persist in asserting their inner freedom, no matter what restrictions might be imposed by the government.

2.37 Manasie Manaipik, *Good Spirit*, 1969, Pangnirtung, Northwest Territories, Canada. Whale vertebra, 12½ × 18⅝ ×7½ ins (32 × 48 × 19 cm). Macmillan-Bloedel Limited, Vancouver.

SPACE

In art, as in life, space is an intangible element. Yet artists work quite consciously with spatial aspects of our existence to achieve the effects they desire. Those we will explore here are the ways in which three-dimensional art controls space, the differing ways space is handled in two-dimensional work, the concept of scale, and the mystery of spatial illusions.

THREE-DIMENSIONAL ART IN SPACE

On the most basic level, three-dimensional art physically occupies space. It has its own very obvious spatial reality—the volume of air it displaces. Less obvious are other ways in which certain works exist in space.

Some works delineate forms in space, shaping the intangible into contoured areas. In Manasie Manaipik's *Good Spirit* sculpture (**2.37**), the open area in a whale's vertebra that once housed the spinal cord is brought to our attention as an interesting form in itself. The hard edges of the opening and its regular contours help us to "see" the form of the unfilled space. Certain architectural forms work the same way, defining a volume in space by enclosing it. In the great Byzantine church of Hagia Sophia (**2.39**), the central interior space is a vast domed square rising 183 feet (56 m) above the floor. A model of the interior (**2.38**) reveals the form of this space as though it were a solid mass. This delineated space surrounds worshippers—originally restricted to the emperor, his court, and the clergy—with an awe-inspiring microcosm of the vastness of the universe and the greatness of its Creator.

2.38 Model of the interior space of Hagia Sophia.

2.39 (right) Hagia Sophia, Istanbul, AD 532–37. Dome 183 ft (56 m) high.

2.40 Joseph Cornell, *The Hotel Eden*, 1945. Assemblage with music box, 15⅛ × 15⅝ × 4¾ in (38.3 × 39.7 × 12.1 cm). National Gallery of Canada, Ottawa. Photo by Bruce C. Jones, courtesy of Xavier Fourcade, Inc.

Some sculptures carve out their own small world in a confined space. Joseph Cornell has done many works of this sort, defining an area by means of a glass case and then building up enigmatic compositions within it from FOUND OBJECTS. In his *The Hotel Eden* (**2.40**), there is a sense of faded Victorian romance—the exotic paper parrot, listings in French, the remains of a poster for what appears to be a large seaside hotel. Beyond these relatively identifiable clues to content, the identity, meanings, and relationships of the found objects exist in a private fantasy world of the artist. Why the ball? The concentric circles to which the parrot holds a string? The glass of white cylinders? Cornell collected all sorts of objects that delighted him, from marbles and toys to sky charts, and created small scenes with them that tempt the mind beyond its usual frame of reference. Within a space so defined and set apart, everyday objects lose their usual identities and become whatever the artist and viewers' imaginations perceive them to be.

It is possible for a three-dimensional work to "control" an area larger than it physically occupies. Sculptures with pointed linear projections may seem to activate the space around them, as if the lines continued for some distance into that space. The bold lines of Mark di Suvero's sculpture *She* (**2.41**) are so strong that their commanding presence is felt beyond the edges of the steel. Furthermore, it is a participatory sculpture with three movable parts to swing on. When these swinging members are in motion, the sculpture seems to command an even greater volume of space.

It is also possible for three-dimensional art to control us in space. Architecture provides defined rooms and halls and stairways that guide our movements. Gardens may also be planned to manipulate people's movements through space, using pathways and barriers. In the Japanese garden shown in Figure **2.42**, the way across the pond is defined by a path and then by stepping stones, all carefully arranged to imitate nature. The artistry of Japanese garden design leads us to step in specific places, at a specific pace, so that we are invited to enjoy artfully composed views of the landscape. When these devices work well, we are unaware of being manipulated.

2.41 Mark di Suvero, *She*, 1976–9.
Steel, 55 ft (16.76 m) long.
Collection: Eugene M. Klein.

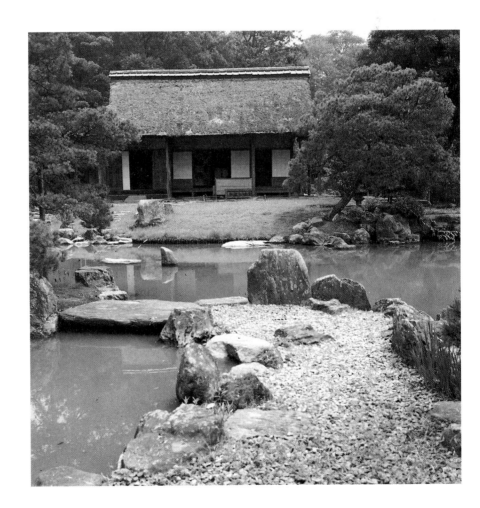

2.42 Garden of Katsura Palace, Kyoto,
Japan, Edo Period, early 17th century.

TWO-DIMENSIONAL SPACE

The two-dimensional surface is by definition a flat plane. This plane may be referred to as the GROUND; if a discrete shape is placed on it, it may be called a "figure on a ground," or a FIGURE-GROUND RELATIONSHIP. In the most direct case of a figure-ground relationship, the ground is unworked and the figure can be clearly distinguished as lying on top of it. In **2.43**, the painted Aboriginal spirit is the positive figure; the bark on which it is painted is the ground, which seems to lie behind it in space. Since there is a strong contrast in colors between figure and ground, we can discern an edge where they meet and we interpret it as belonging to the figure. However, even in this case, the spatial relationship between figure and ground is not necessarily so straightforward. As a

second look at this Australian Aboriginal bark painting will reveal, the figure is not fully demarcated from the ground by an outline; the figure is open, leaving some mystery about where the spirit stops and the surrounding environment begins. Indeed, they may not be entirely separate.

If figure and ground are approximately equal in area, artists can create a FIGURE-GROUND REVERSAL in which either color can be interpreted as lying on top of the other. Is a checkerboard red on black or black on red? Those of us who are accustomed to reading black type on white paper may initially assume that when we see black and white work, black is the figure and white the ground. The poster for *"Master Harold" . . . and the Boys* (**2.44**) calls this assumption into question, for we can continually flip between seeing the black head of Master Harold as a positive

2.43 Attributed to Dick Nangulay, *Spirit Figure*, 1972, Western Arnhem Land.
Ocher on bark, 14½ × 22½ ins (37 × 57 cm).
Copyright by The Asia Society Galleries and the South Australian Museum.

2.44 David McNutt, designer, "Master Harold" . . . and the boys, 1985. Poster for the Department of Theater Arts, California State University, Los Angeles. Courtesy of the artist.

2.45 Mu-ch'i, *Six Persimmons*, Southern Sung dynasty, China, late 13th century. Ink on paper, 14½ ins (37 cm) wide. Daitoku-ji, Kyoto, Japan.

figure and seeing it as the background for a white figure. The white itself alternately reads as the African continent and a white boy's head. In this case, the visual puzzle not only holds our attention but also draws us into the theme of the play: race relations in South Africa.

Two-dimensional picture planes are often treated to create the impression of space that recedes from the viewer—or sometimes even extends forward. A number of devices have been developed that fool the eye into thinking it is looking into a space that has depth. As illustrations, we will use works that primarily use only one device, though many pieces of three-dimensional art use all of them at once.

One such device is the placement of images on the picture plane. In general, we tend to interpret figures that are lower on the picture plane as being closer to

us in space. In Mu-ch'i's *Six Persimmons* (**2.45**), we do not interpret the fruits as floating in the air. Even though there is no visible surface for them to be sitting on, we perceive them as resting on something because of their placement in relationship to each other. We see the one that is lowest as closest to us, implying a surface that extends at least as far forward as the fruit seems to come. The other persimmons line up behind it at slightly different depths in space, with the highest one in the center seeming farther away than the ones to either side. The artist tells us to look from object to object, observing the many subtle ways they differ, including their very slightly differing placement in space.

Another device giving the illusion of spatial depth is OVERLAPPING: the obscuring of images to be interpreted as farther away from us by objects designed to appear closer to us. In Romare Bearden's collage, *She-Ba* (**2.46**), even though the cut-out shapes are flat and intentionally ambiguous, the obscuring of some parts by others offers clues to their

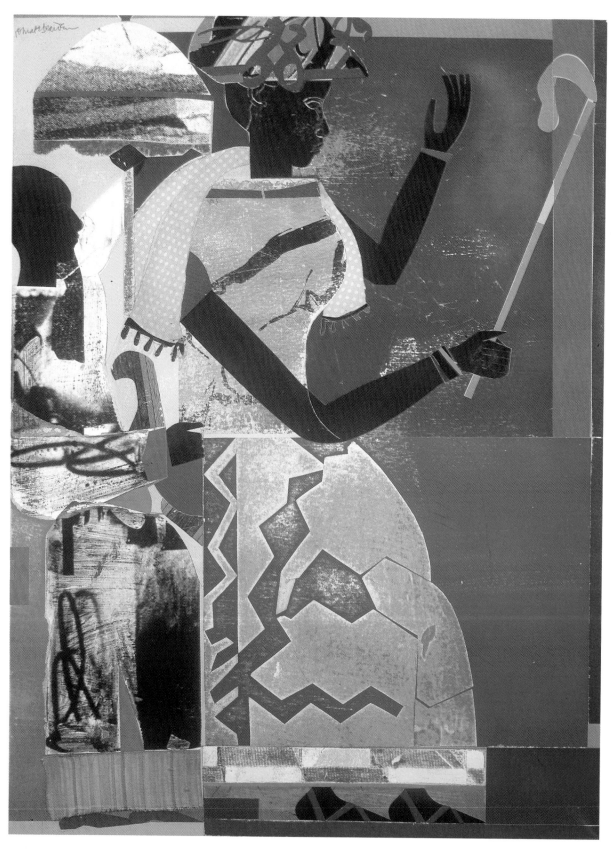

2.46 Romare Bearden, *She-Ba*, 1970. Collage on composition board, 48 × 36 ins (122 × 91 cm). Wadsworth Atheneum, Hartford. The Ella Gallup Summer and Mary Catlin Summer Collection.

2.47 Pieter Bruegel the Elder, *Hunters in the Snow*, 1565.
Oil on canvas, 3 ft 10 ins × 5 ft 4 ins (1.17 × 1.62 m).
Kunsthistorisches Museum, Vienna.

relative positions in space. Across the queen's torso, for instance, overlapping tells us that her scarf is in front of her sleeve, which is in front of her right arm, which is in front of her breasts, which are in front of the other side of her scarf, which is in front of her left arm. The staff is not floating in the air, for part of her hand is in front of it and there is a suggestion that the ends of her fingers are hidden by it in the back.

A device which adds a tremendous feeling of depth to a two-dimensional painting is SCALE CHANGE. In art, the term "scale" refers to relative size. One of the most dramatic examples of the use of scale change is Bruegel's *Hunters in the Snow* (**2.47**). We perceive the large figures to the left as closest to us in space because they are by far the largest of the human figures. The people down on the frozen pond are pushed way back in space because they are so much smaller in comparison. The same kind of rapid scaling down can be traced in the houses and the trees from foreground to distant background. Bruegel makes us feel that we are looking across an immense distance, all the way to another village with a church spire and even beyond that.

Another device used to create the illusion of extremely deep space is LINEAR PERSPECTIVE. This technique was refined and translated into precise mathematical terms by Renaissance artists in the fifteenth century. It portrays all parallel horizontal lines of forms that recede from the viewer's position as converging diagonally toward the same VANISHING POINT in the distance (in simple ONE-POINT perspective), determining the changing scale of the

103

2.48 One-point perspective drawing.

forms. Figure **2.48** demonstrates the effect of standing on a railroad track while holding a window before one's eyes. This window represents the PICTURE PLANE—the flat surface on which a two-dimensional work is created. The tracks, which are parallel in actuality but perpendicular to the picture plane, appear on the picture plane as lines drawn toward a single point at a great distance. The horizontal line on which they seem to converge appears as the horizon; it is at the height of the viewer's EYE LEVEL LINE. A dramatic demonstration of this principle can be seen in Anselm Kiefer's *Athanor* (**2.49**), in which architectural lines rapidly converge toward an eye-level line somewhere beyond the doors of this war-ravaged Third Reich building.

When parallel lines appear to diverge toward two different vanishing points (as when we look at the corner of a building or the intersection of two hallways), the visual illusion is known as TWO-POINT PERSPECTIVE (**2.51**). The engraving of the *Crystal Palace* shown in Figure **2.50** is rendered in two-point perspective. The parallel lines of the hall to the right seem to converge toward one vanishing point, while those in the hall to the left apparently converge

2.49 Anselm Kiefer, *Athanor*, 1983–4. Oil, acrylic, emulsion, shellac, and straw on photograph mounted on canvas, 7 ft 4½ ins × 12 ft 5⅝ ins (2.25 × 3.8 m). Private collection.

2.50 Joseph Paxton, *The Crystal Palace*, London, 1851. Engraving by R. P. Cuff after W. B. Brounger, 18¼ × 25¼ ins (46.5 × 64 cm). Drawings Collection, Royal Institute of British Architects, London.

toward another, both on the same eye-level line. Note that the vertical lines of the supports remain of even width from top to bottom, for they are parallel, rather than perpendicular, to the picture plane. But if the picture plane is tilted somewhat, parallel vertical lines will also seem to taper together toward a vanishing point above or below the eye-level line, creating THREE-POINT PERSPECTIVE (**2.52**). Drawings

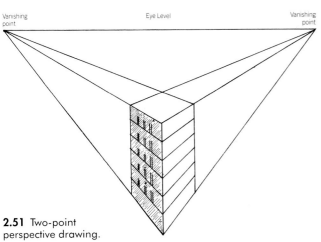

2.51 Two-point perspective drawing.

2.52 Three-point perspective drawing.

2.53 Albert Bierstadt, *The Rocky Mountains, Lander's Peak*, 1863.
Oil on canvas, 6 ft 1½ ins × 10 ft ¾ ins (1.86 × 3.06 m).
The Metropolitan Museum of Art, New York. Rogers Fund, 1907.

based on these visual illusions of linear perspective may be used to create highly spatial imagery on what is actually a flat picture plane.

Artists may also use ATMOSPHERIC (or "aerial") PERSPECTIVE, by representing the tendency of things in the distance to be less sharply defined in form, hues, and value contrast than forms that are closer to us, because of the effect of atmospheric haze. This device is used naturalistically to push areas back in space, especially when a truly vast scene is depicted, as in Albert Bierstadt's scene from the Rocky Mountains (2.53). In contrast with the details of the Shoshone Indian encampment in the foreground, the land gradually loses sharpness and value contrast to the point where the details of the mountains in the distant background are so faint as almost to blend with the sky.

Aerial perspective is a rather subtle spatial clue and may sometimes be overridden by use of the stronger illusory devices: overlapping, scale change, and linear perspective. In Al Held's *Vaporum VI*

(2.54), the latter three devices create a great sense of depth, despite the paradoxical placement of the brightest colors to the rear rather than in the foreground, contradicting expectations that colors will become grayer as they recede from us. Strong use of multiple-point linear perspective steers the eye through a complex maze of imagined structures. However, Held notes, the perspective lines "are not systematized—they're empirical."[10] That is, like many artists, he uses linear perspective in a way that reminds us of our experience in a three-dimensional world rather than abiding by theories about precisely where and how lines should converge.

In working two-dimensionally with illusions of three-dimensional space, artists also manipulate the POINT OF VIEW. By the angle from which they show us figures, they are telling us exactly where we are placed in spatial relationship to them. The invention of the camera encouraged artists to experiment freely with the points of view they used, rather than rely on conventional frontal views.

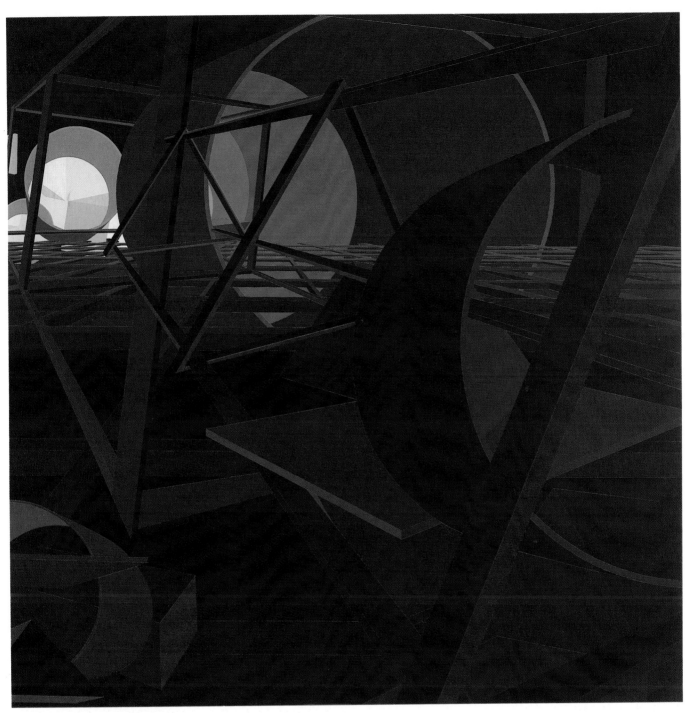

2.54 Al Held, *Vaporum VI*, 1988.
Acrylic on linen, 7 ft × 7 ft (2.13 × 2.13 m).
Andre Emmerich Gallery, New York.

Edgar Degas explored unusual points of view in many of his works. In *Dancer with a Bouquet* (2.55), we can barely see the bouquet. What we see instead is the fan of the woman whom Degas has placed between us and the ballerina, telling us exactly where we are sitting: behind and to the left of the woman with the fan, perhaps in a box slightly above the stage. Degas even makes it very clear where we are looking: down and back across the stage. This precise and unexpected point of view brings us intimately into the scene, as though we were really sitting at the ballet rather than looking at a picture of a ballet.

Sometimes artists deliberately place us in very improbable points of view. Robert Lawson illustrates the sentence from Munro Leaf's book *Ferdinand*, "He didn't look where he was sitting and instead of sitting on the nice cool grass in the shade he sat on a bumble bee," with a picture that places us under the bull's rump, a bumble bee's eye view (2.56). This perspective emphasizes the great bulk of Ferdinand and actually shrinks our sense of our own size, for we must be very small to fit where Lawson has placed us and to see the bumble bee as it is presented in the original, about three times life size.

2.55 Edgar Degas, *Dancer with a Bouquet*, c. 1878.
Pastel and wash over black chalk on paper, 12½ × 19¾ ins (31.7 × 50.2 cm).
Museum of Art, Rhode Island School of Design, Providence.

2.56 Robert Lawson,
Illustration to Munro Leaf,
The Story of Ferdinand, 1936.

2.57 Janet Cummings Good,
Floor Show, 1983.
Ink drawing,
30 × 40 ins (76.2 × 101.6 cm).

Another relatively recent innovation in points of view is the AERIAL VIEW, perhaps suggested by the photographs taken from airplanes and satellites. It takes considerable visual sophistication to interpret such images as horizontal when they are hung on a vertical surface. Janet Good's *Floor Show* (2.57) may make sense to you if you are holding this book horizontally. But if you tip it to the vertical, as the picture would be if it were hanging on a wall, you must make a strong mental adjustment to recognize that you are looking down on cats who are lying on a wooden floor instead of across at cats splayed against a wall. In such cases, artists require us to use our model of the world to interpret their creations. We just know from experience that cats sleep on the floor, not on the wall.

2.58 Hieronymus Bosch, *The Carrying of the Cross*, c. 1510. Oil on board, 30 × 32 ins (76.2 × 81.3 cm). Musée des Beaux-Arts, Ghent.

We can also examine two-dimensional use of space by considering the extent to which the artist has filled it or left it open. Hieronymus Bosch's *The Carrying of the Cross* (**2.58**) is so full of people that the canvas seems crowded with degenerate life forms. For this crowd effect, Bosch packed more heads into the picture than could actually fit bodily into the space. Amid this leering and hateful mob,

the serene, resigned face of Jesus is a striking counterpoint—the image of the divine unrecognized in the midst of human ugliness.

By contrast, leaving large areas of the picture plane unfilled may be used to create a quiet effect or to draw attention to an image isolated within this emptiness. In traditional Japanese painting, the areas left unfilled were considered just as important as the

2.59 Hasegawa Tohaku, *Pine Trees*, Momoyama Period, Japan, 1539–1610. Ink on paper, 5 ft 1 in (1.55 m) high. National Museum, Tokyo.

2.61 Hans Holbein, *Jane Small*, c. 1540. Watercolor on vellum, 2 1/16 ins (5.3 cm) diameter. Victoria and Albert Museum, London.

2.60 Claes Oldenburg, *Stake Hitch*, 1984. Aluminum, steel, urethane foam, 53 ft 6 ins × 15 ft 2 ins × 44 ft 6 ins (16.3 × 4.6 × 13.6 m). Dallas Museum of Art, commissioned to honor John Dabney Murchinson, Sr., for his arts and civic leadership, and presented by his family.

filled areas. The sixteenth century Japanese artist Hasegawa Tohaku dares to leave two of the large panels of his painted screen (2.59) almost completely unfilled and provides only suggestions of form in the others to create the effect of trees fading into the mist. By a supremely subtle use of contrast, the unfilled areas and the barely-seen, washed-out tree forms heighten our appreciation of the darkest strokes.

SCALE

We are accustomed to objects that are "life-sized." When an artist presents a familiar form in an unfamiliar size, our interest is often heightened, for the experience is immediately something out of the ordinary.

Claes Oldenburg presents mundane objects—such as a clothespin, a lipstick, a hamburger, a baked potato—as colossal monuments to the familiar banalities of our lives, greatly exaggerated in scale. By their great size, these inflated monuments to the ordinary make viewers feel dwarfed. Visitors to the Dallas Museum of Art discover that *Stake Hitch*

(2.60) is so huge that the 20-inch-thick (51 cm) rope runs all the way to the vaulted roof of the gallery and the point of the stake is "hammered through" the floor and can be seen in the basement. Oldenburg sketched and proposed far more monuments than municipalities have dared to build. Approaching the absurdities of modern civilization with humor as a survival tactic, Oldenburg explained his first inspiration:

> The first suggestion of a monument came some years ago as I was riding in from the airport. I thought: how nice it would be to have a large rabbit about the size of a skyscraper in midtown. It would cheer people up seeing its ears from the suburbs.[11]

By contrast, vast scale is often used to evoke awe and reverence. Such is the case with the many colossal statues of the Buddha in Asia. The great dying Buddha in Polonnaruwa, Sri Lanka (2.62) is 46 feet (14 m) long, dwarfing devotees and inspiring a sense of the greatness of the eternal Buddha principle.

At the other end of scale exaggerations are MINIATURES, artworks that draw us in because they

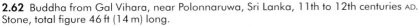

2.62 Buddha from Gal Vihara, near Polonnaruwa, Sri Lanka, 11th to 12th centuries AD. Stone, total figure 46 ft (14 m) long.

2.63 Attributed to Li Ch'eng, *Buddhist Temple in the Hills after Rain*, Northern Sung dynasty, China, c. AD 940–67. Ink and slight color on silk, 44 × 22 ins (111.8 × 55.8 cm). William Rockhill Nelson Gallery of Art, Atkins Museum of Fine Arts, Kansas City.

are so much smaller than we would expect. We are accustomed to seeing paintings scaled down to sizes that fit conveniently onto book pages. But when we recognize that Hans Holbein's miniature portrait of Jane Small (**2.61**) was actually painted in the same size as it is shown here, we can begin to appreciate the extreme delicacy and skill required for its creation. Imagine how small a brush Holbein must have used to paint the details on the cuffs and neckpiece. Despite the minuscule scale of this meticulous work, it is considered one of the world's great portraits. Precise miniature paintings were very popular as illustrations for medieval European and Persian manuscripts and as jewelry pieces for sixteenth-through eighteenth-century English aristocrats.

Scale may also be used to make a statement about the relative importance of forms within a work. In *Buddhist Temple in the Hills after Rain* (**2.63**), as in many early Chinese landscape paintings, the figures of pilgrims are tiny and unobtrusive in comparison with the impact of the mountains. In Taoist thought, this scale reflected the importance of humanity in the universe—a barely significant part of the totality, subordinate to nature. By contrast, religious works from the Christian tradition tend to emphasize human forms, especially those of holy figures. In the large altarpiece, *Madonna Enthroned with Angels and Prophets* (**2.64**), the Madonna is larger than life and larger than the angels on either side and the prophets below, a spatial device that speaks of her importance on the throne of heaven.

SPATIAL ILLUSION

One intriguing way in which some artists work with space is to twist it into situations that seem at first glance to work but turn out on closer inspection to be quite impossible, given what we know of the three-dimensional world. William Hogarth's frontispiece for Kirby's *Perspective* (**2.65**) is a visual game with space as its subject. For instance, the fishing pole held by the man at the far right cannot possibly be long enough to reach all the way out to the pond, where it is shown neatly catching a fish. The scale of the sheep rounding the corner at the left is exactly backwards: Those farthest away are the largest. To introduce the study of perspective, Hogarth has humorously created a scene full of spatial "mistakes." It may look initially plausible, but the longer you examine it, the more spatial impossibilities you will discover.

2.64 Cimabue, *Madonna Enthroned with Angels and Prophets*, c. 1280–5. Tempera on wood, 12 ft 6 ins × 7 ft 4 ins (3.85 × 2.23 m). Galleria degli Uffizi, Florence.

2.65 William Hogarth, frontispiece to Kirby's *Perspective*, 1753.
Engraving, 8¼ × 6¾ ins (21 × 17.1 cm).
Victoria and Albert Museum, London.

2.66 M. C. Escher, *Relativity*, 1953.
Lithograph, 10¾ × 11½ ins (27.3 × 29.2 cm).
Print on loan to Gemeentemuseum, The Hague by the Escher Foundation.
© 1990 M. C. Escher Heirs/Cordon Art, Baarn, Holland.

The Dutch graphic artist M. C. Escher was fascinated with spatial illusions. In his *Relativity* (**2.66**), many surfaces serve three purposes at once—wall, ceiling, and floor—depending on the angle from which the figures approach them. The remarkable staircase to the right has figures walking both on the top and underside of its treads. Each segment is plausible unto itself but becomes spatially improbable when compared to adjoining areas. For Escher, his art was not a game but a serious inquiry into infinity—the point beyond which human concepts of space and time have no meaning.

117

TEXTURE

The TEXTURE of a work of art is its surface quality—how it would feel if we touched it. From our experiences in the world, we are quite familiar with a great range of textural qualities: coarse, slimy, bristly, smooth, furry, matted, scratchy, wrinkled, and so on. Our hands are equipped with sensitive nerves for distinguishing textures, and we find sensual joy in feeling certain surfaces. Artists know this, and often use textures as a major influence on our response to a piece.

The sculptor Henry Moore encouraged people to touch his works. His *Reclining Figure* (**2.68**) makes us want to do so. Its highly polished wood surface reminds us visually of the smoothness of taut skin and invites caressing. Despite the abstraction of the form, the prominent grain in the elm wood accentuates the visual similarity to a human body by suggesting the curves of muscles.

Some textures are much less inviting, but nonetheless enhance the intended visual impact of a piece. The Batetela mask shown here (**2.67**) was designed for a shaman's use in exciting crowds with fear of the spirit world. Its several textures are in dramatic contrast to each other, from the hairy unkempt quality of the beard, to the geometrically precise incised lines defining the contours of the face, to the furry antennae flopping down over the face like the legs of a dangerous spider. Used in this context, all of these textures become alarming yet fascinating. The effect of the mask in motion must have been truly terrifying.

Textures may toy with our curiosity, using it to lure us into spending time with a piece. Lucas Samaras' *Book 4* (**2.69**) presents us with sharp found objects we know would hurt us if we touched them. What is more, Samaras has placed them in menacing projections. But rather than totally avoiding such dangerous things, we tend to come as close as we dare out of a sense of adventure. The combination of all these sharp materials with an open book increases their perception as textures. Since a book is something we usually hold in our hands, turning the pages, we can readily "feel" these textures.

2.67 African Batetela mask. Wood, fur, and fiber, 16½ ins (42 cm) long. British Museum, London.

2.68 Henry Moore, *Reclining Figure*, 1935–6. Elm wood, 3 ft 6 ins (1.07 m) long.
Wakefield Metropolitan District Council Art Gallery and Museums, Yorkshire.

2.69 Lucas Samaras, *Book 4*, 1962. Assemblage: partly opened book with pins, razor blade, scissors, table knife, metal foil, piece of glass, and plastic rod, 5½ × 8⅞ × 11½ ins (14 × 22.5 × 29.2 cm). Collection, The Museum of Modern Art, New York. Gift of Philip Johnson.

ACTUAL TEXTURE

The textures with which we are most familiar are those we can feel with our hands: ACTUAL TEXTURES. Everything has a surface texture, but some textures tend to stand out as such. The Danish rune stone (**2.70**) is carved as a low relief into rock so grainy that its roughness shows in the photograph. The over-and-under interlacing patterns that wrap around the Christ figure ask to be touched and followed with the fingers, almost bringing us into physical contact with the person who carved the stone.

To create an impressive, magical bust of the war-god Kukailimoku (**2.71**), a Hawaiian artist applied several materials with striking actual textures to a wicker frame. The feathers of tropical birds create a mysterious texture for the skin, pearl shells make a smooth and shining eye, and dogs' teeth make an impressive array of sharp teeth. These textural materials may have been used partly because they were plentiful, but to the eyes of those from other cultures, they give a strange, inexplicable quality to the piece.

Some actual textures are created rather than used just as they are found. In her *Rock Books*, such as the one shown in Figure **2.72**, Michelle Stuart captures

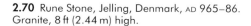

2.70 Rune Stone, Jelling, Denmark, AD 965–86. Granite, 8 ft (2.44 m) high.

2.71 The war-god Kukailimoku, from Hawaii, before 1779. Feathers over wickerwork, pearl shells, and dog teeth, 3 ft 4¾ ins (1.03 m) high. British Museum, London.

the "story of a place" by gathering rocks and dirt there and pounding it into paper, rubbing its surface until it develops a gloss. A series of such "pages" made from diggings at the site are then bound into a "book." The book, in turn, is sealed with a found texture—a feather, a coarse-woven string, a bone. These assemblages bespeak touching the earth, but they do not invite much handling by the viewer because they appear fragile, precious, and even ancient.

120

2.72 Michelle Stuart, *The Pen Argyl Myth*, 1977. Earth and feather from Pen Argyl Quarry, Pennsylvania, rag paper, 13½ × 10½ × 3½ ins (34.3 × 26.7 × 8.9 cm).

2.73 Mary Azarian, *T is for Toad*, from *A Farmer's Alphabet*, 1981. Two-color woodcut, 12¼ × 7½ ins (31.1 × 19 cm).

SIMULATED TEXTURE

Two-dimensional works often create the visual sensations of textural qualities on a surface that would actually feel quite different if touched. If we touched a print of Mary Azarian's woodcut (**2.73**) from the alphabet she was commissioned to create for the Vermont public schools, we would feel only the slight coarseness of the paper and the ink across the surface. But visually, what we perceive is the relative smoothness of grass blades, the filmy delicacy of dragonfly wings, and the bumpiness of the toad's skin. None of these textures is described utterly realistically. For instance, the bumpiness is more hard-edged than the smooth, moist lumps on a real toad. Instead, Azarian uses a visual shorthand

that reminds us of these natural textures, if we are familiar with them. These shorthand simulated textures also provide an interesting series of visual contrasts.

In comparison, certain artists have gone to great lengths to capture the visual effects of textures. One of the masters in this respect is Ingres. In his *Portrait of the Princesse de Broglie* (**2.74**), the facial skin and hair are rather stylized and simplified, in dramatic contrast to the extreme attention to detail in rendering the textures of the fabrics. The lush satiny dress fabric is so realistically painted that we can guess exactly how it feels. One clue is the way it reflects the light, a characteristic of smooth and shiny surfaces. We can see that the lace and gold-trimmed throw have very different textures, though

121

they share with the satin the suppleness of fabric. And the information given to our eyes about the chair allows our fingers to imagine the play of the smooth surface and raised brocade across its plump contours.

This same realism in simulated textural effects has occasionally been achieved in three-dimensional works. One of the hardest of materials—marble—has been lovingly sculpted to suggest the feel of human skin in the *Venus de Milo* (**2.75**) from the Hellenistic period. Not only does it appear soft; it even looks as though it would feel warm to the touch.

When a visual effect is so realistic that it totally

2.76 Marilyn Levine, *Two-Toned Golf Bag*, 1980. Stoneware with nylon reinforcement, 35 × 10½ × 7 ins (89 × 27 × 18 cm).

2.75 *Venus de Milo*, c. 150 BC. Marble, 6 ft 10 ins (2.08 m) high. Louvre, Paris.

2.74 (opposite) Jean Auguste Dominique Ingres, *Portrait of the Princesse de Broglie*, 1853. Oil on canvas, 47¾ × 35¾ ins (121.3 × 90.8 cm). The Metropolitan Museum of Art, New York. Robert Lehmann Collection 1975.

fools our perceptions, it is called TROMPE L'OEIL (literally, "deceive the eye"). We are fascinated with that which deceives us in art. There is probably little innate visual appeal in a golf bag. But the fact that Marilyn Levine has created a life-sized golf-bag (**2.76**) from ceramics makes her piece utterly intriguing. She has carefully studied and captured precisely in the hardness of fired clay the look of pliable worn leather and of metal. If we touched it, the actual feeling of the surface would be shockingly and humorously different from what our mind expects.

TEXTURE-LIKE EFFECTS

Certain works create a visual texture by repetition of elements of design. Imagine a forest seen from a distance. It has an all-over visual texture created by the repetition of tree-forms that is quite different from the actual feeling of tree trunks and branches. But those of us who are familiar with trees and forests may not be aware of this all-over texture, for our familiarity with the particular blinds us to what we are actually perceiving. It is easier for us to perceive a texture-like effect in something unfamiliar, such as the Imperial Edict ("Firman") of Sultan Mustafa IV (**2.77**). Because most of us cannot read the Arabic scripts used for the Imperial Monogram and the edict that is written below it, we can see them as nonobjective designs, each having its own distinct visual texture. Certainly the way that the calligrapher Mustafa Rakim presented the edict reflects his awareness that each line of characters forms a textured shape.

Sometimes even with familiar images the textural effect of repeated elements of design is so strong that we distinguish the individual elements only secondarily. In the portrait of Mao Tse-tung (**2.78**), it is the revolutionary leader we see first; the figures used to create him are so numerous, similar, closely-packed, and small in relationship to the whole that it is difficult to read them as individuals. The visual texture the faceless multitudes create is again a sort of shorthand, with sufficient information given that we translate the image into known textures of hair, eyebrows, lips, ear, and "Mao jacket."

2.77 Mustafa Rakim, *Firman*, early 19th century. 51 × 19⅝ ins (129.5 × 50 cm).

2.78 Hans-Georg Rauch, illustration for *En Masse*, Macmillan Publishing Co., Inc. © Rowoholt Verlag, 1974.

2.79 Henri Edmond Cross, *The Artist's Garden at St. Clair*, c. 1908. Watercolor, 10½ × 14 ins (26.6 × 35.5 cm). The Metropolitan Museum of Art, New York.

VALUE AND LIGHT

Another visual element that may escape our notice, but which is used quite consciously by artists, is VALUE, the relative lightness or darkness of an area. Values are most easily perceived when color hues are subtracted. Black and white photographs of colored artworks translate hues into a range of grays from very dark to very light, as in this reproduction of Henri-Edmond Cross's watercolor *The Artist's Garden at St. Clair* (**2.79**). These value variations help us to understand the effects of lighting and distance despite the abstract quality of the painting. Here, the

overhanging branches seem to create pools of shadow, beyond which values become very light in what appears to be strong daylight, fading to near-white in the distance. In general, as we saw in the section on space, perceived value contrasts are strongest in areas closest to the viewer.

The gradations of value from very dark to very light can be represented by means of a VALUE SCALE. The one shown in Figure **2.80** breaks down the variations into ten equal steps, with black at one end and white at the other. In a work such as *The Artist's Garden at St. Clair*, there are actually many more values than ten, but the value scale is a useful tool for seeing value

2.80 A 10-step value scale.

2.81 Gaston Lachaise, *Standing Woman*, 1932. Bronze (cast 1932), 88 ins × 41⅛ ins × 19⅛ ins (223.6 × 104.3 × 48.4 cm). Collection, The Museum of Modern Art, New York. Mrs. Simon Guggenheim Fund.

gradations lined up sequentially.

In addition to giving spatial clues, values also help us to perceive the modeling of forms. As light falls on a three-dimensional object, such as Gaston Lachaise's sculpture *Standing Woman* (**2.81**), the areas that light strikes most directly are the lightest, showing up as HIGHLIGHTS. As contours curve away from the light source in space, the light dims, making the surface appear darker, until it approaches a true black in areas where light is fully blocked. The strong value contrasts on *Standing Woman* help us to grasp the extent to which the form swells out and draws back in space. In this photograph, strong lighting accentuates these contrasts; in more diffuse light, such as an overcast day, the ins and outs of the form would not be so apparent.

LOCAL AND INTERPRETIVE VALUES

The actual lights and shadows we see on real surfaces are called LOCAL VALUES. Some photographers attempt through techniques of photographing and developing to capture on film the full range of local values, called a FULL TONAL RANGE in photography. Although Katherine Alling confines and twists feathers into interesting shapes in *Feathers #22* (**2.82**), she also emphasizes their visual reality, with all the local values created as they curve from light into shadow. She remarks:

> We generally don't look at a feather that carefully. We label it and that's it. One of the features of photography is that we examine an object more carefully as a visual thing. We don't just say "Feather" and let it go.[12]

With intents other than reproducing visual realities, many artists have manipulated values.

2.82 Katherine Alling, *Feathers #22*, 1984. Toned silver print, 12 × 9 ins (30.5 × 22.9 cm).

127

When they are not handled realistically, they may be called INTERPRETIVE VALUES. One technique is to reduce the degree to which values gradually change, presenting them as more dramatic contrasts. To turn the sculptor Rodin's famous profile into a massive sculptural form, as if the man himself were a monument chipped from black stone, photographer Edward Steichen arranged for both Rodin and his sculpture *Le Penseur* ("The Thinker") to be in shadow, making them appear similarly strong (**2.83**). Their intense confrontation is set off by the white plaster figure of *Victor Hugo* brooding in the background. There are mid-grays in this photograph, but the main focus is on the stark contrast of the black forms to the highlights on *Le Penseur* and the light values of the *Hugo*. The drama of this approach is like hitting chords on both ends of a piano keyboard at once, with none of the notes in between.

Another approach to interpretive value is to emphasize one area of the value scale: lights, darks, or mid-tones. Each carries a different emotional quality. Rembrandt used the dark end of the scale in his self-portrait (1.64), with the light of his face barely emerging from the shadows. Graphic designer Milton

2.83 Edward Steichen, *Rodin: The Thinker*, 1902. Photograph. Collection: The Gilman Paper Company.

Glaser has chosen the light end of the scale to represent Monet on a poster (**2.84**). The choice is appropriate, for the artist emphasized the effects of light in his own work. Here he appears as if in midday light so strong that it has burned away all details except for those disappearing into the shadow under his hat. The fact that Glaser has added slight shadows to the right on Monet's hat and shoulder, an indication that the sun is slightly to the left of directly overhead, keeps the near-abstraction within the realm of the nearly-realistic.

In HIGH CONTRAST works, artists leave out all minor details, turning forms that usually include a range of grays into a dramatic contrast between black and white. The result may be an unrecognizable, seemingly nonobjective design. But in the case of the Guggenheim Museum poster (**2.85**), just enough

2.84 Milton Glaser, Poster for The Monet Museum, Giverny, 1981.

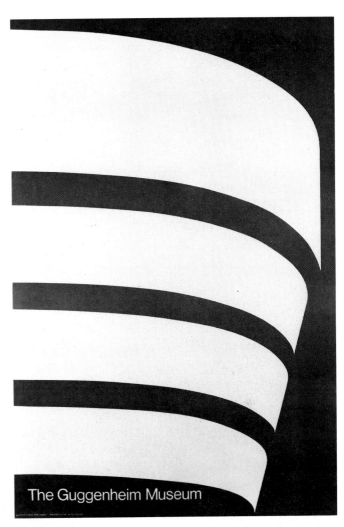

2.85 Malcolm Grear Designers, Poster for the Solomon R. Guggenheim Museum, 1970.

information is left to allow us to fill in the missing edges of the building's famous spiraling form. Presented in high contrast, it is an intriguing abstraction that calls on us to bring our own knowledge to complete the picture.

LIGHTING

The way a subject is lit—by the sun or by artificial lighting—will affect how we perceive it. In the Persian miniature painting to illustrate *The Concourse of the Birds* (**2.86**), as in most Persian miniatures, Habib Allah presents a uniformly lit scene with no shadows. This lighting represents no particular time of day, removing it from the realm of the real into the ideal, mystical setting of the parable, which symbolically illustrates the unity of

2.87 Nancy Holt, *Sun Tunnels*, 1973–6. Total length 86 ft (26.2 m), tunnels each 18 × 9 ft 4 ins (5.48 × 2.84 m). Great Basin, North West Utah Desert.

2.88 Nancy Holt, *Sun Tunnels*, detail. Sunset on summer solstice.

individual souls with the divine. In the *Mantiq at-Tayr* thirty birds undertake a difficult journey in search of the Simurgh, king of the birds, only to discover that they are themselves *sī murgh*, which means "thirty birds."

Many works do, however, contain some reference to the ever-changing reality of light. Three-dimensional pieces placed outside in a natural setting—as well as two-dimensional depictions of the natural world—will appear quite different when lit from the east at sunrise, overhead at noon, and from the west at sunset. The sun's angle changes during the year, also altering where the highlights and shadows fall. Moonlight brings a very different quality to a scene or piece of sculpture, softening edges and blurring distinctions between forms. And on cloudy days and during rain or snow the character of a piece or scene will be dramatically changed.

From antiquity, humans have used objects placed outside to track—and honor—the movements of the sun, moon, and stars. To do so reveals the predictabilities inherent in an otherwise uncertain existence. The sun will come up again tomorrow, though the point of its rising will have moved slightly. The solstices—the points on the horizon and calendar where this movement turns back on itself—have long had particular significance. A contemporary version of the ancient homage to the sun's apparent movements is Nancy Holt's *Sun Tunnels* (2.87). This consists of four enormous concrete tunnels placed on the Utah desert in such a way that the sun shines directly through two of them for ten days at the winter solstice and through the other two during the summer solstice. At other times, holes drilled into the pipes channel the light of sun, moon, or stars into their shaded centers to create the constellations Capricorn, Draco, Perseus, and Columba. Looking directly through the appropriate pipe during a solstice (2.88) one sees a shining circle around a circle whose center is the sun. At other times, one sees encircled darkness studded with starlike points of light, a circular sunwashed openness beyond, and the dark circle of the opposite tunnel at its center.

The use of artificial lighting allows controlled rather than changing effects. Sculptors are very careful how their works are lit, for the shape, size, and position of shadows and highlights depend on the placement of lighting.

Even two-dimensional works can be enhanced or destroyed by lighting. Mark Rothko was extremely particular about the way his large luminous paintings (see 1.34) were illuminated when they were shown. He gave these instructions for a retrospective show of

2.86 Habib Allah, *The Concourse of the Birds*, 1609. Colors, gold, and silver on paper, 10 × 4½ ins (25.4 × 11.4 cm). The Metropolitan Museum of Art, New York. Fletcher Fund, 1963.

2.89 Caravaggio, *The Conversion of St. Paul*, 1600–2. Oil on canvas, 7 ft 6½ ins × 5 ft 9 ins (2.29 × 1.75 m). Cerasi Chapel, S. Maria del Popolo, Rome.

2.90 Charles W. Moore and William Hersey, Piazza d'Italia, New Orleans, 1978.

his work:

> The light, whether natural or artificial, should not be too strong. The pictures have their own inner light and if there is too much light, the color in the picture is washed out and a distortion of their look occurs. The ideal situation would be to hang them in a normally lit room—that is the way they were painted. They should not be over lit or romanticized by spots; this results in distortion of their meaning. They should either be lighted from a great distance or indirectly, by casting lights at the ceiling or the floor. Above all, the entire picture should be evenly lighted and not strongly.[13]

During the Renaissance, European painters developed the technique of CHIAROSCURO (Italian for "light and shade")—the depiction in a two-dimensional work of the effects of light and shadow. Values are manipulated for their dramatic effect. In Caravaggio's *The Conversion of St. Paul* (**2.89**) Saul's body gleams with the reflection of the light of God which blinded him. The divine light is emphasized by the surrounding darkness. Rembrandt, the great master of chiaroscuro, portrays himself (**1.64**) as a softly illuminated form barely emerging from

total shadow.

We are quite familiar with the use of artificial lighting to add drama to a city's skyline or friendly warmth and light to the interiors of our homes. Less familiar is the use of artificial colored lights to change the hues as well as the values in an area. A spectacularly theatrical use of colored neon lights appears at the *Piazza d'Italia* in New Orleans (**2.90**). A celebration of the contributions of Italian immigrants, it is like a stage setting for an opera. Flamboyantly sensual, eclectic and surprising in its architectural forms, it lures visitors to become part of the play. The neon lights throw a great range of colors across the fantastic architecture, for they mix where they overlap, enticing viewers to experience this multi-hued lighting playing across their own bodies.

REFLECTIONS

Another way in which light is used in art is by taking advantage of the fascinating effects of reflections off a smooth surface. Reflected light tends to capture our attention. The reflections of the surroundings on the highly-polished interior of the double-wall bowl (**2.92**) make us aware of this unfilled area. The reflections make this area surprisingly active and the high gloss adds to its sense of preciousness.

To depict reflections convincingly in two-dimensional works takes great skill. Richard Estes has perfected the art of painting the reflections in artificial surfaces such as chrome and glass so realistically that they appear to be photographs. His *Double Self-Portrait* (**2.91**) is a complex tour de force, photorealistically displaying both the reflections in a

2.91 Richard Estes, *Double Self-Portrait*, 1976.
Oil on canvas, 24 × 36 ins (60.8 × 91.5 cm).
Collection, The Museum of Modern Art, New York. Mr. and Mrs. Stuart M. Speiser Fund.

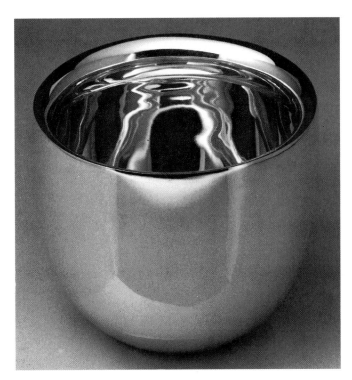

2.92 Labbar Hoagland, Alfonso Soto Soria, and Pedro Leites, *Double-Wall Bowl*, 1985. Silver, 8 × 5½ ins (20 × 14 cm). Manufactured by Tane Orfebres, Mexico.

restaurant's glass wall of the view across the street—including the artist, who is seen taking the photograph from which this painting was done—and the intermingled details of the interior of the restaurant seen through the same glass. In certain lighting situations, some glass will seem to hold reflections on its surface, but this glass allows both inside and reflected outside to be seen at once, as if the outer world were penetrating the interior. To add to the visual puzzle of figuring out what is inside and what is outside, there is a mirrored surface inside the restaurant, in which a second reflected image of the artist appears.

When we see an object reflected in water, it may seem to lose its grounded position on the earth and instead appear to be floating in space. Such reflections hold great fascination for us, for they draw us into a different world of spatial possibilities. When the water outside the Byodoi Temple (**2.93**) is as smooth as it is in this photograph, the temple and its reversed image become a totality apparently floating without support in space. The reversed image is visually exciting in itself as a symmetrical completion of the actual temple.

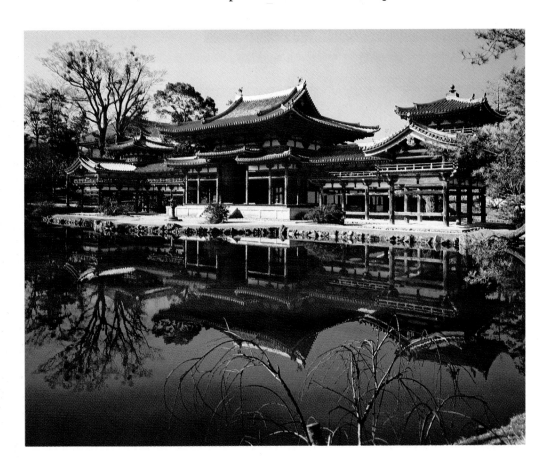

2.93 Hoodo (Phoenix Hall), Byodoi Temple, Uji, near Kyoto, Japan, 11th century AD.

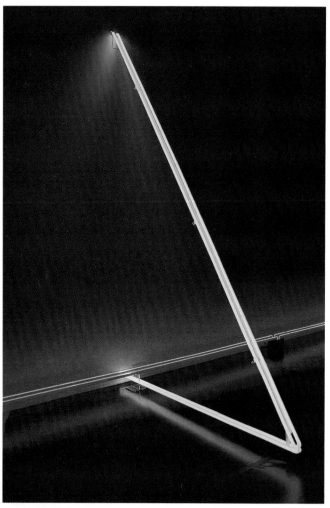

2.94 Stephen Antonakos, *Green Neon from Wall to Floor*, 1969–70. Neon tubing, 8 × 24 × 5 ft (2.4 × 7.3 × 1.5 m).

LIGHT AS A MEDIUM

Light itself may be captured and controlled as an element of design. We humans have always been fascinated by looking at light. It has the power to bring us out of the darkness and to illuminate spaces, both outside and inside us. Artistic presentation of light is of ancient origin. The aesthetic care given to fashioning early clay lamps suggests the reverence and joy with which we regard light.

Since light is energy that tends to diffuse through space, it must be controlled in different ways from corporeal matter. From the familiarity of neon signs—such as the *EAT* restaurant sign—contemporary artists have derived the idea of using neon tubes to create lines of light in space, such as Stephen Antonakos's *Green Neon from Wall to Floor* (**2.94**). The invention of lasers suggested another art form: laser projections thrown against the night sky or a dark wall (**2.95**). Here no structure is needed to confine the light; it is shaped as a needle-thin beam.

Windows provide another way of controlling light for aesthetic purposes. The elaborate use of stone arches allowed great openings to be made in the walls of Gothic cathedrals for stained-glass windows that

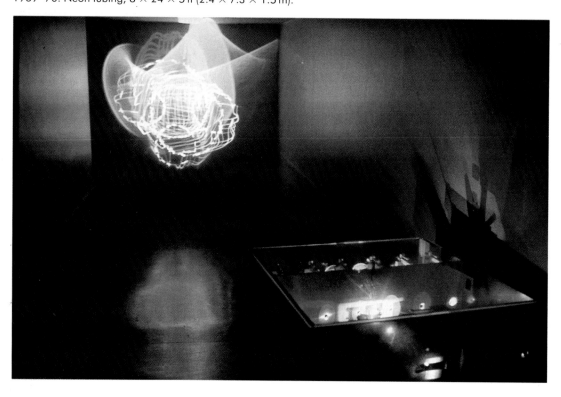

2.95 Laser deflection images, produced by Video/Laser III, 1987. Operated by Professor Lowell Cross at The University of Iowa.

2.96 (opposite) Sainte-Chapelle, Paris, 1243–8.

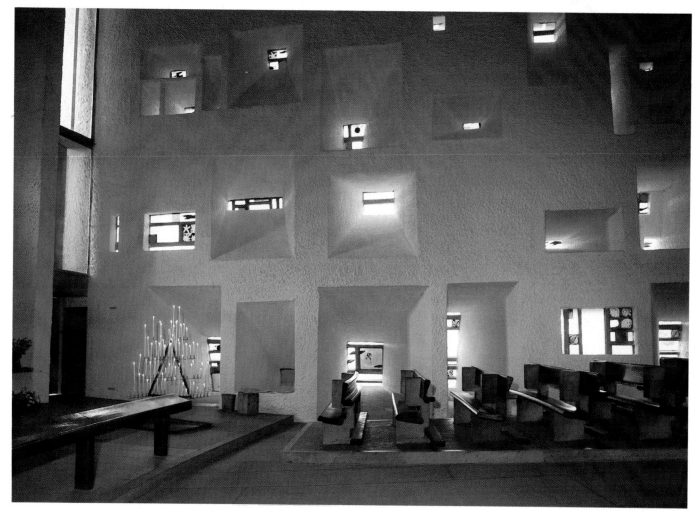

2.97 Le Corbusier, Interior of the chapel of Notre-Dame-du-Haut, Ronchamp, France, 1950–5.

COLOR

told Biblical stories and created a mystical atmosphere for worshippers within, like the breath of the divine. At Sainte-Chapelle (**2.96**), a chapel for the French kings, the interior is suffused with many jewel tones that color the sunlight coming through the intricate stained-glass panes, more brilliant than any flat-painted color could be. The architect Le Corbusier translated this effect into contemporary terms at his *Notre Dame-du-Haut* (**2.97**), placing bits of stained glass within continually varying window openings. As the light bursts through each of these recesses in the thick walls, it creates a series of focal points in complex mathematical relationships to each other. Within the safe thickness of the walls, the light of God breaks through to touch each person physically.

Color is an immediately obvious aspect of a work of art that clearly impresses itself on our consciousness. In describing any work that strikes a particular color note, we inevitably speak of it as "that red cube" or "one of Picasso's blue paintings." Less obvious are the subtle effects of colors on our visual receptors, emotional state, and our perceptions of space, though these effects are under study by scientists and used consciously by many artists. Color may even affect us spiritually, as the Russian nonobjective painter Wassily Kandinsky wrote:

> Color is a power which directly influences the soul. Color is the keyboard, the eyes are the hammers, the soul is the piano with many strings. The artist is the hand which plays, touching one key or another, to cause vibrations in the soul.[14]

2.98 The visible spectrum.

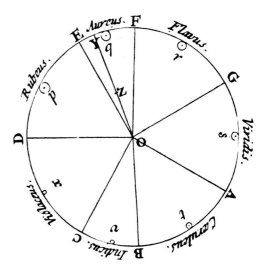

2.99 Newton's Color Wheel, from Isaac Newton, *Optice*, 1706. British Library, London.

A VOCABULARY OF COLOR

From Kandinsky's sublime perception we descend to the need to establish a vocabulary for speaking about differences between the colors we perceive. The first understanding necessary is that what we perceive as the color of an object is actually the reflection of light of a certain wavelength off the surface, as this reflection is received by the retina of the eye and perceived by the brain. It does not "belong" to the object itself. The wavelengths that humans can see (only a tiny fraction of the great spectrum of electromagnetic radiation) are collectively referred to as the VISIBLE SPECTRUM. As shown schematically in Figure **2.98**, the visible spectrum is the rainbow of colors we see when the white light of the sun passes through a prism that breaks up the wavelengths into seven graduating bands of color.

Centuries ago, Sir Isaac Newton proposed that the ends of this band of hues were so similar that they could be joined, pulling the band into a circular model of color relationships that we now call the COLOR WHEEL. Newton's original proposal is shown in Figure **2.99**. The color wheel demonstrates theoretical relationships among HUES, the wavelength properties by which we give colors names such as "red," "blue," and so on. In REFRACTED (light or "additive") colors, there are theoretically three basic hues, from which all other hues can be mixed (**2.100**). These basic hues are called PRIMARY COLORS. In refracted colors, the primaries are red, green, and blue-violet. If you examine a color television picture very closely, you

2.100 Primary and secondary hues in refracted lights.

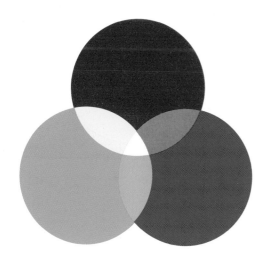

2.101 Primary and secondary hues in reflected pigments.

139

2.102 The traditional color wheel of pigment mixtures.

and yellow, for instance, are complementary to each other, as are blue-green and red-orange.

The problem with Newton's model of color relationships—in addition to the open question of whether the two ends of the spectrum can really be joined—is that it accounts for only one characteristic of color: hue. The colors we perceive also differ in two other ways: VALUE and what is called SATURATION (also known as "chroma" or "intensity"). Value, as we have seen, is a measure of the relative lightness or darkness of a color. It can be conceived as a vertical pole with white at the top and black at the bottom, in terms of grays. Value variations in reds, blues, and so on run a similar course from near-white to near-black, with middle-value reds or blues lying at the middle of the pole. These value variations are shown as a three-dimensional model in Figure **2.103**. To illustrate the effects of value changes in a hue, Georgia O'Keeffe's *Abstraction Blue* (**2.104**) can be seen as a beautiful study in value changes in several hues. At their darkest, the hues of the cloudlike forms are almost black, graduating to pastels that are almost as light as the shape dividing the center of the canvas. At either end of the value scale, different hues are almost indistinguishable from each other.

The three-dimensional model of color relationships (2.103) also illustrates differences in saturation, which is a measure of the relative brightness and purity of a color. The most highly

will see that it is composed entirely of dots of these three hues. There is no yellow in television transmission. Yellow is one of the SECONDARY hues in refracted light mixtures; it is created by mixing red and green light.

This information is hard for many of us to grasp, since the color wheel with which we are more familiar (**2.102**) shows the relationships between REFLECTED hues. Also called "pigment" or "subtractive" hues, reflected hues are those that result when light is reflected from a pigmented surface that absorbs all wavelengths except those that we see. In this case, the primary hues according to traditional color theory are red, blue, and yellow; the secondaries that can be mixed from them are orange, green, and purple (**2.101**). If primary and secondary hues lying next to each other on the color wheel are mixed, they form another level of mixtures: TERTIARY HUES, as shown in Figure **2.102**. Note that there is a circle of gray in the center of the color wheel. If pigments of hues lying opposite each other on the wheel—which are called COMPLEMENTARY HUES—are mixed in equal amounts, they will theoretically produce a neutral gray. Purple

2.103 Relationships in hue, saturation, and value, according to the color theorist Albert Munsell.

2.104 Georgia O'Keeffe, *Abstraction Blue*, 1927. Oil on canvas, 40¼ × 30 ins (102.1 × 76 cm).
Collection, The Museum of Modern Art, New York. Acquired through the Helen Acheson Bequest.

MUNSELL COLOR TREE ILLUSTRATING COLOR SOLID

2.105 The Munsell Color Tree.

saturated colors are those that are the pure hue with none of its complementary added. As more and more of its complementary is added—for instance, as we mix yellow with purple—the color becomes more and more subdued, until, at the center of the vertical axis on this model, it appears as a gray value. O'Keeffe worked with highly saturated, pure hues, though many are shown only in their lighter values to minimize jarring contrasts.

The three-dimensional models shown in Figure 2.103 and in Figure **2.105** were developed by the color theorist Albert Munsell. Munsell found that color relationships could best be explained with a system of five primaries, so his complementary colors do not exactly match those of the traditional color wheel shown in Figure 2.102. Munsell's system is now used as a commercial standard for naming and mixing pigments. His models show that the number of equal steps in saturation, from gray to most saturated, varies from one hue to another, with red having the most possible steps and yellow the least. The Munsell "Color Tree" is therefore asymmetrical.

NATURAL AND APPLIED COLOR

We are surrounded by color in the natural world. Our awareness of its subtleties depends partly on how open our eyes are and partly on where we live. Those who live in snowy areas may become sensitive to the varied hues that can be seen in the "whiteness" of snow, from blue and even green in its shadows to the grayness of "white" flakes seen falling against a pale sky.

Many artists doing three-dimensional work have featured the natural colors in materials rather than covering them with another color. The many hues that lie beneath the bark of wood are often prized by woodworkers. Semi-precious stones may be cut and polished to bring out their colors, and amethyst and citrine quartz crystal clusters are presented as art objects not only because of their unusual crystalline forms but also because of the natural beauty of their translucent colors. Isamu Noguchi dwells on the natural colors of marble, basalt, and wood in the sculptural composition shown in Figure **2.106**. He writes, "I attempt to respect nature, adding only my own rawness."[15]

In diametric contrast to Noguchi's restrained use of natural colors, the opposite attitude is that color applied to materials intensifies the significance of a work. Many classical Greek and Roman marble sculptures were originally painted to bring out the details. Medieval wooden sculptures were also

2.106 Isamu Noguchi, (from left to right)
Small Torso, 1958–62, Greek marble, 13¾ ins (34.9 cm);
Core Piece #1, 1974, basalt, 14¼ ins (36 cm);
Core Piece #2, 1974, basalt, 15¼ ins (38.7 cm).
Photo by Shigeo Anzai.

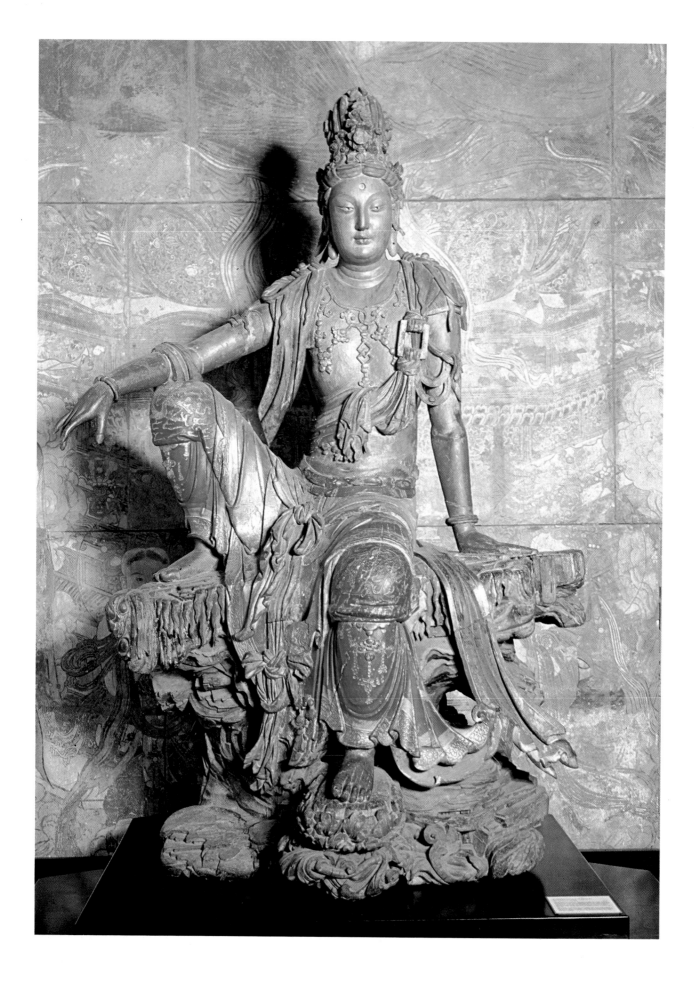

painted, as was the Chinese statue of the Bodhisattva Kuan-yin (**2.107**). Kuan-yin, like other Chinese divinities, had both male and female qualities, and was at various times considered the Bodhisattva of Mercy and the traditional Chinese mother goddess. The gold suggests a rich and spiritual presence; the red and green excite the eye, in addition to carrying connotations of life, fertility, and good fortune. When colors that are complementary to one another, such as red and green, are juxtaposed, they intensify each other's brilliance. Here this effect is used only sparingly, for the garment is chiefly red trimmed with gold, with a green sash draped here and there like a pathway through the red and gold.

LOCAL, IMPRESSIONISTIC, AND INTERPRETIVE COLOR

Many of us are taught as children that objects in our world "are" predictable colors: An apple is red, an orange is orange, a tree has a brown trunk and green leaves, the sky is blue, and so on. These perceptions are called LOCAL COLORS. They are the color an object appears if seen from nearby under normal lighting. Often these ideas of what color an object "is" are used to guide color choices in painting. In Gerard David's *The Resurrection* (**2.108**), boulders are gray, dirt is brown, and grass is green. Although the values of forms in the distance are generally painted lighter than those in the foreground, the hues are still largely local colors. Christ risen from the tomb clearly dominates the composition, not only because of his central position and upright, frontal stance but also because of the intense red of his cloak, heightened by contrast with the greens that surround it.

A fixed mental model of the world can blind us to its subtle and shifting realities, however. The French Impressionists met with tremendous opposition when they trained their minds to perceive the actual colors and forms their eyes were seeing. When Monet painted haystacks, as in Figure **2.109**, he discarded

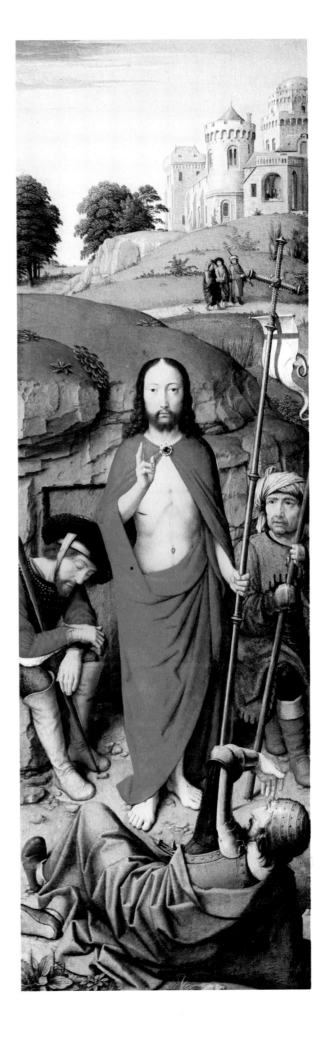

2.107 (left) *Kuan-yin*, Chinese, 11th to early 12th century. Polychromed wood, 7 ft 11 ins (2.41 m) high. Nelson Gallery, Atkins Museum, Kansas City.

2.108 Gerard David, *The Resurrection*, c. 1500. Oil on wood, 34 × 11 ins (86.4 × 27.9 cm). The Metropolitan Museum of Art, New York. Robert Lehmann Collection, 1975.

2.109 Claude Monet, *The Haystack*, 1891.
Oil on canvas, 23⅞ × 39½ ins (60.5 × 100.5 cm). Louvre, Paris.

the idea that hay is yellow and presented what he actually saw in the red light of late afternoon. The surprising, scintillating color impressions tend to dematerialize the form. To capture visual truth as nearly as possible, Monet took his canvases outside to paint in natural lighting, from nature, rather than making sketches with color notations and then working inside. He returned again and again to the same field near his home, from summer into winter, painting the ever-changing effects of lighting on the same haystacks.

An INTERPRETIVE use of color is different from either local or impressionistic color: Here color choices are guided by the artist's intent rather than by any external reality. Color is often used interpretively to set the emotional tone for a work. Picasso's *The Old Guitarist* (**2.110**) was painted during his "Blue Period" (1901–4). During these years, he used blues as the predominant colors in his paintings to express the pathos of poverty. In the West, blue is often associated with a feeling of melancholy. If Picasso

had used other colors—such as the pinks of his "Pink Period" that followed—the tone of the painting would have been more jovial, but that was not his intent.

EMOTIONAL EFFECTS OF COLOR

Colors affect our moods, and we tend to surround ourselves with the psychological atmosphere we want through our choices of colors in clothing and interior design. Research into the effects of colors suggests that a certain pink has a calming effect on us, for instance, whereas red is stimulating. In addition to these physiological effects, we respond to our culture's color associations. In Northern European cultures, white is a symbol of purity. But to the Sioux

2.110 Pablo Picasso, *The Old Guitarist*, 1903.
Oil on panel, 47¾ × 32½ ins (121.3 × 82.5 cm).
The Art Institute of Chicago, Helen Birch Bartlett Memorial Collection.

Indians, white symbolized wisdom and health; and in the Far East white is a symbol of death. As we saw in Picasso's *The Old Guitarist* (2.110), blue is associated with sadness in Western cultures; it is also linked with serenity and humanity and is therefore the color often used symbolically for the robes of the Virgin Mary (see Figures 14.19, 14.22, and 14.28).

While such knowledge is interesting and useful, it does not totally explain the way colors are used expressively in art, for color is only one aspect of the totality to which we respond in a work of art. As an illustration, consider three works, all of which feature red as their dominant color. Considered sensitively, each has a different emotional content. In Matisse's *The Red Studio* (**2.111**), the red is joyous and noisy, the slight accents of other colors make the red seem boisterous. Matisse intentionally subordinated realism to expression in his use of color, explaining, "What I am after, above all, is expression. . . . I am unable to distinguish between the feeling I have for life and my way of expressing it."[16] In Grünewald's *The Resurrection* (**2.112**), a panel from

2.111 Henri Matisse, *The Red Studio*, Issy-les-Moulineaux, 1911. Oil on canvas, 5 ft 11¼ × 7 ft 2¼ ins (1.81 × 2.19 m). Collection, The Museum of Modern Art, New York. Mrs. Simon Guggenheim Fund.

2.112 Matthias Grünewald,
The Resurrection, from
The Isenheim Altarpiece, c. 1510–15.
Oil on panel, 8 ft 10 ins × 4 ft 8 ins
(2.7 × 1.4 m).
Musée Unterlinden, Colmar, France.

2.113 Josef Albers, *Homage to the Square: Board Call*, Fall 1967.
Oil on composition board, 4 ft × 4 ft (1.22 × 1.22 m).
Collection, The Museum of Modern Art, New York. The Sidney and Harriet Janis Collection.

the Isenheim Altarpiece, red has a highly spiritual quality, for it appears as the light radiating from the risen Christ. And in Josef Albers' *Homage to the Square: Board Call* (**2.113**), red has an almost cold and intellectual quality. Albers presents reds in such precisely geometrical gradations, with edges softened by the minimizing of contrast, that his work suggests itself as an object for quiet contemplation. These very different ways of handling the same hue attest to the genius of the artists: that they can make red do whatever they ask, by the way that they use it.

WARM AND COOL COLORS

In addition to—and perhaps linked with—our perceptions of colors as having certain emotional qualities, we also tend to associate degrees of heat or cold with them. Although scientific evidence is inconclusive, we do seem to respond to colors kinesthetically, as though they produced different color sensations in our bodies. Some of us intuitively dress in red to feel warmer and blue or green to feel cooler. Such choices of hues seem independent of

2.114 Interior of Jim and Sandy Howell's home, Washington.

2.115 David Hicks, Sitting room of a house in Oxfordshire, England, 1970s. Courtesy of the artist.

2.116 Interior of Judy and Pat Coady's townhouse, with Marni Bakst stained glass doors, column by Trent Whitington.

2.117 Ellsworth Kelly, *Spectrum III*, 1967.
Oil on canvas in thirteen parts, overall 33¼ ins × 108⅝ ins (84.3 × 275.7 cm).
Collection, The Museum of Modern Art, New York. The Sidney and Harriet Janis Collection.

value differences in the amount of light absorbed or reflected. In general, reds and yellows are considered WARM colors, like those of fire; blues and greens are considered COLD, like icy water. Consider the visual "temperature" of three interiors.

The silvery-blue paleness of Jim and Sandy Howell's living room (**2.114**) has a feeling so cool and airy that even the red of the woodstove does not seem to give off much warmth. The house is designed to draw in a tremendous amount of outside light through broad glass walls and a skylit core. This light is of great importance to Jim, a painter who works with very subtle variations of color and light (one of his paintings hangs on the wall). The warmth and brilliance of the light that floods the house is balanced by the quiet coolness of the blues inside.

By contrast, the reds of the sitting room shown in Figure **2.115** create an extremely warm effect. But when reds, oranges, and yellows are used in small amounts, as accents rather than whole environments, they may not create a sense of warmth. We have already noted the strange coolness of the small fire seen in the woodstove in Jim and Sandy Howell's living room. And the red-purple of the chair and ottoman in Judy and Pat Coady's townhouse (**2.116**) does not change the overall coolness of the room. Rather, the pale pastel green of the door draws our attention to the cool qualities in the focal point: Marni Bakst's stained-glass panels. The amounts in which colors are used, and the areas where our attention is focused, have a strong effect on our response.

ADVANCING AND RECEDING COLORS

Because of the way our eyes see colors, warm colors tend to expand visually, seeming to come toward the viewer in space, while cool colors contract, seeming to draw back in space. But these effects do not exist in isolation. Look carefully at Ellsworth Kelly's *Spectrum, III* (**2.117**). Because the same amount of color appears in each band, careful observation of our own reactions will give us some clues as to which colors seem visually larger and closer. Does the strip of colors seem to bow in or out at any point? Is this effect continuous, or does it change direction on any of the bands? Now try blocking out the white of the page by placing four strips of some other color around the edges of the reproduction. Does the spatial effect of the colored bands change?

The only rule that is always true in dealing with the elusive subject of color effects is this: *All colors are affected by the colors around them.* Our perception of certain colors as closer or farther depends to a large extent on the colors to either side of them. Colors that are closer to the hue and value of the background will seem to lie on the same plane as the background; the more that colors differ in value and hue from the background, the more they will appear to come off or recede into it in space, with the direction depending on other spatial clues. The effect of contrast between individual colors and the background is complicated in the Ellsworth Kelly painting by the interactions between adjacent colored bands. If you look closely and for some time, you will begin to see that along many edges where colors meet, the light one appears lighter and the dark one darker. Colors affect each other optically by "subtracting" their own hue and value from that of their neighbor.

COLOR COMBINATIONS

Because colors affect each other, in our perceptual apparatus, theorists have noted that the distance between colors on a color wheel has a predictable effect on how harmonious they will be if placed together. Using the traditional color wheel, they have distinguished several common patterns of color combinations, as shown in **2.118**. These patterns apply to any sets of colors, and not just the ones shown as illustrations in the figure and the examples that follow. Such orderly relationships do not exhaust the possibilities but provide a basic framework for some designers' color choices.

When only one hue is used, perhaps in different values and saturations and perhaps with small amounts of other colors as accents, the color combination is said to be MONOCHROMATIC. Andrée Putman's interior design for a New York apartment (**2.119**) focuses primarily on yellows, with neutral black. Values of one hue harmonize very closely with each other.

Another kind of close harmony occurs when ANALOGOUS colors—hues lying next to each other on the color wheel—are used. Blue and green are analogous colors, with minimal contrasts. Blues and green predominate in El Greco's *View of Toledo* (**2.120**), interspersed with neutral blacks, whites, and browns. Even the whites are bluish, and the browns are tinged with green.

In contrast with the peaceful coexistence possible between closely related hues, hues that lie opposite each other on the color wheel have a jarring or at least exciting effect on the eye when they are juxtaposed. These high-contrast combinations are called

2.118 Color combinations.

154

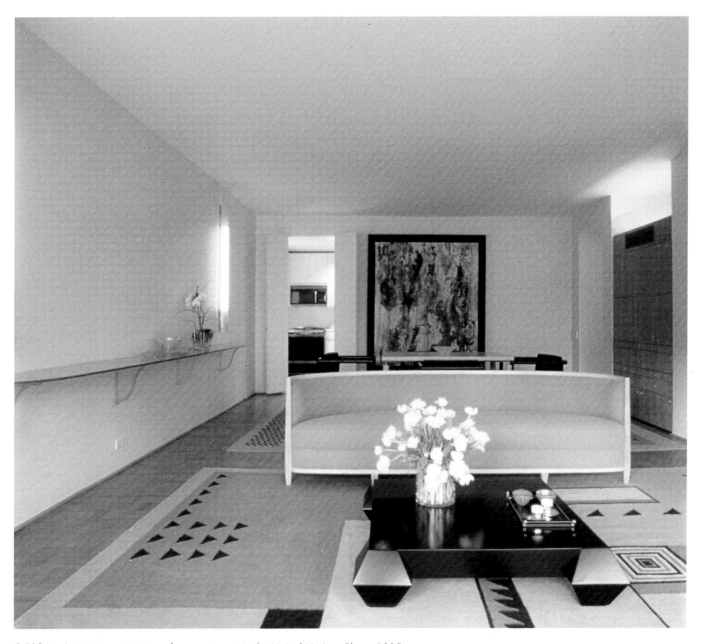

2.119 Andrée Putman, interior of an apartment in the United Nations Plaza, 1985.

COMPLEMENTARY color schemes. In the Chinese statue of Kuan-yin (2.107), the juxtaposition of red and green, which are complementary to each other, creates a sensation of vibrant life. Redon gave his *Orpheus* (2.35) an enhanced atmosphere of mystical space by juxtaposing purple and yellow where mountains meet sky, creating a sense of vibration between them. It is possible to capture the visual excitement of a complementary color combination without over-stimulating the eye, if this is the artist's intent. Anni Albers' weaving, *Pasture* (**2.121**), combines a series of green values and red most effectively by using very small amounts of red to bring the greens to life.

A similarly stimulating combination is a TRIAD color scheme, in which three colors equally spaced around the color wheel are used together. The yellow, blue, and red of the lovely Ottoman embroidered envelope (**2.122**)—a container for royal gifts, messages, and documents—are far enough apart on the color wheel to provide vigorous contrast for each other, but not so far apart that their hues clash.

2.120 El Greco, *View of Toledo*, c. 1597.
Oil on canvas 3 ft 11¾ ins × 3 ft 6¾ ins (1.21 × 1.08 m).
The Metropolitan Museum of Art, New York.
Bequest of Mrs. H. O. Havemeyer, 1929. The H. O. Havemeyer Collection.

2.121 Anni Albers, *Pasture*, 1958. Mercerized cotton weaving, 14 × 15½ ins (35.6 × 39.4 cm). The Metropolitan Museum of Art, New York.

2.122 Embroidered envelope, Ottoman, 16th century. Velvet with silk, gold and silver wire, 7½ × 16⅛ ins (19 × 41 cm). Topkapi Sarayi Museum, Istanbul.

INTERACTION OF COLOR

The highly contrasting effects of complementary colors juxtaposed may be exactly what an artist desires. When highly saturated complementaries are used in the right amounts next to each other, the interaction between the color sensations in our brain may create some extraordinary optical phenomena. The complementaries may seem to enhance each other's brilliance, the edges between them seem to vibrate, and ghost colors may appear where they meet. Op Art, a movement of the 1960s, used these phenomena extensively in nonobjective, hard-edged, geometrical works that create fascinating illusions in our perceptual apparatus. In Op Artist Richard Anuszkiewicz's *Splendor of Red* (**2.123**), the juxtaposition of green and blue lines, and then blue lines alone, with a uniform red ground creates vivid optical illusions that transcend what has actually been painted. The red is the same throughout, but

what we perceive is a diamond of very intense red popping forward from a less brilliant red diamond against an even less brilliant red. That blue halo around the center diamond occurs solely in our perceptions; it has not been physically painted.

No one can yet state with certainty how these effects happen. Scientists have long tried to determine how we see colors, but only theories are yet available. Color perception seems to involve the one hundred million rods and six and a half million cones in the retina at the back of the eye. The rods and cones are specialized photoreceptive cells that glean information from light striking the retina and pass it along to the brain through a series of nerve fibers. In the brain, almost a third of the gray matter of the cerebral cortex is devoted to integrating the information from the two eyes.

We do not know quite how the brain perceives colors; we do not even know what triggers the information about different hues in the cones. There

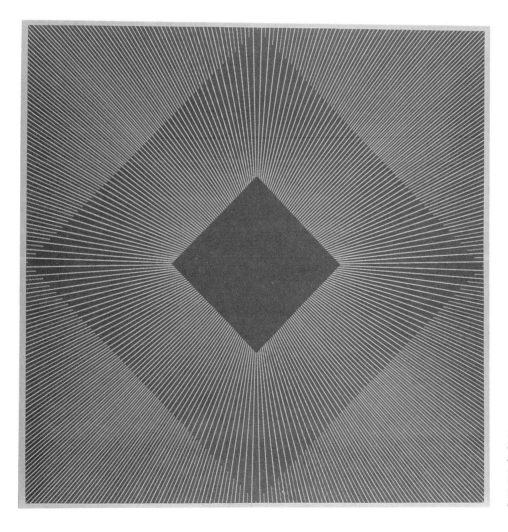

2.123 Richard Anuszkiewicz, *Splendor of Red*, 1965. Acrylic on canvas, 6 ft × 6 ft (1.83 × 1.83 m). Yale University Art Gallery, New Haven CT. Gift of Seymour H. Knox.

2.124 Optical illusion from value contrast.

are light-sensitive pigments in the cones, but we are not certain how they respond to different wavelengths, which correspond to different hues. One of the current theories is that there are three kinds of pigments in the cones: one senses the long wavelengths (reds), one the middle-range wavelengths (greens), and one the short wavelengths (blue-violets). All other colors perceived are mixtures of these primaries in light mixing.

Be this as it may (for there are many other theories), it seems clear that color perception operates by comparison of one colored area with another. For this reason, it is easily "fooled." Consider a simple case of contrast in value. If a medium gray value is seen next to a darker area, it appears light; if the same medium gray is seen against a lighter field, it appears dark. In Figure **2.124**, the central line is actually the same value throughout, but the eye-brain mechanism does not see it that way.

Color perception is not like a camera; it is not a simple registering of information from the outside world. If you were shown a green light in a dark room,

you would be able to identify it as green by comparison with the surrounding blackness. But if that same green light were then presented amidst many other green lights, it would be very difficult to select which one had been shown to you first, for there would not be sufficient contrast to judge by.

In addition to effects of contrast, certain optical effects seem to happen when the photoreceptors are fatigued. If we look at one bright hue for a while—overstimulating those photoreceptors—and then look away, we will "see" its complementary hue briefly in an illusion of the same shape. If you stare at some of the blue-green circles in Larry Poons' *Orange Crush* (**2.125**) and then glance into the orange area, you are likely to perceive more brilliant illusory dots of orange there as after-images. Goethe, who in addition to being a great writer was also a major color theorist, proposed that this illusion arises from an inborn desire for wholeness:

> When the eye sees a color it is immediately excited, and it is its nature, spontaneously and of necessity, at once to produce another, which with the original color

2.125 (above) Larry Poons, *Orange Crush*, 1963. Acrylic on canvas, 6 ft 8 ins ×
6 ft 8 ins (2.03 × 2.03 m). Albright-Knox Art Gallery, Buffalo, New York.
Gift of Seymour H. Knox, 1964.

2.126 (above right) Georges Seurat, *Seated Model*, 1887. Oil on board, 9½ ×
6 ins (24 × 15.2 cm). Louvre, Paris.

comprehends the whole chromatic scale. A single color excites, by a specific sensation, the tendency to universality.[17]

Whether the explanations are psychological or physiological, the unusual effects known to occur when colors are juxtaposed have led to some interesting artistic experiments. For instance, some artists and color theorists have tried to mix colors optically rather than physically. The Post-Impressionist painter Georges Seurat studied the science of color perception in depth and created a technique called POINTILLISM. Using dots of primary and secondary colors in close juxtaposition, he coaxed the eye to mix other colors from them, as in his *Seated Model* (**2.126**). Seen from a distance, the dots tend to blend into colors other than those of the dots, such as flesh tones and their shadows. The effect suggests scintillating lights, rather than flat pigments.

A remarkable and effective contemporary approach to optical mixtures of colors was developed by Arthur Hoener. Working with the interactions among colors and the ground against which they are shown, he created optical color mixtures in the areas between colored figures. In his unique color theory, called SYNERGISTIC COLOR MIXING, the primaries are orange, green, and violet. Violet and green mix optically to form blue, orange and green are mixed to produce yellow, and violet and orange mix to form red. Although these combinations are quite different from those of the traditional Newtonian color wheel shown in Figure 2.99, they do work surprisingly well. In Hoener's painting *Tenuous* (**2.127**), the "yellow" wedge you see is actually made from orange and green, and the "red" wedge is made from violet and orange. These color effects are difficult to reproduce, however, because color printing devices tend to be fooled by them, as is the human eye.

Color interaction effects also depend on the willingness of the viewer to perceive them. They are

160

2.127 Arthur Hoener, *Tenuous*, 1974. Acrylic on canvas, 23½ × 23½ ins (59.7 × 59.7 cm).
Collection of Mr. and Mrs. Walter Tower, Newton MA.

most apparent to those who know to look for them or who relax and allow their immediate experiences to register. Others may use their brains to override their sensory experiences; if they know that no yellow has been physically painted in *Tenuous*, they may not perceive it as a visual reality. Some color interactions happen very quickly and are compellingly "real;" others are more subtle and take time to develop.

161

Josef Albers
on
THE COMPLEXITY OF COLOR

Josef Albers (1888–1976) is widely considered the greatest twentieth-century teacher of the use of color in art, as well as being a great colorist himself. Albers created a great number of paintings called *Homage to the Square* (Figs. 2.113 and **2.129**). In them he held the composition constant—nesting squares of certain proportions—but altered the color relationship in such a way that each painting has a unique effect.

The exercises Albers created for his students at Yale University forced them to recognize the startling optical changes that can be wrought by color interactions. In Figure **2.128**, which is a student solution to a problem given by Albers, two different colors (shown below) are made to look nearly identical by surrounding them with carefully selected colors. Albers did not begin by teaching the optics of color perception or theories of formal relationships between colors. He began by forcing his students to look carefully at colors, to pay attention to what they were actually seeing rather than what they thought they were seeing. He said:

"I like to recall a discovery of Gestalt psychology, that 80 if not 90 percent of our perception is visual. This makes it clear that our sensory contact with the world is first of all visual, that is, through our eyes. And this contact is going on uninterruptedly all day long, as long as there is light and our eyes remain open.

Obviously, but also unfortunately, this continuous and most intensive connection with the surrounding world is not appropriately recognized in education, which remains predominantly auditory."[18]

"In visual perception a color is almost never seen as it really is—as it physically is. This fact makes color the most relative medium in art.

In order to use color effectively it is necessary to recognize that color deceives continually. The aim of such study is to develop—through experience—by trial and error—an eye for color."

"If one says 'Red' (the name of a color) and there are fifty people listening, it can be expected that there will be fifty reds in their minds. And one can be sure that all these reds will be very different. Even when a certain color is specified which all listeners have seen innumerable times—such as the red of the Coca-Cola signs which is the same red all over the country—they will still think of many different reds.

Even if all the listeners have hundreds of reds in front of them from which to choose the Coca-Cola red, they will again select quite different colors. And no one can be sure that he has found the precise red shade.

And even if that round red Coca-Cola sign with the white name in the middle is actually shown so that everyone focuses on the same red, each will receive the same projection on his retina, but no one can be sure whether each has the same perception."

"We are able to hear a single tone. But we almost never (that is, without special devices) see a single color unconnected and unrelated to other colors. Colors present themselves in continuous flux, constantly related to changing neighbors and changing conditions."

"If one is not able to distinguish the difference between a higher tone and a lower tone, one prob-

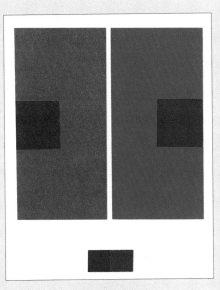

2.128 Two physically different colors can be made to appear nearly identical by careful choice of colored grounds.

2.129 Josef Albers, *Equivocal*, from *Homage to the Square: Ten Works by Josef Albers* © 1962 Ives Sillman, New Haven, Connecticut. Silk-screened print, 11 × 11 ins (27.9 × 27.9 cm). Collection of Arthur Hoener.

ably should not make music.

If a parallel conclusion were to be applied to color, almost everyone would prove incompetent for its proper use. Very few are able to distinguish higher and lower light intensity between different hues. After some training one might easily agree on light relationship, that is, which of two colors is lighter and which is darker. However, there is rarely agreement on color intensity, that is, which among a number of reds is the reddest red."

"Usually, illustrations of harmonic color constellations which derived from authoritative systems look pleasant, beautiful, and thus convincing. But it should not be overlooked that they are usually presented in a most theoretical and least practical manner, because normally all harmony members appear in the same quantity and the same shape, as well as in the same number (just once) and sometimes even in similar light intensity.

When applied in practice, these harmony sets appear changed. In addition to quantity, form, and recurrence, wider aspects exert still more changing influences. These are changed and changing light—and, even worse, several simultaneous lights; reflections of lights and of colors; direction and sequence of reading; presentation in varying materials; constant or altering juxtaposition of related and unrelated objects. With these and other visual displacements, it should not be a surprise that the sympathetic effect of the original 'ideal' color combination often appears changed, lost, and reversed.

Good painting, good coloring, is comparable to good cooking. Even a good cooking recipe demands tasting and repeated tasting while it is being followed.

And the best tasting still depends on a cook with taste."[19]

163

2.130 Frank Stella, *Katsura*, 1979. Oil and eposxy on aluminum, and wire mesh, 115 ins × 92 ins × 30 ins (292.1 × 233.7 × 76.2 cm). Collection, The Museum of Modern Art, New York. Acquired through the Mr. and Mrs. Victor Ganz, Mr. and Mrs. Donald H. Peters, and Mr. and Mrs. Charles Zadock Funds.

LIMITED AND OPEN PALETTE

We leave the complex subject of color with a final measure of ways that artists use color: the range of colors used in a single work of art. An artist who works with an OPEN PALETTE draws from the full range of colors, as Frank Stella does in *Katsura* (**2.130**). His color choices seem completely unrestrained, in a composition held together by repetition of shapes such as French curves and other drafting tools. At the other extreme is the very LIMITED PALETTE used by

Picasso in his *A Woman in White* (**2.131**). The painting is quite rich in color, however, despite the immediate impression of white. The hues Picasso uses are primarily reds and blues, in values so light that they approach white. In general, there is an obvious difference in emotional impact between the two approaches. A more open palette tends to be busy and exciting, especially when colors are used at full saturation. A more limited palette creates a far more subdued, tranquil emotional atmosphere. This is generally true even if those colors are red (2.113).

2.131 Pablo Picasso, *A Woman in White*, 1923. Oil on canvas, 39 × 30½ ins (99 × 77.5 cm).
The Metropolitan Museum of Art, New York. Rogers Fund 1951.

2.132 Column of Trajan, Rome, AD 113. Marble, 125 ft (38.1 m) high.

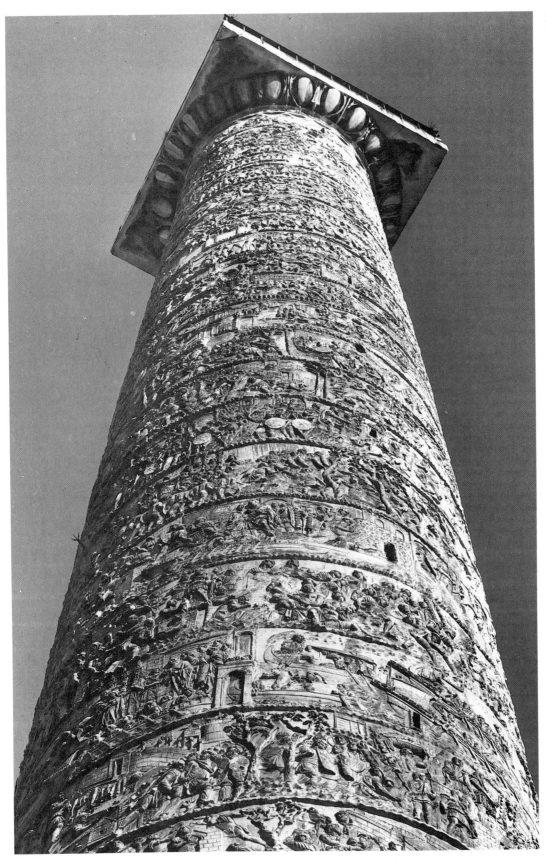

TIME

Thus far we have been exploring visual elements that exist in space: line, form and shape, texture, value and light, and color. But art exists in time as well as space, and time can be considered an element in itself. Ways in which artists work with time include manipulations of viewing time, actual movement, the illusion of movement, capturing a moment in time, using time as the subject of a work of art, and bringing attention to change through time.

VIEWING TIME

A certain amount of time is required for the viewing of any work of art. It is said that the average person spends only ten seconds looking at each work in a gallery or museum. This is not nearly long enough to really "see" them.

Some works have ways of calling us to spend more time with them. One way of doing so is to get us to walk all the way around a three-dimensional piece.

The Roman *Column of Trajan* (**2.132**) does more than that: It lures us to walk around the column again and again, reading the story of Trajan's campaigns to expand the Roman Empire across the Danube. The low relief narrative is carved in marble as a 625-foot-long (190 m) spiraling band that gets broader near the top to improve its visibility. Reading the 150 separate events thus chronicled, working out who and where the figures are and what they are doing, is time-consuming but was presumably possible for those who were familiar with the stories.

Whereas the sculptor of Trajan's Column asks us to walk around the outside of his work, the designers of the *Water Garden, Fort Worth* (**2.133**) entice us to spend time walking not only around the perimeter of the artificial falls but also down through them to the pool at their center. The broad stepped slabs provide varying surfaces over which the patterns of the water change as it descends. The water is finally channeled into torrents as it gathers from the whole area and plunges into the pool. Many of us are fascinated by the patterns of moving water and will happily spend

2.133 Philip Johnson and John Burgee, Water Garden, Fort Worth, Texas, 1974.

2.134 Bridget Riley, *Crest*, 1964.
Emulsion on board, 5 ft 5½ ins × 5 ft
5½ ins (1.66 × 1.66 m).
Private collection.

time beyond mind watching them change.

An entirely different kind of viewing time is demanded by works of Op Art, whose reliance on the distortions introduced by visual fatigue requires that we look at them for a long time in order to experience their effects. In works that juxtapose bright complementary colors, effects such as vibrating edges and color halos appear as the retina tires of the contrast. In black and white Op Art, such as Bridget Riley's *Crest* (**2.134**), one's perception of mere black and white lines lasts only briefly. If you stare at it a bit longer, allowing the image to weave its hypnotic spell, continually changing optical phenomena will occur, including movement, wavy moiré patterns, and perhaps even the appearance of brilliant colors. Try focusing and unfocusing your eyes, shifting the ways you look at it, to see how many different effects you can experience.

Auguste Rodin
on
THE ILLUSION OF MOVEMENT

The sculptor Auguste Rodin (1840–1917) worked intently with naturally-moving living models, creating vigorously realistic sculpture that flew in the face of prevailing French academic traditions. His marvelous *Monument to Balzac* (**2.135**), though commissioned by the Society of Men of Letters, was rejected by the Society because it did not coincide with their ideas of what a portrait should look like. Yet his genius in coaxing apparent life into cast metal and sculpted marble is now highly celebrated. The following are excerpts from conversations with his friend Paul Gsell, on the illusion of movement in sculpture:

"I have always sought to give some indication of movement. I have very rarely represented complete repose. I have always endeavored to express the inner feelings by the mobility of the muscles.

Art cannot exist without life. If a sculptor wishes to interpret joy, sorrow, any passion whatsoever, he will not be able to move us unless he first knows how to make the beings live which he evokes. For how could the joy or the sorrow of an inert object—of a block of stone—affect us? Now, the illusion of life is obtained in our art by good modeling and by movement. These two qualities are like the blood and the breath of all good work."

"Note, first, that *movement is the transition from one attitude to another*. ... You remember how in Dante's Inferno a serpent, coiling itself about the body of one of the damned, changes into man as the man becomes reptile. The great poet describes this scene so ingeniously that in each of these two beings one follows the struggle between two natures which progressively invade and supplant each other.

It is, in short, a metamorphosis of this kind that the painter or the sculptor effects in giving movement to his personages. He represents the transition from one pose to another—he indicates how insensibly the first glides into the second. In his work we still see a part of what was and we discover a part of what is to be.

The sculptor compels, so to speak, the spectator to follow the development of an act in an individual.... Have you ever attentively examined instantaneous photographs of walking figures? What did you notice? If, in instantaneous photographs, the figures, though taken while moving, seem suddenly fixed in mid-air, it is because, all parts of the body being reproduced exactly at the same twentieth or fortieth of a second, there is no progressive development of movement as there is in art.

It is the artist who is truthful and it is photography which lies, for in reality time does not stop, and if the artist succeeds in producing the impression of a movement which takes several moments for accomplishment, his work is certainly much less conventional than the scientific image, where time is abruptly suspended."

"Note besides that painters and sculptors, when they unite different phases of an action in the same figure, do not act from reason or from artifice. They are naively expressing what they feel. Their minds and their hands are as if drawn in the direction of the movement, and they translate the development by instinct. Here, as everywhere in the domain of art, sincerity is the only rule."[20]

2.135 Auguste Rodin, *Monument to Balzac*, 1897. Bronze, 8 ft 10¼ ins × 3 ft 11½ ins × 4 ft 2½ ins (2.70 × 1.20 × 1.28 m). Musée Rodin, Paris.

ACTUAL MOVEMENT

Rather than requiring movement on the part of the viewer, some three-dimensional works move through time themselves. They are often called KINETIC SCULPTURE. Famous examples are the MOBILES of Alexander Calder—constructions suspended by a system of wires so that their parts circle around the central point when pushed or moved by air currents. This aspect of the movement of a mobile such as *Lobster Trap and Fish Tail* (**2.136**) is partly predictable, but intriguing as we watch the different parts passing in front of us. More surprising are the unpredictable ways that the individually suspended parts turn around each other and on their own axes. Spatial relationships among the shapes will change continually, as long as the mobile is in motion.

ILLUSION OF MOVEMENT

In two-dimensional works, movement obviously cannot happen in real time. It can only be suggested. How to do so was an intellectual and artistic challenge to the French artist Marcel Duchamp. He chose the device of showing a single figure in a sequence of motions, rather like stop-action photographs, for his famous and controversial *Nude Descending a Staircase* (**2.137**). Some scientists today feel that this is actually the way time moves: by little jerks, a series of barely different frames, rather than a continuously changing flow. So far we have no way of knowing which model of time is true. But when Duchamp painted *Nude Descending*, the European artists who called themselves "Futurists" were insisting that modern art should reflect modern life, which is fast, fragmented, and in constant change. In their *Futurist Manifesto* of 1910, they asserted:

> The gesture which we would reproduce on canvas shall no longer be a fixed *moment* in universal dynamism. It shall simply be the *dynamic sensation* itself. Indeed, all things move, all things run, all things are rapidly changing. A profile is never motionless before our eyes, but it constantly appears and disappears. On account of the persistency of an image upon the retina, moving objects constantly multiply themselves; their form changes like rapid vibrations, in their mad career. Thus a running horse has not four legs, but twenty, and their movements are triangular.[21]

2.136 Alexander Calder, *Lobster Trap and Fish Tail*, 1939. Hanging mobile: painted steel wire and sheet aluminum, about 8 ft 6 ins high × 9 ft 6 ins diameter (2.60 × 2.90 m). Collection, The Museum of Modern Art, New York. Commissioned by the Advisory Committee for the stairwell of the Museum.

2.137 Marcel Duchamp, *Nude Descending a Staircase #2*, 1912. Oil on canvas, 58 × 35 ins (147 × 89 cm). Philadelphia Museum of Art, Louise and Walter Arensberg Collection.

NU DESCENDANT UN ESCALIER

2.139 Henri de Toulouse-Lautrec, *Cirque Fernando: The Ringmaster*, 1888.
Oil on canvas, 3 ft 3⅜ ins × 5 ft 3⅜ ins (1 × 1.61 m). The Art Institute of Chicago.

THE CAPTURED MOMENT

Although it is difficult to represent the passage of time in a single two-dimensional image, some images clearly refer to motion by capturing a moment of it in time. In Fragonard's *The Swing* (**2.138**), we see a young woman being swung by an obliging but naive old cleric at the behest of her hidden admirer, whose gaze she teasingly acknowledges by kicking off her shoe toward him. The sensuous swirling of her clothes, the dynamic positions of her limbs, and the curve of the ropes create a great sense of continuing motion in a fleeting, erotic moment.

With the invention of photography, some artists began selecting and framing their views of life as if seen through the lens of a camera. As we saw in discussing point of view, Degas did so to bring us into

the intimacy of the ballet theatre (2.55). Considerably influenced by Degas, Toulouse-Lautrec used a photographic cropped effect to create a sense of motion in his *Cirque Fernando: The Ringmaster* (**2.139**). We see only what we could see if we were in the ring to the ringmaster's right, watching the horse almost from behind as it gallops around. We could not see much above the dancer's head without raising our glance, so the top of a clown standing on a stool is out of our sight, as is the left side of the clown to the left. Toulouse-Lautrec makes it clear that we are following the horse visually through time, of which only one moment is shown, and he gives the horse a large open area into which to move, increasing the impression of its movement.

In the early days of action photography, cameras were capable of capturing moving forms at speeds of up to ½₅₀₀ of a second (in the case of the single-lens

2.138 Jean Honoré Fragonard, *The Swing*, 1766.
Oil on canvas, 32 × 35 ins (81.3 × 89 cm).
The Wallace Collection, London.

2.140 Jacques Henri Lartigue, *Grand Prix of the Automobile Club of France*, 1912. Photograph.

camera brought out in 1899 by Guido Sigriste). But they used a FOCAL PLANE SHUTTER, which was a curtain with a slit that travels across in front of the film to expose it. If the subject is moving rapidly or the camera is being turned to follow the action, the image will be distorted in ways that give the impression of great speed, as in Lartigue's photograph of the Grand Prix (**2.140**). Unlike the Fragonard (2.138) and the Toulouse-Lautrec (2.139), this image does not show the area ahead of the action. This truncated space visually increases the sense of speed: the automobile is moving so fast that it has almost disappeared before the moment could be captured on film.

Not all captured moments deal with movement. Some references to moving time center on the ephemeral and precious nature of the present moment, which will never recur in exactly the same way. Juan Gonzales's exquisite pencil drawing *Sara's*

Garden (**2.141**) shows us a fleeting glimpse of tiny dewdrops along fragile threads seemingly strung like cables to hold up lilies whose blossoms are at their peak. The "cables" are imaginary, as are the "pearls" at their junctions, according to the artist, who used them to break up the space and suggest poetic allusions in the mind of the viewer. The work is executed so realistically that we can sense the fragility of the moment, fully expecting that the slightest wind will break the gossamer threads, and the lilies will wither and die in the natural cycle of life. But here, captured, is the beauty of the moment.

2.141 (right) Juan Gonzales, *Sara's Garden*, 1977. Graphite on paper, 22 × 18 ins (56 × 46 cm). Nancy Hoffman Gallery, New York.

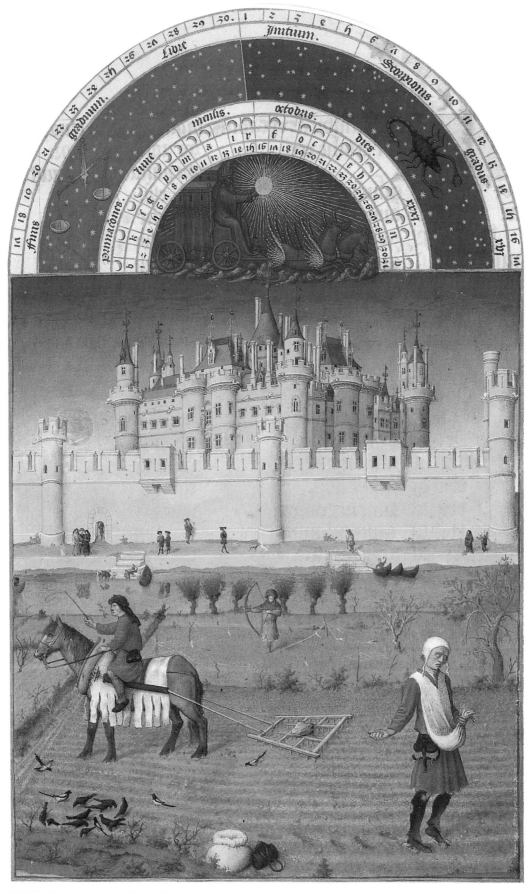

2.142 The Limbourg Brothers, *October*, from *Les Très Riches Heures du Duc de Berry*, 1413–16. Illumination, 8½ × 5½ ins (21.6 × 14 cm). Musée Condé, Chantilly, France.

2.143 Gentile da Fabriano, *The Adoration of the Magi*, 1423. Tempera on wood panel, 9 ft 11 ins × 9 ft 3 ins (3.02 × 2.82 m). Galleria degli Uffizi, Florence.

TIME AS THE SUBJECT

Yet another way in which artists work with time is to make it the central subject of their piece. In uncertain times, such as the Hundred Years' War in France, artworks that bespeak the orderly, predictable passage of time have a special significance. During that war, the three Limbourg brothers created for the Duke of Berry a remarkable Book of Hours—a private devotional book giving the Catholic prayers for each part of the day, from Matins to Compline, plus other liturgical duties and calendars for local feast days. Each month has a detailed miniature painting of what the peasants or aristocracy should be doing during the month. For October, shown here (**2.142**), the peasants are planting winter wheat. Above the scene are notations and symbols of the zodiac signs for the month—with images of Libra and Scorpio—and the reassurance that the chariot of the sun will be making its yearly rounds.

In addition to our desire for life's certainties as time inevitably brings changes, we also like to be told stories about events happening *through* time. Works that tell a story using pictures rather than words are often called NARRATIVE works. Many were used to teach the illiterate the traditions of church or state; some are simply to entertain, such as Fragonard's *The Swing* (2.138).

While these paintings summarize a whole story in one image, others show progressive frames of action occurring through time, rather like a cartoon strip. In Gentile da Fabriano's *The Adoration of the Magi*

(**2.143**) we see beneath the primary painting small scenes of the birth of Jesus, the flight to Egypt, and the visit of the Magi in a contemporary setting, with depictions of the trip of the Magi to Bethlehem above culminating in the crowd spilling into the canvas for the moment in which the Three Kings actually kneel in adoration before the Christ child.

CHANGE THROUGH TIME

All works of art themselves change through time. Usually they gradually deteriorate, some so slowly that the change is barely noticeable. But some are purposely fragile, so that witnessing their decay is part of the art experience itself. CONCEPTUAL ART deals with ideas and immediate experience rather than with permanent form. Even clay, one of the most durable of media, can be handled conceptually as a temporary experience that changes through time, if the clay is not fired to hardness. George Geyer and Tom McMillin's installation, *Surface Erosion* (**2.144**), was set up quickly when the tide was out and then inexorably destroyed by waves as the tide returned. To be touched by this work, one would have to stand close by, watching its disintegration until the forces of nature had again cleared the area of human efforts, leaving only the primordial sea, sand, wind, and rocks.

2.144 George Geyer and Tom McMillin, "*Surface Erosion*" *Laguna Beach*, California. Clay, wood, steel, water, and sand.

3

ORGANIZING PRINCIPLES OF DESIGN

The visual elements examined in Chapter 2 are manipulated by artists to form compositions that have a certain coherence, or UNITY. If these elements work well, they contribute to a whole that is greater than the sum of the parts. In trying to determine what holds an effective work together, theorists have distinguished a number of principles that seem to be involved. They include repetition, variety or contrast, rhythm, balance, compositional unity, emphasis, economy, and proportion. Another principle that artists use, but that theorists generally overlook, is the relationship of a work to its environment.

Not all of these principles are emphasized in a single work. And certain artists use them more intuitively than intellectually, using nonlinear thinking while sketching, planning, and manipulating design elements—until everything feels right. Nevertheless, the principles give us a basis for understanding the form of certain

3.1 Nathalie du Pasquier, Fabric, 1985. Silk. Manufactured by Memphis/Tino Cosmo, Italy.

compositions. Often these formal considerations help to express the content of the work and can best be understood when the content as well as the form is taken into account.

REPETITION

One of the basic ways that artists have unified their designs is to repeat a single design element, be it a kind of line, shape, form, texture, value, or color. As the viewer's eye travels from one part to another, it sees the similarities, and the brain, preferring order to chaos, readily groups them as like objects. Nathalie du Pasquier of the Milan-based Memphis design group presents imaginary animals as cut-out shapes tumbling across her fabric design (**3.1**). The turning of the same amusing shape to many different positions

makes the design lively and interesting, while its repetition holds the design together in the viewer's perception.

In three-dimensional work, repetition of a single design element can have a powerful effect. *Backs* (**3.2**), by Polish fiber artist Magdalena Abakanowicz, has a disturbing emotional impact on viewers, not only because of the headless, limbless quality of the hunched-over, hollowed-out torsos, but also because there are so many of them. The artist explained: "I needed 80 to make my statement. At first I made six, but then I saw I must have 80 of them—to show a crowd, a tribe, or a herd, like animals."[1] She leaves their interpretation to viewers, preferring universal to specific references, but they clearly reflect human oppression, as experienced by one who grew up in a war-ravaged, enemy-occupied country.

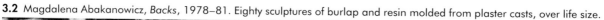

3.2 Magdalena Abakanowicz, *Backs*, 1978–81. Eighty sculptures of burlap and resin molded from plaster casts, over life size.

3.3 José Clemente Orozco, *Zapatistas*, 1931. Oil on canvas, 45 × 55 ins (114.3 × 139.7 cm). Collection, The Museum of Modern Art, New York. Given anonymously.

3.4 (right) Repeated figures in *Zapatistas*.

The repeated figures in Abakanowicz's *Backs* and du Pasquier's fabric seem to stand alone, despite their similarity. By contrast, in José Clemente Orozco's *Zapatistas* (**3.3**), the similar figures in the peasant army merge into a unified whole. As shown in the diagram (**3.4**), our eye picks out the diagonals of the standing figures and their hats as beats in a single flowing movement to the left, with bayonets as counterthrusts pointing to the drum-like repeated beats of the large hats above. We can see that even if one revolutionary falls, the mass of the others still moves inexorably forward.

3.5 Henry Wilson, Wallpaper, 1898.

Many paintings use repetitions of some design quality to unify complex compositions. In *Mont Sainte-Victoire* (2.29), for example, Cézanne uses the repetition of similar brush-strokes to help tie the work together. If you page through the illustrations in this book, you will find many more examples—some obvious, some quite subtle.

In purely decorative works, such as fabric and wallpaper designs, repetition of design elements is often used to build up an all-over PATTERN, a series of images that is repeated in an orderly way. When a whole wall is papered in Henry Wilson's wallpaper (**3.5**), one sees a pattern of interlocking stylized trees with flowers both separating and unifying them.

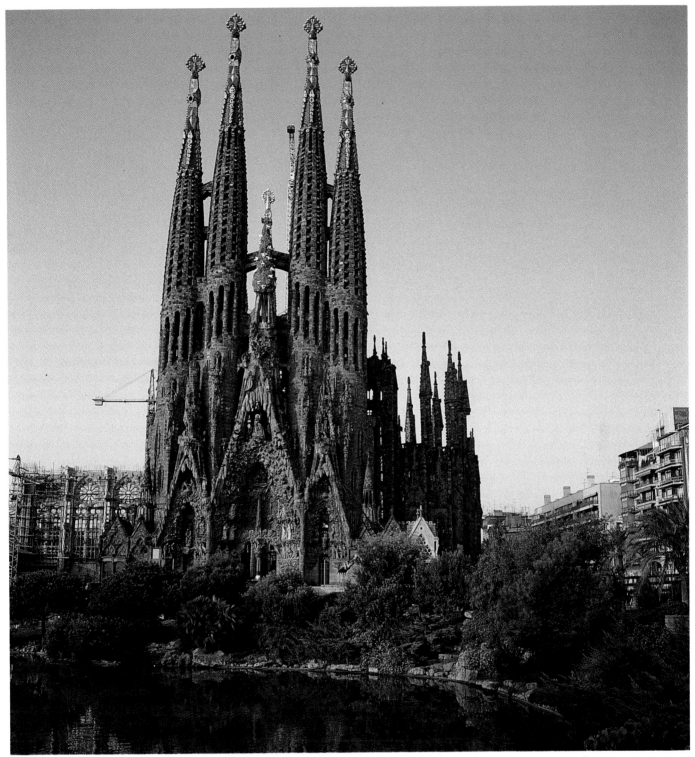

3.6 Antonio Gaudi, Church of the Holy Family (*Sagrada Familia*), Barcelona, Spain, 1883–1926. Photo from Mas, Barcelona.

VARIETY

The companion of repetition is VARIETY: change rather than sameness through space and time. Variety often takes the form of subtle variations on the same theme: Du Pasquier's animals (3.1) vary in position and each of Abakanowicz's backs is slightly different (3.2). Antonio Gaudi's uncompleted church of the *Sagrada Familia* in Barcelona (**3.6**) is a fantastic conglomeration of many architectural styles. Yet it is

183

3.7 Helen Frankenthaler, *Essence Mulberry*, 1977. Woodcut, edition of 46, 40 × 18½ ins (101.6 × 46.9 cm).

3.8 (opposite) Balega Mask, Africa. Wood with pigment and fiber, 8 ins (20.3 cm) high. Private collection.

held together visually by its spires, which vary in form but resemble each other in their tapering upward reach.

Another way in which variety is expressed is through TRANSITIONS, or gradual changes from one state to another. For example, one color may gradually blend into another, a line may change in character, or a form may dissolve into unfilled space. Helen Frankenthaler's woodcut *Essence Mulberry* (**3.7**) presents a beautiful transition from mulberry to a gray that echoes the gray of the ground. She also works with variety in the form of CONTRAST—an abrupt change. Here the gradual vertical color change of the upper portion is played against the sudden horizontal of gold on the bottom. Frankenthaler is also working with contrasts in scale and shape, between the hard-edged geometry of the large golden rectangle and the soft-edged amorphous shapes above.

Contrast is often used to enhance our appreciation of both things being compared. The gold and the mulberry hues are so different that each brings out the other's richness by contrast. In a Balega mask (**3.8**) the rough, random fibers of the beard accentuate the smooth, fast lines of the head. The Church of Taivallahti, excavated as an underground space within living rock in Helsinki (**3.9**), calls us to appreciate both the organic roughness of the stone and the elegant refinement of the organ pipes, the earthiness of the walls and the light of the sky brought in beneath the great copper dome. Through a continuing series of contrasts, the stone church wakes up our perceptions and sharpens our awareness of each visual sensation.

Although it might seem logical that highly contrasting passages in a work would disorganize it, detracting from its unity, often the opposite is true. The roughness of the Balega mask beard keeps referring us to the smoothness of the face, tying the two together visually like an egg in a nest. In any work that makes us look from one passage to another and back, it is that act of comparing on the part of the viewer that is the unifying factor. Even if parts seem diametrically opposed to each other, they can be unified in the viewer's mind as two ends of the same continuum. Opposites have a certain unity, complementing each other like black and white, night and day, masculine and feminine.

Artists may also use contrast to create a certain visual tension that adds excitement to a work. There

3.9 Timo and Tuomo Suomalainen, Interior of Taivallahti Church, Helsinki.

is a fine point where things fight with or pull away from each other as far as they possibly can without destroying the unity of the composition. Tintoretto seems to have found this point in his *Leda and the Swan* (**3.10**). As diagrammed in Figure **3.11**, Leda and the observer form strong arcs actively pulling away from each other and twisting through space, accentuating Leda's movement toward her lover Zeus, who has appeared in the form of a swan. Tintoretto worked out his compositions by posing small wax figures in boxes, as if on a stage. He then translated the three-dimensional scene to two

3.10 Jacopo Tintoretto, *Leda and the Swan*, c. 1570–5. Oil on canvas, 5 ft 3¾ ins × 7 ft 1¾ ins (1.62 × 2.18 m). Galleria degli Uffizi, Florence.

3.11 Compositional arcs in *Leda and the Swan*.

dimensions by drawing the figures on a grid placed across the stage and then enlarging them from this grid to the scale of the painting. Not only has he depicted the figures as pulling away from each other; each of the bodies is also twisted in a flowing serpentine movement called *serpentinata* in Italian, an exaggeration of the figure-posing used in High Renaissance art. First developed by classical Greek sculptors, the technique involves twisting areas of the body in counterpoised opposition to each other. The twisting movement adds to the dramatic effect. Tintoretto was one of the so-called Mannerist painters, who exaggerated gestures for their theatrical impact.

RHYTHM

A third organizing principle found in many works is RHYTHM. Repetition and variety in design elements create patterns that are analogous to rhythms in music, from the predictable drumbeats of a marching band to the swirling rhythms of romantic symphonies to the offbeat intricacies of jazz timing. The same element—such as a line, form, or color— may be repeated visually through space, or groupings may be repeated so that the eye picks out recurring patterns, such as small-large-medium, small-large-medium. Such patterns, which may be easily perceived or complex and subtle, create repeated visual accents with spaces between them, like

3.12 (right) *Apsara*, Northern Wei dynasty, China, early 6th century. Gray limestone, 25 ins (63.5 cm) wide. Victoria and Albert Museum, London.

3.13 Ugolino di Nerio, *Last Supper*, c. 1322. Tempera and gold on wood, 13½ × 20¼ ins (34.3 × 51.4 cm). The Metropolitan Museum of Art, New York. Robert Lehmann Collection, 1975.

upbeats and downbeats, or waves and troughs. The *apsara*, or divine water nymph, shown in Figure **3.12** in fact appears to be part of the flowing rhythm of the ocean, and of the song being played on the instrument. There is a continued repetition of upswept lines, and within these arcs secondary melodies repeat the theme with variations. These melodies within melodies are particularly visible on the right side of the piece, where wavy lines dance within the upward arcs. The nymph's body, too, is turning rhythmically in space, with face frontal, hips turned sideways, and feet so turned that we see the soles. Even the fingers are treated rhythmically, like notes in counted measures.

Rhythm in a work satisfies the desire for order, for it brings a familiar sense of the pulsing of life. In the *apsara*, the pulsing is playful and free, but ordered nonetheless. In the *Last Supper* altarpiece by the medieval artist Ugolino di Nerio (**3.13**), the rhythm formed by the repetition of the circles of the haloed heads of the disciples is as regular as drumbeats. This easily-perceived regularity is broken by the wider space separating Christ from the others, the grieving position of John the beloved, and the absence of a halo around the head of Judas. These dramatic elements are like crossbeats to the rhythms of the rest of the painting, another being produced by the alternating placement of reds.

Rhythms may flow continuously through time, without the measured pauses seen in Ugolino's *Last Supper*. As we noted in examining the Thonet rocking chair (2.15), its lines flow rhythmically through long curves, never stopping fully except at the delicate ends of the "tendrils." For the most part, the only changes we "hear" in the visual music of the chair are shifts in volume and speed, with slight crescendos through the center of the curves and slowing decrescendos as the lines change direction.

In freely-stroked works, each line reflects the rhythm of the breath and movements of the artist. The Levha calligraphy by Sami Efendi (2.1) is created with single brush movements, precisely controlled for a free-flowing effect. The calligrapher cannot lift pen or brush before completing a stroke, for its subtly varying width depends on the movement and angle of the writing implement. Traditional Chinese and Japanese painters were trained to use the whole arm to create brush-strokes. They practiced brush movements for years to develop the control and flexibility needed to create free-flowing lines that

3.14 Remedios Varo, *Toward the Tower*, 1961. Photograph courtesy of Christie's, New York.

were also even and continuous. The wrist was used only in drawing very delicate lines.

The rhythm of certain works is like orchestral music, a complex interweaving of voices into a coherent progression in time. Remedios Varo's *Toward the Tower* (**3.14**) is full of dreamlike mysteries, but the artist holds these incongruous parts together visually like the music produced by an orchestra. The towers are like dull booming bass notes, with the smaller rounded forms such as the nuns' heads and bicycle wheels as higher, faster counterpoints. With more nuns coming out of the towers and the birds inexplicably flying in and out of the pedlar's pack, the music seems to be continuous, like a rondeau. Looking at it, one can almost beat out the timing of each of the parts and hear them fitting together into a symphony.

BALANCE

A fourth design principle is BALANCE—the distribution of apparent visual weights so that they seem to offset one another. We subconsciously assign VISUAL WEIGHT to parts of a work, and we tend to want them to be distributed through the work in such a way that they seem to balance each other. The sense of forms held in balance against the pull of gravity is psychologically pleasing; imbalances may give us an unsettled feeling, a reaction that is not usually the artist's desired effect.

Reading horizontally across a piece, the balancing of visual weights is like a seesaw. As diagrammed in Figure **3.15**, this kind of balancing of equal forces around a central point or axis is called SYMMETRICAL or FORMAL BALANCE. An example of absolutely symmetrical balance is the chest from the Haida

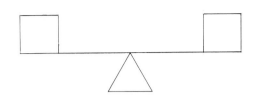

3.15 Symmetrical horizontal balance.

culture of Queen Charlotte Island off the north-west North American coast (**3.16**). If an imaginary vertical axis were drawn right through the center of the piece, the two halves of the central figure and the geometric animal motifs extending to the sides would be exact mirror images balancing each other. If a horizontal line were drawn through the center of the piece from left to right, the upper and lower halves would also consist of symmetrically balanced, though not identical, visual components.

3.16 Chest for clothes and jewelry of the Haida tribe, of Queen Charlotte Island off north-west coast of North America, 19th century. Wood inlaid with shells and animal tusks. British Museum, London.

3.17 William Blake, *The Last Judgement*, 1808. Tempera, 19⅞ × 15¾ ins (50.3 × 40 cm). Petworth House, Sussex, England.

Symmetrical balance can occur even if images on each side of the vertical axis are not exactly the same. In William Blake's dramatic painting of *The Last Judgement* (**3.17**), those who have erred are descending to the flames of hell on the right side, balanced by those blissfully ascending to the throne of God on the left side. The fact that the right side of the painting is darker than the left adds to the visionary drama. Although the value difference would imbalance the work otherwise, it is balanced by the symmetrical circular motion of the figures, as if radiating outward from the point between the two central beings blowing horns, and by the strong vertical axis created by the patterns of the figures rising through the center. The continuing movement of the figures reflects Blake's view that our fortunes are ever-shifting and that those who have sinned are not eternally damned.

Elements may also be symmetrically arranged around a central point in all directions, in which case the composition may be referred to as RADIAL BALANCE. In the Buddhist Wheel of Life (**3.18**), each circle represents a different aspect of existence, with the whole wheel surrounded by the monster of death and impermanence. Note that even his parts are symmetrically arrayed around the center.

191

When the weights of dissimilar areas counterbalance each other, the result is called ASYMMETRICAL or INFORMAL BALANCE. Expressed as a simple diagram (**3.19**), a large light-colored area might be balanced by a small dark-colored area, with the fulcrum off-center. Dark colors generally seem heavier than light ones, busily detailed areas heavier than unfilled ones, bright colors heavier than dull ones, large shapes heavier than small shapes, and objects far from the center heavier than those near the center.

Consider Thomas Gainsborough's *Mr. and Mrs. Andrews* (**3.20**). The painting is obviously asymmetrical, for both important figures are on the left side, with nothing but their lands to the right. The balancing point is established by the vertical thrust of the tree, well to the left of center. The pair carry considerable visual weight because they are visually interesting and detailed human figures, because they are looking at us and holding our attention, because they and the tree trunk are the largest and closest objects in the composition, and

3.19 Asymmetrical horizontal balance.

192

3.20 Thomas Gainsborough, *Mr. and Mrs. Andrews*, c. 1749. Oil on canvas, 27½ × 47 ins (69.8 × 119.4 cm). National Gallery, London.

because their clothes are the brightest colors in the painting. The breadth of the fields to the right is not a wasted area in the composition, for Gainsborough needed a great expanse of less detailed space to balance his strong figures. Note that the fields recede into deep space. To a certain extent, Gainsborough is setting up a balance that extends into—as well as across—the picture plane. And those fields serve a purpose in the content as well as the form of the painting: They demonstrate the wealth of this couple, whose lands seem to stretch as far as the eye can see.

Sometimes artists violate the principle of balance intentionally to create tension in their works. Nancy Graves' *Trace* (**3.21**) is not visually "safe;" it appears to be extremely fragmented and precariously balanced, about to fall over in the direction that the three slender "legs" are bent. Its three-point anchor in a heavy base actually makes the piece quite stable, but visually it seems to be dynamic and fragile. Contemporary aesthetics and materials allow an artist to push balance to limits never seen before.

3.21 Nancy Graves, *Trace*, 1979–80. Bronze, steel, patina, and paint, 8 ft 11 ins × 9 ft 8 ins × 4 ft 2 ins (2.71 × 2.92 × 1.27 m). Collection of Mr. and Mrs. Graham Gund, Boston.

3.22 Pietro Vanucci, called Perugino, *The Crucifixion with Saints*, c. 1485. Oil, transferred from wood to canvas, middle panel 39⅞ × 22¼ ins (101.3 × 56.5 cm), side panels 37½ × 12 ins (95.2 × 30.5 cm). The National Gallery of Art, Washington D.C. Andrew W. Mellon Collection.

COMPOSITIONAL UNITY

Artists can also hold compositions together by creating strong attachments between elements within the work. They may physically touch each other, like the cut-out shapes forming Matisse's abstract *Snail* collage (2.30). They may be held together by the energy of opposition, like the magnetism of opposing arcs in Tintoretto's *Leda and the Swan* (3.10). Or the artist may have arranged the lines of the work—both actual and implied—in such a way that they lead the viewer's eye from one area to another, visually tying the work together.

A common formula for unifying compositional lines is the implied triangle. Standing on its base, a triangle is a highly stable shape. Christian sacred art has often used the solidity of a double triangle pattern, with a strong primary triangle counterbalanced and filled out by a weaker inverted secondary triangle, as in Figure 3.23. The central panel of Perugino's *The Crucifixion with Saints* altarpiece (3.22) illustrates a complex series of these compositional triangles. As shown in Figure 3.24, the major triangle is crowned by the head of Christ and bounded on its lower corners by the pointed feet of the mourners. A secondary inverted triangle is formed by the horizontal of the cross and implied lines joining it from the diagonal stakes pointing upwards at the base of the cross.

Another set of triangles is created by the eyelines among the figures, as diagrammed in Figure 3.25. Jesus' head is inclined down toward Mary, whose downcast eyes lead us to a diagonal stake, which points us up to the face of John, whose gaze is directed up to Jesus' face. This circuit completes and reinitiates a diamond pattern that is divided into two triangles across the middle by the horizon. We can also read our way round and round each of these triangles. For instance, in the lower one, we read from Mary's gaze down to one stake, up through the other to John's head, and then across along the horizon back to Mary's face. Even the folds in the saints' robes contribute to the triangular patterns. Perugino carefully leads us through the composition, bringing us back again and again to the major figures and thus tying them together both in form and in emotional

3.23 Double triangle composition.

3.24 Double triangle composition in *The Crucifixion with Saints*.

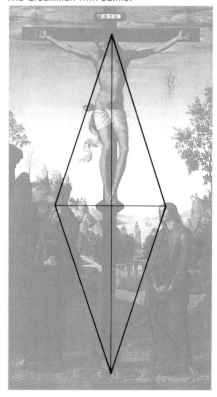

3.25 Implied triangles in *The Crucifixion with Saints*.

content. The balance and compositional unity of the work are entirely appropriate for an altarpiece forming the focal point of a symmetrically planned church. But it is not rigid. Notice, for instance, the off-center arrangement of the lake and hills in the background, placing John's head against water and sky and Mary's against rock. This interesting asymmetry is possible because the composition is so well unified by the triangular patterns in the foreground.

In later works, compositional unity is often achieved by less formulaic means. Renoir's Impressionist painting *The Boating Party* (**3.26**) uses a series of devices to unify the many individual figures. The first is the subject matter: These people are relaxing together at a pleasure garden overlooking the Seine. They are unified into small groups because we see them talking to and looking at each other.

The friends having lunch together in the foreground are not in conversation with each other—Aline Charigot, who was to become Renoir's wife, is paying more attention to her dog—but they are held together by being at the same table. The man standing and bending toward the table at the right brings the groups in the background into relationship with those seated at the table. The canopy over the whole group pulls them together visually, as does the bracketing of the figures by the two boatmen. Placed strategically at the right and left margins of the canvas, they stand out from the others because of their large size and matching athletic clothes. Their gazes cross the canvas, encompassing the whole space.

Three-dimensional works are often unified by compositional lines as well, though they cannot be fully appreciated in a two-dimensional photograph

3.26 Pierre Auguste Renoir, *The Boating Party*, 1881.
Oil on canvas, 4 ft 3 ins × 5 ft 8 ins (1.29 × 1.73 m).
Phillips Collection, Washington D.C.

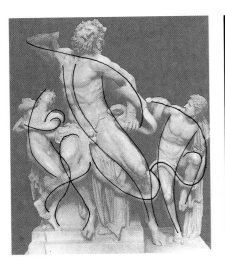

3.28 Three-dimensional compositional lines in the *Laocoön*.

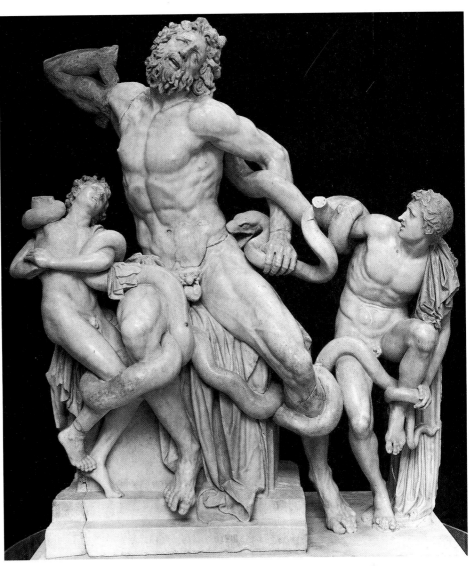

3.27 Hagesandrus, Athenodorus, and Polydorus, *Laocoön*, 1st century AD. Marble, 8 ft (2.44 m) high. The Vatican Museums, Rome.

from a single point of view. The sculptors of the Hellenistic marble *Laocoön* group (**3.27**) wrapped a continuing series of lines around the anguished figures of Laocoön and his sons. Most obvious are the lines of the sea serpents winding through the group. They were said to have sprung out of the sea to attack Laocoön, a Trojan priest, and his sons for defying Apollo or for warning that the Greeks' Trojan horse was a ruse. In addition to the serpents' horrifying way of connecting the figures, the lines of the three straining humans form a continuing series of related curves, as suggested two-dimensionally in Figure **3.28**. They are further tied together by the eyelines from the sons to the father.

EMPHASIS

A further organizing principle in many compositions is that of EMPHASIS—the predominance of one area or element in a design. By its size, position, color, shape, texture, or surroundings, one part of a work may be isolated for special attention, giving a focus or dramatic climax to the work.

When awareness is drawn to a single place, it is called the FOCAL POINT of the composition. In Leonardo da Vinci's *The Last Supper* (**3.29**), Christ is clearly the central focus of the work. The most obvious device used to emphasize him is his placement at the exact center of the painting.

3.29 Leonardo da Vinci, *The Last Supper*, c. 1495–8. Mural painting, 15 ft 1⅛ ins × 28 ft 10½ ins (4.6 × 8.6 m). Refectory, Monastery of Santa Maria delle Grazie, Milan.

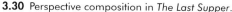

3.30 Perspective composition in *The Last Supper*.

Leonardo has formally lined up the figures along one side of the table, opening the space in front of them so that they all face the audience, as it were, rather than using the arrangement favored by Ugolino (3.13). On this stage, Christ's central position is emphasized by the perspective lines, which all come to a point in or behind his head, as shown in Figure **3.30**. Many of the disciples enforce this movement toward the center by looking at Christ. Even those who are turning away from him to talk among themselves of his tragic announcement point to him with their hands.

Finally, Christ's head is framed within the central window at the back of the room and by the arch over it.

Sacred architecture often develops a single focal point to center worshippers' attention on the forms used to represent divinity. In the small chapel (**3.31**) reconstructed at the Cloisters in New York from twelfth-century sources, the altar is clearly the focal point, with its candles, marble ciborium (canopy), and statue of the Madonna and child. In addition to being the most visually interesting area of this simple chapel, the altar is emphasized by the domed arch in the architecture, the windows to either side that highlight the area, the contrasting value of the curtain behind the statue, and the raised platform on which the altar rests. These devices also symbolize the sacredness of the spiritual, elevating it above the mundane.

Not all works of art have a focal point. In a wallpaper or fabric pattern, the same design motif may be repeated again and again with equal emphasis, scattering the attention in the interest of creating an overall effect. If the repeating unit has a particularly strong visual element, it may appear as

198

3.31 Chapel, from the church of Notre Dame du Bourg, Longon, Bordeaux, France, after 1126. Marble ciborium from the church of San Stefano, near Finao Romano, Rome, 12th century. The Metropolitan Museum of Art, New York. Cloisters Collection.

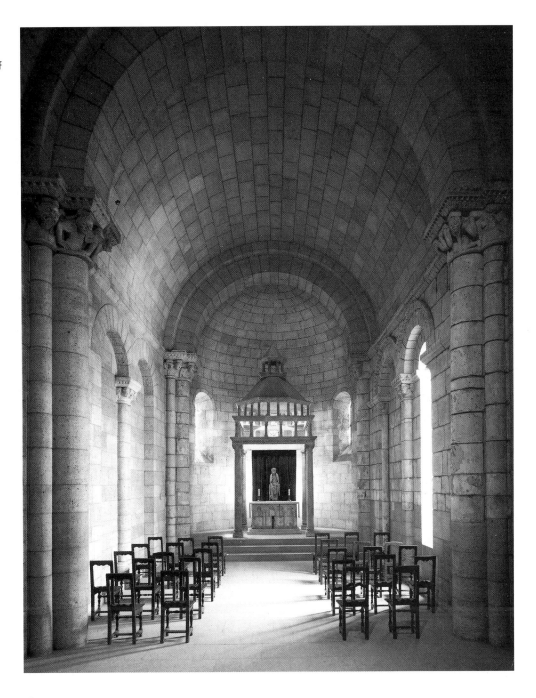

accents within the larger pattern. Many pieces of sculpture also lack a single focal point, for the intention may be to lead the viewer to examine the work from all angles, unlike two-dimensional images in which many elements must be unified across a single plane. Sometimes the entire sculpture becomes a focal point, as it were. Imagine how Brancusi's *Bird in Space* (1.12) would look if it were displayed by itself in a darkened room with a single spotlight gleaming off its polished bronze surface. In most museum settings, works are shown in the midst of many others rather than being emphasized by isolation in a dramatic setting. Altarpieces, for example, were originally intended as the focal points of symmetrical churches. Much of their emotional impact is lost when they are hung on the walls of museums, flanked by other pieces to which they are visually unrelated, and seen under uniform lighting.

3.32 Liang K'ai, *The Poet Li Po*, 13th century.
Ink on paper, 42⅞ × 13 ins (109 × 33 cm).
Tokyo National Museum.

3.33 Vase (*Ching-te-chen* ware). Ch'ing dynasty, China, probably
K'ang-hsi period, 1662–1722. Porcelain, *sang di boeuf* glaze,
7⅞ ins (20 cm) high. The Metropolitan Museum of Art, New York.
Bequest of Mary Clark Thompson, 1924.

ECONOMY

The principle called ECONOMY OF MEANS refers to the ability of some artists to pare away all extraneous details, presenting only the minimum of information needed by the viewer. Economy is a hallmark of some contemporary design, and also of artists influenced by Zen Buddhism. In his portrait of the poet Li Po (**3.32**), Liang K'ai captured the man's spiritual essence as well as his voluminous form with a few quick brushstrokes. This was considered inspired art, possible only when the artist was in direct communion with the Absolute. Nevertheless, to develop the technique of the "spontaneous" brushstroke took many years of practice.

Economy is not limited to figurative art that suggests real forms by using a minimum of clues. The principle can also be applied to nonobjective art. In contrast to the decorative approach of those who paint marble sculptures or cast saltcellars in the forms of the gods (1.48), it is possible to create objects of great beauty by severely limiting the design elements used. The elegant porcelain vase from Ch'ing Dynasty China (3.33) eschews any ornamentation in order to focus attention on the gracefulness of the form and the subtle crackles and color changes in the oxblood glaze. The intensity of the red gets our attention, but in its simplicity, the vase becomes an object for quiet contemplation.

Isamu Noguchi, whose spare aesthetic is apparent in his unadorned rock sculptures (2.106) and his point-balancing cube (1.40), speaks of the difficulties of reducing art to the minimum:

> The absence of anything is very beautiful to me. That is to say, emptiness is very beautiful to me. And to desecrate that emptiness with anything takes nerve. So you might say, well, I'm not a lover of art. But I am, you know. I'm always in a quandary. Too much is not good. Too much of anything is not good. With my attitude, it makes it rather difficult to do anything at all. Nevertheless, I'm rather prolific.[2]

As in the Bauhaus dictum, "Less is more," it is possible to suggest very complex forms or ideas with very few visual clues. Graphic designers are challenged to do so when they are commissioned to create logos. A successful LOGO is a highly refined image that bespeaks the nature of an entire group or corporation with an absolute minimum of marks. The logo Peter Good designed for the Hartford Whalers hockey team (3.34) immediately suggests the tail of a sounding whale, completed by a fluid "W" for the Whalers and a figure-ground reversed "H" for Hartford implied in the unfilled white space. Open to the surrounding space, the "H" has a dynamic flowing quality through the upper portion, with squared-off legs giving strength to the base. If you look very closely at the outer corners of the feet of the "H" you can see LIGHT WELLS there—tiny outward swells that counter the eye's tendency to round off the corners. The light wells actually make the lines of the "H" look straighter. The light pouring in through the opening seems to collect in these corners, creating vibrant effects and perhaps even colors in the eyes of some viewers. In what is actually only two simplified filled areas, this economic logo gives us the initials of the town and team, suggests the derivation of the Whalers name, and gives the impression of liveliness, strength, and speed.

PROPORTION

A further principle in composing artworks is that all parts should be in pleasing proportions to each other. From our experiences in the three-dimensional world, we have a learned sense of "correct" size relationships. In representations of the human figure, we expect the head, feet, arms, and fingers to be a certain size in relationship to the rest of the body. These expectations have been institutionalized in certain schools of art. In the art of China and Japan, for instance, one set of conventions for drawing the human figure was to make the standing body seven times the height of the head, the seated body three times the height of the head, the head itself twice the size of the open palm, and so on. These same schools taught proper proportions for representing on a panel the illusion of the vastness of landscapes, called *Shan-Shui,* or "mountain-water" pictures in Chinese. According to one convention of proportions, if a mountain were shown ten feet (3.1 m) high, a tree should be one foot (30.5 cm) high, a house a tenth of a foot (3.05 cm) high, and a human the size of a pea.

In addition to these artistic conventions about proportion in figurative art, there have been theories that we have an innate abstract sense of ideal proportion. The Greeks formulated this idea of mathematical perfection as the GOLDEN RECTANGLE: one in which the short side is to the longer side as the long side is to the sum of the two sides. This ratio

3.34 Peter Good, Logo for the Hartford Whalers Hockey Club, 1979.

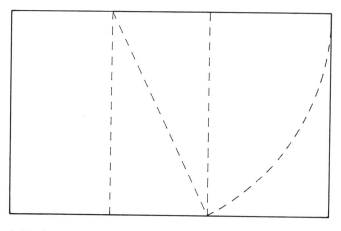

3.35 The Golden Rectangle.

3.36 Ictinus and Callicrates, The Parthenon, Athens, 447–438 BC.

works out to approximately 1 to 1.618, as shown in Figure **3.35**. It is a now-familiar shape, for its proportions of length to height have been used for centuries as an approximate format for paintings.

Although the Greeks worked out the Golden Rectangle as a mathematical formula, they also recognized that our visual perception is not flawless and that it is influenced by our mental assumptions. Ictinus and Callicrates, the architects of the Parthenon (**3.36**), therefore used an astonishing series of "optical refinements" in the proportions of the building to make it appear perfectly regular and they appear to bear (a subtle principle called ENTASIS), and the illusion of regular spacing among the columns is created by having their spacing actually differ. The result is what we perceive as the most perfectly proportioned building ever created.

Artists who are able to create satisfying proportions may thus be working with the actual visual "feel" of objects rather than mathematical precision. The lovely chalice by Timothy Brigden (**3.37**) is divided into three areas that are approximately—but not exactly—the same size: the cup, stem, and base. The base is actually slightly shorter in height than the cup and stem, but with its outward flare it would appear awkward if it were any higher. Brigden has also forsaken exact regularity in the area just below the bottom of the cup, making it straighter than the curves of the rest of the stem. It serves as a transition from the straighter lines of the cup to the undulations of the stem. If it had a more rounded curve, there would be "too many" curves. As it is, the chalice appears just right to the human eye.

Mathematical precision in proportions can actually be found in nature. The seeds in a sunflower head, the florets in a daisy, and the chambers in a nautilus shell (**3.38**) grow in spiraling increasing patterns in the mathematical relationship called a *Fibonacci series*. The ratio of the size of one unit to that of the following unit is 0.618... (an infinite, irrational number); the size of any unit divided by the size of the preceding one is 1.618..., the Greeks' GOLDEN SECTION, on which the Golden Rectangle is based.

3.37 Timothy Brigden, Chalice, late 18th or early 19th century. Pewter, 8⅞ ins (22.5 cm) high. The Metropolitan Museum of Art, New York. Gift of Joseph France, 1943.

rectangular to the human eye. Exact measurement of the Parthenon has revealed many apparently intentional deviations from regularity and rectangularity. Because the Greeks recognized that our visual apparatus perceives vertical lines as sloping and horizontal lines as sagging in the center, they corrected for these human errors in perception. The platform and steps actually curve upward. So does the ENTABLATURE (the horizontal element above the columns), though to a lesser degree, presumably because it was farther from the viewer's eye. The columns and entablature also slope inward slightly to prevent their appearing to slope outward. At the corners, the columns are thickened slightly to counteract the optical thinning effect of their being silhouetted against the sky. The form of the columns bulges out by two-thirds of an inch (1.7 cm) part way up to accommodate the human assumption that the columns will be slightly compressed by the weight

3.38 Diagrammatic section of a Nautilus shell.

3.39 Wassily Kandinsky, *Painting #199*, 1914. Oil on canvas, 5 ft 4⅛ ins × 4 ft ⅜ ins (1.626 × 1.227 m). Collection, The Museum of Modern Art, New York. Nelson A. Rockefeller Fund.

Wassily Kandinsky
on
UNDERLYING HARMONY

The Russian nonobjective painter Wassily Kandinsky (1866–1944) began his adult career in the realm of principles, as a budding professor of law. But he gave that up for painting, and as a painter he worked to free himself from attempts to copy the world of outer appearances or abide by traditional ideas of aesthetic harmony. A mystic, he believed that expressions of a higher inner harmony could be presented through the pure language of colors and forms, with no references to the objective world. Excerpts from his book, *Concerning the Spiritual in Art*, follow:

"The need for coherence is the essential of harmony—whether founded on conventional discord or concord. The new harmony demands that the inner value of a picture should remain unified whatever the variations or contrasts of outward form or colour. The elements of the new art are to be found, therefore, in the inner and not the outer qualities of nature."

"The spectator is too ready to look for a meaning in a picture—i.e., some outward connection between its various parts. Our materialistic age has produced a type of spectator or 'connoisseur,' who is not content to put himself opposite a picture and let it say its own message. Instead of allowing the inner value of the picture to work, he worries himself in looking for 'closeness to nature,' or 'temperament,' or 'handling,' or 'tonality,' or 'perspective,' or what not. His eye does not probe the outer expression to arrive at the inner meaning.

In a conversation with an interesting person, we endeavour to get at his fundamental ideas and feelings. We do not bother about the words he uses, nor the spelling of those words, nor the breath necessary for speaking them, nor the movements of his tongue and lips, nor the psychological working on our brain, nor the physical sound in our ear, nor the physiological effect on our nerves. We realize that these things, though interesting and important, are not the main things of the moment, but that the meaning and idea is what concerns us. We should have the same feeling when confronted with a work of art. When this becomes general the artist will be able to dispense with natural form and colour and speak in purely artistic language."

"New principles do not fall from heaven, but are logically if indirectly connected with past and future. What is important to us is the momentary position of the principle and how best it can be used. It must not be employed forcibly. But if the artist tunes his soul to this note, the sound will ring in his work of itself.

The 'emancipation' of today must advance on the lines of the inner need. It is hampered at present by external form, and as that is thrown aside, there arises as the aim of composition—construction. The search for constructive form has produced Cubism, in which natural form is often forcibly subjected to geometrical construction. . . .

The harmony of the new art demands a more subtle construction than this, something that appeals less to the eye and more to the soul. This 'concealed construction' may arise from an apparently fortuitous selection of forms on the canvas. Their external lack of cohesion is their internal harmony. This haphazard arrangement of forms may be the future of artistic harmony. Their fundamental relationship will finally be able to be expressed in mathematical form, but in terms irregular rather than regular."[3]

3.40 Rock Garden of Ryoanji Temple, Kyoto, Japan.

There are also proportional relationships that are entirely intuitive, based totally on the individual's innate sense of aesthetics. An extreme example is the perfection of the Zen rock garden in Ryoanji Temple (**3.40**). The relationships of sand (raked in lines to represent the sea) to rocks (representing mountainous islands, like the islands of Japan), rock to rock within each grouping, and rock group to rock group are the result of a meditative attunement to the perfection of the universe, rather than obedience to any human system of perfection.

RELATIONSHIP TO THE ENVIRONMENT

A final principle with which artists must often work is the relationship of a piece to its intended environment. When we see art on the pages of a book or on the walls of a museum, we cannot grasp this dimension, for it can only be appreciated in the midst of the living setting for a work of art.

To appreciate the relationship of St. Peter's Church (**3.41**) to its midtown Manhattan setting, one must imagine the great height of the skyscrapers all about, the passing traffic, and the driven attitude of the pedestrians on the Lexington Avenue sidewalk. Under the shadow of the huge Citicorp tower, amid the power plays of banks and publishing houses and the wealth showcased at the Waldorf Astoria and the Racquet and Tennis Club, the tiny church raises its rose-gray granite angularity to the heavens, suggesting a haven of peace in the midst of the fast life.

Artists must work within the limitations and features of whatever settings their commissions involve.

3.41 Hugh Stubbins Associates, St. Peter's Church, New York, 1977. Photo © Peter Aaron/ESTO.

3.42 Frank Lloyd Wright, Kaufmann House (*Fallingwater*), 1936–9. Bear Run, Pennsylvania.

Architect Frank Lloyd Wright, asked to build a house near a creek in Pennsylvania, chose to build it on top of the falls (**3.42**), "not simply to look at the waterfalls but to live with them." Preserving and capitalizing on the beauty of the waterfall, Wright cantilevered the decks of the house right out over it. The horizontal lines of the building mirror the slabs of rock below, echoing their pattern of linear, light-struck mass punctuated by deeply shadowed recesses. His ideal was what he called "organic architecture"—that which respects and merges with the natural environment. Wright wrote:

> When organic architecture is properly carried out no landscape is ever outraged by it but is always developed by it.... Fallingwater is a great blessing—one of the great blessings to be experienced here on earth. I think nothing yet ever equalled the coordination, sympathetic expression of the great principle of repose where forest and stream and rock and all the elements of structure are combined so quietly that really you listen not to any noise whatsoever although the music of the stream is there. But you listen to Fallingwater the way you listen to the quiet of the country.... [4]

PART 2

TWO-DIMENSIONAL MEDIA AND METHODS

Since humans first approached their cave walls to scratch and paint images of the animals they hunted and spirits they sensed, flat surfaces have lured us to record our impressions of life. Across the millennia, we have appropriated everything from plaster walls to computer screens for this purpose.

4

DRAWING

Appreciating the technical aspect of art requires knowing what to look for. Each MEDIUM—a term we use in its broad sense as the material with which the artist works, such as watercolor, oil paint, or stone—and the methods by which it is used have unique characteristics that can be seen in certain works, though some artists use their medium so skillfully that they transcend its limitations and can make it do anything they choose. In this chapter we will examine a variety of media that have been used in drawing.

APPROACHES TO DRAWING

Drawing is perhaps the most direct of all the arts. The marks the artist lays down in a drawing reflect the movements and skillfulness of the arm and hand. This aspect is somewhat different from the visual quality of the lines themselves. Aubrey Beardsley's Ali Baba (**4.1**) is composed of elegant flowing lines, but to get this free-flowing effect with pen and ink took tremendous manual control on Beardsley's part. Even the letters are elegantly controlled drawn lines.

Drawings are often created as illustrations, such as Beardsley's illustration for the book *The Forty Thieves*. Techniques of book printing are easily adapted to reproduction of drawn lines, and they resemble and complement the lines of letter forms, as in the Ali Baba cover.

Another way in which artists have often used drawing is in studying natural forms in preparation for rendering them in another medium. Artists do not typically paint or sculpt a human figure, for example, by starting at the head and working down, filling in

all the details as they go along. Rather, they first analyze the general form, the underlying structure and relationships between parts. They study the figure in terms of volume, values, proportions, lines, and the dynamics of gestures. What they see they may then draw in a preliminary series of sketches—thinking on paper, as it were. Before painting the Sistine Chapel ceiling (15.19–15.25), Michelangelo made numerous drawings to work out the

4.1 Aubrey Beardsley, Cover design for *The Forty Thieves*, 1879. Pen and black ink, brush, and black chalk, 9⁷⁄₁₆ × 7¹³⁄₁₆ ins (24 × 19.7 cm). Fogg Art Museum, Harvard University, Cambridge MA. Grenville L. Winthrop Bequest.

4.2 Michelangelo Buonarroti, Preparatory drawings for *The Creation of Adam*, Sistine Chapel ceiling, 1511. Red chalk over black chalk, 8⅜ × 11 ins (21.3 × 27.9 cm). Teylers Museum, Haarlem, The Netherlands.

musculature and gestures of the figures. The sketch page shown here (**4.2**) includes his working out of the famous arm of the Lord that we see infusing Adam with life in the celebrated *Creation of Adam* (15.22) portion of the ceiling. Michelangelo's technique in these drawings is alternately free and "sketchy," and tighter and more refined, with God's arm modeled in considerable detail.

A third way in which drawings may be used is in presentations, as models for future works. Claes Oldenburg's proposed colossal clothespin monument drawing (**4.3**) was a tongue-in-cheek entry in a competition for a Chicago memorial, 45 years after the fact, although he did actually erect a similar clothespin in Philadelphia in 1976. Such

presentation drawings are now considered collectable works of art in their own right. Christo often sells his drawings of proposed earthworks to help finance his projects, such as *Running Fence* (2.7).

In today's broad aesthetic, all of these kinds of drawings—illustrations, sketches, and presentation drawings—are appreciated and hung as works of art. Many artists also create finished drawings as ends in themselves. The many media now at their disposal are explored in the following sections. Those described are not an exhaustive list; some contemporary artists are drawing with new media such as felt-tip pens. Neither are these categories absolute. Chalks, crayons, charcoal, and pastels are quite similar, and pastel work is often classified as

4.3 Claes Oldenburg, *Late Submission to the Chicago Tribune Architectural Competition of 1922: Clothespin (Version Two)*, 1967. Pencil, crayon, and watercolor, 22 × 23¼ ins (55.9 × 60.3 cm). Des Moines Art Center. Gift of Gardener Cowles by exchange and partial gift of Charles Cowles, New York, 1972.

painting rather than drawing because it involves laying down masses of color rather than lines.

Note that most of the illustrations of drawings are of relatively recent works, for the medium on which most drawing is done—paper—has only been readily available since the early 1500s. At that time, increasing urbanization concentrated the population, and the manufacture of less expensive yard goods coupled with growing affluence led people to throw away clothes as they were worn, outgrown, or out of style. Rag collectors moved through the cities buying the used fabric and selling it to paper manufacturers, enabling paper to be produced in greater quantities than in the past and bringing its price down. Today the best artist's papers are still made with rag; less expensive papers, made from woodpulp, yellow and deteriorate with time and don't hold up well under repeated working.

DRY MEDIA

GRAPHITE PENCIL

The pencils commonly used by artists are quite similar to those used as writing tools. They are simply thin rods of GRAPHITE—a soft form of carbon, mixed with clay, baked in a kiln and encased in wood or some other material as a holder. Though now commonplace, the graphite (or "lead") pencil was not widely used in drawing until the end of the eighteenth century, when techniques for varying the hardness of graphite were developed. Values range from silver-gray to black depending on the proportional relationship of clay to graphite. The hardest grades of graphite produce the palest, finest lines; the softer grades tend to produce darker, broader lines and to glide more smoothly across the paper. A lighter touch with a soft pencil can also be used to create paler values.

Artists may use many grades of graphite or varying techniques with a few grades to create a range of values in a single drawing. In Corot's *Città Castellana* (**4.4**), soft grades of graphite have been used to create very black filled-in areas. For lighter gray values, Corot has used parallel lines of hatching.

4.4 Jean Baptiste Camille Corot, *Città Castellana*, 1826. Graphite pencil on beige paper, 12¼ × 15⅜ ins (31 × 39 cm). Louvre, Paris.

213

4.5 Stuart Caswell, *Chain Link Disaster*,1972.
Pencil on paper, 22 × 28 ins (55.9 × 71.1 cm).
Minnesota Museum of Art, St. Paul.

And on the right side of the drawing, he has used the side rather than the point of a pencil to lay down broad areas of graphite, which are then rubbed for an overall gray tone. These value gradations create contrasts that remind us of the continual variations between darks and lights in a deciduous forest. Corot has used a visual shorthand for trees, leaves, stream, and rocks, but gives enough information for us readily to perceive the representational scene.

Whereas graphite is laid down in quite a free fashion in Corot's drawing, it is used with great precision in Stuart Caswell's *Chain Link Disaster* (**4.5**). Whether real or imaginary, this view of mangled sections of chain link fencing is photorealistic in its precisely described values and interwoven, overlaid lines. Pencil drawings are more typically used as quick studies; this kind of tight rendering is extremely time-consuming.

SILVERPOINT

The advent of the graphite pencil greatly lessened the use of SILVERPOINT, which had been popular in the fifteenth and sixteenth centuries. Silverpoint drawings are made with hard, finely-pointed rods of silver in a holder. The paper is first coated with some medium such as opaque white pigment or rabbitskin glue with bone dust to prepare a rather abrasive surface that will scrape off and hold minute grains of the metal. The lines made as the silverpoint tool is run across this prepared ground are silver at first but soon oxidize to a darker, duller color with a special light-reflecting quality. Copper, gold, and lead have also been used in the same way. As shown in Roger van der Weyden's delicate silverpoint, *Head of the Virgin* (**4.6**), shadows and textures are usually built up using parallel lines.

CHARCOAL

In contrast to the tight, thin lines produced by silverpoint, CHARCOAL is a medium that moves very freely across the paper, depositing broad, soft lines. Charcoal is made of charred wood or vine in sticks of varying width and hardness. The marks it makes are easily smudged. Though this possibility is often exploited by artists in toning an area, charcoal drawings are coated with a fixative when finished to

4.6 Roger van der Weyden, *Head of the Virgin*, c. 1455.
Silverpoint.
Louvre, Paris.

prevent further accidental smudging.

Käthe Kollwitz's uses of charcoal in her *Self-Portrait with a Pencil* (**4.7**) demonstrate the great versatility of the medium. She has given a faint tone to the paper with a slight deposit of charcoal. The charcoal has also been used sideways with a light touch to create broad strokes across the chest. Laid down this way, the charcoal dust sits on the surface of the paper, allowing the grainy texture of the paper itself to show through. The side of a soft piece of charcoal has been worked into the paper with great strength along the arm, creating lines of a darker value whose boldness bespeaks the creative energy of the artist at work. The tip of the charcoal has been used to create lines describing the artist's features.

And Kollwitz has used the tip of a harder, finer piece of charcoal to complete the upper contour of her head.

Because charcoal is such a soft and free medium, the tendency is to use it in a quick way, as Kollwitz has done. The spontaneity of the act of drawing is revealed and celebrated in this very natural use of the medium. But it is also possible to use charcoal in a more controlled manner. Richard Lytle's charcoal study, *Norfolk* (**4.8**), is a rare example of a very refined charcoal drawing in which the paper is left totally white in places. Whereas many charcoal drawings use only a range of mid-values, Lytle creates very rich blacks whose juxtaposition with true white makes them sing. He comments:

4.7 Käthe Kollwitz, *Self-Portrait with a Pencil*, 1933.
Charcoal, 18¾ × 24⅞ ins (48 × 63 cm).
The National Gallery of Art, Washington D.C. Rosenwald Collection.

4.8 Richard Lytle, *Norfolk*, 1976.
Charcoal, 22½ × 30 ins (57.1 × 76.2 cm). Collection of the artist.

Most people use charcoal since it is a very forgiving medium. You can rub it off, in contrast to the immutability of ink. But I use charcoal with a mentality that was evolved through my work with ink. The imagery in this piece is slow in revealing itself, suggesting a bit of mystery, with the dark areas worked densely to a pure velvet black and the floating white areas developing volumes.[1]

CHALK

Chalk is a naturally-occurring deposit of calcium carbonate and varying minerals, built up from fossil seashells. Powdered, mixed with a binder and compressed into sticks, it has long been used as a soft drawing medium. Renaissance, Baroque and Rococo artists used white, red, and black chalks to work up and down the value scale on a tinted surface which served as a mid-tone. This technique is beautifully illustrated by the cartoon for *The Virgin and Child with St. Anne and St. John the Baptist* (**4.9**) by Leonardo da Vinci. A CARTOON was a full-sized drawing done as a model for a painting. The lines from the cartoon were transferred to canvas or wall by pressing charcoal dust through holes pricked in the major line of the cartoon. But this cartoon is so striking in its own right that it is displayed by itself in a special dark room of the National Gallery in London, with lighting designed to keep the paper from deteriorating. To indicate volumes rounding in

space, Leonardo used black chalk lines to separate the figures from the tone of the paper and then used dark tones within the figures to indicate areas receding from the viewer in space. Areas that are to be seen as closest are lightened with white chalk. Notice how much flatter the areas that were not yet worked out—such as the upraised hand and the feet—appear without this use of values. Leonardo's very subtle value gradations were called SFUMATO, Italian for the smoky appearance that softens the lines of the contours and gives a mysterious hazy atmosphere to the image. He achieved the same effect in his paintings, such as *The Virgin of the Rocks* (14.22).

PASTEL

Often confused with chalk, which is harder, PASTEL is a chalky stick made of powdered pigment plus filler bound with a small amount of gum or resin. When rubbed onto a rough-textured paper with enough "tooth" to hold the particles, it deposits masses of color. Pastel drawings are very fragile until treated with a fixative; if they are shaken before they are fixed, some of the powder will fall off. But an overabundance of fixative will deaden or spot the drawing; the only way to assure the permanence of a pastel is to seal it under glass.

The word "pastel" is commonly associated with pale tones, and pale pastels are well suited for creating light and romantic images. In the hands of Degas, pastels became a brilliant medium, like paints, but with their own special powdery effect. *After the Bath* (**4.10**) is one of his many major works in pastel. Because pastels are so soft, most artists smudge and blend them on the paper; Degas handles them as lines of color that reveal the act of drawing.

4.9 (left) Leonardo da Vinci, *The Virgin and Child with St. Anne and St. John the Baptist*, 1510. Black chalk heightened with white on paper, 4 ft 7¾ × 3 ft 5 ins (1.42 × 1.04 m). National Gallery, London.

4.10 Edgar Degas, *After the Bath*, c. 1895–8. Pastel on paper, 27½ × 27½ ins (70 × 70 cm). Musée d'Orsay, Paris.

Degas was able to lay one coat of pigment on top of another without their blending, using a special fixative between layers. The formula for the fixative has since been lost, and it is now difficult to build up layers with pastels using contemporary fixatives without dulling the brightness of the colors. In addition to his special fixative, Degas used pastels made with a high ratio of pigment to filler, juxtaposed at maximum strength so they intensify each other's brilliance.

CRAYON

Several media carry the name "crayon." CONTÉ CRAYON, named after the person who invented it in the eighteenth century, is a fine-textured grease-free stick made of powdered graphite and clay to which red ocher, soot, or blackstone has been added to give it a red, black, or brown color. Children's crayons are made of pigmented wax. Oil-based crayons come in brighter colors than wax crayons and can be blended on the paper, rather like oil paints. Lithographic crayons are made of grease for use in lithographic printing, but have been adopted for drawing by contemporary artists who like the pleasing way they glide across the paper. Each has its unique qualities, but crayons in general tend to skip quickly across paper. This quickness—and the humor it brings out in the artist—is apparent in Toulouse-Lautrec's *Équestrienne* (**4.11**). To see how differently the mass of the horse is described when the artist is using drawn lines rather than painted masses of color, compare this crayon drawing with Toulouse-Lautrec's oil painting of a similar subject shown in Figure 2.139.

4.11 Henri de Toulouse-Lautrec, *Équestrienne*, 1899. Crayon, 19¼ × 12⅜ ins (48.9 × 31.4 cm). Museum of Art, Rhode Island School of Design, Providence.

4.12 Pablo Picasso, *Three Female Nudes Dancing*, 1923. Pen and ink, 13⅞ × 10⅜ ins (35.2 × 26.3 cm). National Gallery of Canada, Ontario.

LIQUID MEDIA

PEN AND INK

While the drawing media discussed so far are all DRY MEDIA, it is also possible to draw lines with a LIQUID MEDIUM: usually ink. Today's drawing inks are made of pigment particles, shellac, and water. In traditional China, Japan, and Europe during the Middle Ages and Renaissance, ink was made from ground lampblack mixed into a weak glue. Ink is usually applied with pens made of steel, quills, reeds, or bamboo. Depending on the shape of its point, a pen may produce either lines of uniform width or lines that vary in width according to the direction and pressure of the pen.

Pen and ink drawings are difficult to execute, for the point of the pen may catch on the surface of the paper and splatter ink unpredictably. Today's technical pens can move more easily across the paper, like fine ballpoints, but it is still difficult to create so free-flowing a line as Picasso has used in his *Three Female Nudes Dancing* (**4.12**). If you follow the lines, you will see areas where the ink came out in spurts rather than a continuous flow, but the lines keep moving with utter assurance.

Whereas most ink drawings are dark lines on a white or toned surface, Hyman Bloom creates the texture and form of fish skeletons (**4.13**) by working in white ink against maroon paper. By varying the amount of white laid down in an area, Bloom creates a range of values that gives an in-and-out spatial

4.13 Hyman Bloom, *Fish Skeletons*, c. 1956.
White ink on maroon paper, 16¾ × 22¾ ins (42.5 × 57.8 cm). Collection of Mr. and Mrs. Ralph Werman.

4.14 Claude Gellée, called Claude Lorraine, *Campagna Landscape*, 1660.
Pen and bister with wash, 12⅝ × 8½ ins (32 × 21.6 cm).
British Museum, London.

4.15 Rembrandt van Rijn, *Sleeping Girl*, c. 1660–9. Brush drawing in brown ink and wash, 9⅝ × 8 ins (24.5 × 20.3 cm). British Museum, London.

quality that borders on both realism and fantasy.

Pen and ink is essentially a line medium; tone or shade is conveyed by the use of special techniques such as stippling (dots), scratching, hatching or cross-hatching (see Bittleman's *Martyred Flowers*, Figure 2.13). As an alternative, ink can be thinned with water or spirit and brushed on as a WASH to suggest the tone. The wash can be applied to penned line which is still wet to soften and dilute it. If it is added to a dry drawing the original pen marks usually remain hard and dark.

In Claude Lorraine's *Campagna Landscape* (**4.14**), brown ink has been watered down and used to fill in varying brown tones, without overpowering the darker penned lines used to describe the trees and rocks. The tower, however, is described by a darker wash accented by drawn marks, and the distant hills are suggested by a very thin wash alone that almost blends into the light values of the sky.

BRUSH AND INK

The final step into liquid media that can still be classified as a "drawing" is the application of ink with a brush without any penned marks. Developed to a fine art by Oriental schools, this technique is used in a near-abstract manner by Rembrandt in his sketch of a sleeping girl (**4.15**). The action of making each wet stroke is clearly evident, including passages where the ink on the brush was spent and the white of the paper began to show through. Above the girl's head an area of the background is suggested with a brushed wash. Note the attention to the placement of the figure on the ground, a consideration that is particularly important when large areas of the ground are left unfilled and will be perceived as flat shapes in themselves. The wash tends to contradict such an interpretation, softening and pushing the largely unworked area back in space.

COMPUTER AS DRAWING MEDIUM

There is no limit to the tools artists could use to draw with and surfaces to draw on: anything that will make a mark and anything that can be marked on can be used.

COMPUTER GRAPHICS

A major new medium capable of producing drawings unlike any ever done before is COMPUTER GRAPHICS. Rapidly-evolving innovations in miniaturized memory, screens with extremely fine resolution and the ability to display over sixteen million colors at the same time, high-resolution color printers and plotters that can produce a continuous range of values of the same hue, and sophisticated programming are opening up previously unimaginable possibilities to artists. Some artists are treating the computer as a tool for handling conventional techniques very rapidly and perfectly. Other contemporary artists find that the computer is an entirely new medium in itself, opening up entirely new approaches to art.

Some computer drawing programs allow the artist to work rather conventionally, by drawing with an electronic stylus on a digitizing tablet that transfers these marks to the screen as lines between PIXELS. Pixels are points where X and Y coordinates meet on the invisible grid which allows the computer to assign mathematical references to all places on the screen. Higher-resolution screens are those with more pixels. This indirect method of drawing requires that the artist develop some unfamiliar eye-hand coordination skills, for the image appears on the screen as one draws it, rather than directly under the stylus. Additional "tools" on the computer screen allow the artist to do painterly things like filling in, blending, or "spraying" colors.

A less direct method of building up computer images is to use mathematical formulas—programs—to communicate with the computer and printer. In this case, art is created solely by numbers, and it takes a lot of them just to make a line. For example, a very simple BASIC program that tells a plotter to draw 25 random lines in color looks like this:

```
10   HGR:FOR Z = 1 TO 25: HI = RND(1)•270:V1 = RND(1)•190
20   H2 = RND(1)•270:V2 = RND(1)•190: HCOLOR = INT(RND(1)•8)
30   HPLOT H1, V1 TO H2, V2
40   NEXT Z
```

These instructions establish a series of points on X and Y axes that when connected form lines. Very complex figures can be thus described, rotated for viewing from all sides, blown up or reduced in scale.

Although it may take many hours to program the computer to draw a complex image, once the information is installed, the artist can manipulate it indefinitely, unlike a drawing done with any other medium. Images can be flipped, stretched, compressed, added to or subtracted from; lines can be widened or narrowed, and their texture and color altered ad infinitum. Intricate drawings become possible which no one would attempt by hand, such as Eudice Feder's *Swarm* (**4.16**). She has equipped her plotter with hand-drawing tools—ballpoint, felt tip, and ink pens—but then given it information to create images that transcend anything ever done by human hand.

As illustrated by *Ornamental Mutation* (**4.17**), a computer can even be programmed to "know" how to create the impression of three-dimensional form on a two-dimensional surface, by using visual clues such as shading, overlapping, and scale change. Often such work takes the combined skills of an artist and a computer programmer, as in the three-person team that created this image.

Moral and legal issues arise: What state of this process is the work of art? Can it be freely duplicated by the artist? In traditional print media, a series of prints are pulled from one block and each print is numbered. If further editions are made from the same block, they must be marked as second or third editions. Otherwise, the block must be scored so that it cannot be re-used. If the art consists in programming a computer disk, must the program be erased after an edition is printed out (as in *Swarm*) or photographed from the electronics of the computer (as in *Ornamental Mutation*)? Should the disk itself be sold? Can the purchaser make changes in it? Does the work only exist as art if it is seen in real time on a computer monitor or video screen? These are new questions evoked by an entirely new set of artistic circumstances.

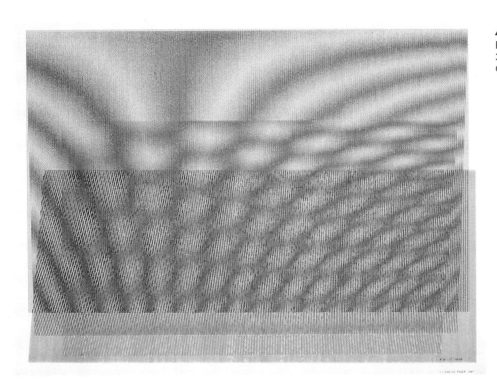

4.16 Eudice Feder, *Swarm*, 1988.
Plotter drawing, ballpoint, felt tip, ink,
30 × 25 ins (76.2 × 63.5 cm).
Courtesy of the artist.

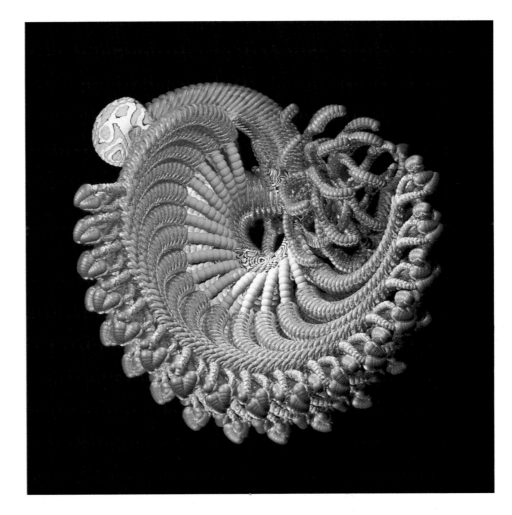

4.17 William Latham, *Ornamental
Mutation* (third variation), 1992.
Created at IBM UKSC. Courtesy of the
artist/Computer Artworks.

5

PAINTING

APPROACHES TO PAINTING

Painting is the process of coating a surface with colored areas by using a hand tool such as a brush or a palette knife. There is no absolute demarcation between drawing and painting. Some drawing techniques, such as pastel, can also be used to create areas of color, and a brush may be used for drawings, such as brush and ink drawings. There is a slight

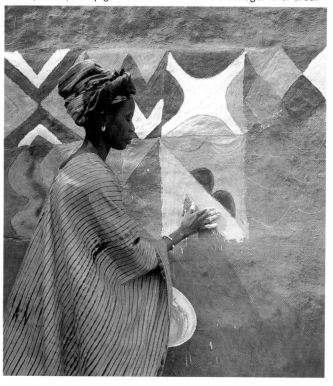

5.1 Silla Camara painting the wall of her family compound, Soninke village, Djajabinnit, Mauritania. Paste of ground white kaolin, water, and pigments collected from the Senegal River area.

difference in approach however: Drawing is primarily linear mark-making. The media discussed in Chapter 4 are usually considered drawing media, while encaustic, fresco, tempera, oil, watercolor, gouache, and synthetics are considered paint media.

We now tend to associate the word "painting" with a flat, movable surface to which paint has been added, such as a canvas which can be hung on any wall, but paint was probably first applied directly to stationary surfaces such as the walls of caves and buildings. The women of West Africa still maintain a dramatic wall-painting tradition of unknown antiquity. They use their hands to paint liquid clays mixed with plant and mineral colors onto the mud and clay walls of their houses and shrines (**5.1**). Each rainy season these vibrant clay paintings dissolve and are then reapplied, usually by groups of women using patterns handed down from mother to daughter.

Over the years and around the world, many different technical solutions have been devised to allow the spreading of colored PIGMENTS (particles of color) across a surface. In general, painting is made possible by suspension of pigments in a liquid medium, plus a BINDER that makes them adhere to a surface. The surface on which the paint (that is, pigment plus medium) is spread is called the SUPPORT, be it a wall, a piece of wood, or a stretched canvas.

Through time, varying media have been developed to improve properties such as ease in working, drying time, permanence, or brilliance. Each form of painting thus evolved—often referred to as MEDIA, in reference to the varying vehicles that distinguish them—has its own strengths and difficulties. Most are still in current use, though sometimes only by a few artists who are willing to tolerate the technical difficulties for the sake of the special effects possible.

5.2 Agnolo Bronzino, *Portrait of a Young Man*, c. 1550. Oil on wood panel, 37⅝ × 29½ ins (95.7 × 74.9 cm). The Metropolitan Museum of Art, New York. H. O. Havemeyer Collection.

Approaches to painting have changed as well. In general, the older approach was to plan carefully and execute a painting in stages, beginning with drawing studies of the forms to be represented. Once the drawing satisfied the artist, it was transferred to a support and the forms were developed in a series of stages. In this INDIRECT method, used for works such as Bronzino's *Portrait of a Young Man* (**5.2**), perfection in technique was a painstaking matter but was capable of representing subtleties such as the textures of wood and fur and the translucent appearances of skin. Such effects involved a process of sketching, UNDERPAINTING to define the major forms and values, and then a series of OVERPAINTINGS to tint and describe the forms.

Another approach—the DIRECT method—is to paint imagery directly on the support without staged underlayers. This approach may allow the paint—and the painter—to reveal their presence. Oil paint, for instance, has a lush, creamy quality. Van Gogh laid down his paint with heavy IMPASTO strokes that reflect the spontaneity of his gestures. His paintings (such as *The Starry Night*, Figure 1.35) have appreciably three-dimensional surface textures. Oil paints now available also carry sensually rich colors. In Pierre Bonnard's *Nude in a Bathtub* (**5.3**), the

5.3 Pierre Bonnard, *Nude in a Bathtub*, 1941–6. Oil on canvas, 4 ft × 4 ft 11½ ins (1.22 × 1.51 m). The Carnegie Museum of Art, Pittsburgh. The Sarah Mellon Scarfe Family.

5.4 James Brooks, *Anteor*, 1981. Acrylic on canvas, 5 ft × 5 ft (1.52 × 1.52 m). Collection Exxon Corporation.

model's body is almost obscured by the way the dabs of paint juxtapose varied colors, breaking up the outlines of the forms. The colors are playful, sensual delights rather than reports of actual local colors; the shapes they "describe" are flattened, abstracted.

Direct painting, as practiced by contemporary artists, does not necessarily call attention to the texture of the paint or the activities of the painter, however, and may not even be used to describe forms.

Whereas canvases are usually treated with a glue solution to hold the paint on their surface and white-lead (GESSO) to keep oils from rotting the canvas, certain nonobjective painters in the twentieth century have worked on UNSIZED canvases so that the paint would be absorbed, with no noticeable surface texture and no trace of the artist's hand. Their works (Fig. **5.4**) are created with an appreciation for the essential quality of pigment as pure, flat color.

5.5 Leonardo da Vinci, *Mona Lisa*, c. 1503—6.
Panel, 30¼ × 21 ins (76.8 × 53.3 cm). Louvre, Paris.

Leonardo da Vinci
on
CHIAROSCURO

Leonardo da Vinci (1452–1519) was one of the major figures of the Italian High Renaissance. His subtle *Mona Lisa* (**5.5**) is perhaps the world's most famous painting, but Leonardo was an inventor, sculptor, and architect as well as a painter, and he had far-reaching curiosity about all natural phenomena. His intensive studies of human anatomy involved dissection of corpses, from which he created detailed drawings of musculature, bones, and joints. He also wrote extensively on art, anatomy, machinery, and natural history, but his voluminous writings were never published during his lifetime. His statements about the use of lights and darks in painting help us to understand why the boundaries of Mona Lisa's facial features are soft and undefined (though undoubtedly the darkened dirty state of the varnish now obscures the original colors of the painting):

"The first intention of the painter is to make a flat surface display a body as if modeled and separated from this plane, and he who most surpasses others in this skill deserves most praise. This accomplishment, with which the science of painting is crowned, arises from light and shade, or we may say *chiaroscuro*."

"Shadow is the privation of light. Shadows appear to me to be supremely necessary in perspective, since without them opaque and solid bodies will be ill defined. Those features that are located within their boundaries—and their boundaries themselves—will be ill defined if they do not end against a background of a color different from that of the body. In addition to this, these shadows are in themselves of varying degrees of darkness because they represent the loss of varying quantities of luminous rays, and these I term original shadows, because, being the first shadows, they clothe the bodies to which they are attached. From these original shadows there arise shadowy rays which are transmitted throughout the air, and these are of a quality corresponding to the variety of the original shadows from which they are derived. And on this account I will call these shadows derived shadows, because they have their origins in other shadows."

"Shadow shares the nature of universal things, which are all more powerful at their beginning and become enfeebled towards their end. When I speak about the beginning of every form and quality, discernible or indiscernible, I do not refer to things arising from small beginnings that become greatly enlarged over a period of time, as will happen with a great oak which has a modest start in a little acorn. Rather, I mean that the oak is strongest at the point at which it arises from the earth, that is to say, where it has its greatest thickness. Corresponding, darkness is the first degree of shadow and light is the last. Therefore, painter, make your shadow darker close to its origin, and at its end show it being transformed into light, that is to say, so that it appears to have no termination."

"That body will exhibit the greatest difference between its shadows and its lights that happens to be seen under the strongest light, like the light of the sun or the light of a fire at night. And this should be little used in painting because the works will remain harsh and disagreeable.

There will be little difference in the lights and shadows in that body which is situated in a moderate light, and this occurs at the onset of evening or when there is cloud, and such works are sweet and every kind of face acquires grace. Thus in all things extremes are blameworthy. Too much light makes for harshness; too much darkness does not allow us to see. The medium is best."[1]

5.6 *Young Woman with a Gold Pectoral*, Egypto-Romano (Coptic) c. AD 100. Encaustic, 16½ × 9½ ins (42 × 24 cm). Louvre, Paris.

PAINT MEDIA

ENCAUSTIC

A very early method of painting that was used by the Greeks, Romans, and early Christians in Egypt, ENCAUSTIC involves the mixing of pigments with wax. The wax must be kept hot as it is applied, to keep it liquid. Knowledge of the technique used to make such luminous works as *Young Woman with a Gold Pectoral* (**5.6**) was lost for many centuries, though temptingly described by writers such as Pliny. Leonardo da Vinci, ever the experimenter, may have

5.7 Diego Rivera, *Creation*, 1922–3. Encaustic and gold leaf, Anfiteatro Bolivar, National Preparatory School, Mexico City.

tried to revive the process in 1503, but his attempts failed. Early in the twentieth century, the great Mexican muralist Diego Rivera studied books in Paris describing the techniques of the ancient

Greeks, Romans, and Egyptians and experimented with combining hot wax and pigments. He was searching, he said, for "the traditional encaustic with its solidity, purity, depth, and richness of colors."[2]

Rivera mastered the difficult encaustic process sufficiently to use it for the first of his immense murals, *Creation* (**5.7**), and then switched to fresco for all his other major works.

5.8 Ambrogio Lorenzetti, *Allegory of Peace*, 1339, detail. Fresco. Palazzo Pubblico, Siena, Italy.

FRESCO

The FRESCO technique was developed by the ancient Mediterranean civilizations, refined to a supreme art by the Italian Renaissance painters, and used with great vigor by twentieth-century Mexican muralists. The word "fresco" means "fresh" in Italian, for fresco paintings must be created quickly and spontaneously, with little room for error. They are wall paintings in which pigments in a water base are painted onto freshly applied plaster. The immediacy of this method is apparent in the lively feeling of the figures in Ambrogio Lorenzetti's *Allegory of Peace* (**5.8**). As indicated in Figure **5.9**, which is a reconstruction of the progress of Lorenzetti's fresco, the wall is first given two or three layers of plaster. Once the last of these is dry, the cartoon of the intended image may be traced or freely sketched by the artist onto the wall. Transparent paper is then used to make a copy of this cartoon; tiny holes are made along the lines of the copy with a perforating

wheel. When the final layer of plaster, the INTONACO, is applied, a fine powder ("pounce") is tapped along the perforations of the tracing to transfer the sketch

5.9 Layers in a fresco.
1. Masonry wall 2. Underlayers of plaster 3. Cartoon of image
4. Fresh *intonaco* with pounced cartoon for the day's work
5. Previously completed portion.

5.10 Diego Rivera, *México del Presente (Present-day Mexico)*, 1929–45. Mural on the stairway of the National Palace, Mexico City.

onto the wet wall. The intonaco is applied over the underlying cartoon in sections small enough to be painted that day while the plaster is still damp, so that the paint is immediately absorbed into the plaster. Once it is dry the fresco is as permanent as the plaster of the wall. Over the centuries, chunks of the plaster may fall away, as in *Allegory of Peace*, but fresco is by and large a very permanent method of painting, so long as it is indoors. Outdoor frescos are vulnerable to air pollution and to wearing away by wind-blown particles.

Fresco is usually an intense collaborative effort involving a team of plasterers and assistants as well as the artist. For Diego Rivera's huge murals of Mexican political history (**5.10**), plasterers covered a wall with two coats of plaster, and then Rivera sketched with red chalk or charcoal directly on this rough "brown" coat. Assistants traced this sketch onto transparent paper and ran a perforating wheel over the copy. Very early in the morning, a third coat of plaster was applied to the part of the wall to be painted first that day, and the sketch was pounced with lampblack powder. Rivera had specified the area, following the lines of the shapes rather than a uniform square, so that all figures could be finished rather than trying to match colors another day.

Once the plaster had dried to the proper humidity, Rivera was awakened, usually about dawn. The plaster would remain sufficiently wet for six to twelve hours, depending on the weather, and his method was to paint the same area twice in one day. The first painting was to establish black modeling of the figures, the second to add colors. Even as he worked, usually sitting on a scaffolding, another team of plasterers was preparing a second section of the wall. Rivera would continue painting until evening, when there was no longer enough natural light to work by. Examining the day's work by the dim light, he often decided it was not quite right, and would instruct his assistants to remove it all. The same lengthy process would begin again the next morning.

235

5.11 Andrea Mantegna, *Dead Christ*, after 1466.
Tempera on canvas, 26¾ × 31⅞ ins (66.8 × 81 cm). Pinacoteca di Brera, Milan, Italy.

5.12 Layers in a tempera painting. 1. Wood panel 2. Gesso and perhaps linen reinforcement 3. Underdrawing 4. Gold leaf 5. Underpainting 6. Final tempera layers.

TEMPERA

Another old and very demanding painting technique involves the mixing in water of pigments with water-soluble egg yolk or some other glutinous material. The resulting TEMPERA paint dries very quickly to a matt finish that will not crack, as can be seen in Andrea Mantegna's *Dead Christ* (**5.11**). Unlike later paints, tempera colors will not blend or spread well. The artist must painstakingly lay down tiny individual brushstrokes side by side, hatching or cross-hatching to cover an area with pigment (**5.13**). The painting of the final surface follows lengthy preparation procedures.

As diagrammed in Figure **5.12**, a simplified detail of Ugolino's tempera painting of the Last Supper

5.13 Detail of Cimabue's *Madonna Enthroned* (2.64), 1280–90, showing handling of tempera paint.

(3.13), the support used—wood or canvas—is first coated with GESSO. This is a fine white substance that gives the panel a smooth, brilliant eggshell finish that accepts paint readily and has enough "tooth" to allow control of the brush. After the gesso dries, the cartoon of the drawing is scratched onto it. These scratched outlines can sometimes be seen beneath the paint in the finished work. If there are to be gold areas in the work, they are covered with a light coating of red gilder's clay, BURNISHED (rubbed) to a gloss. Extremely thin leaves of gold are applied over the gilder's clay in

layers, each of which is also burnished. As the gold leaf wears off, patches of the red gilder's clay underneath may show through.

Then comes UNDERPAINTING. Most areas are first underpainted with a base tone of their local colors. But to keep flesh tones from appearing too flat, the painting guilds of the Middle Ages worked out a system of underpainting flesh passages with *terre verte* (green earth). In the final layers of the painting, the flesh areas are covered with pink pigment; the bits of green that show through make the complementary reds of the skin seem more vibrant. A faintly greenish cast that persists can often be seen in the finished work.

It is so difficult to create lively, fresh paintings with tempera that most artists eventually switched to oil paints. But a few contemporary artists still use this old medium quite skillfully, most notably Andrew Wyeth (**5.14**).

5.14 Andrew Wyeth, *The Virgin*, 1969.
Tempera on canvas, 46 × 36 ins (116.8 × 91.4 cm).
Brandywine River Museum, Chadds Ford, Pennsylvania.

5.15 Jan van Eyck, *The Madonna of Chancellor Rolin*, c. 1433–4.
Oil on panel, 26 × 24⅜ ins (66 × 61.9 cm). Louvre, Paris.

OIL

Tempera is a LEAN MEDIUM—a uniform thin film. By contrast, paint that uses oil as a binder for pigment is called FAT. It can be piled up in thick globs and dries very slowly, allowing the artist to blend colors right on the canvas. The use of oil paints by artists began in the fifteenth century, flowering brilliantly in the work of Jan van Eyck, who applied oil and varnish glazes over tempera. As is apparent in van Eyck's *The Madonna of Chancellor Rolin* (5.15), oils opened great vistas to painters. Now they could simulate textures, portray the effects of light and shadow, model three-dimensional forms, add tiny bits of colors as highlights, and work from the darkest to the lightest tones without losing the brilliance of the pigments.

Using oils, artists could work with optic realism, for as they began to recognize, we do not necessarily see figures distinctly. Unless the air and light are very clear, colored areas may blend together visually. In Tintoretto's *Leda and the Swan* (3.10). which was painted entirely in oils, the attendant's dress merges into the dark tones of the background, as do Leda's left arm and hair, emphasizing her radiant torso as the central focus of the painting.

This radiance or luminosity is another special characteristic of traditional oil paintings. The flesh of Correggio's *Danae* (5.16) actually seems to glow. Even the shadows glow with life. These striking effects were the result of underpainting and then overpainting with layers of GLAZES (films of pigments suspended in a transparent medium) to build up color tints and details of form. A very light passage, such as Danae's body, might be thickly underpainted with white and then glazed with skin tones; a dark passage

5.16 Antonio Correggio, *Danae*, c. 1532.
Oil on canvas, 64½ × 29 ins (163.5 × 74 cm). Galleria Borghese, Rome.

5.17 Leonado da Vinci, *The Adoration of the Magi*, begun 1481. Underpainting on panel, 8 ft × 8 ft 1 in (2.44 × 2.46 m). Uffizi Gallery, Florence.

such as the shadows of the room might be underpainted with brown and then glazed with thin layers of a darker gold-brown.

An unfinished painting by Leonado da Vinci (**5.17**) allows us to see how he has blocked out certain areas by underpainting before building up details and optical effects with glazes. The painting appears much flatter than his completed works, such as *The Virgin of the Rocks* (14.22). Underpainting and then overpainting deepens the shadows of dark areas and also gives more tinting power to lighter and brighter pigments. Layers may also be used to create a more lifelike color sensation, with green beneath red, for instance, to bring out its brilliance by complementary contrast.

Oil paint is itself luscious and can become part of the visual focus of a work. Hans Hofmann's *Rhapsody* (**5.18**) is a celebration of the sheer vitality and flexibility of the medium. Color passages are

built one atop the other, by scumbling (brushing one opaque layer of paint on top of a dried lower layer in such a way that some of the undercolor still shows through) and heavy IMPASTO strokes that leave such a thick deposit of the medium that the strokes of brush or palette knife are recorded as an actual texture on the surface. When layered wet, oil colors can be blended; if the underneath hue is to be kept the same, it is allowed to dry before the next layer is applied.

Highly saturated hues in prepared tubes of paint were a nineteenth-century innovation. Earlier oil paintings were built on a more subdued palette created from natural pigments, ground and mixed with oil by apprentices who devoted years to learning how to formulate paint.

5.18 Hans Hofmann, *Rhapsody*, 1965. Oil on canvas, 7 ft ¼ ins × 5 ft ½ ins (2.14 × 1.54 m). The Metropolitan Museum of Art, New York. Gift of Renate Hofmann, 1975.

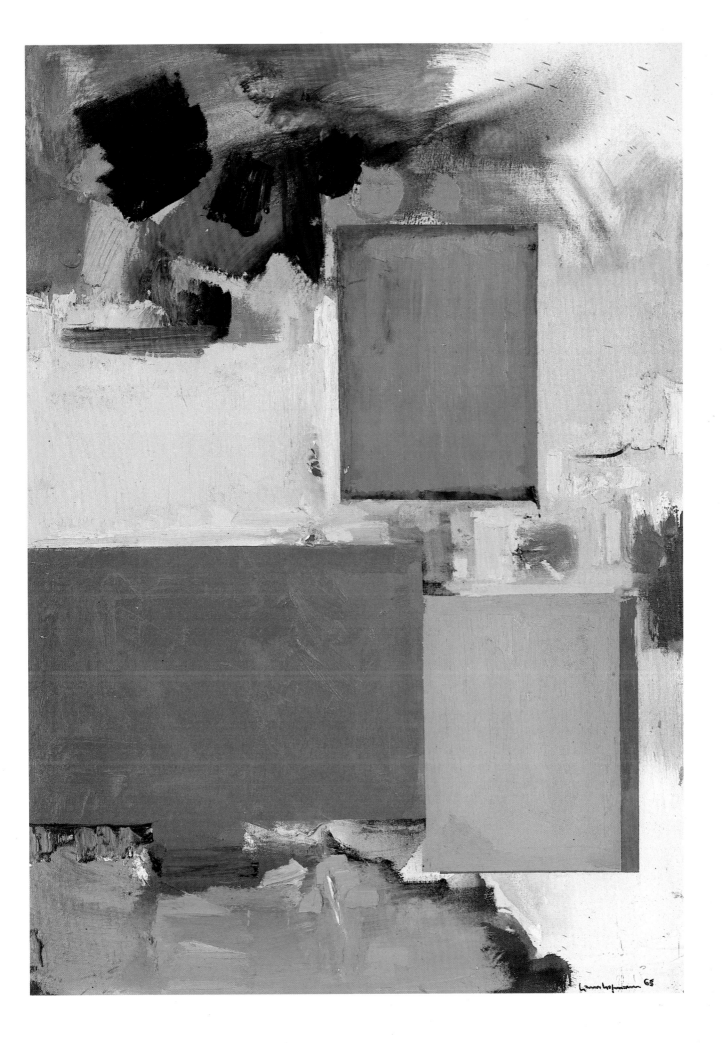

WATERCOLOR

An extremely fluid and transparent medium—WATERCOLOR—is created when pigments are bound with a water-soluble binder such as gum, thinned with varying amounts of water, and applied wet to paper. The white of the paper is usually allowed to shine through the thinned pigment in some areas. Whereas the white usually appears as the background against which images have been worked, Richard Lytle brings the white into the foreground as the color of flower petals in his *Spring Thaw on Goose Pond* (**5.19**). Note how well watercolor adapts itself to portraying the transparency of water and sky here, with one tone blurring into another.

Although watercolor can be applied with a "dry brush" it is generally a very runny medium, so hard to control that Lytle's tight rendering is exceptional. Watercolor cannot be extensively corrected and reworked, unlike oil paint, so the artist is committed to each stroke, which must be made quickly, before the paper dries. This necessity becomes a virtue in the hands of artists like Turner, whose *A Whale Aground* (**5.20**) uses the medium's liquid freedom of gesture and transparent airiness to the fullest. The heaviness of the whale is barely suggested by the shadowed area in this powerful and free abstraction.

A more traditional approach to watercolor is exemplified by Winslow Homer's *The Gulf Stream* (**5.21**). The paint looks very wet, as if freshly painted, but bleeding into the paper and blending of colors are carefully controlled, with the white of the paper revealed as a significant design element.

5.19 Richard Lytle, *Spring Thaw on Goose Pond*, 1986. Watercolor, 30 × 41½ ins (76.2 × 105.4 cm).

5.20 Joseph Mallord William Turner, *Looking out to Sea: A Whale Aground*, 1845.
Pencil and watercolor on paper, 9⅜ × 13¼ ins (23.8 × 33.5 cm). Tate Gallery, London.

5.21 Winslow Homer, *The Gulf Stream*, 1899. Watercolor, 11⅜ × 20 ins (28.9 × 50.9 cm).
The Metropolitan Museum of Art, New York.

5.22 Joan Miró, *The Beautiful Bird Revealing the Unknown to a Pair of Lovers*, 1941. Gouache, 17 × 15 ins (43 × 38 cm). Collection, The Museum of Modern Art, New York. Acquired through the Lillie P. Bliss Bequest.

GOUACHE

In contrast to the transparency of watercolor, GOUACHE is an opaque medium. It, too, is water-soluble, but in this case it is mixed with inert pigments such as Chinese zinc white or chalk for opacity, with gum arabic as the binder. This combination makes painting with gouache feel like spreading not-quite-melted butter, in contrast to painting with oils, which flow like melted butter. Some artists use opaque gouache passages to strengthen their otherwise transparent watercolors: some paintings referred to as "gouache" are actually watercolors painted over an opaque white ground.

Gouache cannot be piled up like oil paint, for it will crack if heavily built up. But it will stay opaque as it ages, rather than becoming more transparent as watercolor tends to do. This means that it can be worked over a colored ground and be counted upon to cover it thoroughly.

In Joan Miró's *The Beautiful Bird Revealing the Unknown to A Pair of Lovers* (**5.22**), the fantastic galaxy of lines and shapes sits atop a toned ground without any bleed-through of the underlying color. In Miró's hands, gouache was the instrument of a spatially flat other-worldly vision.

Gouache is quite flexible, however, and can also be used to create realistic illusions of depth and form. And whereas Miró painted dark over light, the artist using gouache can also paint light colors over dark without bleed-through. In Bill Martin's *Abalone Shells* (**5.23**), a tour de force of realistic gouache painting, light highlights sit atop darker areas.

Gouache dries very quickly by water evaporation, in contrast to the slow drying of oils by oxidation. Gouache is usually painted in immediate, spontaneous, direct ways; wet can so soon be painted over dry that blending of adjacent colors is difficult. The paint is also flat and non-reflective. Despite these characteristics of the medium, Bill Martin has painstakingly juxtaposed soft-edged areas of similar hues to create striking pearlescent illusions of light-reflecting glossy surfaces. The opaque gouache gives the shells a convincing solidity: even the paint has the appearance of thickness. This is a special characteristic of gouache. Even though it cannot be built up deeply like oils, it forms a film of paint on a surface, unlike watercolor, which sinks into the paper.

5.23 Bill Martin, *Abalone Shells*, 1982. Gouache, 11⅞ × 15¾ ins (30.2 × 40 cm).

SYNTHETICS

Several decades ago, SYNTHETIC MEDIA created chemically rather than derived from natural substances were introduced as part of the artist's tool kit. The form most used today—called ACRYLIC EMULSION, or ACRYLICS—is a water-based medium that can be used straight from the tube with techniques similar to those of oil paints, thinned and blown out as a fine spray through an AIRBRUSH, or thinned right down to the consistency of watercolor. Acrylics dry quickly, and for this reason are preferred by some artists to oils. This property not only allows the artist to complete a painting quickly, but also makes it possible to create special effects, such as painting hard-edged shapes by laying a line of masking tape over previously painted, already dried areas. Even without tape, acrylic stops where the brush stops, unlike oil, which spreads slightly into the canvas. A retarder may be added to extend the period during which the acrylic paint is workable.

Very bright, pure colors can be formulated with synthetics; without the pigment, the medium itself would dry clearer than glass. The colors do not yellow with age, as oils tend to do. Acrylics are also permanent and fade-proof; in theory, even if the support rots away, the acrylic paint won't. Its molecular structure is similar to that of the superglues, so it has tremendous bonding power and can be used on many different grounds. Not all artists

5.24 Chuck Close, *Frank*, 1968–9. Acrylic on canvas, 7 ft × 9 ft (2.13 × 2.74 m). The Minneapolis Institute of Arts.

5.25 Helen Frankenthaler, *Hint from Bassano*, 1933.
Acrylic on canvas, 7 ft 1 in × 18 ft 11¼ ins (2.16 × 5.77 m).
Collection of Mr. and Mrs. David Mirvish, Toronto, Ontario.

have switched from slow-drying oils to acrylics, however, for acrylics have a different feel and optical quality and are less easy to blend on the canvas. They do not have the sheen of oils, and whereas oils flow from the brush like softened butter, acrylics have a slight drag.

Airbrushing with acrylics can be used to create very even gradations in value. As used by some fantasy illustrators and commercial artists, these transitions are flawless rather than more realistically irregular. But by precisely controlling the gradations, Chuck Close is able to create photorealistic human heads of monumental proportions, such as his *Frank* (**5.24**), which is nine feet (2.75 m) tall. Close begins with a photograph which he blows up and transfers to the canvas by a grid system and then re-creates in minute detail, complete with facial blemishes and slightly fuzzy areas where the close-up photograph was out of focus.

Helen Frankenthaler's *Hint from Bassano* (**5.25**) demonstrates how synthetic paints behave when thinned to the consistency of very fluid watercolors.

The paint can get so runny that Frankenthaler often works with her canvases on the floor rather than on an easel. Unlike watercolors, acrylics can be painted in layers, allowing the preservation of the hue of an underlayer rather than the blending that occurs when two watercolor hues are laid on top of each other wet. Frankenthaler's thinned acrylics sink into the unsized canvas and become part of that ground itself, rather than sitting on top of it. She had earlier used a similar technique with oils thinned with turpentine, but the turpentine left a halo where it spread into the canvas. The striking freshness of the results is a quality for which she aims:

> A really good picture looks as if it's happened at once. It's an immediate image. For my own work, when a picture looks labored and overworked, and you can read in it—well, she did this and then she did that, and then she did that—there is something in it that has not got to do with beautiful art to me. And I usually throw those out, though I think very often it takes ten of those over-labored efforts to produce one really beautiful wrist motion that is synchronised with your head and heart, and you have it, and therefore it looks as if it were born in a minute.[3]

COLLAGE

A relatively new art form, introduced in 1912 by Picasso, is COLLAGE. Though technically classified with paintings, a collage does not necessarily involve the application of paint to a surface. Rather, it is built up two-dimensionally, or as a relief, by selecting and gluing to a surface varying flat materials, such as the colored papers, leaf, and Polish stamp in *Connecticut Remembered* (**5.26**). For the artist, it is exciting to collect materials that are interesting in themselves—such as old documents and drawings—and then combine them into an effective whole. Having ready-made areas of colors, textures, and shapes that can be physically moved around allows a very experimental approach to design. One item compels the artist to lay another next to it. For the viewer, the excitement comes first in responding to the work as a whole and then trying to figure out the original identity of its parts. As in a successful recipe, one

5.26 Paul Zelanski, *Connecticut Remembered*, 1986. Collage, 8 × 10 ins (20.3 × 25.4 cm).

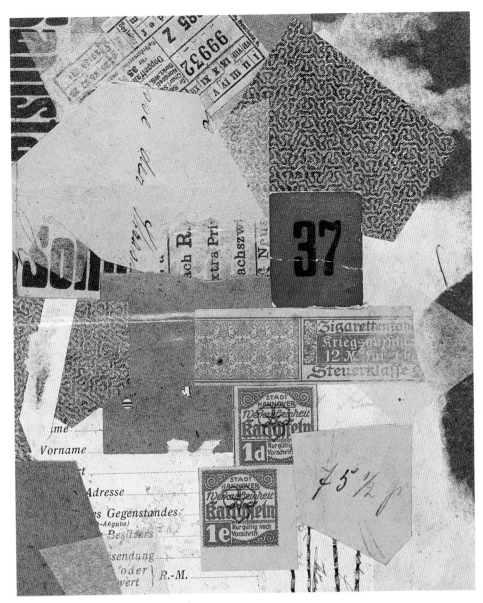

5.27 Kurt Schwitters, *Merz 19*, 1920.
Collage on paper, 7¼ × 5⅞ ins (18.4 × 14.7 cm).
Yale University Art Gallery, New Haven, Connecticut.

does not at first notice the different spices used as ingredients.

Kurt Schwitters, a master of collage, often used bits of paper with writing or printing that read first as abstract design elements and then, as one examines the work more closely, as cryptic clues to meaning. Schwitters was working in the very strange period after World War I in Germany, in which inflation was so great that stamps were overmarked from 5 marks to 5 million marks, and houses were wallpapered with money since it was so worthless. But Schwitters has given these discarded fragments of a disordered life a kind of dignity by the way in which he has put them together.

In a successful collage, such as *Merz 19* (**5.27**) the fragments appear to be spontaneously laid down, but are actually chosen and juxtaposed very carefully. If one more thing were added to this collage, it would be too much; if one thing were subtracted, its visual unity would fall apart.

5.28 *The Battle of Issus*, 2nd to 1st century BC. Mosaic, 8 ft 11 ins × 16 ft 9½ ins (2.72 × 5.13 m). Museo Archeologico Nazionale, Naples.

MOSAIC

An ancient and long-lived technique for creating two-dimensional imagery, MOSAIC is composed of small pieces of colored ceramic tile, glass, pebbles, marble, or wood. These are actually imbedded in cement along the surface of a wall, floor, or ceiling of a building. The subtleties possible with this process are illustrated by *The Battle of Issus* (**5.28**), an impressive Roman mosaic that was buried by the eruption of Vesuvius in AD 79 and not unearthed until the eighteenth century. The image is a lively depiction of Alexander the Great's defeat of the Persians (Alexander is bare-headed at left, with the Persian King Darius in retreat in his chariot). Its vigorous realism seems all the more surprising when we recognize that the colors are composed of small TESSERAE, cubes of natural stone that can more readily be distinguished in the detail (**5.29**). The hues are limited to black, white, yellow, and red, but stones of varying values in each hue have been used to suggest spatial modeling and to provide details for the forms.

5.29 Detail of Alexander from *The Battle of Issus*.

Mosaics were common in the early civilizations of Sumeria, Greece, and Rome and were used to decorate early Christian and Byzantine churches until the fourteenth century, when the cheaper medium of fresco was introduced. But the technique has not been lost. Visionary architect Lluís Domènech i Montaner used it lavishly and playfully in the decoration of architectural structures such as pillars in his Palau de la Música Catalana in Barcelona (**5.30**). An exhilarating feast for the senses,

the building borrows from the Byzantine, Moorish, and Gothic styles of Catalonia's past. The architect's exuberant use of the mosaics on the pillars almost negates their function. Pillars are usually convincingly solid visual evidence that they are holding up heavy structures. We don't expect them to appear so flowery and airy as these do. Here the tiles are much larger than in the Roman mosaic and no attempt is made to hide their identity as individual cubes.

5.30 Lluís Domènech i Montaner, Balcony of the Palace of Catalan Music (*Palau de la Música Catalana*), Barcelona, Spain.

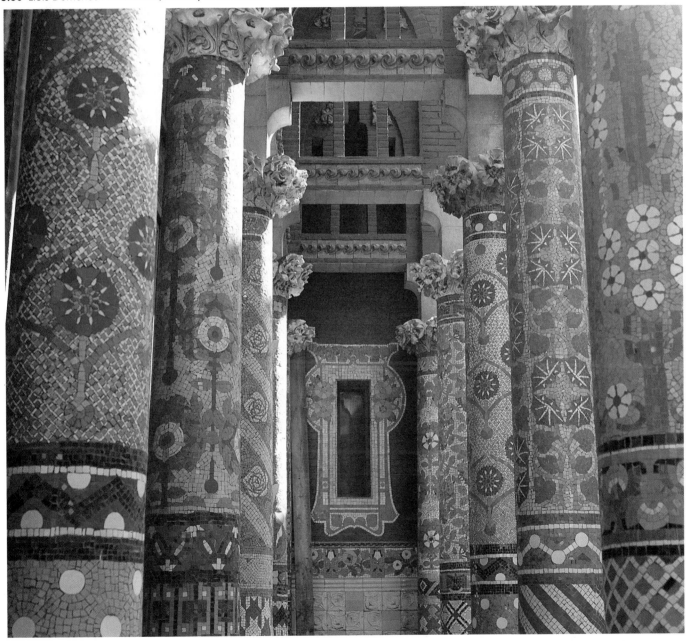

COMPUTER PAINTING

In a sense, computer painting is an extension of mosaics, for the computer screen is divided into a grid of tiny cells. These are "colored" by electronic instructions which have become so sophisticated that computer artists can now mimic hand-painted work, if they so choose. Many commercial programs are available that allow the artist to draw an image on a digitizing tablet which transfers it to the computer monitor as in computer drawing; areas can then be "painted" on the screen by making choices from a "palette" of over sixteen million colors, in the case of high-end equipment.

Another starting point is to use a colored photograph as a source image which is electronically scanned as a BITMAP reporting the predominant color of each small area (**5.31**). These can be reproduced with realistic color-matching, or the colors can be changed at will, including the option of limiting rather than extending the palette. Colors can be "painted" in with brush-like strokes of any size or direction. Edges can be "pushed" to exaggerate the contrast between colored areas, to develop three-dimensionality. The whole background can be "washed" with color, as if toning a canvas, and additional images can be overlaid. Three-dimensional illusions of forms can be created with realistic or skewed "lighting" effects and visually textured surfaces, even if the forms are unlike any ever seen on earth.

With FRACTAL GEOMETRY, astonishingly realistic landscapes can be created arithmetically without reference to any known landscape. This mathematical modeling of complex and random patterns in nature was developed in the late 1970s by the mathematician Benoit Mandelbrot. He based his computer models on the concept of "self-similarity"—the observation that large natural forms consist of visually similar smaller forms. Richard Voss's fractal images, *Changing the Fractal Dimension* (**5.32**), demonstrate this logic: Using the same program, Voss changed the fractal dimension of this computer-simulated landscape to be more and more attenuated, thus altering the roughness of the smallest details along with the large forms. Fractals have been taken up with great enthusiasm by many artists who are also mathematicians—or mathematicians who also have aesthetic sensibilities.

To create traditional painting-like results, artists may choose to print "hard copies" of their computer paintings, using film, plotters, or printers onto art paper, canvas, or textiles.

5.31 Bitmap scanning. The scanner looks at the image square by square. If there is a lot of dark color in the square it registers a black dot. If the square is mostly white it registers nothing. The finer the imaginary grid of squares the better the resolution and the better quality the bitmapped image. For a color halftone it scans three times: using red, green, and blue filters.

Bitmap

Color filters

Lens

5.32 Richard Voss,
Changing the Fractal Dimension, 1983.
Cibachrome prints, each
10 × 14 ins (25.4 × 35.6 cm).
Courtesy of the artist.

MIXED MEDIA

Art forms no longer fit neatly into the traditional categories. We live in a period of great experimentation with all media, and some artists are introducing media and art forms that have never existed before. Often media are mixed, crossing all previous boundaries. Robert Rauschenberg mixes media with glee, combining fine art techniques such as painting and printmaking with a great variety of ready-made and partially altered bits of popular culture, in ways that suggest meaning, even if one cannot be quite sure what it is. His *Monogram* (**5.33**) features a stuffed ram within a tire mounted on a base of Abstract Expressionistic paintings. Rauschenberg says the point is to:

> begin with the possibilities of the material and then you let them do what they can do. So that the artist is really almost a bystander while he is working. The hierarchy of materials is completely broken down.[4]

5.33 Robert Rauschenberg, *Monogram*, 1959.
Stuffed ram, automobile tire, collage, and acrylic, 4 ft × 6 ft × 6 ft (1.22 × 1.83 × 1.83 m).
Moderna Museet, Stockholm.

6

PRINTMAKING

PRINTS—images made by transference of ink from a worked surface onto a piece of paper, usually in multiples—were originally used as illustrations in books and other kinds of printed matter. Books, in turn, were largely dependent on the appearance of inexpensive, readily available paper. Aside from hand-illustrated, one-of-a-kind treasures (such as the Duc de Berry's Book of Hours, shown if Figure 2.142),

books were illustrated with images printed from durable blocks of wood, metal plates, or stones worked by hand. Even after photo-mechanical methods of reproduction removed this need for prints, the printmaking arts continued to be practiced, for prints became valued as artworks in themselves. Now artists can print a limited edition of an image and sell each one as an original.

6.1 Antonio del Pollaiuolo, *Battle of the Ten Nude Men*, c. 1460. Engraving, 15⅛ × 23¼ ins (38.4 × 59 cm). The Metropolitan Museum of Art, New York. Purchase 1917, Joseph Pulitzer Bequest.

6.2 Detail of Figure 6.1, *Battle of the Ten Nude Men*, c. 1460.

Processes used for the creation of transferable images allow great variety in artistic styles. Some prints are similar to tightly rendered representational drawings. Antonio del Pollaiuolo's influential *Battle of the Ten Nude Men* (**6.1**) is a highly skilled example of this approach. All of the muscular human forms and foliage in this line engraving are built up through a series of small lines, as shown in the detail view (**6.2**). The painstaking effort involved in making such a work is not immediately evident because of the great vigor of the image as a whole. Pollaiuolo's skillfulness as an engraver apparently derived from his training as a goldsmith, but his genius in conceiving this dramatic composition of opposing lines far transcends mere manual skill.

A far freer approach to the block is apparent in Hokusai's *Southerly Wind and Fine Weather* (**6.3**), one of his famous views of Mt. Fuji. With stylized simplification of natural cloud and tree forms into flat shapes and a limited palette of hues, it creates an atmosphere all its own that expresses the respect of

6.3 Hokusai, *Southerly Wind and Fine Weather*, late 1820s. Woodblock print, 10 × 14¾ ins (25.5 × 37.5 cm). British Museum, London.

6.4 Mary Frank, *Untitled*, 1977. Monotype on two sheets, printed in color, 35½ × 23¹³⁄₁₆ ins (90.2 × 60.4 cm). Collection, The Museum of Modern Art, New York. Mrs. E. B. Parkinson Fund.

the Japanese people for their most-loved mountain. The color woodcut print was highly developed in Japan as a way of illustrating popular picture books. Hokusai, one of the greatest of the practitioners of the art, created tens of thousands of such prints, each of which was reproduced in multiples and usually sold very cheaply. These mass-produced UKIYO-E woodcut prints were not considered fine art until pages from one of Hokusai's illustrated books turned up in Paris in 1856 as packing material for a shipment of valued porcelains.

Printmaking has usually been defined as a method for creating multiple identical copies of an image by repeatedly inking and printing a worked plate. An alternative introduced in the seventeenth century is MONOTYPE, a printmaking process in which the artist paints an image directly onto a sheet of metal or glass with printer's ink or paint and then presses paper onto it to transfer the image. Some ink or paint may be left on the surface, as a ghost of the image which can then be re-inked and reprinted. Each time the image may change slightly, so no two monotype prints will be exactly alike. And the fact that the artist is printing and improvising freely, perhaps even wiping off areas with turpentine and adding something else, rather than scratching fixed lines, gives the monotype an entirely different quality from other prints, as is evident in Mary Frank's soft and fresh rendering of an amaryllis in bloom (**6.4**).

Another departure from traditional definitions of printmaking is the possibility of making an image that is transferred without any ink. Covers of some books are BLIND EMBOSSED, pressed against an uninked cut plate of metal to create an image that can only be seen when it is turned against the light to bring out the shadows in its indentations.

There are many ways of preparing a plate to be printed. Most can be grouped into four major categories: relief, intaglio, planographic, and stencil. Each is explored below.

PRINTMAKING PROCESSES

RELIEF

In a RELIEF technique, a block of wood, metal, linoleum, or even a found object is carved so that lines and areas to be printed are raised above areas that will stay blank. A simplified diagram of the process is shown in Figure **6.5**.

The classic relief process is the WOODCUT. Typically, a drawing of the intended image is created on or transferred to a smooth block of softish wood—though some artists develop the image directly on the block, as they cut it. Everything that is to remain as an inked line or area is left intact; all other wood near the surface is carved away with a knife along the edges of lines. Gouges are used to remove large areas

6.5 Cross-section of a relief block.

6.6 Albrecht Dürer, *Saint Christopher*, 1511. Woodcut.
The Metropolitan Museum of Art, New York. Fletcher Fund 1919.

6.7 Antonio Frasconi, *Portrait of Woody Guthrie*, 1972.
Woodcut, 23½ × 38¾ ins (59.7 × 98.4 cm).
From Antonio Frasconi, *Frasconi—Against the Grain*,
Macmillan Publishing New York, 1972.

of wood. All cut-away areas will be shallower and will not pick up ink when it is applied to the surface with a roller. After the woodblock is inked, a sheet of paper is pressed onto it in such a way that it picks up, in reverse, the inked image.

Traditional European woodcuts used intricate lines of HATCHING and even CROSS-HATCHING to build up tones and textures, rather like ink drawings. Although it is much more difficult and indirect to carve wood away from lines than to draw them, this approach to the medium was handled with superb technical and aesthetic proficiency by Albrecht Dürer. Although Dürer was personally skillful at woodcutting, like many artists of the period he often prepared only the drawing, delegating the actual cutting of the block to some of the finest artisans of the time. Dürer's *Saint Christopher* (**6.6**) illustrates the range of tones and flowing lines these collaborators were able to coax out of the stiff, flat wood. Some were used as book illustrations; others were sold as single sheets so cheaply that the middle classes could afford to buy them.

Although the woodiness of the block is well hidden in Dürer's work, some contemporary artists

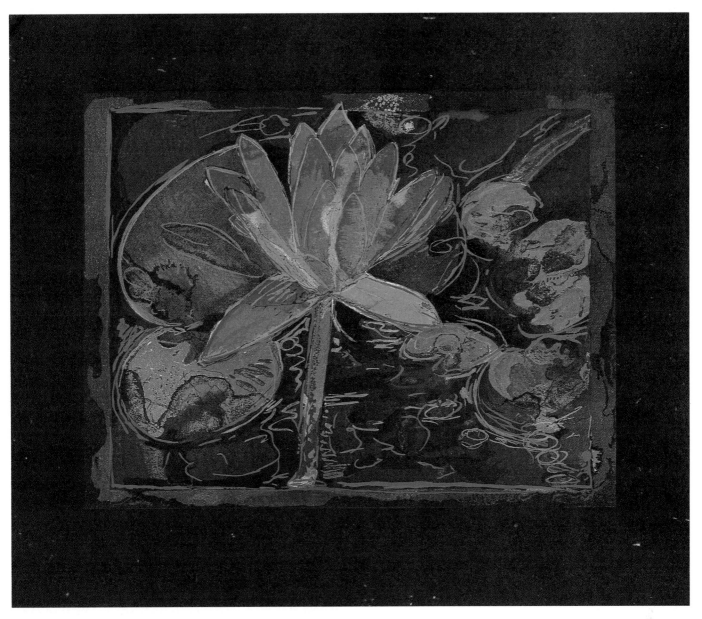

6.8 Joseph Raffael, *Matthew's Lily*, 1984. 28-color woodcut, edition of 50, 32 × 37 ins (81.3 × 94 cm).

have chosen to reveal the character of the wood. Different kinds of wood have very different grain patterns, which appear as lines in the printed areas. Wood from the beech tree and fruit trees—such as cherry, apple, or pear—is uniformly hard and even-grained. These woods are often used when the artist wants to create fine details that will stand up to hundreds of printings of the block and to avoid obvious grain lines. Certain species of pine, on the other hand, have wood that varies considerably in softness and hardness from one ring to another, producing strong grain lines that the artist may choose to exaggerate in order to create visual textures in the print. The grain may be heightened by scraping

a wire brush across it so that it will be sure to print. In Antonio Frasconi's *Portrait of Woody Guthrie* (**6.7**), the woody quality is a quiet visual pun that accentuates the rough-cut, homespun character of the folk guitarist. The grain—which can clearly be seen running horizontally through the work—is also used to indicate tones and textures, in a rather serendipitous fashion. Whites with bits of grain printed through them become optically grayer.

Woodcuts can also be executed in colors, as in Joseph Raffael's *Matthew's Lily* (**6.8**), in which the image is composed of 28 colors. The traditional way of adding extra colors—developed to a precise art by the Japanese *ukiyo-e* printmakers—is to cut a series of precisely matched blocks, each having only the area to be printed in a certain color raised as a printing surface. To match the blocks, a master or "key" block with the essential details is first cut and inked, and numerous reference prints are made from it. Areas that are to be printed in different colors are then indicated on these prints. These guides are glued face-down onto new blocks, one for each color, and everything except the intended colored areas is cut away. At the corners, beyond the edges of the print, registration guides are also cut to help in precise placement of the paper used for the final printing of the entire image. After all the blocks are cut, the same piece of paper is printed by each of the blocks, usually working from lighter to darker tones. The ink is somewhat transparent, and where two colors overlap they will blend. Interestingly, although Germany and Japan had little contact with each other until the mid-nineteenth century, their artists had devised very similar ways of printing color woodcuts from a series of blocks. The chief difference in the result was the more delicate values of the Japanese prints, which were made with water-soluble rather than oil-based inks. As an alternative to the use of separate blocks, some woodcuts were hand-tinted, one-by-one.

When the end-grain rather than a lengthwise slab of wood is cut, the process is called WOOD ENGRAVING. The cross-section of a tree trunk is less likely to splinter than a lengthwise plank and can be incised directly with burins and gravers.

As Figure **6.9** indicates, wood engraving tools are solid rather than having grooved cutting lips like woodcutting tools. The engraved lines become areas that do not print, and are therefore white in the print.

6.9 (left) Wood engraving tools. (right) Wood cutting tools.

6.10 Fritz Eichenberg, *Ecclesiastes*, "*And in her mouth was an olive leaf*", 1945. Wood engraving, 12 × 6 ins (30.5 × 15.2 cm).

Wood engravings are typically conceived as white lines cut directly, rather than black lines from which the wood to either side has been cut away. The difference in these two approaches becomes apparent by contrasting Dürer's classic woodcut style (6.6) with the wood engraving of Fritz Eichenberg (**6.10**). Ecclesiastes's beard, hair, and musculature are all described primarily with white lines within areas left black. Of wood engraving, Eichenberg says:

> I have made thousands of drawings for many purposes, I have made many etchings and lithographs, but nothing can compare to the excitement when again I hold in my hand a beautiful block of close-grained, polished boxwood. I caress the silky surface before the burin touches it, digs in lightly, and then glides smoothly through the wood. A little curl rises from the groove in the path of the tool. I am in control, I am happy.
>
> Wood engraving is a contemplative medium; it gives one time to think, to meditate, to listen to good music. As the graver cuts into the darkened surface, it creates light, order, beauty, out of a piece of a living thing, a tree perhaps much older than the artist himself. There are no shortcuts as the artist conjures out of a small square of wood a microcosm of life.[1]

Wood engraving was adopted for printing illustrations in books and newspapers until it was replaced by photographic methods at the end of the nineteenth century. When illustrations were needed quickly for new stories, a team of wood engravers who had been trained to use the same style were given different parts of an image to cut, and then their blocks were bolted together and printed as a unit. The engraved blocks could be clamped into place at the same height as type and the two printed together to make illustrated texts.

In the twentieth century, linoleum blocks have been added to the printmaker's options. Linoleum cuts, commonly referred to as LINOCUTS, lack the directional character of woodgrain. Lines can be cut equally smoothly and uniformly in any direction, and uncut areas can print in a strong solid black, as in Stephen Alcorn's *Don Juan* (**6.11**). When lines are made directly with a gouge, rather than being what is left after the surrounding wood is carved away, the image is often conceived as white lines within a black area, rather than vice versa. Lines tend to be free-flowing and bold, reflecting the speed of the direct cuts. Although linoleum is easy to cut, it is also somewhat crumbly and cannot be used for ultra-fine lines.

6.11 Stephen Alcorn, *Don Juan*, 1984. Linocut, 12⅞ × 10 ins (33 × 25.2 cm). From *The Bibliophile's Calendar*, 1986, Meriden-Stinehour Press.

Linocuts have been eschewed by some serious artists because of their association with children's art, but using the medium well is actually quite difficult. Stephen Alcorn, who also works in other printmaking and painting media, explains:

> I was attracted to linoleum by the uncompromising discipline it requires. It is not a flexible medium. Whatever tonal gradations, ornamentation, and pattern appear in the finished print have to be deliberately invented, in contrast to media such as charcoal or lithography, where the artist can hide a lack of structure in the drawing by creating facile atmospheric effects, or oils, where the possibilities for creating subtleties with transparent glazes are endless. Linoleum is a bold and healthy medium. It requires vigor, decisiveness, and solidity in drawing. And to experiment to find ways to enrich the initially barren uncut surface, to make it come to life, is very exciting.[2]

6.12 Pablo Picasso, *Bust of a Woman after Cranach the Younger*, 1958.
Color linocut, 25¼ × 21⅛ ins (64.1 × 53.7 cm).

6.13 Lucas Cranach the Younger, *Portrait of a Woman*, 1564. Oil on wood, 32⅝ × 25⅛ ins (83 × 64 cm). Kunsthistorisches Museum, Vienna.

Some prints have historically been used as a means of reproducing works of art originally executed in other media. Picasso plays with this method in his color linocut *Bust of a Woman after Cranach the Younger* (**6.12**). It is loosely derived from Cranach's sixteenth-century painting, *Portrait of a Woman* (**6.13**). Note that the linocut image is the mirror opposite of the painting; Picasso apparently worked it with the same orientation as the painting, but when the sheet was pulled off the inked block, the image was reversed. Picasso's linocut version is also obviously much more direct and playful. For the multiple colors of his linocuts he developed the REDUCTION PRINT method of continually cutting away areas on a single block, inking the surface a different color at each stage rather than cutting a series of registered blocks.

INTAGLIO

The second major category of printmaking methods is INTAGLIO, a term derived from the Italian word for engraving. As shown in Figure **6.14**, it is the exact opposite of relief techniques. In intaglio prints, the image is cut into the surface of a plate. These depressed lines are printed by applying thin ink to the plate with dabbers that force the ink into all the grooves. The plate is then wiped so that no ink remains on the surface, and a sheet of dampened paper is pressed onto the plate so that it picks up the ink that remains in the sunken areas. For special tonal effects or softening of the lines, the plate may first be rubbed lightly with a piece of gauze or muslin, lifting small amounts of ink from the incisions. This technique, most often associated with etchings, is called RETROUSSAGE.

On an intaglio print, the paper beneath the lines is slightly raised because it has been pressed very firmly and uniformly into the grooves to avoid missing any part of the image. A strong roller press—traditionally hand-operated but now mechanized—is therefore used for intaglio prints, in contrast with the lighter

pressure exerted by the screw press or hand-rubbing used to transfer ink from block to paper for relief prints. There is a slight sculpting of the paper as it is pressed in a damp state into the plate.

The earliest intaglio process developed was LINE ENGRAVING. In this relatively direct method, the image is drawn on a plate of metal. Copper was generally used from the sixteenth century until the nineteenth century, when steel was chosen for its ability to hold an image sharply for a greater number of printed copies. Steel, however, was much harder to engrave than copper, so a method of applying a steel facing to already-engraved copper plates was developed in the late 1850s. A BURIN is used to cut the lines. This is a bevelled steel rod with a sharpened point and a wooden handle. A similar tool is used for wood engraving, which is a relief process. Because line engraving is an intaglio process, the ink is forced into the v-shaped grooves cut by the burin, and these become the printed lines.

Line engravings, like wood engravings, were traditionally used for illustrations and reproductions of works of art before photography took over this function. The translation of an image from one medium to another is never precisely accurate. In the steel engraving (**6.15**) of Turner's oil painting *Snow Storm: Steamboat off a Harbor's Mouth* (**6.16**), the engraver has skillfully created a complete range of values from black to white, with many mid-tones, by engraving a tremendous number of tiny lines that vary in width, length, and proximity to other lines, as shown in the enlarged detail of waves (**6.17**). Every area of the engraving is executed with great skill. But even though the values and shapes are similar in the reproduction and the original, the two versions differ tremendously in attitude. The engraving is necessarily conceived in terms of precise lines; the painting is a swirling mass of free-moving brushstrokes, depicting the wild and ever-changing elements as almost obliterating the identity of the steamboat. Another obvious difference, of course, is that the painting is executed in color, whereas line engraving is traditionally a black-and-white medium.

A second major intaglio technique is ETCHING. A copper, zinc, or steel plate is coated with a waxy, acid-resistant substance called a RESIST. The design is drawn through this coating with an etching needle,

6.14 Cross-section of an intaglio plate.

6.15 After Joseph Mallord William Turner, *Snow Storm*. Steel engraving, 1891. British Museum, London.

6.16 Joseph Mallord William Turner, *Snow Storm: Steamboat off a Harbor's Mouth*, 1842. Oil on canvas, 36 × 48 ins (91.5 × 122 cm). Tate Gallery, London.

6.17 Detail of engraving of *Snow Storm*.

6.18 Henri Matisse, *Young Woman, Goldfish and Checkered Cloth*, 1929. Etching, printed in black, paste, 5 × 7 1/16 ins (12.8 × 17.9 cm). Collection, The Museum of Modern Art, New York. Purchased.

baring the surface of the metal. The plate is then bathed in an acid solution that bites grooves into the metal in the areas where the needle has cut through the resist. These grooves are then inked and printed as in engravings. Because the waxy resist offers much less resistance to the etching needle than a metal plate does to a burin, the lines in an etching can be quite freely drawn, as they are in Matisse's *Young Woman, Goldfish and Checkered Cloth* (**6.18**).

Another unique characteristic of etchings is the possibility of varying tones by withdrawing the plate from the acid bath, "stopping out" certain areas with varnish to keep them from being etched any deeper (and therefore printing darker) and then returning the plate to the bath for rebiting of the unstopped areas. If printed individually, each stage is called a STATE. Rembrandt, whose etchings helped to establish the process as a major art form, printed five states of his *Three Crosses*, of which three are illustrated here

(**6.19–21**). The second state is printed on VELLUM, a fine parchment made of animal skin, rather than paper. The vellum blurs the lines, giving a softer, more paint-like quality to the composition. The fourth state reveals a tremendous amount of reworking. As the states proceed, the work becomes more abstract, with the masses milling below the crosses receding into the shadows (**6.22–24**).

In addition to being stopped out and rebitten, etching plates may also be touched up directly with a DRYPOINT tool—a sharp-pointed, perhaps even diamond-tipped device for scratching lines directly into a copper plate. In an etching, touching up with drypoint techniques eliminates the need for re-applying the resist in order to make changes and is a way to work more value and textural variations into the basic design. The long, dark, parallel lines in the later stages of Rembrandt's crucifixion etchings were obviously added after the original plate was cut.

6.19 Rembrandt van Rijn, *The Three Crosses*, 1653, State II. Drypoint and burin etching, on vellum, 15⅛ × 17¾ ins (38.4 × 45 cm). The Metropolitan Museum of Art, New York. Gift of Felix M. Warburg and his family.

6.20 Rembrandt van Rijn, *The Three Crosses*, 1653, State III. Drypoint and burin etching, 15⅛ × 17¾ ins (38.4 × 45 cm). British Museum, London.

6.21 Rembrandt van Rijn, *The Three Crosses*, 1653, State IV. Drypoint and burin etching, 15⅛ × 17¾ ins (38.4 × 45 cm). British Museum, London.

6.22, 6.23, 6.24 Details of States II, III, and IV of *The Three Crosses*.

6.25 Mary Cassatt, *The Caress*, 1891.
Drypoint, 7¹¹⁄₁₆ × 5¾ ins (20 × 15 cm).
The Metropolitan Museum of Art, New York. Gift of Arthur Sachs, 1916.

Drypoint cutting can also be used by itself to scratch lines into a blank copper plate. When inked and printed, the plate yields what is called a DRY-POINT PRINT. Mary Cassatt's *The Caress* (**6.25**) is a lovely example of the directness and sensitivity of this process. The darkness of lines is directly determined by the depth to which they are cut. Drypoints also have a characteristically soft and furry line quality. This softening of the line is created by the burr of metal pushed up by the drypoint tool. The burr tends to hold ink when the plate is wiped. Because the burr does not hold up under repeated prints, editions of drypoints are usually small.

A fourth method of intaglio printing is called MEZZOTINT. In this process, the copper plate is first scored with a rocking device, creating a burr across

6.26 Prince Rupert, *The Standard Bearer*, 1658.
Mezzotint.
The Metropolitan Museum of Art, New York. Harris Brisbane Fund, 1933.

the whole surface. The burr is then smoothed and scraped to varying degrees to create variations in tone and texture. The lightest tones will appear in areas that are smoothed the most. Gradations from very dark to white are possible, and the print will have a rich velvet visual texture, as in Prince Rupert's *The Standard Bearer* (**6.26**).

Another intaglio printing method is called

AQUATINT. Like mezzotints, aquatints are capable of creating toned areas rather than the lines to which line engraving, etching, and drypoint are limited. The aquatint process is like etching tones instead of lines. Transparent areas of ink that resemble a wash drawing are created by allowing acid to penetrate a porous covering of powdered resin. Where the surface of the copper or zinc plate is not protected by the resin

6.27 Anne Sobol-Wejmen, *Boyka Fable*, 1979.
Aquatint, 9¼ × 11½ ins (23.5 × 29.2 cm).
Collection: Annette Zelanski.

6.28 Frank Boyden, *Changes #IV*, 1986.
Lithograph, 8 × 9¾ ins (20.3 × 24.7 cm).

particles, the acid etches pits in the metal, producing the grainy tones characteristic of aquatints, as in Anne Sobol-Wejmen's *Boyka Fable* (**6.27**).

In the traditional aquatint method, the whole surface is first dusted with the resin and then variations in tone are created by repeatedly stopping out areas with varnish to vary the degree to which the acid bites into the plate. Linear details are usually added using line engraving or drypoint. A version of this process that allows more spontaneous, direct work on the plate is called SUGAR AQUATINT. In this method, the composition is painted onto the resin-coated plate with a sugar solution. The plate is then varnished and immersed in water. The water swells the sugar, which bursts the varnish in the painted areas and exposes the metal there. When the plate is bathed in acid, the previously painted areas will have the grainy aquatint texture, while the varnished areas will remain white.

PLANOGRAPHIC

The major PLANOGRAPHIC or "surface" process of printmaking is LITHOGRAPHY. In lithography, prints are made from a perfectly flat surface rather than one that is raised (as in relief methods) or incised (as in intaglio). Adopted as an art medium in the late eighteenth century, the method is based on the observation that grease and water will not mix. A design is drawn on a slab of fine-grained limestone (or a metal or plastic plate) with a greasy substance, such as a litho crayon made of wax, soap, and lampblack. The stone is chemically treated to fix the grease and make the open areas more porous, and then it is dampened. When oily lithographic ink is spread across the surface, it is repelled by the wet areas but sticks to the greasy areas.

Lithography can easily reproduce both lines and tones. The dark areas in the prints pulled from a lithographic plate can be very lush, in contrast to darks that must be built up by lines. Artists find it a very free way to work, and one that mirrors the gestures of their drawings exactly. Although many lithographs are freely drawn, creating dark lines against the white ground of the paper, it is also possible to work in a *manière noire* ("black manner") by brushing a broad area of grease onto the plate and then scratching lines and tones into it. Frank Boyden

6.29 James Rosenquist, *Iris Lake*, 1975.
Nine-color lithograph, 36 × 52 ins (91.4 × 132 cm).

explains how he used this time-consuming process to develop his exquisite lithograph, *Changes #IV* (**6.28**):

> What you see as the black image was brushed out on a stone with autographic ink—a very fine oil- or grease-based emulsion. The lines along the sides are where the brush dragged along. Then I went back into it. The salmon was done with etching needles. The gray of the raven was removed with a very sharp razor blade, like an Exacto knife, to expose the stone just a very little bit. To get those kinds of gradations took about five hours of work, just in that area. Fiddling, just scraping and scraping and scraping. Then the ribbed sorts of things were drawn back over that, with an etching tool and also a razor blade for just a little bit more contrast. You don't often see this kind of work, because it's a horrible drag. And *manière noire* is very difficult to print, because it's so difficult to hold the values.[3]

Like many contemporary lithographers, Boyden has his work printed by a fine-printing lithography house. They work together to get a satisfactory print, on which the artist writes BAT, for *"bon à tirer"* ("good to pull"); all prints pulled are compared to that model in order to be approved for the edition.

Although fine lithographs are printed in limited editions, a great number of prints can be pulled from a single stone or plate, so modern versions of the lithographic process are widely used for commercial printing of everything from cigar labels to books. In OFFSET LITHOGRAPHY, the process used to print this book and most others today, illustrations are converted to systems of dots that give the effect of different tones. The dot patterns are created by photographing the image through a screen of crossed lines. You can see the dots if you examine one of the black-and-white illustrations in this book with a magnifying glass. Screened illustrations and typeset text are then transferred photo-chemically to plates for printing. Ink is picked up—"offset"—from the cylindrical plates onto a rubber roller and thence transferred to paper so that the final image is the same way around as that on the plate, rather than reversed, as in most art printing processes.

In both original works of art and commercial printing processes, lithography can also be adapted to multiply colored images. In prints that originate as lithographs, such as James Rosenquist's nine-color *Iris Lake* (**6.29**), a separate plate is made for each color. Each plate is marked so that it can be carefully aligned to match the others during printing. In commercial reproduction of colored images created by other processes, such as those in color in this book, *color separations* are done on a computerized *color scanner*. It reads a *transparency*—a flexible transparent photograph of the work—to translate the colors into mixtures of the four colors that will be used to print it on a *four-color press*: yellow, magenta (red), cyan (blue), and black. Each color is printed from a separate plate; the pages of this book that have color illustrations have received four precisely registered printings. Figure **6.30** illustrates the process and results of four-color printing. In highly specialized printing, additional passes may be used for purposes such as varnish, metallic inks, intensification of reds, or use of mixed inks specified by the designer.

6.30 The color separation process. Color separations from a 1970 poster by graphic designer Peter Good, employing a photograph by Bill Ratcliffe. Printer: The Hennegan Company.

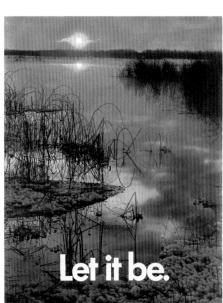

STENCIL

The fourth major printmaking process is *stenciling*—masking out areas that are not to be printed. The form of stenciling now most often used both by fine artists and commercial printers in this increasingly sophisticated medium is the SILK SCREEN or SERIGRAPH. A fine silk or synthetic fiber screen stretched across a wooden frame is masked in places by a cut paper or plastic stencil or by lacquer, glue, or lithographic crayon. High-contrast photographs may also be transferred to special film whose glue-like emulsion is adhered to the screen as a stencil. When ink is brushed across the screen with a squeegee, it passes through the unmasked areas to be deposited on the paper or other surface to be printed below. A multi-colored image can be created by use of successive screens with different colors and different masked areas. Precise registration (placement of successive screens) is necessary to prevent gaps or overlapping. But in his silkscreened photo-emulsion self-portraits (**6.31**), Andy Warhol allowed slight mis-registrations to reveal the mass-production "non-art" derivation of the medium, as an exercise in Pop Art.

In addition to flat colored shapes, graduated tones can also be created in a silkscreen print by means of a photomechanical screen of dots. Andy Warhol deliberately enlarged the dots in his self-portraits to reveal this mechanical process.

Paints used in silkscreens may be transparent or opaque. Colors can blend into each other through a *split fountain* technique, in which different paints are placed at different ends of the squeegee and blended where they overlap as they are pushed across the screen.

6.31 Andy Warhol, *A Set of Six Self-Portraits*, 1967.
Oil and silkscreen on canvas, each 22½ × 22½ ins (57.2 × 57.2 cm).
San Francisco Museum of Modern Art. Gift of Michael D. Abrams.

6.32 Francisco de Goya, *And there is no remedy*. Plate 15 from *Los Desastres de la Guerra*, 1808–20. Etching and aquatint. National Gallery of Art, Washington, D.C. Rosenwald Collection.

MIXED MEDIA

Although we have examined the major printmaking processes separately, in practice they are often mixed with each other. Relief, intaglio, planographic, and stencil plates can be alternately printed on the same surface. Francisco de Goya has used both etching and aquatint in his *And there is no remedy* (**6.32**), for a combination of dark, scratchy etched lines and gray tones.

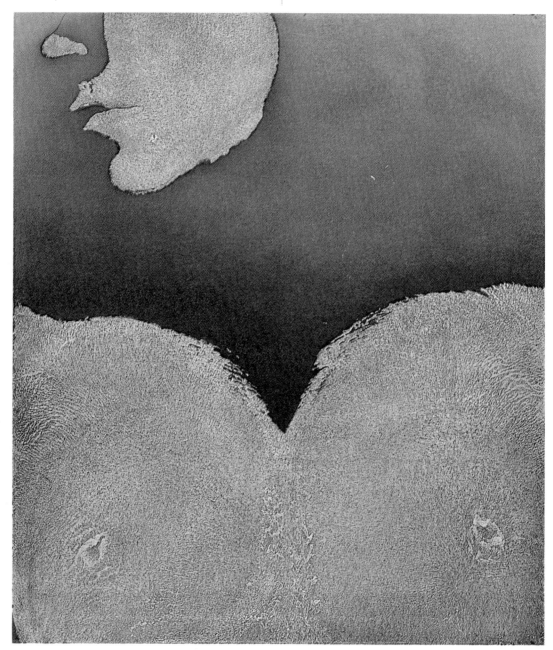

6.33 Janet Cummings Good, *Cerulean Sky*, 1990.
Mixed media, 12 × 11 ins (30.5 × 27.9 cm).
Courtesy of the artist.

In today's wide-open experimentation, some artists are even combining printmaking with other media.

Janet Cummings Good coats parts of her own body with gesso, presses herself against paper, and then works into the texture of the resulting monoprint with oil paint and drawing media (**6.33**). Sometimes she cuts up the impression and reassembles the parts.

She began these body prints after a period of doing very tight drawings of the body. Good reports:

I felt I had taken the realism of the body as far as I could. I wanted to get more personal, more expressive with the subject. I was unsatisfied with representing the surface. The irony is that the way to get beyond my fixation with surface was to deal with it even more directly and immediately, by literally placing my body on the surface of the paper.[4]

7

GRAPHIC DESIGN

The term "graphic designer" is a rather new label in the history of art. It is applied primarily to those who design two-dimensional images for commercial purposes, from advertisements, packaging, and corporate images to the pages of books. Their challenge is to catch the eye of an already optically saturated public, conveying information in a memorable way.

Graphic designers must have their fingers on the ever-changing public pulse, staying one step ahead of shifting tastes and interests. This does not necessarily mean that effective designs are always futuristic. For a logo for New York's Russian Tea Room (**7.1**), Milton Glaser has combined contemporary honed-down, hard-edged lines with a more lyrical, nostalgic invented type style that is reminiscent of the Cyrillic alphabet, bespeaking the wealth of Czarist Russia. The gradually thinning lines around the border and the implied lines that run outward from the center on the corners give the center shape and letter forms greater impact by making them appear to project toward the viewer in space.

In line with the current public mood, many designers are packaging food in ways that make it appear more "natural." To market a new pasta sauce as if it were home-made from an old family recipe using all-natural ingredients, Duffy Design Group suggested bottling the sauce in traditional canning jars, complete with raised measurement marks along the side. The labels they designed for the jars (**7.2**) have the rustic appearance of hand-cut, hand-tinted woodcuts, adding to the home-made image. Through words and imagery, the designers develop a certain feeling toward the product in the attitude of the consumer.

7.2 Charles Spencer Anderson, designer/illustrator, Duffy Design Group, Packaging for Prince Foods' Classico pasta sauce range.

7.1 Milton Glaser, Logo for the Russian Tea Room, from Milton Glaser, *Graphic Design*, The Overlook Press, Woodstock New York, 1983.

Peter Good
on
THE ART OF GRAPHIC DESIGN

Peter Good is an internationally known graphic designer and illustrator. His studio, Peter Good Graphic Design, works on assignments for corporations, small businesses, and arts organizations, including several ballet troupes and The National Theatre of the Deaf (**7.3**). He is best known for his posters. Good observes:

"Things are constantly changing. How do you become a graphic designer? I think we need to begin by constantly being open to new ways of seeing things. Everything depends on context; everything is a

7.3 Peter Good, *Poster for the National Theater of the Deaf, King of Hearts*, 1988. 25 × 25 ins (63.5 × 63.5 cm). Courtesy of the artist.

reaction to what is in the present. The designer works to communicate another person's ideas. The artist is usually someone who has his own ideas.

If there's anything that can go in two directions [as art and as commercial design], it's posters. They act like paintings—they're on a wall. But there is information on a poster—it has to perform a certain function. After the function is over and people put it on a wall as art, you no longer have the informational requirements."

"There are a few American designers who use ambiguity as Tomaszewski, the father of Polish posters, does. But the American culture is not receptive to that kind of imagery, that use of metaphor and levels of meaning. It's not as sophisticated. I face this all the time with clients. I say, 'Well, don't you see? Someone will think about it and will become engaged in it, and therefore it will be a stronger communication.' But people tend to think you have to be obvious in all cases. Sometimes the obvious can work, but other times ambiguity enhances the communication. You see that in European and other cultures. Perhaps they have more design education; perhaps it's because multi-lingual areas rely more on visual language.

On the other hand, something that works really well may seem obvious. Even though you never saw it before, it seems understandable, it seems right. It is real genius to

take something that's right before our noses and to do something with it that works so well that everyone says, 'Oh, my God!'"

"The worst thing for a young designer is freedom, because the best design, the best art, comes from limitations. There are too many options. There are many different solutions to design problems, some more successful than others. If you start with the broadest possible range, you can't possibly explore all those possibilities. You have to make certain decisions to narrow the range, so you begin to explore the possibilities within a smaller realm, and then you narrow it further, until you get into a manageable form to deal with. But if you don't know that process of self-limitation—from experience or talent or whatever—this process becomes arbitrary. I see that happening with the possibilities opened up by computer graphics. If you have an area of land to explore—say, an acre of land—you can't possibly explore it in detail. But if you have a square foot, you can get down to molecules, down to very fine things.

I feel graphic designers work much better if they get involved with things that are not design. If you're doing something for a hospital, to go to the hospital and see the people and see what the real problems are. Otherwise you're working blind. Empathy is one of the greatest tools a designer has—to always put yourself in someone else's position."[1]

The graphic designer works with visual ideas. Paul Rand, considered one of the world's greatest and most influential designers, observes that:

> Graphic design is essentially about visual relationships—providing meaning to a mass of unrelated needs, ideas, words, and pictures. It is the designer's job to select and fit this material together—and make it interesting. The problem is not simple; its very complexity virtually dictates the solution—that is, the discovery of an image universally comprehensible, one that translates abstract ideas into concrete forms.[2]

Rand's catalog cover for a show of Picasso's work (**7.4**) catches the eye with its two bold lines, which still look freshly-painted today, and uses Picasso-esque hand-written information at a time when everyone else was using uniform machine-set type. Picasso's photograph ever so slightly overlaps the circular line at the chin, setting up a delightful three-dimensional spatial illusion. He appears to be looking out at us from inside the catalog, enticing us to open it. The individual elements seem quite simple and uncluttered, but putting them together so that they work so well takes great mastery of design.

7.4 Paul Rand, a proposed catalog cover.

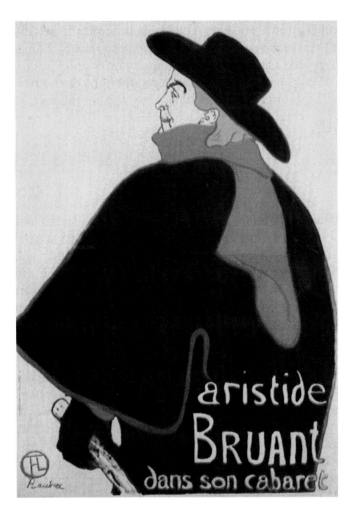

7.5 Henri de Toulouse-Lautrec, Poster, *Aristide Bruant dans son Cabaret*, 1893. Color lithograph, 54½ × 39 ins (138 × 99 cm). The Metropolitan Museum of Art, New York. Harris Brisbane Dick Fund, 1932.

Graphic design is usually aimed directly at consumers, though there is often an art director and a marketing team between the designer and the end user. But its commercialism has not kept some graphic design from being treated as fine art. Some is created by recognized artists who have distinguished themselves in other media, such as Toulouse-Lautrec, whose lithographed posters for dance-halls and cabarets (**7.5**) raised the poster to an art form. They were so admired by collectors that they were stolen as fast as they were put up.

The poster, like most graphic design, was initially conceived as an ephemeral piece to be thrown away once its commercial purpose was finished. But posters are often so visually compelling that someone saves—or buys—them and hangs them as one would a painting. They have become a relatively inexpensive way to bring art into one's home. Whereas a few decades ago, those who couldn't afford original works of art hung reproductions of them in their homes, many people now display posters by renowned designers, such as Henryk Tomaszewski (2.36).

TYPOGRAPHY

The two major ingredients of graphic design are letters and images. Typography is the art of designing, sizing, and combining letter forms on a printed page. The choices the graphic designer must make are subtle and complex. Hundreds of TYPEFACES that can be used for printing the Roman alphabet have been developed over the years. Most can be grouped into two large categories: SERIF and SANS SERIF typefaces. A serif is a fine line that finishes the larger "stroke" used to make a letter form. Originally used in the classical Roman alphabet on which modern letters are based, serifs tend to lead our eye through a word, tying it together visually, as well as giving elegant calligraphic flourishes to the individual letter-forms. Most books, including this one, are printed in one of the many serif typefaces. Many modern typefaces eliminate the serifs, however, for a more contemporary look. These sans serif ("without serif") type styles are often chosen when an upbeat, forward-looking message is desired. Figure **7.6** illustrates the general difference between these two categories: Baskerville is a serif typeface originally designed in the eighteenth century by John Baskerville, while Gill Sans is a twentieth-century sans serif typeface often used on modern English signs. Eric Gill based its proportions and shapes on the classic Roman letter-forms, but made the rules for their creation so simple that even the least skilled signwriter could follow them perfectly.

When a typeface is designed, each letter is carefully constructed, with attention to the balance between

7.6 Baskerville (left) and Gill Sans (right) typefaces.

7.7 Albrecht Dürer, page from *Underweisung der Messung*, 1525. Victoria and Albert Museum, London.

stressed (thicker) and unstressed (thinner) portions. Albrecht Dürer, influential in so many of the visual arts, published in 1525 *Underweisung der Messung mit dem Zirckel und Richtscheyt* ("A Course in the Art of Measurement with Compass and Ruler"). This book included instructions for applying geometric principles to the construction of letter-forms. In the page shown in Figure **7.7** Dürer relates each letter to a square, with a ratio of ten to one between the height and width of the letter strokes. Not only are his letters lovely; the page as a whole is beautifully designed, with pleasing contrast between the scale of the text type and the display type, and enough white space around the printed text to allow it to breathe.

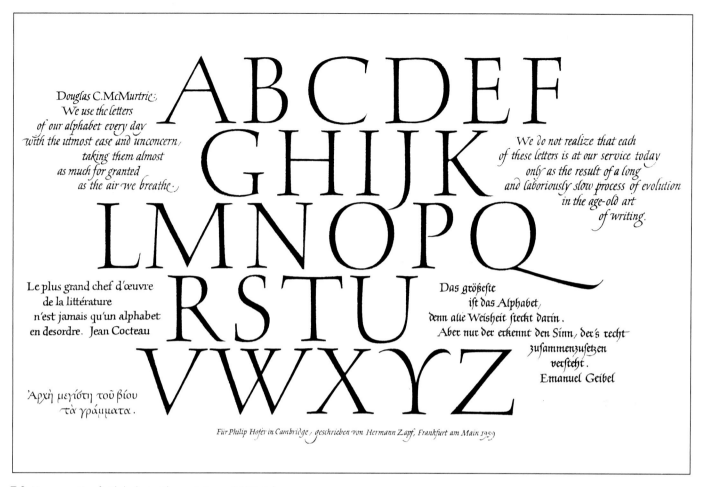

Douglas C. McMurtrie:
We use the letters
of our alphabet every day
with the utmost ease and unconcern,
taking them almost
as much for granted
as the air we breathe.

We do not realize that each
of these letters is at our service today
only as the result of a long
and laboriously slow process of evolution
in the age-old art
of writing.

Le plus grand chef d'œuvre
de la littérature
n'est jamais qu'un alphabet
en desordre. Jean Cocteau

Das größeste
ist das Alphabet,
denn alle Weisheit steckt darin.
Aber nur der erkennt den Sinn, der's recht
zusammenzusetzen
versteht.
Emanuel Geibel

Ἀρχὴ μεγίστη τοῦ βίου
τὰ γράμματα.

Für Philip Hofer in Cambridge, geschrieben von Hermann Zapf, Frankfurt am Main 1959

7.8 Hermann Zapf, Alphabet with quotations, 1959. Ink.
Mr. and Mrs. Philip Hofer Collection, The Houghton Library, Harvard University.

Typesetting has largely been turned over to computerized photocomposition processes rather than handsetting of metal type. But the art of the beautifully designed letter and page is being maintained by aficionados of fine printing. Hermann Zapf has designed over 50 typefaces adapted to twentieth-century technologies, but he maintains a poetic sense of the aesthetics of typography, as is evident in the alphabet sampler done in his own calligraphic hand (**7.8**), and in these remarks:

> Typography is fundamentally two-dimensional architecture. The harmony of single proportions, the grouping of lines of type, the judging of contrast and balance, the symmetry and dynamic tension of axial arrangement—all these are the shaping tools, so employed by the typographer in a given task as to bring the reader a text in its most appealing form.... The letters' indwelling wealth of form is a fresh, unending astonishment.[3]

In addition to having unique characteristics if examined closely, each typeface creates a slightly different value when printed in blocks on a page. In Herb Lubalin's cover (**7.9**) for the typographic newsletter *U&lc* (Upper and Lower Case), each article in the right column is summarized in a different typeface, revealing noticeable differences in blackness and grayness. Lubalin, a highly resourceful graphic designer who often creates his own typefaces to make images of words and letters, has managed to integrate 59 different units of varying typefaces, seven illustrations, and 16 rules (lines) into a page that works well as a whole.

7.9 Herb Lubalin, cover for *U&lc*, 1974. Reprinted with permission from *U&lc* magazine, International Journal of Typographics published by the International Typeface Corporation.

ILLUSTRATION

The other major ingredient in graphic design is illustration. Because graphic design is basically a functional art, illustrators must keep the character of what they are illustrating clearly before them. This need is especially true in advertising, where the intent is to portray the client's product as compellingly as possible. At one extreme, the illustration of the product may dominate the presentation. At the other extreme, an elegant and well-known product sometimes lends itself to considerable understatement, as in the refined Audi ad (**7.10**). Looking down, as if from the point of view of the gods, we are beckoned into the car by the slightly open door and the aureole of glowing light. Most of the brochure cover consists of unfilled space. This extremely restrained use of color, image, and type suggests the message that the benefits of this product are so well known that they need not even be mentioned to genteel clients.

Any kind of image may be used, from photographs to woodcuts. The style of illustration and typography must be harmonious. To illustrate Chaucer's

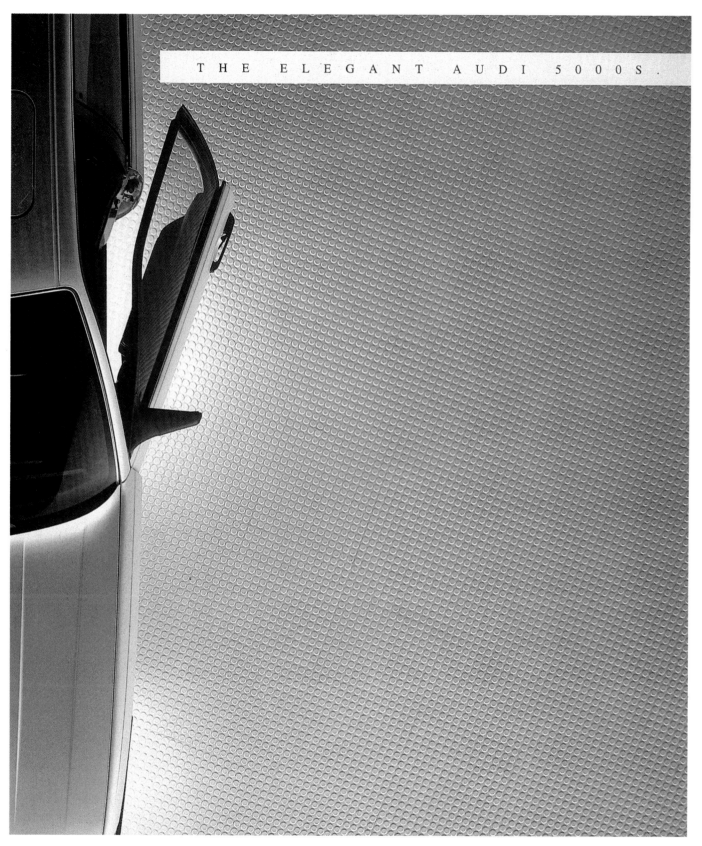

THE   ELEGANT   AUDI   5000S .

7.10 Barry Shepherd and Steve Ditko of SHR Communications,
Brochure for Audi of America, 1985.

7.11 William Morris and Edward Burne-Jones, page from the Kelmscott Press *Works of Geoffrey Chaucer*, 1896. Victoria and Albert Museum, London.

Canterbury Tales, William Morris created a special Gothic typeface, surrounded it with intricate borders, inset woodcuts of drawings by Edward Burne-Jones, and embellished the whole with large illuminated capital letters, as shown in one of the 556 pages of the monumental book (**7.11**). In its brief life from 1891 to 1898, Morris' Kelmscott Press created 18,000 copies of 53 books, all hand-crafted. Their quality and lavish decoration revived interest in fine printing as an art form, at the same time that commercial printing was becoming increasingly mechanized. Morris, who also designed wallpaper, furniture, stained glass, interiors, and industrial products, had a great love for the beautiful object, carefully made of the best materials available. He wrote:

> The picture-book is not, perhaps, absolutely necessary to man's life, but it gives us such endless pleasure, and is so intimately connected with the other absolutely necessary art of imaginative literature that it must remain one of the very worthiest things towards the production of which reasonable men should strive.[4]

Fine printing of illustrated works continues today, often with very different decorative approaches from Morris'. For example, Lance Hidy used handset italic type and a tremendous amount of unfilled white space around his delicate flower etching to present Andrew Marvell's poem, *The Garden* (**7.12**). An

7.12 Lance Hidy, page from Andrew Marvell, *The Garden*, 1970. Etching and letterpress, edition of 115.

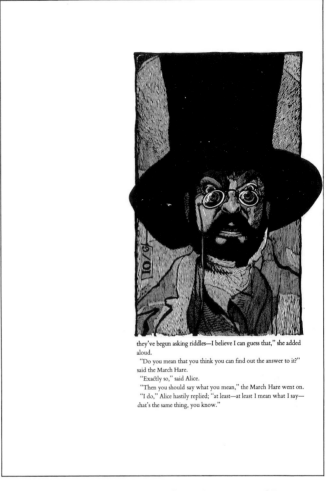

7.13 Barry Moser, *The Mad Hatter*, from The Pennyroyal Press *Alice's Adventures in Wonderland*, 1982. Wood engraving.

entirely different approach was taken by Barry Moser in his bold wood engravings and asymmetrical page layouts for *Alice's Adventures in Wonderland* (**7.13**). The illustration takes up most of the column and even breaks out of its own rectangle, spreading toward the "gutter" or central seam of the book. The head of the Mad Hatter is opposed to the strength of the white border, metaphorically illustrating the illogical frustrations and tensions built up in the story.

8

PHOTOGRAPHY, PHOTOCOPY, AND FILMMAKING

Although photography (the Greek word for "writing with light") and filmmaking are now so much a part of our visual world that we take them for granted, they are relatively recent inventions. From the time of the Renaissance, many artists had used the CAMERA OBSCURA to draw forms and linear perspective accurately. A camera obscura was a dark room or box with light entering through a tiny hole, perhaps focused by a lens. An inverted image from the world beyond would be thrown on the opposite wall or side, and its outlines could be traced on paper. But it was not until the first half of the nineteenth century that several researchers working independently of each other found ways to capture this image permanently.

Later in the nineteenth century, sequences of still pictures began to lead to "movies." By the mid-twentieth century, the technology of capturing moving images from the world had evolved to wireless television broadcasts. And now computer video graphics have opened up a vast new range of possibilities that may or may not originate in the world that we see.

PHOTOGRAPHY

One of the early developers of what became photography was William Henry Fox Talbot. Longing to be able to capture images from his travels and everyday life that he did not have the skill to draw, this English scientist experimented with various techniques. One yielded what he called a *photogenic drawing*, or PHOTOGRAM, created by laying objects on paper coated with light-sensitive chemicals and then exposing it to light. The result is a negative, in which the objects appear light and the paper turns dark. In addition to his scientific resourcefulness, Fox Talbot obviously had an eye for design, as is evident in one of his early photogenic drawings (**8.1**).

At the same time that Fox Talbot was carrying on his experiments, several French researchers had been developing processes that worked along similar lines. After years of secret experimentation, Joseph Nicéphore Niépce (an inventor) and Louis Jacques Mandé Daguerre (a painter of stage sets) began collaborating to produce the process that Daguerre named DAGUERROTYPE in 1837 after Niépce's death. The public was awed by the new ability to preserve actual images in precisely accurate detail. The process was not yet perfect, of course. One problem was the lengthy time needed for exposures. Daguerre's picture of a Paris boulevard (**8.2**) makes it appear to be deserted except for a shoeshiner and his customer. This strange effect occurred because although there were other people on the streets and sidewalks, they were moving too fast for their images to be recorded. In the excitement over the new

8.1 William Henry Fox Talbot, *Botanical Specimens*, 1839. Photogenic drawing. The Metropolitan Museum of Art, New York. Harris Brisbane Dick Fund, 1936.

8.2 Louis Jacques Mandé Daguerre, *A Parisian Boulevard*, 1839. Daguerrotype. Bayerische National-museum, Munich, Germany.

8.3 Anonymous photographer, *Portrait of a Landowner*, India, c. 1900. Painted photograph. ARCOPA (Archival Centre of Photography as an Artform), Bombay, India.

invention, improvements appeared quickly, including the ability to create multiple copies of a single image, based on Fox Talbot's work with the negative.

One of the exciting possibilities opened up by the invention of photography was that of having one's portrait captured for posterity. There had long been portrait painters, of course, but a perfect likeness was both rare and expensive. Many of the surviving early photographs are portraits, such as that of an Indian landowner (**8.3**). Intricately hand-painted before the advent of color photography, it is both subtly beautiful and strangely flat to Western eyes, perhaps because the apparently painted backdrop behind the sitter is not painted in accurate linear perspective (the lines on the door, for instance, all point upwards instead of converging toward a single vanishing point). Even the floor seems to recede up rather than back in space, a spatial convention from traditional Mughal miniature painting.

8.4 Julia Margaret Cameron, *Iago*, 1867. Albumen print. National Museum of Photography, Film and Television, Bradford, England.

8.5 Dante Gabriel Rossetti, *Jane Morris*, 1865. Photograph. Victoria and Albert Museum, London.

8.6 Dante Gabriel Rossetti, *Rêverie*, 1868. Colored chalks, 33 × 28 ins (83.8 × 71.1 cm). Private Collection.

In the hands of some photographers, the portrait photograph became an opportunity to capture an essence or atmosphere rather than a superficial likeness of a person. One of the British gentlewomen who took up the new hobby of portrait photography was Julia Margaret Cameron. Her portraits appear out of focus, for during her long exposures (three to seven minutes) her subjects may have moved, and sharpness was not her object anyway. Her *Iago* (8.4) illustrates the emotional and spiritual depth of her photographs. Although Iago was the villain of Shakespeare's *Othello*, we respond to this man as a complex and compelling human being, investing him with our own ideas about what he is feeling.

In addition to being enthusiastically embraced by the public as a new way of capturing images of the world, photography was adopted by many artists as a helpful tool for creating representational works in other media. As we have seen, painters such as Degas and Toulouse-Lautrec developed unusual perspectives and cropping of figures in response to the camera's-eye-view of external experience. Then, as now, some artists also used photographs as the initial study from which to develop drawings or paintings. Rather than having William Morris' wife, Jane, pose through long sittings, Dante Gabriel Rossetti had her photographed as he posed her (8.5) and then developed his chalk drawing *Rêverie* (8.6) from the photograph. Note that he did not imitate it slavishly; the artist's license he took is obvious when the two images are compared. Even after posing her himself, he changed her posture in the drawing, creating a pleasing circular flow of light across her neck, down her right arm, up her left arm, and back to the Classical styling of her face.

Whenever a new medium appears, artists often try to increase its acceptance by making its products approximate those created with earlier, familiar media. This was true in photography as well. At the turn of the century, the "Pictorialist" movement in photography sought, by elaborate printing techniques, to make photographs look like paintings, emphasizing the hand of the artist at work rather than the sheer duplicating ability of the camera. Edward Steichen used layered prints created with different chemicals to create the misty atmosphere of *Moonrise, Mamaroneck, New York* (8.7).

Although such painterly effects were dramatic, Steichen and Alfred Stieglitz, both leaders of the Pictorialist movement, also evolved strong interest in exploring the potentials that were unique to photography. One was the ability to capture a specific moment in time. Stieglitz's *The Terminal* (8.8) is an ephemeral scene of a horse-drawn trolley being turned on a wintry morning. The steamy breath and

body heat of the horses, the dusting of snow, and the man walking out of the picture in the background give a sense of immediacy to the image.

Willingness to abandon the search for beauty in favor of the straight *documentary* photograph made it possible for sympathetic photographers to share what they had seen of humanity. Documentary photographers—some of them hired by the Farm Security Administration in the United States— wakened public concern for social welfare by recording the plight of the poor, from children working in mines and sweatshops to migrant workers living under wretched conditions. Dorothea

8.7 Edward Steichen, *Moonrise, Mamaroneck, New York*, 1904. Platinum, cyanotype, and ferroprussiate print, 15^{15}⁄16 × 19 ins (38.9 × 48.3 cm). Collection, The Museum of Modern Art, New York. Gift of the photographer.

8.8 Alfred Stieglitz, *The Terminal*, 1915. Photograph.
Gernsheim Collection, Harry Ransom Humanities Research Center, The University of Texas at Austin.

Lange's photograph of a migrant mother and her children (**8.9**) was reproduced in thousands of newspapers and magazines across the country. According to Lange's field notes, this mother, who spoke to the heart of every mother, was "camped on the edge of a pea field where the crop had failed in a freeze. The tires had just been sold from the car to buy food. She was 32 years old with seven children." So effective was this memorable image in waking public sympathy and support for government welfare projects that the death of the mother decades later was publicly honored.

Documentary photographs are not necessarily so direct in their impact. Alex Webb has used a palette of pleasing blue and pinks for *Killed by the Army* (**8.10**) from his *Port-au-Prince* series of 1987, and has purposely underexposed the human figure and kept it in a corner. The viewer is initially drawn in by the colors, textures, shapes—and then comes the secondary realization that the man is dead. One is given no information about who he is or why the killing; with no visible weapons, he seems a symbol of the multitudes of innocent, nameless, hidden victims of the Haitian government.

Sociological photo-reporting has not dwelt exclusively on scenes of human misery. Even among

291

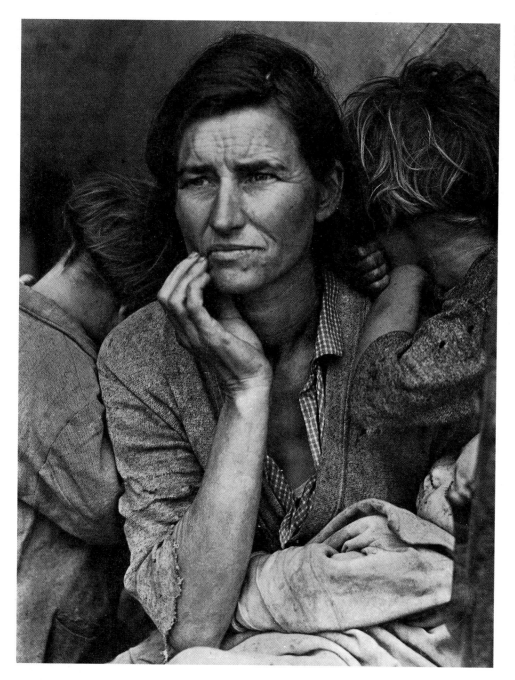

8.9 Dorothea Lange, *Migrant Mother. Nipomo, California*, 1936. Gelatin-silver print, 12½ × 9⅞ ins (31.75 × 24.9 cm). Collection, The Museum of Modern Art, New York. Purchase.

the poor, photographers have often captured moments of great integrity, ecstasy, or humor. Henri Cartier-Bresson specialized in images of everyday life around the world that are emotionally familiar to people from all cultures. His genius lies in his ability to catch the "decisive moment" when a naturally shifting scene of unposed people clicks into place as a strong composition. In his *Sunday on the Banks of the Marne* (**8.11**), everything is placid and staid, from the calm surface of the water to the short, round

forms of the well-fed torsos. The only action we sense is the business of eating, a central theme in these people's lives.

Photographs have also been used to preserve views of the earth's natural landscape that are continually threatened by the expansion of population and industry. In the United States, the work of the great landscape photographers, such as Ansel Adams, has played a major role in wilderness conservation efforts. Adams was a leader in the "f/64 Group,"

8.10 Alex Webb, *Killed by the Army*, from the *Port-au-Prince* series, 1987.

8.11 Henri Cartier-Bresson, *Sunday on the Banks of the Marne*, 1939. Gelatin-silver print, 9⅛ × 13¾ ins (23 × 34.9 cm).

8.12 Ansel Adams, *Clearing Winter Storm, Yosemite National Park*, 1944. Photograph.

which used a small lens opening (such as f/64) in the interests of exceptional clarity, sharpness of detail, and depth of field (sharpness of detail at all distances from the viewer), as illustrated by Adams' *Clearing Winter Storm, Yosemite National Park* (**8.12**). Such arresting images were largely the result of careful planning at the photographing stage rather than manipulation in the darkroom. Adams' full tonal range, from lush blacks, through many grays, to pure whites, is also a hallmark of his work.

In addition to introducing armchair travelers to human and natural landscapes they had never seen, the eye of the camera has also been used to examine familiar objects in such a way that they became unexpected visual pleasures. Barrie Rokeach presents an aerial view of a marsh with a road running through it (**8.13**) as a hauntingly beautiful play of colors, very much like a nonobjective Rothko painting (1.34).

8.13 Barrie Rokeach, *Aerial Photograph of Suisun Marsh, Solano County, California*, 1979.

8.14 Olivia Parker, *Four Pears*, 1979.
Photograph.

Many variables can be juggled for the effect the photographer desires: lighting, type of camera and lens, point of view, exposure time, film, paper, and developing and printing options. Olivia Parker uses these options to create an unfamiliarly heightened sense of realism in her photographs of "familiar" objects. Trained as a painter, she composes her images carefully before photographing them, adding the near-fluorescent red strings to the shriveled fruits of *Four Pears* (**8.14**). Parker comments:

> Although we think of photography as more "real" than the other visual arts, it allows for transformation of objects in ways I find especially interesting. The substance of an object can be altered by removing it partway through an exposure. Light can change form and structure. Objects or figures can exist as shadows yielding only some of their information to a piece. Color can be the color of an object as we think of it, the color of light around an object or a new color caused by filtration, additional projected colored light or the peculiar way a certain film and print material see color.[1]

It is one of the wonders of photography that the camera can capture details that the eye does not perceive. Many of us have seen halved artichokes, but as photographed at close range by Edward Weston (**8.15**), this familiar object becomes a world unto itself, a sensual, evocative vision of secret recesses. One of the most influential members of the f/64 Group, Weston used a classic large format 8 × 10 inch (20 × 25 cm) camera and did not enlarge his prints beyond that size, to avoid any distortion of the carefully previsualized image. Such photographs reveal the artist's love for the photographed object and inspire the same feeling in us.

8.15 Edward Weston, *Artichoke Halved*, 1930. Photograph.

Edward Weston

on

PHOTOGRAPHY AS A WAY OF SEEING

Edward Weston (1886–1958), one of the great figures in American photography, initially created out-of-focus, dreamy portraits. But in the 1920s he began a movement he called "straight photography," in which objects are shot in sharp focus, with attention to their details. He particularly loved the "sculptural" forms of vegetables, rocks, trees, the human figure. For him photography was an intense way of seeing, as well as the technical expertise to capture what he saw. The following are excerpts from his daybooks:

"B. sat to me again. As she sat with legs bent under (**8.16**), I saw the repeated curve of thigh and calf,—the shin bone, knee and thigh lines forming shapes not unlike great sea shells,—the calf curved across the upper leg, the shell's opening.

These simplified forms I search for in the nude body are not easy to find, nor record when I do find them. There is that element of chance in the body assuming an important movement: then there is the difficulty in focussing close up with a sixteen inch lens: and finally the possibility of movement in an exposure of from 20 sec. to 2 min.,—even the breathing will spoil a line.... My after exhaustion is partly due to eyestrain and nerve strain. I do not weary so when doing still-life and can take my own sweet time."

[He imagines explaining himself to his friend, the painter Henrietta Shore:] "You see, Henrietta, with the Graflex I cannot possibly conceive my complete, final result in advance,—as you can. I hold to a *definite attitude of approach*, but the camera can only record what is before it, so I must await and be able to grasp the right moment when it is presented on my ground glass. To a certain point I can, when doing still-life, feel my conception before I begin work, but in portraiture, figures, clouds,—trying to record ever changing movement and expression, everything depends upon my clear vision, my intuition at the important instant, which if lost can never be repeated. This is a great limitation and at the same time a fascinating problem in photography.

Imagine if you had to create in, at the most a few seconds of time, without the possibility of previsioning, a complete work, supposed to have lasting value. Of course my technique is rapid, and serves me if coordinated at the time with my perception."

"Point Lobos! I saw it with different eyes yesterday than those of nearly fifteen years ago. And I worked, how I worked! I did not attempt the rocks, nor any general vista: I did do the cypress! No one has done them—to my knowledge—as I have, and will. Details, fragments of the trunk, the roots,— dazzling records, technically

8.16 Edward Weston, *Knees*, 1927. Gelatin-silver print, 6¼ × 9⁹⁄₁₆ ins (15.9 × 23.4 cm). San Francisco Museum of Modern Art. Albert M. Bender Collection. Bequest of Albert M. Bender.

superb, intensely visioned.... Amazing trees—those stark, bone-white, aged ones, storm-swept and twisted into the most amazing forms. This sounds all too picturesque,—but wait—I have seen them with *my* eyes, at my best."

"I am the adventurer on a voyage of discovery, ready to receive fresh impressions, eager for fresh horizons, not in the spirit of a mili-tant conqueror to impose myself or my ideas, but to identify myself in, and unify with, whatever I am able to recognize as significantly part of me: the 'me' of universal rhythms. Nature must not be recorded with a viewpoint colored by psychological headaches or heartaches.... [I want] an honest, direct, and rever-ent approach when granted the flash of revealment."

"I have been training my camera on a cantalope,—a sculptural thing. I know I shall make some good negatives for I feel its form deeply. Then last eve green peppers in the market stopped me: they were amazing in every sense of the word,—the three purchased. But a *tragedy* took place. Brett ate two of them!"[2]

The integrity of real objects, landscapes, and people is only one possible arena for the photograph.

There are limitless ways of altering the realism of photography. Elizabeth Sunday uses reflective surfaces to elongate forms (**8.17**), to convey spiritual truths that are not apparent in conventional photographs. Sunday explains:

Using elongations allows me to go beyond the world of right angles into an inner place of emotions, where we live. We are so used to seeing the world as it appears in the material manifestation—in surfaces. I want to go behind and through that to someplace else.[3]

Sunday's photographs reveal a world in which everything is dynamic; nothing is as solid as it appears on the surface. In this lively unseen world,

8.17 Elizabeth Sunday, *Life's Embrace*, 1989. Silver print, 40 × 30 ins (101.6 × 76.2 cm). Courtesy of the artist.

8.18 David Hockney, *Gregory Loading his Camera, Tokyo, February 1983*. Photographic collage, 21 × 14 ins (53.3 × 35.5 cm).

whose truth is accepted as fact in modern physics, there are no sharp boundaries between humans and their environment.

Whereas we have tended to be very precious with photographs, handling them carefully by the edges, some artists have violated this taboo to cut into their pristine surfaces. David Hockney has done a series of photographic collages, in which the same image is photographed from varying perspectives and then the results cut and pasted together. The pieced images in Hockney's *Gregory Loading his Camera* (**8.18**) create a sense of process, of the event of seeing as well as of photographing unfolding through time, in a single unmoving two-dimensional framework.

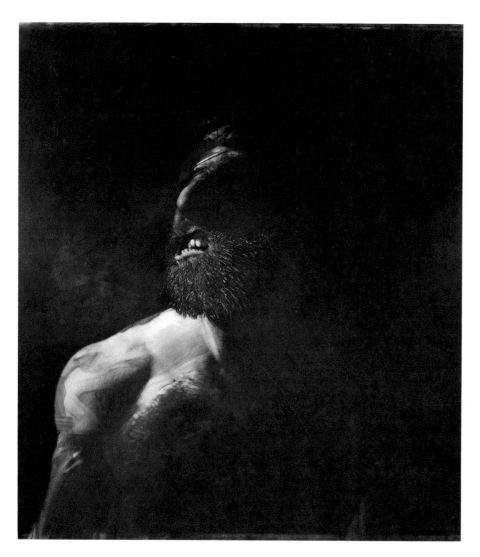

8.19 William E. Parker, *The Temperaments (Choleric II)*, from *Der Wilde Mann Series*, 1985. Handcolored black and white silver print—oil, aquamedia, wax crayon, graphite on Kodak Type N. polyfiber paper. Frame size 4 ft 1 in × 3 ft 9 ins (1.24 × 1.14 m), image size 3 ft 8 ins × 3 ft 4 ins (1.12 × 1.01 m). Eileen Cohen Collection, Great Neck, New York.

An artist can also work directly on the surface of a photograph, as William Parker has done in his "Wild Man" series (**8.19**). He photographs a person, makes a "grand-scale" photographic print from the negative, and then makes hand-colored alterations on the print with oil paint, wax crayon, pastels, and graphite sticks or powder. Why? In addition to the visual drama of such work, Parker says he wants to get beneath the emotionally vacant slickness of the Western male to reveal "a primal expressiveness, the energy that has been suppressed in the man who cannot express emotions."[4]

Computer manipulation of photographic images is another new field with yet unimagined possibilities. Japanese designer Susumu Endo takes photographs of everyday objects and natural scenes and then works with a computer operator to digitize and then transform them into magical visions which challenge our understanding of spatial relationships. In *Space and Space Forest 91A* (**8.20**), a forest photograph changes in hues and values, and is turned into sharp-edged blocks which appear, disappear, and spill beyond their edges. In the center, the imagery becomes so visually dense that it creates an ambiguous series of shadows, as if it were a three-dimensional object. Endo says he seeks to "explore and create new space, to express the co-existence of normal space and the space beyond focus where different planes are fused together."[5]

Technological advances in cameras and films are increasing the range of images that can be captured and manipulated. Stephen Dalton, for example, has developed high-speed photography as an exquisite art to capture images that usually pass unnoticed by the naked eye. Although our visual perception mechanism is fairly good at judging size, form, distance, and color, it cannot see what is happening when things are moving quickly. Moving objects tend to be seen as blurs; the retina cannot pass information to the brain or the brain interpret the information quickly enough to keep changing imagery in sharp focus. By contrast, the camera needs only to record an image; the brain of the viewer can interpret the arrested movement at leisure. Technological innovations such as high-speed electronic flash units now allow us to see what we could not see before.

Stephen Dalton's photograph in Figure **8.21** reveals the dropping of spores by a common horsetail plant. He has controlled values and composition in such a way that this seemingly commonplace occurrence becomes an elegant ballet; rather than appearing frozen in time, the cascading of the spores appears to be happening as we watch. Dalton insists that it is the observant eye of the artist which is most important in any form of photography:

> Clearly, equipment will not produce pictures on its own— the make and complexity of the camera have little to do with the final results and more often than not, the simpler the equipment the better. ... The beauty of the natural world can only be revealed to the eye and camera spending time in the field. Above all, it requires patience, light and an understanding of nature.[6]

8.20 Susumu Endo, *Space and Space Forest 91A*, 1991. Offset lithograph, 23½ × 23½ ins (60 × 60 cm). Courtesy of the artist.

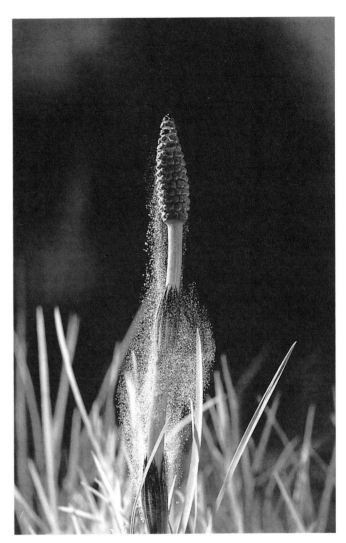

8.21 Stephen Dalton, Spores falling from the common horsetail. Photograph © Stephen Dalton.

PHOTOCOPY AND FAX ART

PHOTOCOPYING (also called "xeroxing," after an early trade name) is named after photography, though the process is based on a different technology. An original of some sort is exposed to a bright light; the light reflects off the white areas, is totally absorbed by the dark areas, and is reflected to varying degrees by gray and colored areas. In "indirect photocopying," this light image is focused by a lens onto an intermediate surface to form an image composed of electrical charges. These charges attract toner (photocopy ink)

8.22 Alcalacanales, *La Corrida de Cannes*, 1989. Xerox art, 3 ft 5 ins × 7 ft (1.04 × 2.13 m).
Courtesy Fernand N. Canales, Coleccion Museo Internacional de Electrografia, Universidad de Castilla.

which is transferred onto copy paper. "Direct photocopying" digitizes the light image—including analysis of colors—and prints them at high resolution by lasers.

Like photography, photocopying technology was not originally created as an art process, but artists have been quick to discover and experiment with its possibilities. Anything that fits into the imaging area can be copied; it can be moved during the copying process, creating blurred results. Color xeroxes can be over-copied, with colors mixing where they lie atop each other. Xeroxed images can be worked on, cut up, assembled, re-xeroxed. Alcalacanales' *La Corrida de Cannes* (**8.22**) is a photocopy collage created from a family photograph, manipulated repeatedly with layers of colors and drawings building up textural and spatial effects.

Anything that can be photocopied can also be faxed—sent electronically by telephone to a facsimile receiving machine anywhere in the world. David Hockney, who gained fame and fortune as a painter and photographer (see 8.18) became very uncomfortable with the astronomical prices some paintings—including his own—now command, so he switched to xerox and fax art. He explains:

On one hand, there is a movement towards unbelievable prices in art. On the other is a countermovement—fax art is essentially a Xerox copy, isn't it? What's it worth? Nothing. That makes the art world very nervous. They don't know what to do with it. But to me, that's what makes it great: You can send the exhibition anywhere. You don't really need much of a gallery. You can glue fax art on almost any wall.... You can give them away, or you can send them to Brazil or to Moscow—anywhere there's a telephone, fax machine, and a bit of paper.[7]

FILM

In photography a work usually consists of a single shot, but in a motion picture film a single frame is only one of a great number of consecutive shots. Viewed individually, each is like a still photograph, as in the sequences Eadweard Muybridge shot in the nineteenth century to analyze the components of animal and human motion. To photograph the movement of a horse galloping (to answer the question of whether all four feet were ever simultaneously off the ground) or a man turning cartwheels (complete with interference from a pigeon—**8.23**), Muybridge set up a line of 12 cameras whose shutters were tripped as the subject rushed by. Putting the images side by side in a strip suggested the idea of viewing them through the whirling toy called a *zoetrope*. This was a topless drum with slits around its sides through which a series of images seemed to merge in the viewer's perception as a continuous movement. The reason for this phenomenon is the *persistence of vision*. Our perceptual apparatus retains images for about a tenth of a second after they have disappeared. In a professionally-made film, images are typically presented to us at the rate of 24 frames per second.

Late in the nineteenth century, French inventions made it possible to record successive movements on a single strip of film; George Eastman turned this strip into durable celluloid. By the end of the century, means of projecting these images onto a screen for public viewing had been developed. Thus was laid the base for the use of moving pictures as an art medium: CINEMATOGRAPHY.

Cinematography is broadly defined as the application of photography to moving images. As an art, it involves the technical considerations of photography—such as the control of lighting, color, camera angle, focal length, and composition for desired emotional and atmospheric effects. In addition, it involves relationships between shots and scenes, and between images and sound (which is carried on a separate track alongside the images). These choices are made by a team. In addition to the

8.23 Eadweard Muybridge, *Headspring, a Flying Pigeon Interfering,* June 26, 1885. Victoria and Albert Museum, London.

person behind the camera, the team typically includes a director, a designer, a music director, a sound mixer, and an editor.

The ability to manipulate the elements of cinematography has been used to a certain degree in all films. When these manipulations make little or no attempt at the illusion of realism, films are often termed EXPRESSIONIST. One of the most extreme examples is *The Cabinet of Doctor Caligari* (**8.24**), which came out of the German Expressionist movement in the arts. Everything in the film was stylized to evoke a mood of dread, the world seen through the eyes of a madman. The sets were painted in stark black and white, with delirious diagonal lines, distorted perspectives, and strange painted

shadows. The spatial wrenching was mirrored by jerky, mechanical acting, portraying the nightmarish control of a sleepwalker's mind by the hypnotist Caligari.

The term *avant-garde* or *experimental* film has been applied to a great variety of works intended to make a philosophical or artistic statement with little regard for public taste. Some, such as *Un Chien Andalou* by Salvador Dali and Luis Buñuel, have even gone out of their way to shock. Conceived in rebellion against the art of "witty, elegant, and intellectualized Paris," as Dali wrote in his *Secret Life of Salvador Dali*, the film begins with a literal eye-opener: a close-up of a woman's eye about to be slit by a razor (**8.25**). This shot is followed by one of a

8.24 Robert Wiene, *The Cabinet of Doctor Caligari*, Germany, 1919. Decla-Bioscop (Erich Pommer).

8.25 Luis Buñuel and Salvador Dali, *Un Chien Andalou (An Andalusian Dog)*, France, 1928.

cloud crossing the moon, and then a close-up of the slitting of the eye (actually that of a dead animal). It was the Russian director Sergei Eisenstein who had pioneered this technique of MONTAGE—the splicing-together at editing stage of a variety of shots of brief duration to produce a complex visual statement. Although all the scenes in this film—which makes no visual reference to any dog—are composed of photographs of actual objects, they are as disorderly and yet as surrealistically vivid as images in dreams.

Even in more apparently realistic films, visual effects may be carefully manipulated to control the audience's response. Orson Welles' still-fresh *Citizen Kane* (**8.26**) is the portrayal of the life of a powerful press magnate. This classic work is a showcase for cameraman Gregg Tolland's brilliant use of *deep focus shots* (in which the viewer's eye can travel across subjects in many different spatial planes, all in focus), symbolic camera angles (such as the tilting of the image shown here to suggest the distorted nature of the politics in the film), *wide angle shots* that make people standing near each other seem widely separated in space, and expressionistic use of dark and light values.

In *Rashomon* (**8.27**), the famous Japanese director Akira Kurosawa's training as a painter is evident in the careful compositions of figures and the elegance with which the camera lingers over lights, shadows, textures, and visual rhythms. As in *Citizen Kane*, the

307

enigmatic narrative proceeds by *flashbacks* to previous events, as four characters each retell the story of a woman's rape and her husband's murder in a different way, leaving the audience to draw their own conclusions.

The ability to manipulate what the viewer sees—and knows—has often been used to create sensations of suspense or surprise. Alfred Hitchcock, director and producer of thrillers such as *North by Northwest* (**8.28**), observed that to build suspense one doesn't show the bomb exploding; rather, one shows the bomb ticking below the table and the people eating above it, unawares. Hitchcock's incitement of tension often has a sly, knowing humour behind it. In the famous scene shown here, Cary Grant, mistaken for a spy by an enemy espionage group, is being chased across a field by a lethal crop-duster. The horror of the chase is entirely invented: It was filmed with the seemingly terrified Grant running on a sound-stage with most of the scene—including the airplane—projected from the rear onto a transparent screen behind him.

8.26 Orson Welles, *Citizen Kane*, USA, 1941. RKO Pictures.

8.27 Akira Kurosawa, *Rashomon*, Japan, 1951. Daiei.

8.28 Alfred Hitchcock, *North by North-west*, USA, 1959. MGM.

Another general approach to filmmaking is the *documentary*—a true-to-life depiction of real people, rather than actors, living their own true lives, without an imposed story line or fake shots. To create the beautiful 1922 film *Nanook of the North* (**8.29**), filmmaker Robert Flaherty lived with the vanishing native people of northern Canada for 16 months. He shared the hardships of their lives in order to record their everyday activities within a harsh natural environment. The vast arctic whiteness was a constant backdrop for the naturally unfolding narrative.

8.29 Robert Flaherty, *Nanook of the North*, USA, 1921. Revillon Frères. Collection, The Museum of Modern Art, New York, Film Stills Archive.

8.30 Andrei Tarkovsky, *Nostalgia*, Italy, 1982. Opera Film/Sovin Film/RAI.

Finally, there is the film as a poetic image, mysterious and beautiful. The Russian filmmaker Andrei Tarkovsky's films, such as *Nostalgia* (**8.30**), have this quality. Tarkovsky spoke of the difficulty of staying true to the beauty of one's original inspiration when confronted by technical problems and the continual distractions of coordinating the efforts of so many people. He did not rely on editing to fix things; he specialized in *extended takes*, often incorporating entire 12-minute cans of film in the finished work. He did edit and join segments, but with keen awareness of the effect of editing on the viewer's sense of time in what is essentially a time-based art. He referred to filmmaking as "sculpting in time."

TELEVISION AND VIDEO

Television—a staple of the modern age—includes both live broadcasts and playbacks of videotaped sequences. In *live television*, VIDEO (visual) and audio signals are broadcast and read as images and sound on television sets far removed from the transmitter. There is little or no editing. In general, what the camera is recording at the time is what the viewers see. This immediacy can bring the emotional impact of distant events—such as the South Vietnamese Police executing a Vietcong officer (**8.31**)—right into our homes.

8.31 Eddie Adams, *Execution of a Vietcong Officer by the South Vietnamese National Police Chief in Saigon*, 1968.

311

Television camera lenses relay the amounts of light in a scene to a tube that translates light into electric signals. An electron scanner reads the hundreds of lines of signals so rapidly that the entire image is completely read 30 times a second. These signals, along with audio signals, are transmitted through the air by electromagnetic waves or carried by cables to television sets, where the signals are translated into the original pattern of light and sound. The persistence of human vision makes the separately transmitted signals seem to blend into continuous images.

Television signals can also be recorded on magnetic tapes, which can then be read by video and audio heads in a receiving device. Because a permanent recording is made, it can be manipulated electronically for special effects before it is shown. Some of the most innovative video effects are being created for music videos broadcast over special music video cable television channels. Images captured by a video camera can be computer-analyzed, broken down into their components, and then visually altered in an ever-expanding variety of ways.

Use of montage and special effects in television has accustomed us to responding to very complex manipulations of time and space. When viewers were first exposed to split-screen images on television—primarily in televised baseball games, where closeups of players on bases were shown at the same time as the pitcher winding up or the batter getting ready—they could not at first understand what they were seeing. Now multiple images can be presented very rapidly to a visually sophisticated public, and everyone is able to follow what is going on.

Since the 1960s, artists have also been experimenting with video as an expressive art form. Video art is collected and shown by museums, aired in performance spaces, and sometimes broadcast

8.32 Dara Birnbaum, *Rio Video Wall*, 1989. Twenty-five 27 ins (68.6 cm) monitors, installed at the Rio shopping and entertainment complex, Atlanta, Georgia. Courtesy of the artist.

over television channels. Those who are accustomed to the rapid pace of commercial television, with remote control over channel-changing, may find some art video sequences monotonous; their appreciation requires a more flexible sense of time.

The first experiment with outdoor, public video art in the United States has raised some new issues. Dara Birnbaum won an international competition to create a permanent "video wall" in Rio, an upbeat shopping mall and entertainment center in Atlanta (**8.32**). Many difficulties emerged as personnel changed in the overall project and as costs rose. Birnbaum's intention was to have her program playing continuously on a grid of twenty-five monitors. Part of the program is a montage of the natural wooded landscape which was destroyed to make way for the shopping center, which appears near the end of the 15-minute sequence. Birnbaum planned that this relatively restful imagery would be periodically interrupted by the news from a live satellite feed, displayed within the outline of the body of any shopper who happened to walk in front of cameras near the entrance and elevator. Since installation of the video wall in 1989, the "interaction" of shoppers with the news has largely failed to be displayed. The landscape sequence is basically shown by itself, for only 24 hours a week. The rest of the time, commercial interests use the wall for rock videos, advertisements for stores, and various spectacles. Legal negotiations were also necessary to define what comprised Birnbaum's work of art. The corporation paying for it insisted that the art consisted merely of the videodiscs; Birnbaum won her argument that the whole site-specific installation is her work of art.

Video is an art form with untapped potential, and its appearance on the art scene may hold yet more surprises.

COMPUTER VIDEO GRAPHICS

Lively experimentation is also underway in the field of computer-generated video graphics, technically known as *video raster graphics*. In these pieces, imagery is both generated and transformed digitally. The same processes are used as those described in computer drawing and painting, except that the potential for altering colors, reducing, enlarging, and rotating figures through space, and "photographing" them from differing focal lengths, all at great speed, is played out for the viewer in real time instead of creating a single image.

The first feature-length movie incorporating computer-generated animation was *Tron* (**8.33**). The

8.33 Walt Disney Productions, *Tron*, 1982.

8.34 Maureen Nappi and Dean Winkler, excerpt from *Continuum 1: Initiation*, 1989. Computer video created on Silicon Graphics 3130 work station with software including Wavefront 3D animation and Post Perfect object generation.

rapidity of computer calculations enabled the designers not only to design fantasy machines, but also to show them in realistic and continually shifting linear perspective as "light cycles" zoomed through illusionary space.

The same technologies are increasingly used to enhance the visual excitement of television commercials. Computer graphics have also been used to create animated representations of forms in our natural world that no one has yet seen, but that can be deduced from scientific data. These are primarily created for scientific study, but some are aesthetically exciting as well. Melvin L. Prueitt, of the Los Alamos National Laboratory, where this kind of computer imagery is generated, speaks of the beauty of the unseen world:

> The universe is filled with beauty, most of it unseen and unsensed. What does an intense magnetic field look like as it churns and bubbles near a neutron star? ... The narrow spectrum of our vision, our hearing, designed to detect the coordinated motions of molecules under restricted conditions, our sense of smell allowing us to detect only a few chemical compounds in the gaseous state, and our short-range sense of touch give us only a partial view of all there is.... Although science discovered myriad strange phenomena, we could not see them.... By computer graphics we begin to see what we have suspected for some time: that the foundations of the universe are filled with niches of loveliness.[8]

As the new field of video raster graphics grows, designers are also creating dynamic invented forms that tell their own visual stories of change through time and space, from varying "camera angles." They can be programmed for credible if unfamiliar "growth" and movements, such as the seemingly three-dimensional forms based on fractal geometry in *Continuum 1* (**8.34**)—a video allegory about cycles of life by Maureen Nappi and Dean Winkler. Nappi originally trained as a fine artist and then increasingly developed her engineering expertise. She explains that to a certain extent the visual ideas in *Continuum 1* are based on nature and made possible by computer technology ("There is a kind of condensation and abstraction that is not possible in any other medium"[9]). But they transcend both nature and technology, reflecting the artist's creative ideas and aesthetic and philosophical sensitivities.

The newest form of computer-generated experience is *virtual reality* systems in which the viewer also becomes participator in the action. This new technology allows architects to "walk through" buildings they have planned and examine what they will look like, before they exist in reality. Another application is an extension of video games: One enters a fantasy world by donning a headset with a pair of miniature monitors and earphones inside or putting one's head into a tunnel that blocks peripheral vision. A "tactile input device," such as a glove with sensors, transfers the movements of the participant's hand to the computer by fiber optics and a special tracking system. In addition to its potential for providing an expensive way to play in an altered reality, this technology may also prove useful to industrial designers. To make industrial mock-ups, the designer's hand may receive "sensory reaction" feedback to allow manipulation on the screen of "virtual solid objects" by a "virtual hand" (**8.35**). Both hand and object actually exist only as numbers but the designer can "feel" an object and alter it on the computer screen in a still-clumsy approximation of crafting something by hand. Computer technology is evolving so rapidly that these experiences will probably become more and more plausibly life-like. Will they be adapted to artistic purposes?

As computer graphics engineering advances, the question arises: Is computer graphics a new art form that does not require artistic sensibilities? Will the ease of creating complex, rapidly changing, brightly colored images by computer—now familiar to anyone who watches television commercials—change public tastes in art? Does computer art have

8.35 View of virtual reality system with pressure feedback for manipulation of virtual solid objects.
Courtesy of the designer Hiroo Iwata.

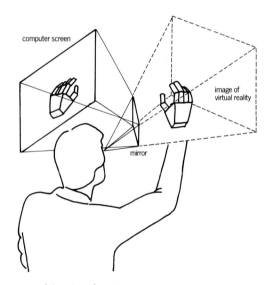

8.36 Set up of the virtual space.

any meaning, or is it just a display of technological brilliance?

Computers were not created as art media; they were mathematical tools designed to generate more mathematics. Those who have recently taken them up to create art are now beginning to explore issues of aesthetics and content in computer-generated art.

Just as early art photographs tried to imitate paintings, a major thrust of computer graphics has been to imitate photographs. Digital representation of familiar objects from the real world is becoming stunningly accurate, but is representational art the highest goal of this new medium? Just because computers can alter images with great speed, is there necessarily aesthetic value in doing so? And once computer artists have struggled to create an image, will they have the discipline to examine it critically from an aesthetic point of view and reject it if it does not work well? Will they use a great variety of colors just because they are available, rather than being more selective? As computer artist John Andrew Berton, Jr., observes:

> Objects created for a synthetic cinema piece generally represent a significant amount of creative effort, at least with today's technology. Thus an artist will often include objects in digital works simply because they are available, whether or not they carry meaning. Like all cinema artists, the digital animator must learn to throw away elements, occasionally, for aesthetic reasons, in spite of the work and technique that went into their creation. ... The computer makes the viewer believe that an object exists, but the artist must make the viewer believe that the object's existence has meaning.[10]

PART
3

THREE-DIMENSIONAL MEDIA AND METHODS

In our daily lives we are surrounded by works of three-dimensional art. Our clothes, buildings, gardens, cars, and functional objects all bear the designer's stamp, with varying artistic success, as do sculptural works whose main purpose is the aesthetic experience.

9

SCULPTURE

The three-dimensional media are not isolated on our walls and television screens. Instead, they exist in our three-dimensional world either as art objects or as our very surroundings. Our exploration of three-dimensional art begins with the fine art of sculpture.

There are four traditional ways of creating sculptures: carving hard materials, modeling soft materials, casting molten materials that will harden, and assembling materials that can be joined. Two other methods that fall somewhat outside these categories are shaping the earth into environmental works and creating sculptures that move through time and space.

CARVING

In the SUBTRACTIVE process of carving, the sculptor cuts away material from an existing piece of some hard material, such as wood, stone, or ivory. Often the original form of the material is totally altered in the process, but in Michelangelo's unfinished *"Atlas" Slave* (**9.1**), we can still see the rectangular block of stone from which he was extricating the form. "Atlas" seems almost to be struggling to free himself from the extra material. Indeed, Michelangelo, like many sculptors, felt that in carving away excess material he was releasing a form already existing inside the block. One of his poems includes these lines:

> The best of artists does not have a concept
> That the marble itself does not contain within it
> Within its surface, and only that is reached
> By the hand obeying the intellect.[1]

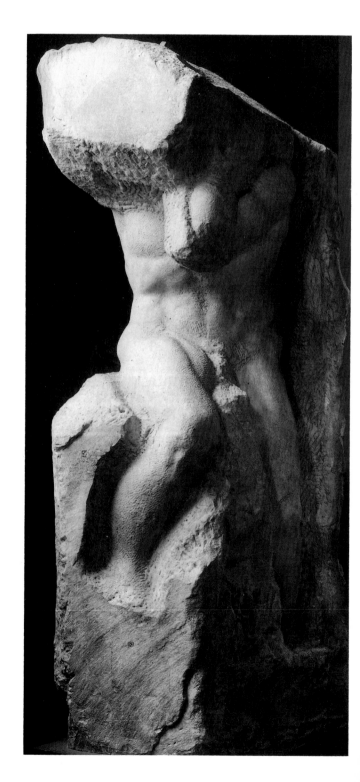

9.1 Michelangelo Buonarroti, *"Atlas" Slave*, c. 1513–20. Galleria dell'Accademia, Florence.

Michelangelo Buonarroti
on
MARBLE-QUARRYING

Michelangelo Buonarroti (1475–1564) was a true "Renaissance man"—sculptor, painter, architect, and poet. As a sculptor, he is best known for some of his earliest work, especially the colossal *David* (**9.2**) and the tender *Pietà* (14.21), both of which were executed when he was in his twenties. Whereas the *David* was carved from a huge block of marble that had been unsuccessfully begun by another sculptor, Michelangelo took personal responsibility for supervising the quarrying of other blocks of marble he was to use, as well as having them transported. In some cases he hired *scarpellini* (stonemasons) to do the initial rough carving of the forms. The following excerpts from his letters suggest some of the difficulties he faced in these processes:

March, 1518: "As the marbles [in the mountains of Seravezza] have turned out to be excellent for me and as those that are suitable for the work at St. Peter's are easy to quarry and nearer the coast than the others, that is, at a place called Corvara; and from this place no expense for a road is involved, except over the small stretch of marsh land near the coast. But for a choice of the marble for figures, which I need myself, the existing road will have to be widened for about two miles from Corvara to Seravezza and for about a mile of it or less an entirely new road will have to be made, that is, it must be cut into the mountains with pickaxes to where the said marbles have to be loaded."

April 2, 1518: "Commend me to his Magnificence and beg him to commend me to his agents in Pisa, so that they may do me the favour of finding barges to transport the marbles from Carrara. I went to Genoa and got four barges sent to the quayside to load them. The Carrarese bribed the masters of the said barges and are bent on balking me, so that I achieved nothing. . . ."

April 18, 1518: "These scarpellini whom I brought from Florence know nothing on earth about quarrying or about marble. They have already cost me more than a hundred and thirty ducats and haven't yet quarried me a chip of marble that's any use. . . . In trying to tame these mountains and to introduce the industry into these parts, I've undertaken to raise the dead."

December, 1523: "When I was in Rome with [Pope Julius], and when he had given me a commission for his Tomb, into which a thousand ducats' worth of marbles were to go, he had the money paid to me and sent me to Carrara to get them. I remained there eight months to have the marbles blocked out and I transported nearly all of them to the Piazza of St. Peter, but some of them remained at Ripa. Then, after I had completed the payment for the freight of the said marbles, I had no money left from what I had received for the said work, but I furnished the house I had in the Piazza of St. Peter with beds and household goods out of my own money, in anticipation of the Tomb, and I brought assistants from Florence, some of whom are still living, to work on it, and I paid them in advance out of my own money. At this point Pope Julius changed his mind and no longer wanted to go on with it."[2]

9.2 Michelangelo Buonarroti, *David*, 1501–4. Marble, approx. 18 ft (5.5 m) high. Galleria dell'Accademia, Florence.

Tools from hammer and chisel to chainsaw can be used to "liberate" the form conceived in the block. Sculptors may begin with drawings and a small clay or plaster model, or MAQUETTE, of the intended work.

The studio of the late Henry Moore (**9.3**) was filled with such maquettes. He explained to a visitor:

> Everything I do is intended to be big, and while I'm working on the models, for me they are life-size. When I take one in my hand, I am seeing and feeling it as life-size. ... When I've got the model in my hand, I can be on all sides of it at once and see it from every point of view—as a sculptor has to do—instead of having to keep walking round it.[3]

Working at full-scale, the artist then continually takes clues from the material itself as the form emerges. The form must fit within the bounds of the original block of stone or log of wood. Carvings often therefore have rather compact contours, to minimize the labor involved in removing excess material. A lengthy projection—such as an outstretched arm—requires a tremendous amount of labor in cutting away open space above and below it. Projections also present structural problems in materials with low TENSILE STRENGTH, such as stone. Tensile strength is the ability of the material to resist forces tending to

9.3 Maquettes at Henry Moore's studio at Hoglands, Courtesy Henry Moore Foundation, Hertfordshire, England.

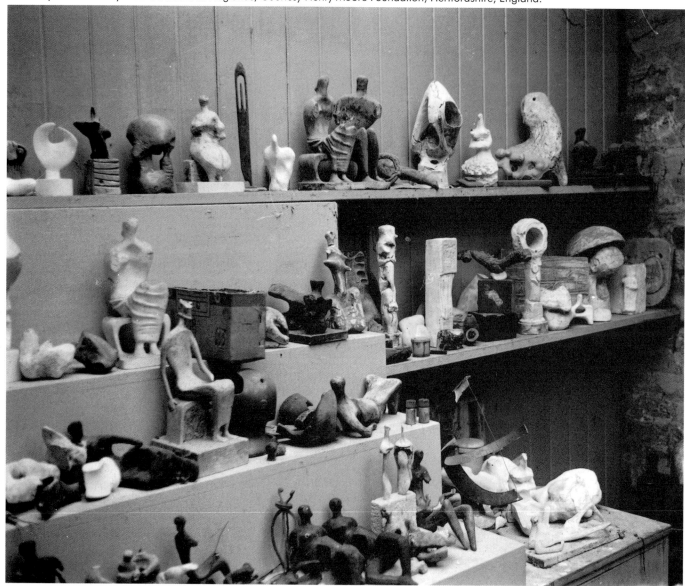

tear it apart—such as gravity, which pulls at thin unsupported pieces. Often a support is integrated into the design, perhaps disguised as clothing or a tree-stump.

Wood is a highly personal medium, warm and organic to the touch, rhythmic in its unfolding growth patterns, and requiring respect for the natural direction of its grain. If wood is protected from weathering and insects, it can be very long-lived. Beautifully carved wood reliefs over 4000 years old survive from ancient Egypt.

In the subtractive process of carving away, taking away too much is disastrous. To keep track of where they are in the block, wood sculptors may draw the outline of the intended piece on it and first remove any excess material that clearly lies outside of the outline, perhaps with a hand saw or even a chainsaw. A medium-sized gouge struck by a mallet may then be used to start working in toward the final form, with the block held in a vise. After this *roughing out* process approximates the desired final form, smaller gouges may be used to create fine details. For the finest of these, the gouge may be hand-driven rather than struck with a mallet. This is done across the grain in shallow strokes to avoid lifting fibers of areas that are to remain positive in the final piece. The sculptor continually reads and works the piece in the round, often referring to elevations previously drawn of the desired appearance from many sides. Finer details are often sketched on the wood itself as the form emerges. Donna Forma carved *Ode to Life* (**9.4**) from a large pine tree trunk some four feet (1.22 m) in diameter, removing a tremendous amount of excess material. She notes:

You have to visually imagine in your mind which are the furthest points out and then leave those and come in from them. In *Ode to Life*, I used just the basic chisel and mallet to come in to the form. A lot of people use a chainsaw when there is so much extra material, but I like using the chisel. It took a long time. It's always a problem no matter what size you work in—there's always that taking away the excess in order to show the form. Actually, you can't think of it as a problem, or you'll never do anything. From the very beginning, the whole time you are working on the form—it's just different steps. There are parts of it that are right out on the surface, whereas in other areas—such as under the bend of an arm—there is so much excess. But you are working all around the form so you're not just concentrating on one spot. Each person does it their own way—but I find that in working all around, it comes together better for me.[4]

9.4 Donna Forma, *Ode to Life*, 1988. Pine, 9 ft (2.27 m) high, original diameter of log 4 ft (1.22 m). Photo by Tom Forma.

Linda Howard

on

COMPUTER-AIDED SCULPTURE DESIGN

Florida-based sculptor Linda Howard (b. 1934) has been commissioned to create large-scale public sculptures that are installed in sites from Sydney, Australia, to Bogota, Columbia, to Fairbanks, Alaska. She assembles her sculptures from aluminum square tubing, welded into mathematically precise forms that nonetheless resemble natural growth patterns. Since this fabrication process is large-scale and demands precision of measuring and placement, Howard now uses a combination of two methods in designing and developing specifications for her pieces: maquette and computer-aided design.

"I first make a little model of styrene strips, perhaps five to ten inches tall. When I'm working on these small maquettes, I visualize them as being the completed size, and visualize myself as being about an inch tall. I never see them as small pieces; I always see them as big pieces. That's the way I think. I like the inside of pieces; I like being able to be inside, looking up, looking out.

Once the model is done, I put it on the computer as a wire-frame drawing. The three-dimensional volume of each square tube becomes four lines. You see it as if it were transparent, and all you are seeing is the edges. I don't see the drawing as solids, for I don't have access to a solids-modeling computer package.

In wire-frame, I can rotate the piece and look at it from different views. Seeing it in the wire frame gives you much more to look at than the solid maquette—the two-dimensional images of the three-dimensional model are very exciting, and they give you new ideas. I don't design new pieces on the computer from these wire-frame drawings, however. Because they are really three-dimensional pieces in three-dimensional space, I still really like a three-dimensional model in real space to work with. But I might see something on the computer that I then want to test out in actual 3-D.

In addition to their visual excitement, the wire-frame computer drawings give me all my shop dimensions, all the fabricating dimensions I need. It doesn't matter who is doing the fabrication—whether I'm cutting it myself or giving the specifications to someone else to cut. The computer provides the shop guide: all the lengths to cut, all the angles to cut.

The wire frame model also reveals how organic these structures are, like the curving growth forms of nature. It happens because of the way I run out the mathematic progression. I nest things. Each point

9.5 Linda Howard, *Centerpeace*, 1991. Aluminum, 14 ft × 24 ft × 16 ft (4.27 × 7.3 × 4.6 m). Bradley University, Peoria, Illinois.

9.6 Linda Howard, CAD wire-frame drawings.

has its own center of radius and they spiral because they are not turning off a common core.

The computer-plotted drawings can even become works of art in their own right. For *Centerpeace* (**9.5**), in cooperation with the Art Department and Engineering Department of Bradley University, we did wire-frame computer images from different eye level points of view. I did one from a central point of view, the way you would ordinarily look at the piece, another higher up, another higher up, and another down from the top. Then I mirror-imaged each one, and we are turning them into lithographs with watercolor backgrounds, named after the four seasons depending on how open or closed the piece felt from that viewpoint. It's a gorgeous sculpture, and the linear wire-frame drawings (**9.6**) are also beautiful in themselves."[5]

9.7 Woodcarving (above) and stone-carving (below) tools.

A number of tools (**9.7**) are used to give the piece a smooth finish, including a scraper with a beveled cutting edge that is drawn across the surface. It shaves off a thin layer of wood, clears the pores of the wood, reveals the grain, and compresses the fibers to make the surface glossy. If desired, the gloss is enhanced with a wax polish. Contemporary woodcarvers often LAMINATE, or bond, many thin layers of wood together before carving them as a block, revealing striations of color on the surface.

Although stone offers much more resistance to the sculptor's chisel than does wood, its permanence, colors, and textures have long been prized for creating subtractive sculptures. Sometimes the original surface texture of the stone is retained. The twentieth-century *Head of a Woman* by Modigliani (**9.8**) is carved directly into a limestone block, celebrating its stony texture with a deliberately "primitive" technique. Some traditional marble sculptures have been carved mechanically, often by hired artisans, by transferring measurements from a maquette to a block of stone, but such a process is not responsive to the uniqueness of the individual block. The sculptor may live with a block of stone for a long time, allowing it to "speak" its own nature before approaching it with a preconceived image.

Stone may be carved and polished to resemble non-stone textures, such as the youthfully smooth skin of Michelangelo's *David* (**9.2**). The nearly 18-foot-high (5.5 m) statue is famous for not only the beauty of its taut-muscled surface but also its ability to suggest a highly lifelike, dynamic energy within the form. The contrapposto attitude of the Biblical shepherd suggests that what is frozen in stone is only a brief moment in time, that David is only temporarily balanced in this asymmetrical fashion while preparing his slingshot for the giant Goliath.

Marble from the quarries at Carrara, Italy, is highly prized for its exceptionally fine, durable, translucent white nature. Granite is hard and more difficult to carve; sandstones and limestones, widely used in northern European architectural sculptures, are more granular. However, all kinds of stone—from the roughest limestone to the finest marble—can be polished to a high sheen, enhancing the stone's color, sealing the surface, and erasing the tool marks. After the lengthy process of carving the form, polishing the surface entails another series of steps. These may include smoothing with a flat chisel, filing remaining rough areas with a file or carborundum stone, sanding with wet sandpaper or an abrasive sanding screen, and rubbing with a polishing agent that seals the surface and makes it glisten. As these steps are taken, previously hidden colors and deeper tones will often appear, but so also may weaknesses in the design, requiring some reshaping of the piece.

The Chinese vase of jade (**9.9**) is painstakingly carved from a single block of the extremely hard semi-precious stone. Jade is so hard and brittle that artists may grind it with a power diamond-tipped bur rather than cut it with hammered chisels, claws, points, and files. Whatever the material, stone-carving is a slow and patient art.

9.8 Amedeo Modigliani, *Head of a Woman*, c. 1910. Limestone, 25¾ ins (65.4 cm) high. The National Gallery of Art, Washington D.C. Chester Dale Collection.

9.9 Magnolia vase, c. 1900. Jadeite, 10½ ins (27 cm) high.

MODELING

At the other extreme from carving hard stone is MODELING—the hand-shaping of soft, malleable materials. Some are so soft, in fact, that they cannot support their own weight and must be built over an ARMATURE, a simple skeleton of harder material, such as wood or wire. *Plaster* is typically built up over an

9.10 Jean-Antoine Houdon, *Bust of a Young Girl*, c. 1779–80. Plaster, 19½ ins (49.5 cm) high. The Metropolitan Museum of Art, New York. Bequest of Bertha H. Busell, 1941.

9.11 Urn Incensario with Figure Seated on Monster Head, Mexico, Tobasco. Classic Maya, AD 250–900. Unslipped buff earthenware, 16⅛ ins (40.8 cm). Indianapolis Museum of Art. The Wally and Brenda Zollman Collection of Pre-colombian Art. Photo by Justin Kerr.

armature by strips of fabric that have been dipped in wet plaster of Paris. The final layer is plaster alone, spread over dampened underlying layers with the hands or hand tools such as knife or spatula. Details—such as the modeling of the hair on Houdon's *Bust of a Young Girl* (**9.10**)—are then worked with a blade.

The use of *clay*—a fine-grained natural deposit—as a modeling medium was common in many ancient civilizations. Worked moist, it can be used to create quite fine details and then be fired to a hard, permanent state. It has more structural integrity than wet plaster, so it will hold slight projections,

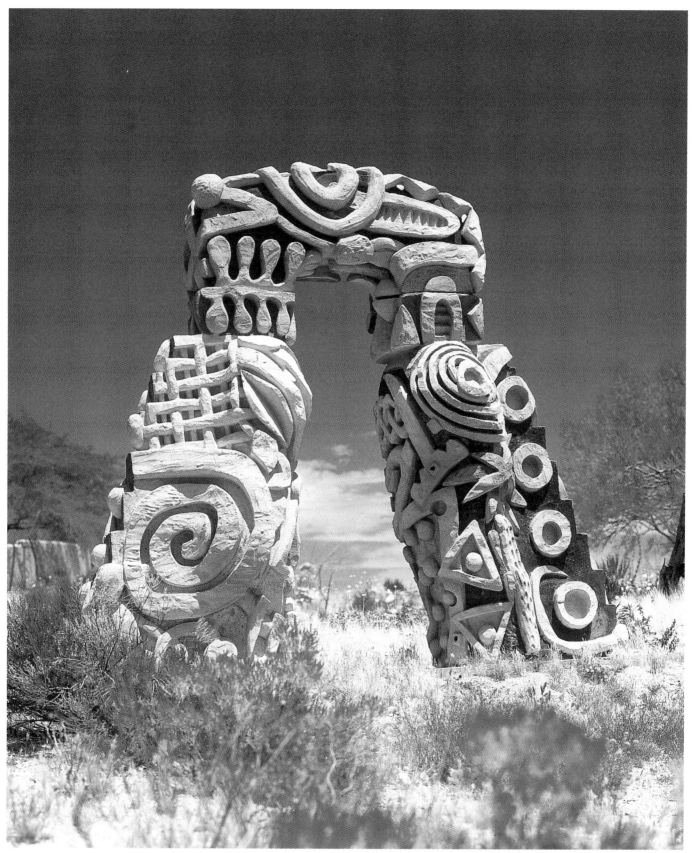

9.12 Arnold Zimmerman, arch for a private residence in Arizona.

such as the serpent and elaborate headdress above a man who may represent one of the two Hero Twins of the Mayan Popul Vuh mythology (**9.11**). The Classic Mayans of Mesoamerica had highly developed clay-modeling skills, sometimes used in creating naturalistic details such as the leg musculature and footgear bindings. In clay modeling, the major form may be coaxed into shape by the fingers; details may be added as lines incised into the form—as in the lines defining the Hero Twin's eyes—or extra bits of clay attached to the piece with SLIP (a mixture of clay and water), as in the Hero Twin's necklace, beard, and headdress.

Whereas free-standing clay pieces have traditionally been rather small, large kilns now allow huge constructions of clay to be fired. Even so, monumental clay sculptures are often constructed and fired in several pieces and then assembled, as can be seen in the joints of Arnold Zimmerman's great ceramic arch (**9.12**).

Wax is very easily shaped and reshaped when warm. It was used by the ancient Greeks for toy dolls and small religious statues and by the Romans to make death masks. But wax is vulnerable to melting when the weather is hot. It is therefore more often used to capture the fresh immediacy of hand-shaping and then cast in some more permanent material, such as the bronze cast of Degas' wax model of a galloping horse (**9.13**). The dabs of wax Degas pressed on to build up the form are clearly preserved in the cast. Some collectors prize such evidence of the artist at work.

9.13 Edgar Degas, *Horse Galloping on Right Foot*, c. 1881. Bronze cast of wax model, 11⅞ ins (30 cm) high. The Metropolitan Museum of Art, New York. Bequest of Mrs. H. O. Havemayer, 1929.

9.14 The lost-wax casting process.

CASTING

In CASTING, easily-shaped materials are used to create a negative mold into which a molten material such as bronze or plastic is poured and then allowed to harden. When the mold is removed, anything that was concave in the mold is convex in the cast form, and vice versa. If the mold is salvageable, multiple copies can be made of the same form.

This process, for which the Bronze Age was named, was refined by the ancient Greeks. They developed the LOST-WAX process illustrated in Figure **9.14**, which is still in use at contemporary foundries. A positive model (a) is used to make a negative mold (b), which is then coated with wax (c). The wax shell is filled with a core of some material such as plaster or clay (d). The mold is removed and metal rods are driven through

the wax into the clay to hold the layers in place, as shown in Figure **9.15**. Wax vents that allow the metal to be poured in and the gases to escape are fitted around the piece. This assembly is then coated with plaster—called the INVESTMENT—and buried in sand (e). The investment and sand are unharmed when this assembly is heated, but the wax melts. It is drained off, leaving an opening between the core and the investment that is filled with molten bronze. When it has hardened, the extraneous investment, tubes, and core are removed (f) and the halves of the cast are reassembled. What remains is a perfect hollow replica in bronze of the original pattern. Solid casting of large pieces does not work well, and hollowness economizes on bronze and weight. Even cast hollow,

bronze is quite strong enough to support the open, extended forms of arms and legs.

Despite their complexity, casting processes are capable of reproducing very fine details. In the fifteenth- to eighteenth-century kingdom of Benin in western Africa, intricate bronze castings such as the *Altar of the Hand* (**9.16**), which celebrated the divine king (the figure whose large head symbolizes his intelligence and power), were made by highly skilled

9.15 (left) Rods are driven into the wax replica to hold the outer investment in proper relationship to the core.

9.16 Altar of the Hand, Benin, Nigeria, Africa, 1550–1680. Bronze, 17½ ins (44.4 cm) high. British Museum, London.

9.17 Apollonius, *Seated Boxer*, c. 50 BC. Bronze, 4 ft 2 ins (1.27 m) high. Museo Nazionale Romano, Rome.

members of a respected professional guild under the direction of the king. While the Altar of the Hand is quite stylized, casts are also capable of reproducing very naturalistic detail, such as the anatomical and psychological accuracy of the Greco-Roman *Seated Boxer* (**9.17**). His musculature is superbly defined, and yet this is not an heroic, idealized portraiture. In the boxer's hunched, tired posture, broken nose, scarred body, and sidelong glance we can read a very human story, perhaps involving exhaustion, defeat, battered pride, or introspection about the emptiness of victory.

Benvenuto Cellini
on
A NEAR-DISASTROUS CASTING

The Florentine Renaissance artist Benvenuto Cellini (1500–1571) was one of the world's greatest goldsmiths (see his famous Saltcellar, Figure 1.48) and also a bronze sculptor whose *Perseus with the Head of Medusa* (**9.18**) is considered an amazing tour de force. His casting techniques were difficult and unique to himself, and the fact that the Perseus came out intact seemed quite miraculous, considering the dramatic problems that arose. In his autobiography he describes the drama that unfolded after the waxed, clay-encased, air-vented and drained mold was lowered into the pit of a specially built furnace:

"At last I called out heartily to set the furnace going. The logs of pine were heaped in, and my furnace worked so well that I was obliged to rush from side to side to keep it going. The labour was more than I could stand; yet I forced myself to strain every nerve and muscle. To increase my anxieties, the workshop took fire, and we were afraid lest the roof should fall upon our heads; while, from the garden, such a storm of wind and rain kept blowing in, that it perceptibly cooled the furnace.

Battling thus with all these untoward circumstances for several hours, and exerting myself beyond even the measure of my powerful constitution, I could at last bear up no longer, and a sudden fever, of the utmost possible intensity, attacked me. [In despair he announced to his helpers that he thought he was dying, left them with instructions for finishing the project, and went to bed, racked with fever.]

While I was thus terribly afflicted, I beheld the figure of a man enter my chamber, twisted in his body into the form of a capital S. He raised a lamentable, doleful voice, like one who announces their last hour to men condemned to die upon the scaffold, and spoke these words: 'O Benvenuto! your statue is spoiled, and there is no hope whatever of saving it.' . . . Jumping from my bed, I seized my clothes and began to dress. The maids, and my lad, and every one who came around to help me, got kicks or blows of the fist, while I kept crying out in lamentation, 'Before I die I will leave such witness to the world of what I can do as shall make a score of mortals marvel.'

[Cellini made his way back to the workshop, where he discovered work stopped because the metal had caked. He ordered hotter-burning oak wood to be fetched.] When the logs took fire, oh! how the cake began to stir beneath that awful heat. At the same time I kept stirring up the channels, and sent men upon the roof to stop the conflagration, which had gathered force from the increased combustion in the furnace; also I caused boards, carpets, and other hangings to be set up against the garden, in order to protect us from the violence of the rain. . . .

I then ordered half a pig of pewter to be brought and flung it into the middle of the cake inside the furnace. By this means, and by piling on wood and stirring now with pokers and now with iron rods, the curdled mass rapidly began to liquefy. . . .

9.18 Benvenuto Cellini,
Perseus with the Head of Medusa, 1554.
Bronze. Loggia dei Lanzi, Florence.

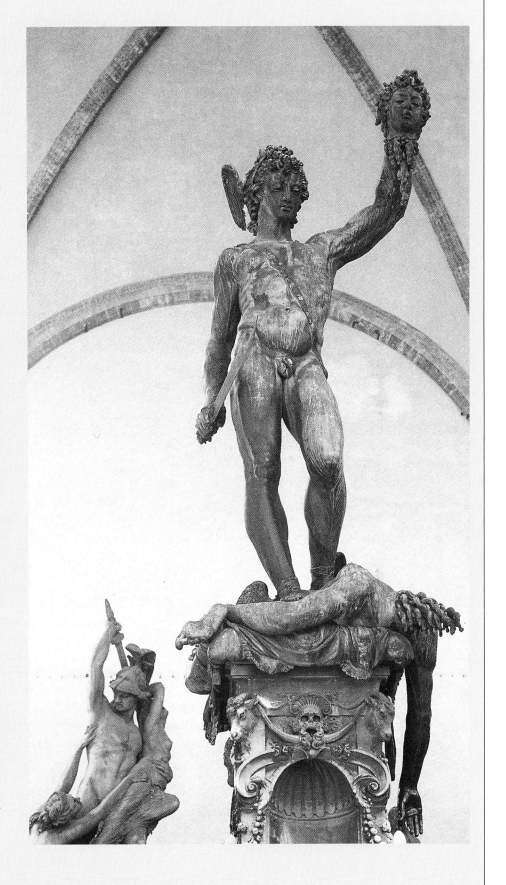

All of a sudden an explosion took place attended by a tremendous flash of flame, as though a thunderbolt had formed and been discharged amongst us. I discovered that the cap of the furnace had blown up, and the bronze was bubbling over from its source beneath. So I had the mouths of my mould immediately opened, and at the same time drove in the two plugs which kept back the molten metal. But I noticed that it did not flow as rapidly as usual, the reason being probably that the fierce heat of the fire we kindled had consumed its base alloy. Accordingly I sent for all my pewter platters, porringers, and dishes, to the number of some two hundred pieces, and had a portion of them cast, one by one, into the channels, the rest into the furnace. This expedient succeeded, and every one could now perceive that my bronze was in most perfect liquefaction, and my mould was filling. ... Seeing my work finished, I fell upon my knees, and with all my heart gave thanks to God."[6]

9.19 Richard Stankiewicz, *City Bird*, 1955–7.
Iron and steel, 27⅛ × 12¼ × 7¼ ins (68.8 × 31.1 × 18.4 cm).
Collection, The Museum of Modern Art. Phillip Johnson Fund.

ASSEMBLING

Another approach to sculpture is to fashion or collect pieces of varying materials and then somehow attach them to each other to form an aesthetically unified whole. Some works are assembled from FOUND OBJECTS, such as the cast-off metal parts assembled by Richard Stankiewicz into *City Bird* (**9.19**). He was a pioneer in the creation of "junk sculpture," in which industrially-manufactured goods which have been thrown away are given new life, new figurative identities. There is a certain poignancy in these homely creations, but also a sense of fun. Stankiewicz spoke of his joy when, in 1951, he first discovered in the yard behind his New York studio:

> a great number of rusty metal objects which seemed so beautiful by themselves that I set them aside as objects to look at.... things that were so decayed and corroded that you couldn't identify them, and of course, it was only a step of the imagination to combine various things together and make compositions from them.... [Found objects are] more provocative than invented effects. Also visual puns, mechanical analogies and organic resemblances in machinery provide a large and evocative vocabulary for sculpture.[7]

When a sculpture is obviously constructed of bits of found objects (not limited to the mechanical discards used in junk sculpture), it may be referred to by the French term, ASSEMBLAGE. Lucas Samaras's *Book 4* (2.69) is assembled from a book, pins, a razor blade, scissors, a table knife, foil, glass, and a plastic rod.

Louise Nevelson assembled large frontal sculptures of bits of turned wood, encased in a series of boxes. In her *Black Wall* (**9.20**), fragments are unified visually by the repetition of the box forms and the uniform black paint. Within this coherent framework, we are invited to explore the differences in form between the wood turnings and the varying ways they relate to each other.

In addition to unifying an assembled work visually, the artist must deal with the mechanical problems of physically joining the pieces so that they will not fall apart. Metal may be welded or bolted; a wooden piece may be held together with glue, nails, and screws. Nevelson has chosen to hide these joining techniques, whereas William King openly reveals the bolts uniting the sheets of aluminum in *Collegium* (**9.21**). In fact, the bolt heads are presented as part of the design interest in these tall-walking college figures.

9.20 Louise Nevelson, *Black Wall*, 1959.
Wood painted black, 9 ft 4 ins (2.84 m) high.
Tate Gallery, London, courtesy of the Trustees.

When an assembled piece seems to lack structural or aesthetic unity, the effect may be intentional. A certain disunity—according to classical principles of design—is an intentional choice of freedom to allow new things to happen in sculpture. This trend is particularly evident in contemporary assembled works and installation pieces. Judy Pfaff, creator of the installation *3D* (**9.22**) explains:

> I want the latitude of shifting thoughts in regard to materials, colors and references. I can't be bound by how they 'should' relate to one another. By going after a certain speed traditionally reserved for painters, I'm reaching for a crossing over of ideas and a weaving of thinking and making....
>
> What's happening now in sculpture seems really wide open and generous.... taking all sorts of permission and running with it, full out.[8]

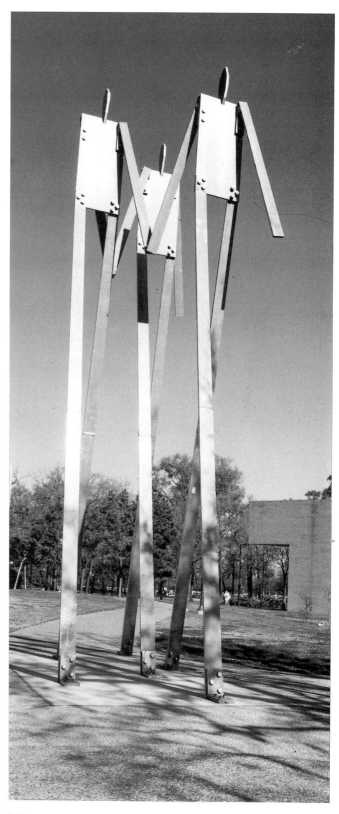

9.21 William King, *Collegium*, 1984.
Cast and plate aluminum, 32 ft (9.75 m) high.
Installation at the University of Houston, Texas, 1984.

9.22 Judy Pfaff, *3D*, 1983.
Installation piece made of mixed media, occupying a room 22 ft × 35 ft (6.7 × 10.7 m). Photo D. James Dee.

EARTHWORKS

Rather than sculpting materials taken from the earth, some artists have used the earth's surface itself as their medium. Robert Smithson's *Spiral Jetty* (**9.23**) is an immense spiral of 6000 tons (6,096,300 kg) of basalt and limestone laid into the primordial red water of Great Salt Lake. He said it was a concrete expression of the "gyrating space" he experienced at the site. The tools of earthwork artists become those of the earthmover, from shovels to bulldozers and dynamite, perhaps with the addition of structurally reinforcing materials, such as the concrete framing Michael Heizer used to strengthen the earth mound of his *City Complex One* (2.25).

Despite the huge amounts of rock and earth that are displaced and rearranged to create earthworks, their existence is often strangely ephemeral. Spiral Jetty has been inundated by the rising water of the lake. Heizer's huge gashes in the earth's surface have filled in again through erosion. Some earthworks now exist as art only in photographs taken when they were new. But permanency is not necessarily a goal of earth artists. Although their medium is the landscape, their subject matter is often mental concepts. Their writings and conversations often tend to be more cerebral than earth-centered. Heizer said he didn't come to the Nevada mesa because of the landscape:

> I didn't come here for context. I came here for materials— for gravel and for sand and for water, which you need to make concrete, and because the land was cheap. The desert is a flat and totally theatrical space. There is no landscape.[9]

Robert Smithson said:

> When you investigate tangible, physical fact this will set up a mental experience which is like the mirror. And how I perceive this is metamorphosed through my mental state, and then I translate that mental state into a physical state. In other words, I'm not just presenting materials, there's a kind of transformation that takes place. So that it's not a return to nature; it's like a subsuming of physical properties, and then gathering them into some kind of coherence, and this coherence can be quite a wilderness that is quite fascinating at the same time. Just like the actual wilderness, but in this case it becomes abstract, and it becomes a kind of entity that points to a lot of different possibilities.[10]

9.23 Robert Smithson, *Spiral Jetty*, 1970. Great Salt Lake, Utah, 1500 × 15 ft (457 × 4.6 m).

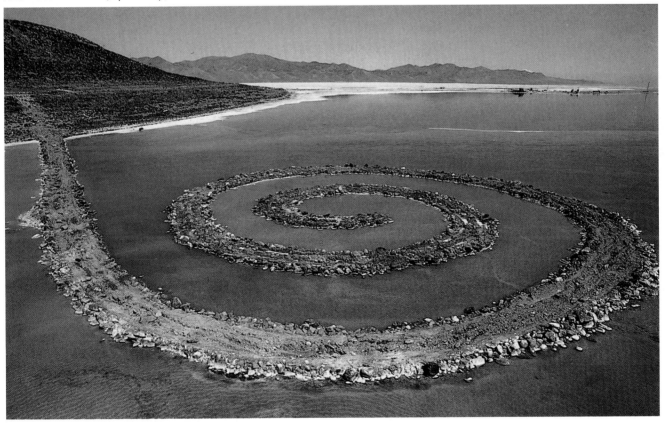

KINETIC SCULPTURE

Anything that will move can be used to create KINETIC SCULPTURE. Kinetic sculpture is not a basic technique, in the same sense that carving, modeling, casting, and assembling are sculptural techniques. But the requirements of making something movable warrant separate consideration. Pieces may have wind-up devices, motors, or be designed to use natural energies. Alexander Calder harnessed the energy of air currents or viewers' hands to propel his mobiles, such as *Lobster Trap and Fish Tail* (2.136). In the age of the mechanical contraption, the Swiss-born artist Jean Tinguely has invented absurd machines to perform artlike activities. The motor-driven arms of *Meta-Matic No. 9* (**9.24**) clamor like a kitchen appliance as they draw a small picture with colored pens. The product of this playful rattling busyness is a random drawing whose expressionistic quality is reflected in the form of the machine itself.

The term kinetic sculpture is now also applied to works made of lights that flash on and off, so that they seem to be alive in time. Contemporary kinetic sculpture may be computer-animated at a high level of technical perfection. But perhaps because we have become so accustomed to the sophistication of computer-driven devices, we may find the bizarre revealed mechanics of Tinguely's little machine all the more whimsically appealing.

9.24 Jean Tinguely, *Meta-Matic No. 9*, 1959.
Motorized kinetic sculpture, 35½ ins (90.1 cm) high.
The Museum of Fine Arts, Houston, Texas.
Purchased from funds by Dominique and John de Mevil.

10

CRAFTS

The appreciation of fine handmade objects is undergoing a rapid renaissance today. This trend may be a reaction to our highly industrialized surroundings, a reassertion of the value of what is made by human hands. Many craftspeople make no attempt to hide their tracks, for the sense of the individual at work may be more highly prized than machinelike perfection and sameness. Even though some craft objects are created in multiples on a semi-production basis, they may still reflect the human touch.

In general, crafts also tend to celebrate the materials from which they are made. One senses that the wood, clay, or fiber has been chosen and worked lovingly. This appreciation for natural colors and textures is contagious. To fill one's home with handcrafted functional items is to turn everyday activities—such as eating and storing food—into sensual experiences of beauty. We feel that these objects have been made slowly, with care, and they can evoke the same unhurried appreciation in us.

The major craft media are clay, metal, wood, glass, and fibers. All have been in use since antiquity, and many of the traditional methods are still employed. At the same time, many craft artists are experimenting with new techniques, materials, and approaches, sometimes to the point of using craft techniques to create nonfunctional works of art.

CLAY

The ancient craft of making objects from clay is called CERAMICS. Clays are found across the globe, but only those clays that are easily shaped and capable of being hardened by heat without cracking or warping are suitable for ceramics. Sometimes several different kinds of clay are mixed to form a *clay body* that has a combination of desirable properties. The most common clay bodies are EARTHENWARE (porous clays such as terra cotta), STONEWARE (clays that become impermeable when fired at high temperatures), and PORCELAIN (a very smooth-textured clay, translucent when fired, and with an extremely smooth, glossy surface).

Clay can be worked by freeform hand modeling, as in pinching a small pot out of a lump of clay. Three traditional methods of building up clay into larger walled vessels have been in use for thousands of years. SLAB BUILDING (**10.1**), used for straight-sided pieces, involves rolling out flat sheets of clay for sides and bottom. The joints are sealed with a rope of clay or with slip, a slurry of clay and water.

10.1 Slab building.

10.2 Coil building.

In COIL BUILDING (**10.2**), the potter rolls out ropes of clay and curls them in spiraling layers on top of a base, welding the bottom layer to the base and joining the coils to each other. Scraping and patting of the outside may be used to obliterate the in-and-out coiled structure. To build up a tall pot, the lower area must be allowed to dry and harden somewhat so that it will support the upper layers. For a narrow-necked piece, the upper layers are gradually diminished and then perhaps pulled out again. The potter must work all around the piece if it is to be uniformly rounded, so it may be placed on a hand-turned base.

The Native Americans, who used the coil method or molds for their pottery, were one of the few pottery-making peoples not to use the third major method: WHEEL-THROWING (**10.3**). The potter's wheel, found in the ruins of ancient Greece, China, and other early civilizations, is a flat disk attached by a shaft to a large flywheel. This lower wheel is kicked by the potter or driven by a motor to make the upper wheel turn. The continuous turning of the wheel allows the potter to literally pull the pot upward, symmetrically. After *wedging* (repeatedly slamming the clay onto a hard surface, cutting and folding it, and throwing it again, to remove air pockets and create an even consistency), the clay is centered on the wheel with the hands while the wheel is being rapidly turned. Working with both moistened hands, the potter then shapes the inside and outside of the pot at the same time by finger pressure applied in just the right places as the wheel is rotating. For a symmetrical form with walls of even thickness, the potter's hands must be disciplined to apply perfectly even pressure. After any of these building techniques—slab, coil, or wheel-throwing—the pot is typically GLAZED (painted with a material that turns glassy when heated) and FIRED (baked in a kiln or open fire) for permanence and water resistance.

10.3 Wheel-throwing.

Facility with such techniques allowed ancient artisans to create vessels that were as beautiful as they were functional. The elegantly proportioned wheel-thrown amphora from Athens (**10.4**) is of the type used to hold the prize of sacred olive oil for the winners of the Panathenic festivals. The foot runners, whose lines carry the eye around the width of the jar, were painted in black and white onto a ground of slip which turned red-orange when fired.

Some contemporary potters have eschewed elaborate ornamentation to bring out the beauty of the natural clays and earth-toned glazes. Karen Karnes' pots (**10.5**) are noted for their simple strength of form and the subtle glazes that emphasize rather than hide the grainy texture of the stoneware.

Another contemporary direction is the use of ceramic techniques for artistic expression rather than the creation of functional pieces. Clay is prized as a very plastic medium for nonfunctional sculpture, although clay processes are not easily mastered. Many variables come into play at every stage, requiring great skill and knowledge if the piece is not to be ruined during the firing stages. However, clay is sometimes built up without firing to create purposely temporary conceptual pieces (2.144) in contrast to fired clay's ability to withstand decay over thousands of years.

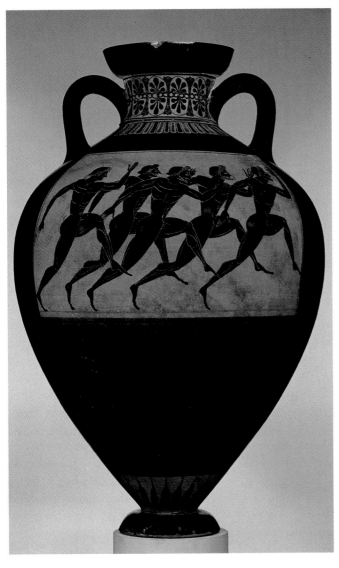

10.4 Attributed to Euphiletos painter, Black-figured prize amphora, Athens, c. 530 BC. 24½ ins (62.2 cm) high. The Metropolitan Museum of Art, New York. Rogers Fund, 1914.

10.5 Karen Karnes, Stoneware pot with lid, 1982.

Paula Winokur

on

WORKING IN CLAY

Paula Winokur (b. 1935), has been working in clay for over 25 years. At mid-century, like most other ceramists, she was creating functional pottery. She has continually evolved along with this rapidly-evolving medium, and has for some time been using clay to express ideas sculpturally. Many of her recent works conceived as fireplace mantels or arches (**10.6**) are in major museums and private collections.

"In college I majored in both painting and ceramics, which was a strange combination at that time. When my husband Bob [also a renowned ceramist] and I moved to a farm in Massachusetts in 1964, I really began to find out about working with clay, because we started doing production pottery [making multiples of the same objects]. That in itself was like going to graduate school, because we made a lot of mistakes and learned a lot.

There is a certain satisfaction in making the same forms over and over again. I used to make fifty cups at a time, which really isn't that much. A good Japanese thrower will make hundreds of something in one day. You would set a goal of how many of what you were going to make in the day, and you would do it, and it was a business.

Simply functional pottery was the accepted mode in the early fifties until Peter Voulkos and that California crew started shaking things up. The material used to be associated with pots and figurines. People didn't think of it as a fine arts material. That's what I grew up with: You made pots, and you made them for use. Now there has been tremendous interest in the material and all of its potentials as a sculptural medium that can be used to describe all sorts of things—political statements, aesthetic statements, one's internal musings. I think what I've done in the past few years is combine my original interest as a painter with what I'm doing in clay, although I'm not using it as a painter—I'm using it more as a sculptor. The things that have happened in the clay world have allowed people the flexibility and opportunity to do whatever they want with it.

Now in my work I'm trying to explore my ideas and use the clay as a vehicle for those ideas. The mantels say something about precipices; as a society, as a species, we are always on the edge, ready to fall off. When I visited Mesa Verde in southwestern Colorado, the peculiar window openings and niches in the canyon walls and the precarious

cliff ledges were of great interest to me. The spirit of the Anasazi, the ancient ones, surrounds the place. I was fascinated by the shapes and forms, some left for hundreds of years, some eroded by time and some arranged by the caretakers. Somehow this is information that I continue to use, sitting here in my East Coast studio on flat ground.

Production pottery was physically demanding; many potters have backaches. Doing unique pieces is also very physical. We make our own clay body. We buy bags of a particular clay, a particular feldspar, silica, and grog, and mix all these things together. That's time-consuming and labor-intensive. At this point, I train students to help me do it. I don't trust just anybody to make my clay body, because in my unglazed porcelain pieces, the clay is the whole thing. If something goes wrong, I can't hide it with glaze.

For these big pieces, I wedge maybe 200 pounds of clay at once and then lay out the slabs, let them stiffen, and put them together. Once I understood that you don't have to make something of clay as a single piece, that you could use many parts and put them together, then scale became no problem for me. The big archways are four or

10.6 Paula Winokur, *Entry I: Sakkara*, 1986.
Porcelain, 102 × 53 × 10 ins (259 × 135 × 25.4 cm). Courtesy of the artist.

five sections on each side, constructed and fired separately, and then put together with grout over an internal structure of pipe that holds it all together. I usually start by making a cardboard template of the different sections. Then if something should break, I can just remake that section. It does happen: I was carrying one piece of one of the fireplaces to the kiln to fire it. I hit it against the side of the table and it went "Kronchh!" and just fell apart.

Despite years of experience, sometimes I still lose things in firing, or sometimes I don't like the way something looks. Clay does have that element of risk, and you wonder why you keep doing this. But I've been committed to this particular material a long time. A lot of people look at someone throwing and say, "Oh, I can do that," and then they sit down at the wheel and realize that to be a really good thrower takes years of practice."[1]

METAL

Like clays, many metals are quite amenable to being shaped. Those used for handcrafted objects have included copper, brass, nickel, pewter, iron, and the precious metals gold, silver, and platinum. They vary in MALLEABILITY (the capacity for being shaped by physical pressure, such as hammering), DUCTILITY (the ability to be drawn out into wire), and hardness. Gold is the most ductile and malleable and is of course prized for its untarnishing color and luster. It is often drawn into wires and shaped into jewelry;

Benvenuto Cellini's masterpiece, the saltcellar for Francis I (1.48), is made of gold and further ornamented with ENAMEL, a glass-like, jewel-toned coating that can be fused to metal by heating.

At the opposite extreme, iron and steel (an alloy of iron and other materials) are the hardest of the common metals and among the least malleable. But they are somewhat ductile and when heated are malleable enough to be FORGED (hammered over an anvil), stretched, and twisted into forms such as

10.7 Joseph L. Brandom, Utensils and Rack, 1982. Stainless steel, rack 39 ins (99 cm) long.

punching, splitting, bending, incising, or REPOUSSÉ (hammering punches against a sheet of metal from the back to create a low-relief pattern). Individually worked pieces of iron can be riveted, screwed, bolted, brazed, or torch-welded together, but purists prefer the traditional hammered weld, with pieces heated to the point at which they will fuse.

Metal can even be coaxed into hollow vessel forms by *raising* (hammering a flat sheet over a stake to raise the sides and work them inward). Douglas Steakley's raised copper vessels (**10.9**) have been purposely textured with marks of punch and hammer to accentuate their handcrafted appearance and add subtle textural interest to their asymmetrically curving surfaces.

10.8 Szabó, Clock, c. 1924. Wrought iron.

Joseph Brandom's kitchen utensils and rack (**10.7**). These combine the sought-after feeling of old-fashioned blacksmithing technology with a light, clean, contemporary design. Note that some of the hammering marks are retained, for the desired handcrafted appearance. If a metalsmith chooses to erase all hammer marks, bulges, and wrinkles from a piece, it can be PLANISHED smooth with a flattening hammer. As metal is worked, it may also need to be continually ANNEALED, or heated to make it more malleable, because many metals harden when they are hammered.

Iron that is worked in a heated state with hand tools is called WROUGHT IRON, in contrast to *cast iron*, in which molten iron is poured into molds. Szabó's extraordinarily crafted wrought-iron clock (**10.8**)—a product of the early twentieth-century rebirth of art metalwork in France—achieves the delicate filigree usually seen only in jewelry fashioned from fine wires. Such decorative details may be created by drawing out, hammering over varied forming stakes,

10.9 Douglas Steakley, Raised vessels.
Copper, left 8 ins (20 cm) high, right 5 ins (13 cm) high.

10.10 "Sea Dog" table, mid 16th century, based on designs by Jean Jacques Androuet du Cerceau. Walnut. Hardwick Hall, Derbyshire, England.

WOOD

Because trees grow in most parts of the world, and because wood is sturdy and fairly easily shaped by saw, chisel, lathe, file, and sanding devices, it has been pressed into service by artisans of most cultures. Its warmth to the touch, smoothness when sanded and polished, rich natural colors, and lively growth patterns give it a highly sensual appeal. It has been used to fashion everything from picture frames and furniture to kitchen utensils, toys, and musical instruments. Many handcrafted wooden objects are now valued as collectors' items, from jewelry boxes with ebony inlays to folk art pieces made of soft woods such as pine and spruce. These soft woods are not necessarily the easiest to work, for they may

splinter. Medium-hard woods include birch, butternut, cherry, pear, and apple; the durable, fine-grained hardwoods include walnut, oak, maple, hickory, teak, ebony, and rosewood.

Wood can be worked into extremely ornate forms, such as the sixteenth-century walnut "sea dog" table (**10.10**) in the Withdrawing Room of Hardwick Hall in England. It may have been a royal gift to Hardwick Hall's original owner, Elizabeth, Countess of Shrewsbury. This extreme elaboration of a table's function is based on the designs of Jean Jacques Androuet du Cerceau, French designer of architecture and fantastic ornamentation.

Some contemporary crafters of wood take a much simpler approach to the medium, allowing it to express the more natural linear qualities of trunk and branch. The large refectory table (**10.11**), designed by Fred Baier and Chris Rose for limited production by Professional Woodworkers, has the lithe grace of a bridge. The curve of the oak slab transforms its heaviness into a dynamic lightness, accentuated by the growing and diminishing lengths of the many cross-members. Although trees grow in relatively straight lines, their wood can be bent into curves when steamed, as in the slab here and the bentwood Thonet chair shown earlier (2.15).

Those who use milled lumber—such as the uniform boards and poles from which the refectory table is built—typically look for clear wood, with no cracks or knots where branches grew out of the main trunk. But some woodworkers purposely seek out and emphasize "defects" in wood for their design interest. Burls—woody hemispherical knobs that grow on the trunks of certain trees—have curling linear patterns that are often used to advantage in veneers (thin overlays of fine woods placed over other woods) and in handcrafted bowls. The art of Mark Lindquist's wood bowl (**10.12**) is less a matter of imposing a design on it than of careful selection of the burl and respectful minimal working to bring out the natural beauty of its sinuous curves.

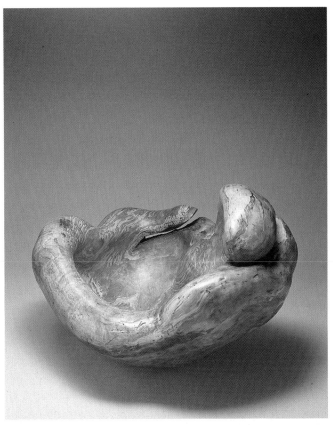

10.12 Mark Lindquist, *Toutes Uncommon Bowl*, 1980. Spalted yellow birch burl, 32 ins (81.2 cm) long. Collection: Duncan and Mary McGowan.

10.11 Fred Baier and Chris Rose, Refectory Table, 1985. Oak, 23 ft (7.1 m) long. Professional Woodworkers Ltd., U.K.

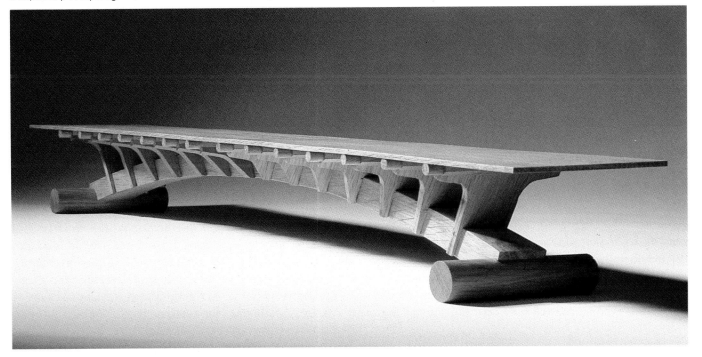

George Nakashima

on

A FEELING FOR WOOD

George Nakashima (1904–1990) was a designer and craftsman of the highest order. Trained as an architect, he began designing handcrafted wood furniture in the 1930s and developed a deep appreciation for the nature of wood from a Japanese woodworker in an internment camp during World War II. When his family was released from the camp, they moved to New Hope, Pennsylvania, where Nakashima established a furniture-making business. His work has many distinctive characteristics, including revealed joinery, architectural bases, and slabs of solid wood (rather than veneers) in which the natural edges are valued. His largest piece is the *Altar for Peace* (**10.13**), installed in the Cathedral of St. John the Divine in New York City as a shrine where people from around the world can pray and meditate. The following excerpts from his writings reveal his attitudes toward his material:

"It is not always ... easy to find the best expression of a piece of wood, and sometimes I will keep an extraordinary piece for decades before deciding what to do with it. This process of selection and usage is the creative act ... of the woodworker. It is this point of personal involvement with personal decision that might be called the essence of the craft. There is always an individuality that distinguishes craftsman-made furniture from mass-produced pieces. There is life there, and it is at odds with the lifelessness of high technology and mass production."

"In commercial lumber, knots and other imperfections are scorned. Only unblemished lumber will command upper-bracket prices. ... Lesser grades of wood have more extensive figuring and many knots and other defects. They are less expensive, and in fact, logs of 'poor' quality may sometimes be had free of charge. To me, however, it is not the economy but the quality of this wood, the 'uniqueness' imparted by the imperfections, that makes these pieces appealing. Some of my most interesting work has come from logs that seemed hopeless to others. They have inspired a creative act and a close relationship with nature.

I search for the pieces with huge knots or with gaping cavities. I am drawn to the root section, which has been underground and has an exceptional quality, offset by one potential problem: Roots often swallow up stones by growing around them. The root of a great tree such as a giant redwood is almost a natural treasure lying underground. It must be dug from the earth carefully, often by hand with machinery doing only the heaviest part of the work. Some roots can remain in the ground for a century and still be usable."

"Searching out the unusual specimens is an adventure. Deciding how to cut them is a challenge. The thickness and direction of the cut will determine the product that comes from them. I often meditate on a piece for many years before making a final decision. Sometimes a dialogue with a client will inspire the cut of a piece."

10.13 George Nakashima, *Altar for Peace*, made for the Cathedral of St. John the Divine, photographed in his New Hope, Pennsylvania studio, 1986.

"Sadly, many of the world's great trees end up as nothing but a common object, cut into paper-thin veneers or parcels of thin wood for novelty boxes or something similar. Part of my destiny has been to intercept this process and give some trees a fitting and noble purpose, helping them to live again in my work."

"As materials and resources become more and more limited around the world, products of beauty and utility will almost have to become more efficient as man confronts the dwindling reserves of nature.... Back in our woods, in New Hope, I continue to make casual objects, objects as simple as a tea bowl. I pursue the path of low technology, away from the murderous syndrome of 'progress.' The fight for beauty has occupied my lifetime, and I have sought to create beauty in a world where little of it seems to exist. My efforts are small points of light within a large light that is still possible and can grow to a great illumination."[2]

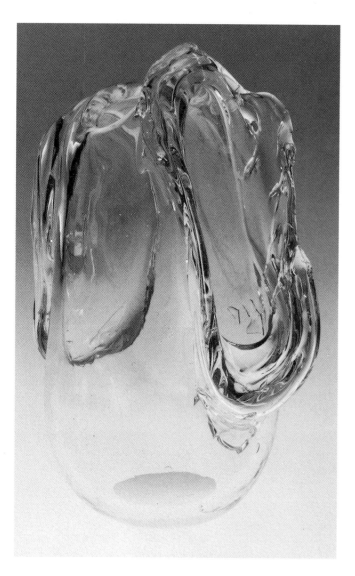

10.14 Harvey Littleton, *Vase*, 1963. Hand blown clear glass, 9¾ × 7½ × 4⅞ ins (24.8 × 19 × 12.4 cm). Collection, The Museum of Modern Art, New York. Greta Daniel Design Fund.

10.15 (right) Dale Chihuly, *#2 Sea Form Series*, 1984. 3 ft 8 ins (1.12 m) wide. Courtesy Foster/White Gallery, Seattle.

10.16 (opposite) René Lalique, *Glass vase*, c. 1905–10. Cast glass, 6 ins (15.2 cm) high. Private Collection, Miami.

GLASS

For all its fragile transparent beauty, glass is made by the surprisingly simple process of melting sand with lime and soda. The technique has been in use for at least 3500 years for creating luxury versions of everyday functional objects.

One of the most common ways of making glass vessels is to scoop up a glob of molten glass with a long metal blowpipe and blow it into a bubble while shaping its form with hand tools. The liquidity of the glass before it hardens is captured in Harvey Littleton's freely blown and draped glass vase (**10.14**). Littleton was a pioneer in the twentieth-century "studio glass" movement, in which fine artists have learned the craft of glassblowing, expanding the medium far beyond traditional concepts of what can be done in glass.

Before the twentieth century, glass production had been done by skilled glassblowers using techniques

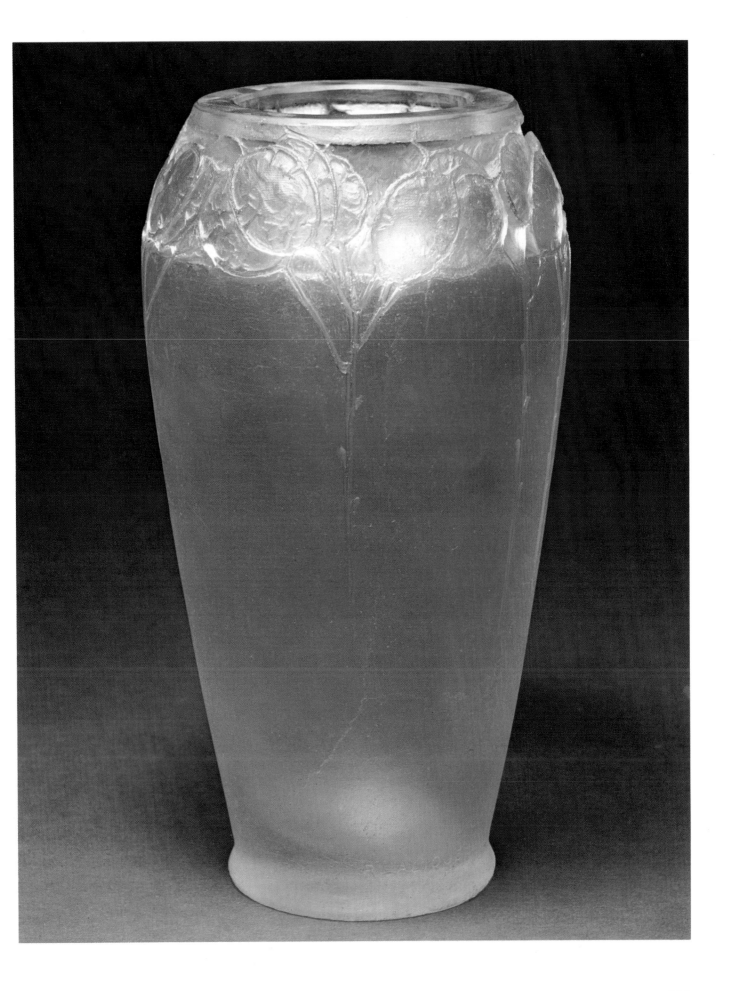

thousands of years old. But industrial techniques were developed that gradually ended the demand for glassblowers. Even in those art glass studios that remained, the process was broken down into a series of steps handled by different specialists.

By the 1920s and 1930s there were only a few traditional glass craftsmen left. Given the rigors of the profession, it is not difficult to imagine why it was largely abandoned. Maurice Marinot, one of the last great glass artists in France, described what it was to work with such a hot medium:

> To be a glassmaker is to blow the substance to transparency into the blind furnace and to reblow it with tools of his art—his lips: to work in the heat, sweating with fever, the eyes full of tears, the hands seared and burnt.[3]

Nevertheless, glass was an enchanting medium with great aesthetic potentials—brilliance, light reflection and refraction, bubbles, iridescence, gem-like colors, extreme malleability when hot. Picking up from Marinot, Harvey Littleton (who had been a ceramist) and a few other artists and technicians held workshops in 1962 to create glass techniques that could be used by individual artists rather than factories. They worked with a new type of glass that was cheap, durable, and easy to melt. The furnace was fitted with a triple hinge; this innovation eliminated the need for an assistant, for the glassblower could close it with just an elbow while holding the blowpipe. The participants were so excited by their discoveries of what could be done with glass that they kept the furnace busy from 5:30 in the morning until midnight.

From this new start, studio glass has become a very dynamic feature of the contemporary art scene. Dale Chihuly is a major figure in today's rapidly evolving art glass field. Many of his pieces take off from traditional ways of forming glass as containers but exuberantly transcend functionality. His *#2 Sea Form Series* (**10.15**) is a dynamic sculptural play of flowing, organic forms, lines, and colors, heightened by the translucent qualities of the glass.

Glass can also be cast. The lost-wax ("cire perdue") process produces one-of-a-kind pieces. René Lalique, one of the great names in glass design, began his studies of the possibilities of glass with the lost-wax casting process. Pieces such as his glass vase shown in Figure **10.16** are prized by collectors not only for their subtle design and the beauty of the glass but also because they retain the human touch: the thumbprints of the modeler, which can be seen in the

flowers. Lalique soon abandoned these unique handcrafted pieces and turned to mass production of beautifully designed glass tableware, vases, bottles, boxes, jewelry, lamps, and panels for luxury cars, trains, and ocean liners.

In addition to blown and cast vessels, glass is also blown or poured into sheets to make two- or three-dimensional works that both admit and transform light, as in lamp shades or cathedral windows. ANTIQUE GLASS, prized for its metal oxide brilliance and its "imperfections" such as bubbles and warps, is blown by a glassblower as a cylinder, cut lengthwise, and heated until it lies flat. For STAINED GLASS, chemical colorants are heated with the base glass in a kiln until they fuse. OPALESCENT GLASS, developed by Louis Tiffany and John La Farge, incorporates soda ash for opacity; the glassmaker swirls bright color oxides through the molten glass as it is poured out into a sheet. To create designs of different colors, pieces of stained glass are cut and then joined by means of soldered lead channeling, copper foil, glue, or heat fusing. Tiffany's virtuosity with glass is especially evident in his windows (**10.17**). They are mosaics of his custom-made glass, thousands of pieces cut and pieced together with dark lead strips—which also serve a design function as outlines defining the shapes. But unlike medieval stained-glass windows, the colors within the shapes are not solid; rather, they are mottled and swirled and juxtaposed to create lush and dynamic interplays of colors. Tiffany refused to paint on the glass, for to do so would inhibit the brilliance of the light effects.

FIBERS

Another ancient craft that is presently undergoing a great resurgence of interest is *fiber art*. This broad category includes everything made of threadlike materials, usually woven or tied into larger wholes. Many of these works are conceived with the functional purpose of maintaining warmth, such as the TAPESTRIES created in many ancient cultures. In Gothic Europe, tapestries were designed to take the chill off the cold masonry walls of castles and cathedrals during medieval Europe's mini-Ice Age. In these heavy handwoven textiles, pictures were woven directly into the fabric. A cartoon of the desired image was drawn on the *warp*, the lengthwise threads strung on the loom. As the crosswise *weft*

10.17 Louis Comfort Tiffany, *Irish Bells and Sentinels*, left panel of triptych window, St. James Country Club, outside Perryopolis, Pennsylvania. 6 ft 8 ins (2.03 m) wide.

10.18 *The Unicorn in Captivity*, from the *Unicorn Tapestries*, c. 1500. Silk and wool, silver and silver-gilt threads, 12 ft 1 in × 8 ft 3 ins (3.68 × 2.51 m). The Metropolitan Museum of Art, New York. The Cloisters Collection, Gift of John D. Rockefeller Jr. 1937.

10.19 Carpet from Tabriz, Iran, Safavid period, 16th century. Wool pile on cotton and silk, 26 ft 6 ins × 13 ft 7 ins (8.07 × 4.14 m). The Metropolitan Museum of Art, New York. Gift of Samuel H. Kress Foundation, 1946.

They were nonetheless treasured family possessions, and in the sixteenth century, Europeans began collecting them as works of art. In everyday use, they can last a hundred years, and the older sun-mellowed ones are much sought-after. The highest quality rugs are made from the wool of sheep grazed at high altitudes. The wool is knotted at densities ranging from 60 to 600 knots per square inch (2.5 cm^2).

Baskets woven of pliable materials are a form of fiber art used by many traditional cultures. A contemporary basketmaker, Susye Billy of the native Pomo people in California, the creator of the lovely tightwoven basket in Figure **10.20**, speaks of the reasons for working traditionally but also of the difficulty of doing so today:

> I feel that the generations before me tried all the different materials and found these to be the best materials, and so I'm pretty strict on that. The materials that we use are the willow. And then we use three main colored fibers: the white material is a sage grass root, and I use the bulrush root for the black fiber, and I use the new shoots of the redbud, and that gives a reddish-brown color. Of course, we have to dig all our own materials. They can't be bought anywhere and it's very hard today to find the places where the materials grow and to be able to gather them. The way that rivers have been dammed up, the way that the waters run different now, wipe out the roots and things that used to grow along the sides of the rivers. And a lot of the willows have been cut down along the roads, where they've put in roads that used to just be dirt roads. ... You have to be very determined to be a basket weaver today.[4]

In addition to carrying on the traditional fiber arts, contemporary artists are also experimenting with nonfunctional "paintings" and sculptures of fibers

10.20 Susye Billy, *Basket*, 1973–85. Edge, redwood, single willow rod foundation, 1¾ × 4¾ ins (4.4 × 12 cm).
Lost and Found Tradition Collection, Natural History Museum of Los Angeles County. The Collection is a gift of the American Car Corporation, now Primerica.

threads of varied colors were woven loosely over and under the warp and then pressed downward, complicated pictures emerged, as in the lovely Unicorn tapestries, of which the last is shown in Figure **10.18**. In the courtly medieval world, these time-consuming works were far more expensive than paintings.

Another prized fiber art is the weaving of Oriental rugs in the Near and Far East (**10.19**). Despite their intricate beauty, the original Persian rugs were used by nomadic peoples to cover the sand within their tents and to wrap their possessions when traveling.

10.21 Norma Minkowitz, *Epicenter*, 1984. Fiber, acrylic, colored pencil, and shellac, 11 × 8 × 6½ ins (27.9 × 20.3 × 16.51 cm).

ranging from cloth and yarns to wire gauze, hog gut, and vines. Basketry and crocheting have been borrowed by fiber artist Norma Minkowitz to create vessel forms that are not intended to hold anything. Minkowitz's *Epicenter* (**10.21**) is crocheted from fibers, delicately colored with pencils, and stiffened with shellac to stand up in forms suggesting the dynamic forces in the center of the earth.

QUILTING, traditionally a way of sewing fabric scraps into colorful, durable, personalized blankets, has also become a medium for fabric works of art that are not intended to cover a bed. Instead, they are meant to be hung on a wall. Sandra Sider's *Focus on the Belvedere* (**10.22**) is only 38 inches (96.5 cm) long and combines traditional quilt piecing techniques with painting on the fabric and printing it with photographic processes. The ideas and techniques she says she was working with in this art quilt are clearly from the world of art for art's sake:

> Photographic processes in my art inspire creative efforts that involve an interplay between light and shadow, an exploration of the graphic relationships of text and image, and experimentation with the visual and emotional impact of color.[5]

Although many of the fiber arts have evolved from handwork done on someone's lap, some contemporary fiber pieces are of tremendous size and weight. To work on the installation of her Bas-relief Wall (**10.23**), Sheila Hicks has to stand on scaffolding. At this scale, there is no historical precedent for what she has done with stuffed silk tubing.

10.22 Sandra Sider, *Focus on the Belvedere*, 1990. Cyanotype chemicals, cotton fabric, fabric paint, photography, painting, machine piecing and stitching, 27 × 38 ins (68.6 × 96.5 cm). Photograph Roberto Sandoval. Courtesy of the artist.

10.23 Sheila Hicks working on Bas-relief Wall (installation), 1975. Sewn, stuffed, wrapped
tubes of silk, 20 × 30 ft (6.09 × 9.14 m). Commissioned for The Galleria, New York City.
Courtesy of David Kenneth Specter, Architect/John Davison Allen.

11

PRODUCT AND CLOTHING DESIGN

In contrast to the unique nature of each handcrafted item, contemporary product design and clothing design usually involve mass-production. But especially for more affluent consumers, artistic sensibilities are often guiding these designs.

INDUSTRIAL DESIGN

In the past, INDUSTRIAL DESIGN was often equated with dreary functionality in appearance. But contemporary designers are taking a new look at the familiar goods used in homes and offices, from furniture and toasters to computers. The result in many cases is a marriage of function and the aesthetics of color, surface texture, line, space, and form.

11.1 Eric Chan toaster prototype. Courtesy of the artist.

The basic designs of many mass-produced objects were conceived some time ago, to accommodate technologies then available. As the innards of electrical appliances change, so can their exterior forms. With miniaturized components, telephones can and do take any form or size. Eric Chan has totally redesigned the toaster, with easy-to-clean nonstick flat surfaces and no place for crumbs to accumulate (**11.1**). As he points out, "Because the hot electric metal coils are hidden within the ceramic-base fiberboard, the threat of electrocution and burned fingers is no longer a problem." New technologies can liberate design, Chan feels:

> Today's climate provides a challenge to explore meaning and feeling rather than just packaging a set of mechanical or electrical components in the most efficient form for mechanical and marketing purposes. I believe my task is to mediate the balance between people and object, poetry and logic, and technology and nature.[1]

New design houses are flourishing in many countries, some of which provide governmental support for their designers as national resources. Today's industrial designers lend their imagination, sense of aesthetics, and awareness of contemporary tastes and technologies to a wide variety of commercial endeavors. For example, Vignelli Associates has offices in New York, Paris, and Milan and provides many firms with designs for graphics, consumer products, furniture, and interiors. Owners Lella and Massimo Vignelli, in conjunction with David Law—a designer of two-dimensional graphics,

11.2 Lella and Massimo Vignelli and David Law, Dinner set, 1984. Stoneware, large plate 10¾ ins (27.3 cm) diameter. Manufactured by Sasaki Crystal, Japan.

11.3 Kazuo Kawasaki, wheelchair.
Lightweight titanium frame, aluminum honeycomb wheels.
Courtesy of eX-Design Inc., Japan.

11.4 (opposite) Hiroshi Morishima, *Wagami Andon*, 1985.
Lamp encircled in a cone of Japanese handmade paper,
29½ × 21½ ins (75 × 55 cm). Manufactured by Time Space Art
Inc., Japan.

packaging, exhibits, furniture, products, interiors, and environmental works—designed the handsome dinnerware shown in Figure **11.2**. They gave great attention to the subtly pebbled "organic" texture of the dishes, the dramatic contrast between the black expanses and the wide white beveled edges, and the sensuously rounded profile of the teapot. It is functional as well as pleasing to the eye, with an easy-to-grasp open handle, good balance in the hand, and a practical spout for pouring hot liquid.

ERGONOMICS, the new science of designing for efficient and comfortable interaction between a product and the human body, attempts to cut down on awkwardness and fatigue in common home and workplace tasks. One offshoot of this new trend is designs that allow physically handicapped people to be as independent as possible.

Kazuo Kawasaki, who was himself paralyzed by a car accident, has redesigned the wheelchair to make it not only more comfortable and energy-efficient, with huge wheels, lightweight titanium frames, and contoured seats but also more fun to look at (**11.3**). There is no reason for those who live independently in wheelchairs to stay with the drab colors of hospital wheelchairs; why not bright colors?

Although many contemporary products are the result of technological innovations in materials and industrial processes, paradoxically, some aspects of high technology make it possible to mass-produce the look of the old and handcrafted. For example, the development of miniature low-voltage halogen lights has allowed designers to eliminate the fuss of wires and fittings in a lamp and to use relatively flammable materials near the light source. Hiroshi Morishima's table lamp (**11.4**) has a gentle handcrafted look, with the light glowing through the soft, random texture of handmade Japanese paper.

Not all product design is for mass production, either. Some small firms make limited editions of pieces that could be called "industrial crafts." They may combine cutting-edge technologies, computer-aided design, and materials with hand labor to create very personal objects sold through exclusive galleries. Kristian Gavoille's "Massai" armchair (**11.5**) looks like an elephant, complete with puffy, gray, wrinkled fabric "skin." But its appealing embrace is tempered by what appears to be a political statement: the feet are turned awkwardly, vulnerably, reminding one that the much-loved elephants are now an endangered species.

11.5 Kristian Gavoille, "Massai" armchair, 1990.
Courtesy Gallery Neotu, Paris.

11.6 YA/YA artist Darlene Francis with her chair and chifforobe.
Courtesy Young Aspirations, Young Artists Inc., New York.

Social justice and up-tempo furniture design are served up together in the expressive one-of-a-kind pieces of YA/YA ("Young Aspirations/Young Artists"). They are formerly problem students from a black vocational high school in New Orleans, inspired and supported by painter Jana Napoli. She encouraged them to paint thrift shop chairs and chifforobes in their own exuberant styles. The chifforobes were conceived as "powerful boxes of hope and fear," painted outside with dreams and inside with hidden fears (**11.6**). The students work up to 30 hours a week after school and on weekends, turning out lively, complex statements that are eagerly sought by collectors in several countries, at prices that are helping the artists save for college.

11.7 Voisard after Desrais, *A Lady of Fashion,* c. 1770. Colored engraving.

CLOTHING DESIGN

Those who design clothes sculpt in fibers, with the human body as a supporting armature. In addition to their aesthetic qualities, our clothes carry symbolic connotations that transcend the sheer function of protecting our bodies from the weather. Naked, we are all much the same. Clothed, we make symbolic statements about our wealth, status, lifestyle, sex role, personality, and taste.

The art of dressing often connotes class rank. Traditionally, the working classes have usually dressed for convenience, with simple sturdy fabrics and designs allowing free movement. Farther up the social scale, wealth and leisure may be demonstrated by a more ornamental than functional approach to design. In addition to demonstrating that the wearer was not involved in manual work, fashions for women have at times turned them into visual display cases. As indicated in the engraving by Voisard (**11.7**), high-born French women of the 1770s were almost immobilized by immense side-paniers, tight-waisted corsets, frilly sleeves, and towering hats and hairstyles that took hours to put together and required that one move very carefully, if at all. Even to be carried in a sedan chair, women so dressed had to kneel on the floor to make room for the height of their headdresses. The hairstyles took so long to

construct that they were maintained for a month or two, with the aid of lard and whiting. Sleeping with them was as hazardous at it was uncomfortable, for mice liked to nibble on them; the solution, a mouse-resistant nightcap, added to the great weight of the concoction.

As well as being calculated to impress others with one's wealth and position, fashions have been used to accentuate one's gender image. To look more desirably feminine, women of some periods and cultures have stuffed themselves into breast-lifting devices and then worn deeply cut gowns to reveal the rounded forms of their pushed-up flesh. Visual attention is drawn to areas with sexual associations, but to make them more desirable they are concealed. Males, too, may dress in ways that flaunt and exaggerate their masculine traits, such as the immense padded shoulders, decorated codpiece, and barely covered legs of Henry VIII's costume (**11.8**). Not only do the artificially broad shoulders emphasize his masculinity; they also bespeak the great political power of the monarch. To a certain extent, such displays were considered *noblesse oblige*; subjects wanted to be proud of their royal families. But Henry VIII obviously enjoyed dazzling audiences with his splendid dress. At his coronation, he wore an ermine-trimmed robe of crimson velvet and a doublet studded with rubies, pearls, diamonds, and emeralds.

Flamboyance in male attire has been rare in Western societies during the twentieth century, with the conservative business suit widely accepted as a uniform. But some cultures drape men with gorgeous fabrics, such as those shown in Figure **11.9**, still the choice of clothing for some of African descent rather than the ubiquitous business suit.

As we become more liberated from traditional social role expectations, we are freer to dress as individuals. Early in the twentieth century, women's emancipation from stricter Victorian standards opened the way for greater freedom in their clothing. The *Delphos* dress of pleated silk by Fortuny (**11.10**) allowed the natural curves of the body to show, without exaggeration or coyness. Its graceful lines— still in demand—were inspired by the draped garments of classical Greece. The pleats travel well and are in fact best maintained by twisting the dress into a knot.

As in the other arts, the world of contemporary high fashion is a mélange of different styles. Its

11.11 Issey Miyake, *Body Sculpture in Rattan*, 1982.

variety is personified by the exuberantly unconventional output of Japanese designer Issey Miyake. His garments range from marvelously loose and flowing pieces that allow and encourage free movement of the body to the open basketwork "coat" (**11.11**). Its cane framework resembles samurai armor, revealing and contrasting with the sensuality of the body. Even Miyake's fabrics are his own invention. To support his broad credo— "Anything can be clothing"—he takes his inspiration for fabrics from everyday images: "leaves, trees, bark, sky, air. Anything. A noodle." Miyake drapes the fabrics over himself to see what they will do. He says:

> Fabric is like the grain in wood. You can't go against it. I close my eyes and let the fabric tell me what to do.[2]

Ever pushing at the boundaries established for fashion by social convention and lack of imagination, Miyake observes that the Japanese word for clothing—*fuku*—also means happiness: "People ask me what I do. . . . I say I make happiness." The wearer of such a garment must have something of the same blithe spirit, a sense of independence and self-confidence. Designed for lithe and sensual movement, the clothes only "work" on a person who moves freely within them.

Some garments—such as those by Issey Miyake— are considered wearable art by collectors. High-quality Chinese and Japanese kimonos are hung as paintings, even though they are also very comfortably functional with their deep-cut arms and loose fit. Indeed, kimono designers old and new have approached this traditional garment as a broad surface for two-dimensional art, such as the intricate embroidered patterns of silk and gold threads worked across the Chinese woman's coat (**11.12**).

In some cultures elaborate handmade garments are among a family's treasures passed down from one generation to the next and worn on special ceremonial occasions. There are also some contemporary attempts to maintain or revive the old labor-intensive costume-making arts as symbols of one's cultural heritage. Cheryl Samuel visited museums from Leningrad to Toronto to study the 11 remaining old-style Kotlean robes woven 200 years ago by natives of the northwest coast of North America, in order to produce a twelfth one (**11.13**). She found that the people had used their basketweaving techniques to twine the robes, working each row from left to right and knotting the weft strands into a fringe on both sides. After each of the concentric geometric patterns was completed, the black weft yarns were left hanging as tassels. When a dancer wearing one of these robes moves, the whole garment sways with the body, and the motion of the dance is accentuated by the swinging of the tassels.

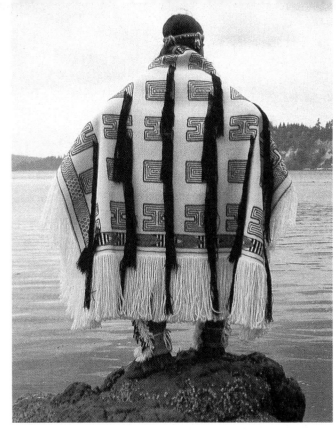

11.13 Cheryl Samuel, Kotlean robe, 1986. Handwoven wool. (From Evan Adams and Cheryl Samuel, *The Raven's Tail*, University of British Columbia Press, 1987.)

11.12 Woman's coat, North or Northwest China, c. 1850–1900. Wool broadcloth, satin borders, embroidered in polychrome silks and gilt threads, 29½ ins (75 cm) long. The Metropolitan Museum of Art, New York. Gift of Dorothy A. Gordon and Virginia A. White, in memory of Madge Ashley, 1973.

12

ARCHITECTURE

Architecture is similar to the other visual arts in aesthetic terms. Visually, buildings are developed from the same elements and principles of design as are other art forms. For example, architects work with form, texture, line, space, and color, using principles such as repetition, variety, and emphasis to unify the results visually. But architecture is a much less direct medium than are other arts. Professor Richard Swibold, architect and professor of art and architecture, observes:

> The architect's is not a one-on-one relationship between conception, design, detailing and construction, the way a painter's or sculptor's is. Once the architect has the idea—assuming all the other relationships with the client and community agencies and codes—then the work is turned over to a contractor to build it. So the architect is cut off, unlike the painter or the sculptor, from that final artistic act of doing it himself. The work is performed usually by people he is never even going to meet. He might go to the construction site once a week to supervise and to look at problems and to evaluate quality work, but for the most part, all these craftsmen—sometimes hundreds or thousands on a really big project—are people he'll never have any personal contact with. So his artistic expression is the result of being able to communicate through drawings and details and written specifications and selecting materials. It relies on that ability to communicate specific intentions—and there are always misunderstandings. Therefore the completed work is almost always a compromise. It's not the pure result of a painter with his idea, his brilliance, completing it with the final brushstroke.[1]

The architect is an artist, but also a social servant. Buildings must not fall down; roofs must not leak. Architects must undergo lengthy specialized

12.1 Kanna hut, Shiv Sadan, Uttar Pradesh, India.

training; their creations must satisfy zoning regulations, building codes, planning committees. Projects must be commissioned and paid for by a client, satisfying the programmatic needs and tastes of the client; they must attempt to accommodate diverse and often contradicting social values. They are executed by contractors and developers, who in today's industrial societies are usually governed by short-range financial considerations. Where does art lie in all of this? Professor Swibold comments:

> The architect's leadership has to be one of persuasion. The initial vision—often a sketch on a napkin at a lunch with a client—that initial conceptual step in the design process undergoes repeated and almost continual refinement and compromise until you finally get approval for construction to start. The need for the client's endorsement and for the approval of everyone else involved is absolute. In this process, the architect can try to stretch the imagination of the client and try to remain responsible to his or her own ideals. And all of this must be accomplished within the limits of a budget! Small wonder that so few buildings can be categorized as truly great architecture.[2]

Architecture must also concern itself with unique functional and structural considerations. These are explored in the pages that follow.

FUNCTION

For comfort in living, we humans have always sought some kind of shelter from the elements. Not only have we clothed our bodies; we have also tried to create miniature environments that are warmer or cooler than our natural setting and that will provide shelter from the elements for ourselves and our possessions.

In the countryside along the Ganges River in India, the local canes and grasses are cleverly woven and bound together into comfortable dwellings that can be erected in two or three days (**12.1**). Although they may last only four or five years, they keep the rain out, cost nothing and are easily replaced as they begin to fall apart.

In most cultures, however, there has been a desire to create larger and more permanent structures. Those designed for group assemblies—such as places of worship, houses of government, and commercial institutions—have required more elaborate technologies in order to stretch roofs over larger interior spaces and protect structures from wind, snow loads, earthquakes, and the like.

12.2 Pantheon, Rome, c. AD 118–28.

Where precipitation is infrequent, such as desert climates, buildings are often flat-roofed. In relatively warm but rainy climates, shallow domes or slightly pitched roofs are sufficient to shed rain. These were used in designing the *Pantheon*, an enormous second-century temple to the gods in Rome (**12.2**). The great central rotunda is roofed by a hemispherical dome; the PORTICO (a column-supported porch, in this case part of an earlier temple) is covered by a pitched roof. When this kind of architecture was attempted farther north in Russia, it collapsed under the weight of snow. A snow-shedding solution devised in the twelfth-century was the "onion" dome (actually intended to look like a candle flame), which was used in fantastic varieties in *St. Basil's Cathedral* in Moscow (**12.3**).

12.3 (opposite) Barma and Posnik, St. Basil's Cathedral, Moscow, 1555–61.

Where environments are hot, people have often designed structures that are dark and cool inside, such as the thick-walled structures of Suq al-Ainau in Yemen (**12.4**) made of packed mud bricks. In such cases, dark interiors are preferable to the heat. In temperate climates, structures may be more open to the outside air and light, as in Frank Lloyd Wright's *Wayfarers' Chapel* in Palos Verdes, California (**12.5**). Wright was highly enthusiastic about such uses of plate glass. In 1955, he wrote:

> By means of glass, open reaches of the ground may enter into the building and the building interior may reach out and associate with these vistas of the ground. Perhaps more important than all beside, it is by way of glass that sunlit space as a reality becomes the most useful servant of the human spirit. Free living in air and sunlight aids cleanliness of form and idea.[3]

In even cooler climates, heating the interior for comfort creates new design considerations. Because heat rises rather than spreading out horizontally,

12.4 Suq al-Ainau, Barat region of the Yemen Arab Republic.

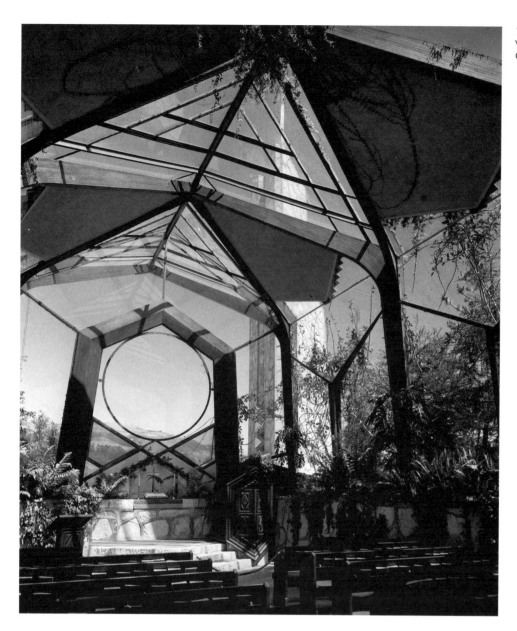

12.5 Lloyd Wright,
Wayfarers' Chapel, Palos Verdes,
California, 1951.

buildings tend to be more vertical, and their skins must keep cold out and heat in. With today's increasing concern about our impact on the environment, architects in cool climates are searching for better ways to capture the natural heat of the sun and prevent heat from leaking out of buildings. Ton Alberts' energy-efficient bank complex in Amsterdam (**12.6**) incorporates special design features such as solar energy panels on its ten towers, cutting energy use to only 25% of that normally used by buildings of the same size. The complex also features a colorful curving interior walkway—a pleasant place no matter what the weather—and "flowforms," sculptures which channel and purify rain water to water the plants in the building.

Functionality is not only physical but often symbolic. Sacred structures, for example, create a devotional atmosphere based on the community's concept of the sacred. Christian cathedrals built in Europe during Gothic times, such as the one at Chartres (**12.7**), attempted to elevate worshippers above the difficulties of mundane existence. Their height was designed to lift one's awareness to the heavens, considered the abode of a distant, awe-inspiring God. Much of the community's resources

12.6 A. (Ton) Alberts and Van Huut Architects, 10-building bank complex, Amsterdam, Holland.

12.7 Chartres Cathedral, France, begun 1194.

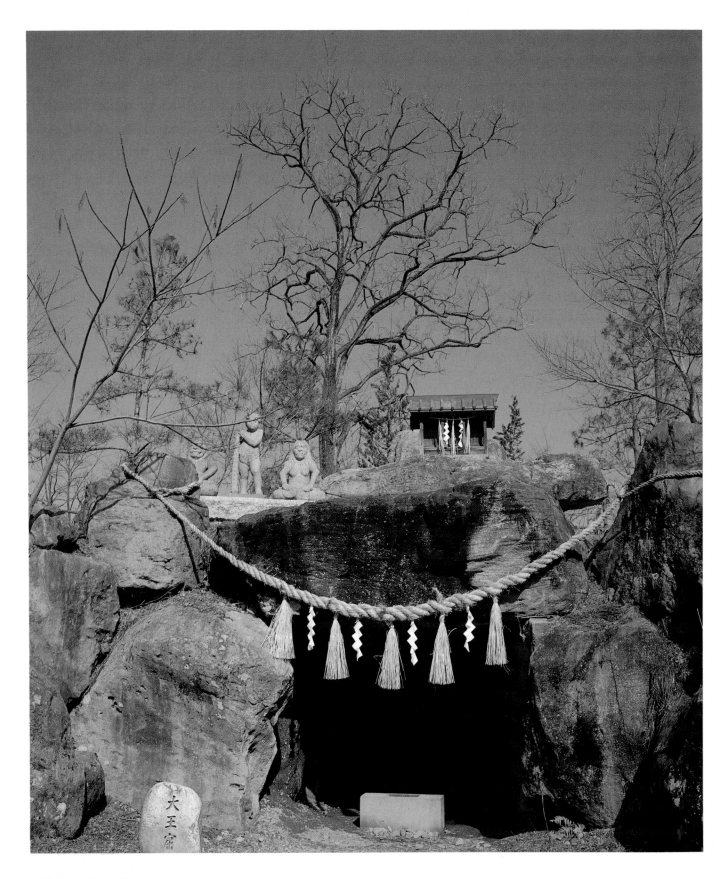

12.8 Small Shinto Shrine at Hotaka, Japan.

were channeled into these great building projects, creating structures that tower far above the surrounding houses and overwhelming those who enter. By contrast, the function of Shinto temples is to honor the many kami, or spirits, who live in nature close to the people. In the mountain top shrine at Hotaka, Nagano-Ken (**12.8**), a special rope demarks the sacred precinct reserved for the spirits. Worshippers are welcome to make offerings outside the shrine, but it is the sacredness inherent in the natural setting which evokes their reverence, rather than structures created by humans.

STRUCTURE

Architectural innovations have usually involved new materials or new ways of putting them together. Stone has been used since ancient times because of its great COMPRESSIVE STRENGTH—the ability to support the pressure of weight without breaking. In India, temples have been carved out of "living" rock as caves or as freestanding structures (**12.9**). The process is like subtractive sculpture—the boulder or mountain is treated as a giant block, and everything not needed is cut away. Metaphysically, their creation is thought to be a divinely inspired act that parallels the process by which material substance is created from ether. The resulting stonework is visually quite lively, expressing its infusion with the divine.

Stone and other materials with a certain compressive strength such as bricks, have more often been used for what is termed BEARING WALL CONSTRUCTION. This is simply stacking one flat block atop another in such a way that the wall thus formed will not topple, and then perhaps placing a roof over the walls by laying logs across the top. Earth that has

12.9 The Dharmaraja Rath and other rock-cut temples, Mahabalipuram, India, AD 625–74.

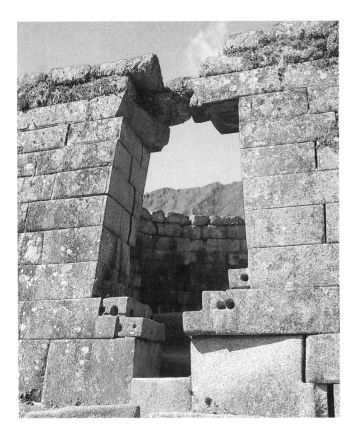

12.10 Machu Picchu stonework detail, Machu Picchu, Peru, c. 1500.

adequate clay content to hold it together has often been shaped into blocks and then built up in this way. Using this technology, the Yemen packed-mud houses (12.4) could rise many stories high. Where wood is more plentiful than clayey soil, people have often flattened and notched the sides of logs and built them up as log cabins. Often some kind of mortar is used between the pieces of a wall construction building to hold them together and fill the cracks. However, the mortarless stones of the famous sixteenth-century mountain-top Incan sanctuary, *Machu Picchu* (**12.10**), were so perfectly cut that centuries later they are still so tightly fitted that in many places a knife cannot be slipped between them.

One of the limitations of bearing wall construction is that walls must be very solid, with imposing separations between living spaces. A more open form of construction is allowed with POST AND LINTEL CONSTRUCTION (**12.11**) which uses strong columns (posts) to support beams (lintels) across which the roofing materials are laid. The horizontal lintel helps to stabilize the posts as well, and the space beneath can serve as an opening, whether door, window, or

12.11 Post and lintel construction.

12.12 The Erechtheum, Athens, 421–405 BC.

A Entablature
B Column
C Cornice
D Frieze
E Architrave
F Capital
G Shaft
H Base
I Plinth

1 Metope
2 Triglyph
3 Guttae
4 Abacus
5 Echinus
6 Volute
7 Fluting
8 Dentils
9 Fascia

Acroterion Raking Cornice Pediment

Stylobate

Stereobate

Greek Doric   Ionic   Corinthian

12.13 The Greek orders.

room. Stone buildings made by this system may be held together by gravity; wooden post and lintel arrangements require some means of notching or bolting the horizontal and vertical parts together.

The classical Greek architects became so confident in their development of post and lintel construction that they could use graceful refinements solely for the sake of visual proportion, such as posts that tapered toward the top. Sometimes they even used columns carved as goddesses bearing the lintels on their heads, as in the *Erechtheum* in Athens (**12.12**). The structures originally designed for wooden temples (partly to keep water from seeping into pillars and foundation) were translated into stone as elaborate sequences of parts known as the "Greek orders" (**12.13**). These started with a base, or

STYLOBATE (which itself is built upon a solid masonry foundation that spreads out the weight of the structure and keeps the building from settling). Atop this were columns, carved vertically with lines to conduct rainwater downward and topped by a CAPITAL on which the lintel rested. Next came the ENTABLATURE (the elaborated lintel), and atop that, the PEDIMENT, the slightly pitched triangular roof support at the end of the temple. The simplest style in the Greek orders was the DORIC. It is thought that it was derived from the flat claypatty and tile that were used atop wooden columns to protect them from rain. More elaborate versions were the scrolled IONIC and the CORINTHIAN, which had capitals carved to look like acanthus leaves pressed outward by the weight of the lintel.

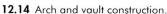

12.14 Arch and vault construction.

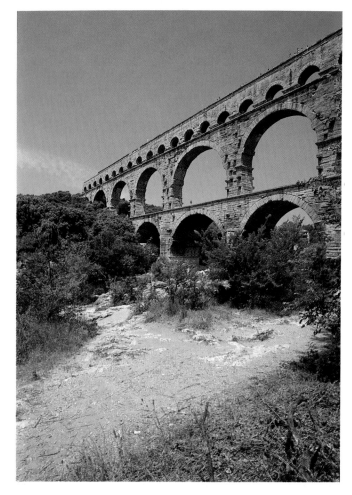

12.15 The Pont du Gard at Nîmes, France.

A major development that appeared in Roman architecture was the ARCH (**12.14**). Crafted of stone by master stonemasons, arches were made of VOUSSOIRS, wedged-shaped stones cut to taper toward the inside of the curve. They are propped up with scaffolding until the KEYSTONE at the top is set in place. The counterpressure they then exert on each other supports the arch, and weight is transferred downward onto the posts. The Romans used the arch to construct an elaborate system of aqueducts, much of which still stands (**12.15**). They also developed ways of combining arches to span broad interior spaces. These three-dimensional arches were widely used in Roman, Byzantine, Romanesque, and Gothic architecture (styles that are explored historically in Chapter 14). They transcended the low tensile strength of stone, which makes it difficult to span a broad area with a single stone beam without its breaking of its own weight; in post and lintel construction the beam must be supported at frequent intervals by posts.

The desire to open greater areas as public spaces without columns getting in the way led to elaborations of arch technology into tunnel-like BARREL VAULTS made of rows of round arches, GROIN VAULTS made of intersecting barrel vaults, and POINTED ARCHES whose width at the base could be varied. Gothic cathedral architects perfected systems of RIBBED VAULTING that carried most of the weight of an arch, allowing lighter materials to be used for the areas between. Seen from within, these cathedrals were symphonies of soaring arched lines and spaces, rhythmically repeated above and to either side of a long central hall, or NAVE (**12.16**).

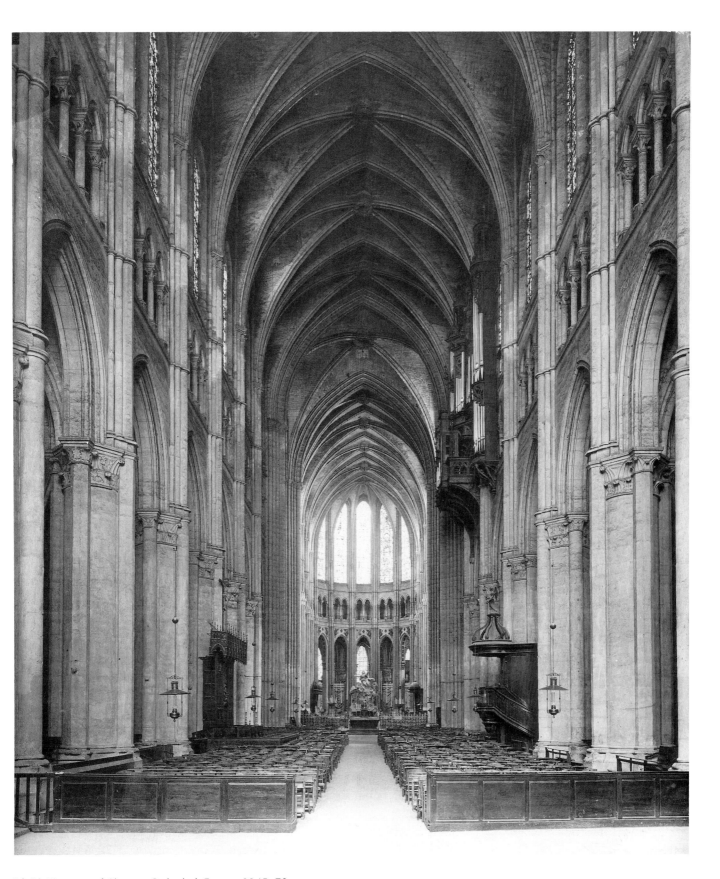

12.16 The nave of Chartres Cathedral, France, 1145–70.

Hassan Fathy
on
INDIGENOUS ARCHITECTURAL INGENUITY

The Egyptian architect, Hassan Fathy (1900–1989), attempted to solve his country's needs for rural housing for the poor by working with materials and technologies already at hand. Given the opportunity to design an entire relocated village for 7000 peasants, New Gourna, Fathy hired two masons from Aswan to carry out the most challenging aspect of building: roofing. Using nothing but adzes and their bare hands to set in mud bricks baked with extra straw for lightness, they quickly created marvelous vaulted roofs (**12.17**) in only a day and a half per room. In his book, *Architecture for the Poor*, Fathy described the great skill with which they worked, despite the material simplicity of their means:

"The masons laid a couple of planks across the side walls, got up on them, took up handfuls of mud, and roughly outlined an arch by plastering the mud onto the end wall. They used no measure or instrument, but by eye alone traced a perfect parabola, with its ends upon the side walls.

Next, one at each side, they began to lay the bricks. The first brick was stood on its end on the side wall, the grooved face flat against the mud plaster of the end wall, and hammered well into this plaster. Then the mason took some mud and against the foot of this brick made a little wedge-shaped packing, so that the next course would lean slightly towards the end wall instead of standing up straight. In order to break the line of the joints between the bricks the second course started with a half-brick, on the top end of which stood a whole brick. If the joints are in a straight line, the strength of the vault is reduced and it may collapse. As they built each completed course, the masons were careful to insert dry packing such as stones or broken pottery in the gaps between the bricks. It is most important that no mud mortar be put between the ends of the bricks in each course, for mud can shrink by up to 37 percent in volume, and such shrinkage will seriously distort the parabola, so that the vault may collapse. . . .

At this stage the nascent vault was six brick-thicknesses long at the bottom and only one brick-thickness long at the top, so that it appeared to be leaning at a considerable angle against the end wall. Thus is presented an inclined face to lay the succeeding courses upon, so that the bricks would have plenty of support.

Thus the whole vault could be built straight out in the air, with no support or centering, with no instrument, with no drawn plan; there were just two masons standing on a plank and a boy underneath tossing up the bricks, which the masons caught dexterously in the air, then casually placed on the mud and tapped home with their adzes. It was so unbelievably simple. They worked rapidly and unconcernedly, with never a thought that what they were doing was quite a remarkable

12.17 (right) Hassan Fathy, architect, Mosque in New Gourna, Egypt. (below) Interior detail of dome. Courtesy of the Aga Khan Award for Architecture, Geneva.

work of engineering, for these masons were working according to the laws of statics and the science of the resistance of materials with extraordinary intuitive understanding. Indeed, to span three meters in mud brick is as great a technical feat as spanning thirty meters in concrete.

Engineers and architects concerned with cheap ways of building for the masses had devised all sorts of complicated methods for constructing vaults and domes. Their problem was to keep the components in place until the structure was completed, and their solutions had ranged from odd-shaped bricks like bits of three-dimensional jigsaw puzzles, through every variety of scaffolding, to the extreme expedient of blowing up a large balloon in the shape of the required dome and spraying concrete onto that. But my builders needed nothing but an adze and a pair of hands."[4]

12.18 Flying buttresses on the side of Notre Dame Cathedral, Paris, 1163–1250.

Because arched vaults transferred pressure not just downward but also outward, the vertical structure had to be either very thick or else firmly braced to keep the sides from being pushed apart. To avoid overly massive walls, a Gothic solution was to engineer systems that gradually transferred lateral pressure to FLYING BUTTRESSES (**12.18–19**) external to the interior space. Figure **12.18** is an overhead view of some of the flying buttresses surrounding Notre Dame Cathedral. It reveals the slender ribs and vaults outside the building, braced against solid masonry piers. Note that each of the piers is capped with a spire that makes it appear less bulky.

When an arch is rotated through 360 degrees, the result is a DOME. The immense dome of the *Pantheon* in Rome (rechristened as the Santa Maria Rotunda since it was converted into a Christian church in the seventh century), was a marvel of engineering and building skills, with COFFERS (sunken panels) used to diminish the weight of the massive concrete roof, and a great oculus—"the eye of heaven"—for natural illumination. Even today, we do not fully understand the structural principles which have allowed the second-century temple to remain intact to the present. But it is known that the concrete mixture the Romans invented hardened into a highly coherent rigid structure, that the width of the drum (the vertical walls) is equal to the height of the dome above, as indicated in Figure **12.20** (so we can suspect some kind of intricate mathematical balance), and

12.19 Flying buttress.

12.20 Section of the Pantheon, Rome.

12.21 Giovanni Paolo Panini, *Interior of the Pantheon*, c. 1740. National Gallery of Art, Washington D.C. Samuel H. Kress Collection.

383

12.22 Cross-section of Byzantine church.

12.24 Balloon-frame construction.

that a series of arches is embedded in the concrete walls of the drum to help support the dome and counteract any possible outward-spreading pressure of the dome. In Byzantine architecture, the lateral thrust of the dome was often transferred to a lower-ceilinged surrounding aisle (**12.22**).

Another approach is FRAME CONSTRUCTION. In wood-framed buildings, pieces of wood are attached at right angles to each other and braced at the top with triangular TRUSSES (such as the one shown in **12.23**). Initially, heavy weight-bearing timbers were used for posts and space-spanning floor and ceiling beams in such structures. But the development of mass-produced nails and sturdy but relatively lightweight milled boards in 2 × 4-inch (10 cm) widths allowed the invention, in the early nineteenth century, of BALLOON-FRAME CONSTRUCTION (**12.24**). In such a

12.23 Truss.

frame, the thin vertical, horizontal, and diagonal roofing boards are closely spaced and nailed together. Stresses are borne by the multi-part frame as a whole rather than by individual posts and beams. The "skin" placed over the frame, such as windows and clapboards, plays no structural role. This system is still predominant in the building of individual houses in areas such as the United States, where wood is fairly plentiful.

In the nineteenth century, industrialization revolutionized architecture. It was found that iron had great tensile strength, with relatively little weight, and could be wrought or cast into columns, beams, trusses, and arches which could be quickly joined into huge skeletons with nothing but glass between the bones. This technology opened new possibilities for what architecture could be used for, and there followed a spate of building great arcades for new kinds of public gatherings, such as trade expositions. The most celebrated of these early iron-skeleton buildings was Joseph Paxton's Crystal Palace (2.50). Built in London for the Great Exhibition of 1851, it was the world's largest building, covering an area 770,000 square feet (71,535 sq m). All of its parts were prefabricated, in standardized repeating units. The entire thing was put up by 2000 workers in three months, and then dismantled after the six-month exhibition. The bits were re-used to build a similar, even larger structure in another part of London (it no longer stands since it accidently burned down in 1936). The "palace" was cleverly engineered not only for speed of construction but also for such functional considerations as shedding of water. The structural columns and beams doubled as a rainwater-conducting system; the structure was entirely watertight.

12.25 Steel-frame skyscraper.

The possibilities of the metal skeleton were developed into steel-frame skyscrapers (**12.25**). As seen in downtown Dallas (**12.26**), the urban landscape of many cities has been transformed during the twentieth century into clusters of these glass-sheathed structures. With real estate extremely expensive in urban areas, the only economically feasible direction to expand was upward. This direction became possible only through the development of steel and concrete frameworks capable of supporting tremendous loads, and of elevators to lift people through the numerous floors. With these frameworks, walls became non-load-bearing curtains and could be made entirely of glass. Interiors also became broad-spanned open spaces within which partitioning could be arranged and moved about according to shifting interior needs rather than the necessity for supporting what lay above.

The steel and concrete framework was mated with an austere approach to design which evolved in the 1920s—the so-called INTERNATIONAL MODERN STYLE. Buildings were constructed along purely functional lines, with largely glass exterior walls, flat roofs, a lack of ornamentation except for horizontal bands

12.26 The Dallas skyline.

defining floors, and symmetrical modular grids. The visual effect of these structures is that of space-filled volume rather than the solid mass associated with earlier architectural forms.

The style was hailed as fresh and honest architecture for the machine age. It was even thought that the new approach to design would liberate humanity itself. For example, the Swiss architect Le Corbusier waxed enthusiastically about the emancipating potential of a new tobacco factory:

> The sheer facades of the building, bright glass and grey metal, rise up . . . against the sky. . . . Everything is open to the outside. And this is of enormous significance to all those who are working, on all eight floors *inside*. The Van Nelle tobacco factory in Rotterdam, a creation of the modern age, has removed all the former connotations of despair from the word 'proletarian.'[5]

Mies van der Rohe and Philip Johnson's Seagram Building (**12.27**) in New York is a classic example of the now-familiar International Style and perhaps its most successful product, with its elegant bronze details and perfect proportions. A large open area has been left beyond the sidewalk for a broad walkway and fountains, allowing a sense of spaciousness and graciousness in the midst of the crowded urban scene. Many large cities now require that skyscrapers be set back from the sidewalk to allow sun to penetrate into the canyons between tall buildings.

Philip Johnson also applied the International Style to the project of designing his own house—a rectangular metal-framed house with glass infill panels (**12.28**). The structure and walls of the house are actually almost invisible; what one sees from within and without are the surrounding trees and vegetation, the pond with fantasy pavilion below, and the valley in the distance. Most of us must use opaque walls and curtained windows to insure our treasured privacy; Johnson's personal life and private paradise is shielded from the curious by a high dry stone wall along the road.

Another unique use of metal to frame a structure with non-bearing walls was developed by the pioneering genius of R. Buckminster Fuller. His brilliant investigations into natural structures led him to develop buildings on entirely different principles than any seen before. He explained:

> I often hear it said that architects build buildings out of materials. I point out to architectural students that they do not do that at all. That kind of definition dates back to the era of men's thinking of matter as solid. I tell architectural

12.27 Ludwig Mies van der Rohe and Philip Johnson, Seagram Building, New York, 1956–8.

12.28 Philip Johnson,
Johnson House,
New Canaan, Connecticut,
1949. Ezra Stoller © Esto.

12.29 Buckminster
Fuller, United States
Pavilion, Expo 1967
geodesic dome.
Photograph © Wayne
Andrews/Esto.

students that what they do is to organize the assemblage of visible modular structures out of subvisible modular structures. Nature itself, at the chemical level, does the prime structuring. If the patterning attempted by the architect is not inherently associative within the local regenerative dynamics of chemical structure, his buildings will collapse. The principles governing structure not only prescribe what man can put together, but they are operative at the molecular level, at the atomic level and at the nuclear level. They are also operative in each of man's life cells and throughout principles of structure in the starry heavens. They are universal, they are purely mathematical, weightless.[6]

Fuller's GEODESIC DOME is a very lightweight but sturdy metal framework in which the bracing strength of triangles is organized into a dome that needs no other support. Such a dome can top a structure or can be the entire structure itself, as in the United States Pavilion for the 1967 World's Fair (**12.29**). Any flat sheet material such as wood, metal, plastic, or glass can be cut into triangles and attached to the frame as a weather-proof skin.

REINFORCED CONCRETE—concrete that is internally strengthened with metal rods or mesh—has also been widely used in twentieth-century architecture. In a post and lintel arrangement, reinforced concrete beams can be CANTILEVERED (**12.30**)—projected beyond supporting posts—if anchored into those posts. Frank Lloyd Wright's Fallingwater (3.42) cantilevers large terraces out over the falls. In addition to flat slabs, reinforced concrete can also be used to create articulated freeform structures unlike any seen before. Italian post-war architectural engineer Pierre Luigi Nervi demonstrated that precast, reinforced concrete sections could be used in ways that were beautiful as well as functional. He applied this aesthetic sensitivity even to aircraft hangars (**12.31**). The famous Sydney Opera House (**12.32**), designed by Danish architect Jorn Utzon, features roof forms resembling ships' sails which cover a complex of separate concert halls and restaurants.

Whereas such structures have to support tremendous COMPRESSIVE (downward-pressing) loads without buckling, the German architect Frei Otto envisioned extremely light structures (**12.33**) where the primary stress would be TENSILE (pulling). Cables are strung under tension among a few anchored masts to support lightweight curving fabric membranes, as in the German Pavilion in Montreal (**12.34**). Such structures have the potential for being easily changed or moved, as needs change, in contrast to the monumentality and permanence long assumed necessary in public buildings.

12.30 Cantilever.

12.31 Pierre Luigi Nervi, Aircraft hangar at Ortbello, Italy, 1939–40.

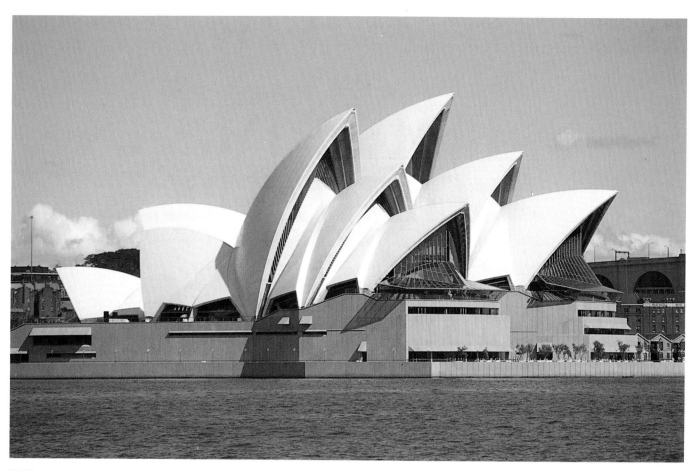

12.32 Jorn Utzon, Sydney Opera House, Australia, 1956–73.

12.33 Drawing of suspended structure.

12.34 Frei Otto, German Pavilion, Montreal, 1967.

Alvar Aalto
on
HUMANIZING ARCHITECTURE

At a time when the impersonal technology of the International Style was predominant, Finnish architect Alvar Aalto (1898–1976) earned global recognition for the warmth and personality of his buildings. They ranged from family homes to total industrial complexes, complete with housing for employees. Aalto was deeply influenced by the architectural traditions of his native Finland, but his designs were highly original. Though extremely varied, they all tended to soften the mechanistic aspects of modern architecture in favor of honoring human needs and using organic materials. His methods of solving architectural problems were a combination of empirical research, original but logical thought, and sheer intuition. Aalto carried on his own research into the special needs of very weak bedridden patients at a sanatorium:

"The experiment showed the room must be different from an ordinary room. This difference can be explained thus: The ordinary room is a room for a vertical person; a patient's room is a room for a horizontal human being, and colors, lighting, heating, and so on must be designed with that in mine.

Practically, this fact means that the ceiling should be darker, with an especially selected color suitable to be the only view of the reclining patient for weeks and weeks. The artificial light cannot come from an ordinary ceiling fixture, but the principal center of light should be beyond the angle of vision of the patient. . . . Ceiling radiators were used but in a way which threw the heat mainly at the foot of the bed so that the head of the patient was outside the direct heat rays. The location of the windows and doors likewise took into account the patient's position. . . .

These are only a few illustrations from an experimental room at the sanatorium, and they are here mentioned merely as examples of architectural methods, which always are a combination of technical, physical, and psychological phenomena, never any one of them alone. Technical functionalism is correct only if enlarged to cover even the psycho-physical field. That is the only way to humanize architecture."[7]

"When I have to resolve an architectural problem I find myself, first of all and without exception, halted by the thought of its realization. What is needed is a sort of '3 a.m. courage,' probably due to the difficulties arising from the weighty importance of the different elements at the moment of conception. The social, human, technical and economic requirements which present themselves side-by-side with the psychological factors and concern each individual and each group, their rhythm and internal friction, are so numerous that they form an entanglement, not lending itself to the methods of rational resolution. The resultant complexity prevents the basic architectural idea from taking shape.

In such cases I work in a completely irrational way. For a while I forget the whole entanglement of problems, clear it from my mind, and occupy myself with something which can best be described as abstract art. I start designing, allowing myself to be guided purely by instinct—and, suddenly, the basic concept is there, a point of departure which gathers together the different, often contradictory, elements which I named above, and puts them in harmony. . . .

Whilst designing the library for the town of Viipuri, . . . I spent a long time making childlike drawings representing an imaginary mountain with different shapes on its sides. . . . Visually these drawings had nothing to do with architecture but from their apparent childishness there arose a combination of plans and sections whose interweaving it is difficult to know how to describe. . . .

I believe that a great number of my colleagues will recognise in all that I have written the familiar characteristics of their own struggles with the problems of architecture. . . . I

12.35 Alvar Aalto, Church at Vuoksenniska, Imatra, Finland, 1958.

believe, rather, am convinced, that at their outset architecture and the other arts have the very same point of departure, which is indeed abstract, but is at the same time influenced by all the knowledge and feelings that have accumulated within us. . . .

Architecture and its detailing are a sort of *biology* and their birth probably takes place in very complicated circumstances. One could compare architecture to the full grown salmon. It is not born full grown, it is not even born in the sea where it swims but far off, where the rivers narrow and divide into tributaries and mountain streams, beneath the first drops of water dripping from the glaciers. It is like the first stimuli of architecture which arise as far from practicality and the finished result as the first impulses of our feelings and instinctive life can be from the everyday toil of our daily bread which binds us, each to the other."[8]

12.36 Kisho Kurokawa, Nakagin Capsule Tower, Tokyo, 1972.

There have also been attempts to use modern factory production-line technologies to pre-package structures and thus cut down on their cost. A common approach is MODULAR CONSTRUCTION. Using standard dimensions with electrical and plumbing connections sandwiched into the walls, buildings can be quickly assembled on-site from factory-made components. In an extreme example of this technology, Kisho Kurokawa created the Nakagin Capsule Building in Tokyo (**12.36**) from a series of stackable prefabricated rooms, each a complete dwelling. Each capsule is only 8 × 12 feet (2.43 × 3.65 m), but includes a bathroom, double bed, desk with typewriter, chair, tapedeck, clock radio, storage space, kitchen, and a heating, ventilation and air conditioning unit. The capsules form a "community" connected to a central water, oxygen, and power supply.

Now that many building technologies are available to support architects' visions, there has been a backlash against strictly functional industrial construction and against repetitive use of lookalike glass boxes. In what is called POST-MODERN architecture, buildings tend to be more expressive and individual, and, some say, less elitist. There is no

one look that defines them all. Some are sensual and decorative, some refer back to historical styles, some are lively and playful. Philip Johnson's shift from International Style buildings to a pastiche of historical references in the American Telephone and Telegraph Building (**12.37**) is an example of this change. Many critics object that Post-Modern architecture is neither structurally inventive nor aesthetically serious.

A more industrial, high-tech approach to architecture persists, though in forms that have broken out of the International Style mold. One of the most extreme examples of HIGH-TECH REVIVAL is

12.37 Philip Johnson and John Burgee, AT & T Building, New York, 1978–84.

12.38 Renzo Piano and Richard Rogers, Pompidou Center, Paris, 1971–8.

the Pompidou Center in Paris (**12.38**) designed by Renzo Piano and Richard Rogers. Designed to house a modern art museum, a public library, exhibition space, and an audio-visual center, it is conceived as an upbeat public gathering place rather than an austere cultural center. Rogers explains its oil refinery appearance: "We wanted it to be fun and easy to read."[9] He and Piano put its mechanical services and functional supports on the outside and color coded them: Water pipes were painted green, electrical ducts yellow, and air conditioning pipes blue. To carry people from one floor to another, they also put the elevator on the outside—a large glass caterpillar that slinks its way up the building and offers a superb view across Paris. Although some critics have condemned the ugliness and high cost of heating and

12.39 The Grameen Bank Housing Programme, Bangladesh. Courtesy of the Aga Khan Award for Architecture, Geneva.

cooling this building turned inside-out, it is indeed popular with the people. Some 30,000 Parisians and tourists visit it every day, more than go to the Eiffel Tower and the Louvre put together.

A very different application of architectural technology that is receiving special attention as we approach the twenty-first century is appropriate use of technology to improve the lives of those who are not wealthy and to minimize damage to the environment. The Aga Khan has established an international architectural award for building projects that use local materials and satisfy true human needs. One recent recipient is the Grameen Bank Housing Programme in Bangladesh (**12.39**).

These simple, sturdy and clean homes combine the old and the new: bamboo supports and siding, corrugated iron roofs, prefabricated concrete floors, and reinforced concrete posts. In five years, almost 45,000 of them have been built by and for residents, with the help of small bank loans. The Aga Khan speaks of the universal desire for good architecture:

> I can think of no human art form which exercises such a permanent influence over our lives. We must demand from our respective national decision-makers, our architects, our planners and our landscape architects an environment in which we live and work harmoniously and to the fullest.[10]

13

DESIGNED SETTINGS

E ven those of us with the most meager of resources tend to make some attempt to organize and design our living environment to suit our sense of order, comfort, and beauty. This chapter will examine aesthetic and functional aspects of interior and environmental design, and conclude with a look at overtly staged settings for the performing arts.

INTERIOR DESIGN

Once a building is erected, there is the issue of selecting and organizing its contents—furniture, fabrics, art objects, functional objects, and personal possessions. In some cases, functionality of furnishings is the prime consideration. The Reading Room of the British Library, London (**13.1**) is a businesslike arrangement of lighted reading tables fanning out like spokes from the central hub—shelves of reference volumes and an information desk. Chairs are upright, with no arms. All space is dedicated to task-solving equipment, with aisles left for convenient traffic flow. This is obviously not a place designed for comfort or conversation, but it efficiently carries out the function of providing reading spaces for a great number of people, with the elegance of a truly functional design.

13.1 The Reading Room, The British Library, London, 1826–47.

13.2 Bedroom from the Palazzo Sagredo, Venice, c. 1718. Wood, stucco, marble, glass, 13 ft (4 m) high.
Painted ceiling by Gaspare Diziani, *Dawn*, c. 1755–60. The Metropolitan Museum of Art, New York. Rogers Fund 1906.

13.3 *Zashiki* or main parlor of a merchant's house, Kyoto, Japan.

By contrast, in our homes we tend to try to surround ourselves with things we consider beautiful or interesting, and furnishings designed to make our lives more comfortable. An extreme example of the opulent extremes to which this endeavour has been taken is the bedroom from Palazzo Sagredo in Venice (**13.2**), now preserved *in toto* in the Metropolitan Museum of Art in New York. The bedroom belonged to Zaccaria Sagredo, a major patron of the Venetian artists of the Late Baroque period. Every surface is richly ornamented, from the painting on the ceiling and the stucco cherubs to the magnificent brocade covering the bed and its headboard. The reds and golds increase the impression of sumptuous, almost royal wealth. The room has the appearance of a stage setting, with the bed raised on a platform, enclosed by an archway, and theatrically lit brighter than the space in front allotted for the "audience."

At the other extreme, is the Japanese tradition that one's home is not used as a place to display material abundance, though it may be a setting for appreciating the beauty of a few carefully selected possessions. The main parlor in a Kyoto merchant's home (**13.3**), lovingly restored along traditional lines by the son who grew up there, is almost entirely bare of furnishings. The simple cushions and table are low to the *tatami*-covered floor, and all other possessions are stored out of sight, with the exception of the single painting within the TOKONOMA alcove out of camera range to the left. This spare aesthetic turns a relatively small space into a quietly spacious sanctuary, a haven from the busyness and crowds of the streets. In the absence of visual noise, inhabitants can develop a heightened awareness of, and appreciation for, the exquisite experiences of the moment. Instead of being submerged in a symphony, in this space one listens keenly to single notes—the scent of a flower, the texture of a cup, the sound of a voice. Kojiro Yoshida, the son, named his family's treasured home *Mumeisha*: "the hall for casting light on the unnamable things of the present."

Frank Lloyd Wright often designed the interior

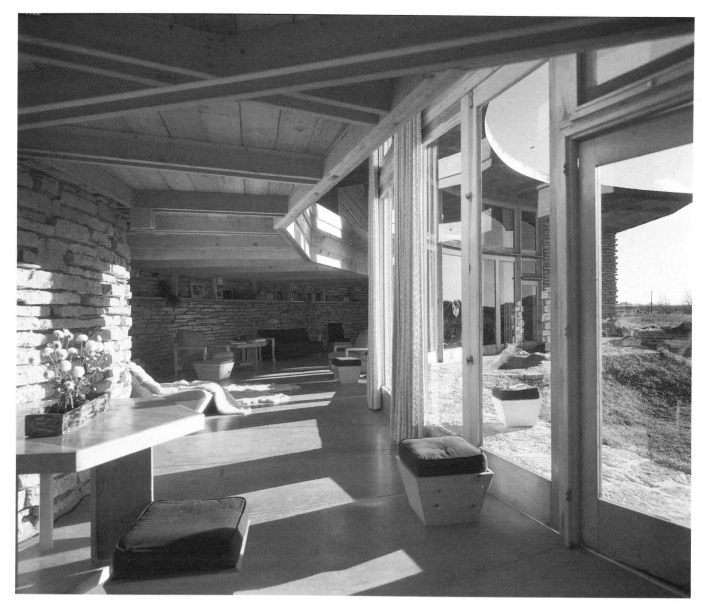

13.4 Frank Lloyd Wright, Herbert Jacobs, "Solar Hemicycle" House, Middleton, Wisconsin, 1944. Living room. Photo 1950 Ezra Stoller, Esto.

furnishings as well as the architectural structure of houses. Typically, he attempted to relate the inside and the outside as a single whole, characterized by use of natural materials. His "Solar Hemicycle" house built in Wisconsin (**13.4**) curves to embrace the sun, drawing it into a cave-like interior in which wood and stone are featured as organic surfaces which match the stone and wood used on the outside. A circular pool at the far end of the patio lies half inside, half outside the glass wall of the house. The simple wooden furniture was also designed by Wright specifically for the house. He insisted:

Furnishings should be consistent in design and construction, and used with style as an extension in the sense of the building which they "furnish." Wherever possible all should be natural. The sure reward for maintaining these simple features of architectural integrity is great serenity.[1]

In contrast to the cozy, natural quality of Wright's house interiors (an effect still being widely emulated in modern homes), business environments may be carefully calculated to make a favorable impression on potential clients as well as employees and to facilitate and symbolize the division of labor. In the renovation of a former shopping mall as the corporate offices of Canberra Industries, a specialized electronics firm, the wide-open expanses were divided by movable partitions into a variety of workspaces. An open plan of mini-offices with low walls that allowed co-workers easy access to each other was used for most clerical and managerial employees, with a few private offices around the edges for corporate officers and conference spaces. Shown in Figure **13.5** is a low-ceilinged area used as a waiting "room" for visitors, backed by the president's receptionist and the offices of the president and senior administrators. Modern nonobjective works of art on the walls announce that this is a forward looking company with good taste. Subdued lighting over couches and an area rug set them off from the brightly-lit business areas beyond,

without isolating them from view of the flow of business activity.

Lighting is itself a major new area of environmental concern. If all homes and businesses in the United States alone changed to existing energy-efficient lighting technologies, there would be a saving of over $30 billion in electrical bills per year and elimination of the need for the energy produced by one hundred twenty power plants the size of Chernobyl. Energy-efficient lighting techniques include substitution of fluorescent bulbs for incandescent bulbs, lamp reflectors, and the introduction of daylight. Use of such money- and energy-saving techniques can also enhance the quality of lighting, which plays a major role in the aesthetics and comfort of interior design.

13.5 Glenn Gregg, architect, Virginia Linburg, interior designer, Virginia McKernan, art consulting design, Executive Offices, Canberra Industries, Meriden, Connecticut, 1984.

13.7 Gianlorenzo Bernini, plan of the Piazza of St. Peter's, Rome, begun 1656.

13.6 (opposite) Nishat Bagh, India. View from the pavilion along the main axis of the garden, 17th century.

ENVIRONMENTAL DESIGN

Beyond our homes and public buildings, we humans have also longed to shape our immediate outdoor environment. Traces of gardens have been found in the ruins of the earliest civilizations. In arid countries, water and lush plantings have been especially prized. On the Indian plains, for example, few wildflowers can survive the fierce sun, but cultivated gardens were mentioned in early Buddhist and Hindu texts. During the great Mughal period of the sixteenth and seventeenth centuries, the emperors had magnificent formal gardens built around their mountain retreats in Kashmir. One of the most beautiful, Nishat Bagh (**13.6**), was built by Asaf Khan, Prime Minister to the emperor Jahangir and brother of his wife. When the emperor saw its lovely green terraces, the sparkling play of water over its stone water-ladders, and its views of the lakes and mountains beyond, he strongly recommended that Asaf Khan give it to him. Asaf Khan demurred, and the emperor in anger cut off the irrigation supply, without which the garden was deprived of much of its soul-soothing beauty. The water was eventually restored, and the garden is today a serenely refreshing oasis open to the public.

From ancient times, societies have also made arrangements for public gathering spaces. In urban areas, plazas and public squares offer a different pace from linear sidewalks crammed with busy people going places. In seventeenth-century Rome, a need was felt for a great open public space to accommodate crowds approaching St. Peter's, the monumental central structure of the Roman Catholic Church. The desired piazza (**13.7**) was designed by Gianlorenzo Bernini, who in addition to being a great painter and sculptor (see Figure 1.36) was also an architect. He planned a huge oval area open at one end and embraced by enormous Tuscan columns lined up to form two giant colonnades, like the arms of the Church welcoming the people. The project was so expensive that it almost bankrupted the Vatican.

Contemporary urban space planning often allows open areas between buildings. The success of their design can be measured by whether people choose to congregate there. By this criterion, Nathan Phillips Square (**13.8**) in Toronto is overwhelmingly successful. Beyond the embrace of the twin towers of

City Hall, a multi-level public space is booked every day with entertainers, from rock concerts to drum majorettes performing their routines, and the area is always thronged with people.

Municipalities have also made provisions for their occupants to benefit from natural settings without having to leave the city, by creating city parks. Some are extensive green belts; some are tiny areas with plantings and benches. In the heart of mid-town Manhattan, the Greenacre Foundation used the space between two buildings for a "vest-pocket" park featuring an artificial waterfall, tables and chairs, and trees to provide shade (**13.9**). To step off the street into the ambiance of this place is a psychological and aesthetic respite from the high-pressure atmosphere of commercial New York. The sound of the waterfall drowns out street noises and its cooling spray adds to the soothing quality of the park.

13.8 Nathan Phillips Square, Toronto, Canada.

13.9 Hideo Sasaki, Greenacre Park, New York, 1979.

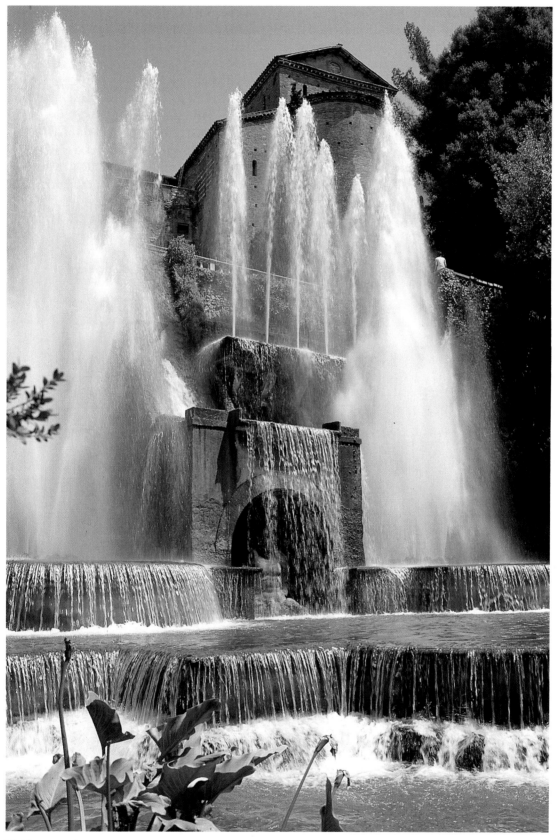

13.10 Water Organ, Villa d'Este, Tivoli, near Rome, c. 1550.

Where water is plentiful, as it is in Rome, it is sometimes used with even greater abandon. An entire river was diverted to feed the Water Organ of the Villa d'Este (**13.10**). This usage is entirely nonfunctional; it is a dynamic environmental sculpture in which water is the medium.

At the grassroots level, some groups are bringing life to the walls of ghettos and otherwise unappetizing cityscapes by painting MURALS. Some are celebrations of ethnic pride; others are humorous illusions, such as *Isle of California* (**13.11**). It was painted by the Los Angeles Fine Arts Squad after a minor earthquake, as a teasing, surrealistically three-dimensional takeoff on a Californian fear: the freeways collapsing into the ocean.

On a broader scale, many people now feel a need to protect the beauty and environmental functions of the natural environment. Lawrence Halprin's sketch for *Sea Ranch* (**13.12**), a planned community on the Californian coast, sets up a series of restrictions that keep houses and roads hidden from view. In landscape design, he specifies use of native materials, forbidding attempts to create artificial grassy lawns, in the interests of preserving the original character of the dramatic setting. These are moral judgments about how what we do to the environment affects the

13.11 Victor Henderson and Terry Schoonhoven, known as the Los Angeles Fine Arts Squad, *Isle of California*, 1972. Enamel mural, 42 × 65 ft (13 × 20 m). Los Angeles.

SEA RANCH

keep house back
from ridge face
so only silhouette
can be seen

no houses in
flat above
road

roads up draws.

Riding
trails   no roads up face

new group plantings

houses at
Edge only where
they cannot be seen
by others

Planting restrictions for Sea Ranch
1- No lawns - ground covers only. ice plant, ceanothus etc.
2- Trees only natives or naturalized ie: Monterey cypress
3- Shrubs - natives ie: toyon, sweet bay, rhamnus.

Architectural restrictions..-
These are harder to establish
1- Stable of arch'ts ? - no review
2- Materials ?
3- submissions; to arch. commission—

13.12 Lawrence Halprin, *Environmental Specifications for Sea Ranch*, 1963. Notebook sketch.

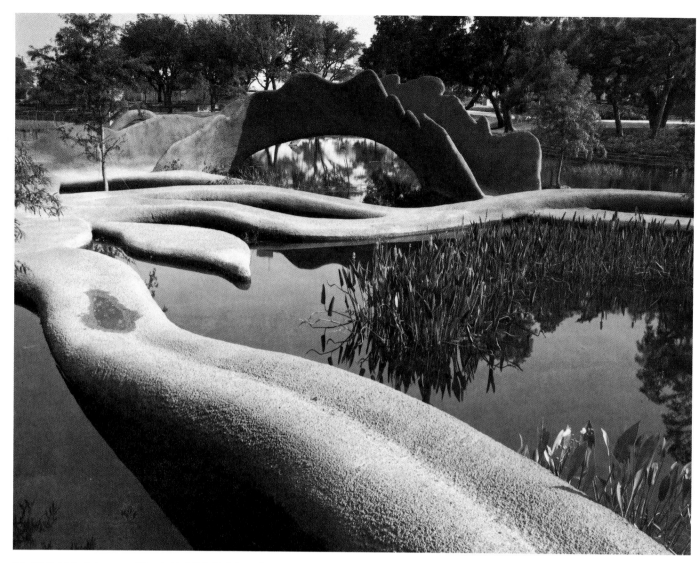

13.13 Patricia Johanson, "*Pteris Multifida*", Fair Park Lagoon, Dallas, Texas. Photograph courtesy of the artist.

quality of our lives, as well as the ecological characteristics of the land.

As environmental awareness grows, increasing numbers of artists are explicitly working to help alleviate environmental problems through planning and innovative designs. Artists are now tackling projects such as sewage treatment and landscaping of garbage landfills, usually aiming for greater visibility than similar projects developed by nonartists. Patricia Johanson "biologically restored" a formerly stagnant lagoon in Dallas (**13.13**) by reintroducing indigenous species of plants, turtles, and fish, and creating bridges and walkways with large plant-like sculptures. Not only do children like her Fair Park but birds are also returning to it. She asserts:

> The reason we [artists] have to participate is that we can do something that's very visual, very poetic; we have the power to sway people to our point of view.[2]

In trying to deduce some general aesthetic principles common to all those cities around the world that are invigorating or pleasant rather than disagreeable, Lawrence Halprin came to the conclusion that good city planning—or happenstance—respects both the old and the new and provides a creative, vibrant environment for the multiplicities of human activities:

> The provocative city results from many different kinds of interrelated activities where people have an opportunity to participate in elegant, carefully designed art and spontaneous, non-designed elements juxtaposed into what might be called a folk idiom, a series of unplanned relationships . . . those chance occurrences and happenings which are so vital to be aware of—the strange and beautiful which no fixed, preconceived order can produce. A city is a complex series of events.[3]

VISUAL ASPECTS OF THE PERFORMING ARTS

While environmental designers use plants, water, earth, stone, paving materials, and screening devices to create pleasant settings for our daily lives, designers connected with the performing arts create artificial settings for make-believe. In the ancient Greek theater, actors initially performed from a flat space at the foot of a hill, with the audience seated on the hillside. There was no scenery. This simple way of separating the imaginary space of the performance from the real space of the audience was later formalized with tiered seating rising up a hillside in a semi-circle around a wooden platform (13.14). Actors entered and exited from a small building called a SKENE, from which we get the words "scene" and PROSCENIUM (in front of the *skene*).

To enhance the illusionary setting for theatrical performances, the area designated as a stage became more elaborate, with fabricated scenery designed to give the illusion of deep space. The chief way of creating this spatial illusion was the use of FORCED PERSPECTIVE, an exaggeration of the speed at which parallel lines converge toward a vanishing point. Shortly after perspective drawings were adopted by Renaissance artists, the device was transferred to the stage. At the *Teatro Olimpico* designed by Andrea Palladio, completed by his pupil Vincenzo Scamozzi in 1585 and still standing today, three elaborate arches opened onto illusionary city streets with their floors raked upwards and rows of models of wooden houses built in forced perspective. All of

13.14 Reconstruction drawing of the Hellenistic theater at Ephesus, Turkey, c. 280 BC, rebuilt c. 150 BC.

13.15 Plan of the Teatro Olimpico.

this elaborate scenery, shown in a frontal view in Figure **13.16** and in plan in Figure **13.15**, was intended to give the illusion of streets intersecting in a public square. Actors were confined to the acting space in front of the scenery; if they were to move up the streets, the falseness of their scale would become apparent.

Shortly after Scamozzi finished the Teatro Olimpico, he invented the form most familiar to us today, in which the entire stage is framed by a single PROSCENIUM ARCH. This arch is used to hide all the mechanics of the stage setting, from the tops of painted sets to light banks and pulleys that allow actors to fly. Within the recessed space of the stage, some of the latest innovations involve computer technologies. Gary English is among those exploring ways in which computer technology can be of use in the visual arts. His projects include theatrical productions such as *Sunday in the Park* (**13.17**), in which all the forced perspective scenery has been designed and painted by computer, and *The Odyssey*, in which a huge computer-animated Cyclops eye watches the actors.

Another major illusionary device used in performing arts is costuming. Even when there is no stage, when performers and audience share the same

13.16 Andrea Palladio and Vincenzo Scamozzi, interior of the Teatro Olimpico, Vicenza, Italy, 1580–4.

13.17 Gary English, (scene designer), *Sunday in the Park*, 1991, Pioneer Theater, Salt Lake City, Utah. Photography by Robert Clayton.

space, performers may assume roles by wearing masks and costumes that hide their everyday identity. The Papuan costume shown in Figure **13.18** transforms ordinary people into spirits attending boys' initiation ceremonies. Such rituals express the beliefs of a culture and are vital to its sense of identity and continuity.

In some traditional African cultures, layers of cloth and wooden masks are similarly used to transform the bearer into a representation of a deceased ancestor, god or goddess. The spirits are thought to be close to the living, but invisible, and to have an active interest in intervening in earthly affairs. Dead ancestors, for example, may still be considered the owners of family property and must be consulted about its use. They influence the weather and the crops, so one must stay in their good graces. Their presence-made-visible is a powerful influence on the behaviors of the living. In the Yoruba language, the word *iron*, which means "theatrical performance," also means "vision." It signifies levels of reality that humans cannot usually see but which they can envision with the mind's eye, inspired by stories and masquerades. When the masqueraders dance, the layers upon layers of cloth whirl about like patterns of energy, dissolving the impression of solidity and physical boundaries.

13.18 Costume of a *kaivakuku* (taboo advisor) from Waima, Papua New Guinea, c. 1900. Bark cloth.

13.19 Scene from *La Bayadère*, Royal Ballet Company, London, 1978. Choreographed by Marius Petipa. Produced by Rudolf Nureyev.

In some performing arts, the bodies of performers are deliberately turned into design elements—elongated lines, opposing or harmonizing forms—like parts of a painting or sculpture that changes through time. This is true in classical ballet; in this scene from *La Bayadère* (**13.19**), the *corps* forms a low circle around the central characters, like a splash radiating outward from the action in the middle. Dramatic high-contrast lighting is used to make the dancers appear as points of light within a dark and otherwise empty space. In Alwin Nikolais' modern dance choreography, all reference to the body as human is deleted. Dancers in his *Sanctum* (**13.20**) move within webs of stretchy fabric, creating an eery grotto of fantasy forms. And Charles Simonds became both sculptor and sculpture in his performance piece *Landscape-Body-Dwelling* (**13.21**), in which he sculpted a clay landscape on his own nude body, complete with miniature dwellings for the "Little People."

The body is used as symbolic mask and gesture by Japanese *kabuki* actors. They wear highly stylized makeup over a white base, transforming their own faces into visages suggesting their roles. They offer their bodies as armatures for costumes weighing up to 50 pounds (23 kg), requiring frequent adjustments by stage attendants who wear black and are therefore

13.20 Alwin Nikolais, *Sanctum*, Nikolais Dance Theatre, New York, 1976.

13.21 Charles Simonds, *Landscape-Body-Dwelling*, 1970.

13.22 Ennosuke Ichikawa III of the Shochiku Kabuki Company, 1981.

not considered visible. These highly trained actors, whose apprenticeships begin at the age of six or seven, assume stylized gestures, freezing momentarily like statues in melodramatic poses (**13.22**) that carry clear meaning for those familiar with *kabuki* conventions. Men play all parts; women were banned in 1629 as part of an attempt by the rulers to restrict the popularity of this art form.

411

13.23 Bread and Puppet Theater, scene from *Passion Play for a Young Tree*. Puppets by Peter Schumann. Photo by Ron Simon.

In puppetry, all is illusion. Figures can be as fantastic as the puppeteer's imagination allows, and designed to hide the hands or bodies that move them. Sculptor Peter Schumann, founder of the Bread and Puppet Theater sees puppetry as:

> ... an extension of sculpture. A professional sculptor doesn't have much to do but decorate libraries or schools. But to take sculpture into the streets, to tell a story with it, to make music and dances for it—that's what interests me.... A puppet may be a hand only, or it may be a complicated body of many heads, hands, rods and fabric.[4]

Many elaborate systems have been devised for remote control of marionettes and puppets, but in the Bread and Puppet Theater's *Passion Play for a Young Tree* (**13.23**), they are life-sized and worn by humans who walk around in them. The figures in the background are "crowd puppets," groups of heads with burlap drapes designed to create a crowd effect with only six to ten people beneath them. In the play, a poplar tree is subjected to a series of trials suggesting those preceding Jesus' crucifixion; after its "death," the broken tree is taken to a pine forest by washerwomen, laid on the ground, and tenderly covered with a sheet. The tree then flies up into the treetops, resurrected and covered with flowers. Shown here is a version of the Last Supper. Elka Schumann, one of the puppeteers, explains the intent:

> Bread and Puppet, one of the oldest alternative theaters in the United States, is not a children's puppet theater, but we like to include children, both in the performances and certainly in our audiences. The themes that we choose for shows are usually of quite a serious nature, dealing with issues that we think are really important to all people, like the nuclear arms race or ecological destruction. We use a very wide variety of puppets, including some very small cut-outs or hand puppets but mostly large or huge puppets that can be manipulated and require big groups of people to run them. Many of our performances are designed to be done outside, in a community or with a community. The Passion Play was a very simple format with no speaking in it. The audience followed the scenes from one beautiful spot to another. By moving with the show, the audience became, in a way, part of the story.[5]

PART

4

ART IN TIME

Change is the one sure constant in art. Over time, art movements typically go as far as they can in one direction and then some artists veer off to explore other approaches. Each work of art also has its own history, with its final appearance the result of many choices made as it evolved from an abstract idea into physical form.

HISTORICAL STYLES IN WESTERN ART

Works of art always express something of the person who created them. They also reflect the views and artistic conventions of the society at the time. Approaches to art have often carried enough similarities among varying artists who were working at the same time, in the same place, for us to be able to categorize them as stylistic movements. These movements lasted a long time at first, since societies were isolated from each other and information passed very slowly from one to the next. Then, as commerce between areas became more common, innovations in one area were more rapidly reflected elsewhere.

Today styles come and go with such speed that the twentieth century alone has been characterized by a great number of artistic movements. Contemporary societies are also far less uniform, supporting a plurality of lifestyles and life views. When the major patrons for art were the state and church, and when the academies dictated whose work was approved and shown, their views dominated what was done. Many stylistic movements now coexist, and many artists are doing work so unique that it does not fit into any group designation.

In this chapter we will trace the chain of the major art styles from earliest times to the present. Although we have examined art from all cultures throughout this book, in this chapter we will limit our focus to the evolution of European and North American art for the sake of clarity. The art of each culture has similarly evolved through many styles, partly through internal innovations and partly through contact with other cultures. Western art has often been influenced by that of non-Western societies—Rembrandt, for instance, was a collector of Near Eastern art, and Picasso was strongly affected by African sculpture. As communications shrink our globe, techniques and approaches to art are increasingly cross-pollinating. Many of the works in Western art discussed earlier are drawn into this discussion and are placed in context on the timelines on the following pages:

page 415 30,000 BC–500 AD Prehistoric to Roman
page 427 500–1500 AD Early Christian to Gothic
page 436 1425–1640 Early Renaissance to Southern Baroque
page 443 1500–1800 Northern Renaissance to Rococo
page 448 1750–1950 Neoclassicism to Surrealism
page 478 1945–1990 Twentieth Century

The accompanying maps indicate the key artistic centers and the location of important buildings of the periods covered. The timeline on pages 416 and 417 covers all the movements from prehistory to the present day and is illustrated with key works of art from this chapter.

Although our society tends to equate the passage of time with progress, some art historians feel that the art of certain periods in our past has never been surpassed. Note, too, that many of the historical groupings of artists are rather artificial constructs that were developed after the fact; others were actual groups of artists working together with a shared vision. Some of these are still called by the derogatory terms given to them by their detractors.

30,000 BC–500 AD	Prehistoric to Roman		
30,000	c. 30,000–10,000 Paleolithic c. 20,000–6000 Mesolithic c. 8000–3000 Neolithic c. 4000 Sumerian civilization emerges in Mesopotamia	c. 20,000 toolmaking c. 9000 domestication of animals c. 4000 Cuneiform script developed in Mesopotamia	c. 30,000–25,000 Venus of Willendorf, Lower Austria (14.2) c. 15,000–10,000 Hall of Bulls, Lascaux, France (14.1)
3000	c. 3000–1000 Cycladic culture, Aegean c. 2780–1085 Kingdoms of Ancient Egypt c. 2000–1100 Minoan civilization, Crete c. 1760–612 Assyrian Empire, Mesopotamia c. 1600–1100 Mycenaean civilization, Greece	c. 3000 hieroglyphic writing, Egypt c. 3000–2000 use of bronze tools/weapons, Sumer c. 2000 "Book of the Dead" first papyrus book c. 1725 horse-drawn wheeled vehicles, Egypt c. 1200 beginning of Jewish religion	2700 Panel of Hesira, Saqqara, Egypt (14.6) 2700–2600 Statuettes from Abu Temple, Tell Asmar, Iraq (14.4) 2500 Cycladic Figure, Amorgos, Greece (14.3) 1450 Senmut with Princess Nefrua, Thebes, Egypt (2.20)
1000	c. 800–650 Geometric period, Greece c. 700–480 Archaic period, Greece c. 500–400 Classical period, Greece c. 500–150 Hellenistic period, Greece 509–31 Roman Republic	c. 900 Ideographic writing, China c. 800 Homer's *The Iliad* c. 700 First Olympic Games 550–480 Gautama Buddha, founder of Buddhism c. 336–323 conquests of Alexander the Great	c. 8th cent. Dipylon vase, Athens, Greece (14.7) c. 5th cent. Warrior from Riace, Greece (1.45) 540–515 Kouros, Anavross, Greece (14.8) 530 Amphora (10.4) 450–400 Spear bearer, Doryphorus (2.21) 448–438 Acropolis, Athens, Greece (14.9) 447–438 Parthenon, Athens, Greece (3.36) 421–405 Erechtheum, Athens, Greece (12.12) 190 Victory of Samothrace, Greece (14.10) c. 20 Augustus of Primaporta, Rome (14.11)
0	31 BC–500AD Roman Empire c. 400 Byzantine Empire begins	c. 30 Crucifixion of Jesus Christ 79 Pompeii and Herculaneum destroyed 98–117 Roman Empire at greatest extent	1st cent. AD Laocoön, Rhodes, found in Rome (3.27) 113 Column of Trajan, Rome (2.132) 118–28 Pantheon, Rome (12.2) 165 Statue of Marcus Aurelius, Rome (2.22) 220–30 Sarcophagus, Rome (1.5) 312–15 Arch of Constantine, Rome (1.16)

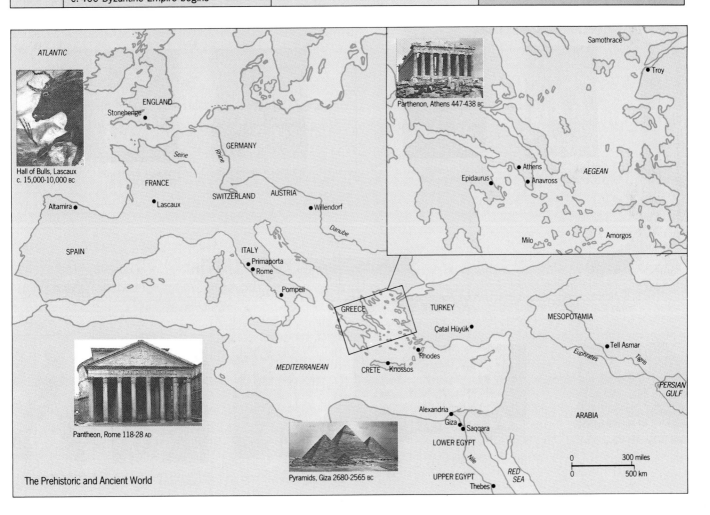

ATLANTIC

Hall of Bulls, Lascaux c. 15,000-10,000 BC

ENGLAND

Stonehenge

GERMANY

Seine

Rhine

FRANCE

Altamira

Lascaux

SWITZERLAND

AUSTRIA

Willendorf

Danube

SPAIN

ITALY

Primaporta

Rome

Pompeii

MEDITERRANEAN

GREECE

CRETE

Knossos

Rhodes

TURKEY

Çatal Hüyük

MESOPOTAMIA

Euphrates

Tell Asmar

Tigris

PERSIAN GULF

Alexandria

Giza

Saqqara

LOWER EGYPT

ARABIA

Nile

RED SEA

UPPER EGYPT

Thebes

Pantheon, Rome 118-28 AD

The Prehistoric and Ancient World

Pyramids, Giza 2680-2565 BC

Parthenon, Athens 447-438 BC

Samothrace

Troy

Athens

Anavross

Epidaurus

AEGEAN

Milo

Amorgos

0   300 miles
0   500 km

TIMELINE

30,000   20,000   10,000   8000   6000   4000   3000   2000   1000   900   800   700   600   500

PALEOLITHIC

MESOLITHIC

NEOLITHIC

MESOPOTAMIA: SUMER   AKKAD, BABYLONIA, ASSYRIA

ANCIENT EGYPT

GREECE: PROTO/GEOMETRIC   ARCHAIC

Venus of Willendorf (14.2)

Lascaux cave paintings (14.1)

Tell Asmar statuettes (14.4)

Portrait panel of Hesira (14.6)

The Dipylon Vase (14.7)

The Parthenon (14.9)

1800   1775   1750   1725   1700   1675   1650   1625   1600   1575   1550

ROCOCO   NORTHERN BAROQUE   NORTHERN RENAIS

NEOCLASSICISM   SOUTHERN BAROQUE   MANNERISM

David, *The Oath of the Horatii* (14.31)

Neumann, Church of Vierzehnheiligen (14.30)

Velásquez, *Las Meninas* (14.27)

Caravaggio, *The Calling of St. Matthew* (14.26)

1825   1850   1875   1900   1905   1910   1915

IMPRESSIONISM   CUBISM

POST-IMP   FAUVISM   FUTURISM

ROMANTICISM   REALISM   EXPRESSIONISM

ABSTRACT

Gericault, *The Raft of the Medusa* (14.32)

Courbet, *The Stone Breakers* (14.33)

Monet, *Rouen Cathedral* (14.35)

Picasso, *Les Demoiselles d'Avignon* (14.40)

Boccioni, *Unique Forms of Continuity* (14.42)

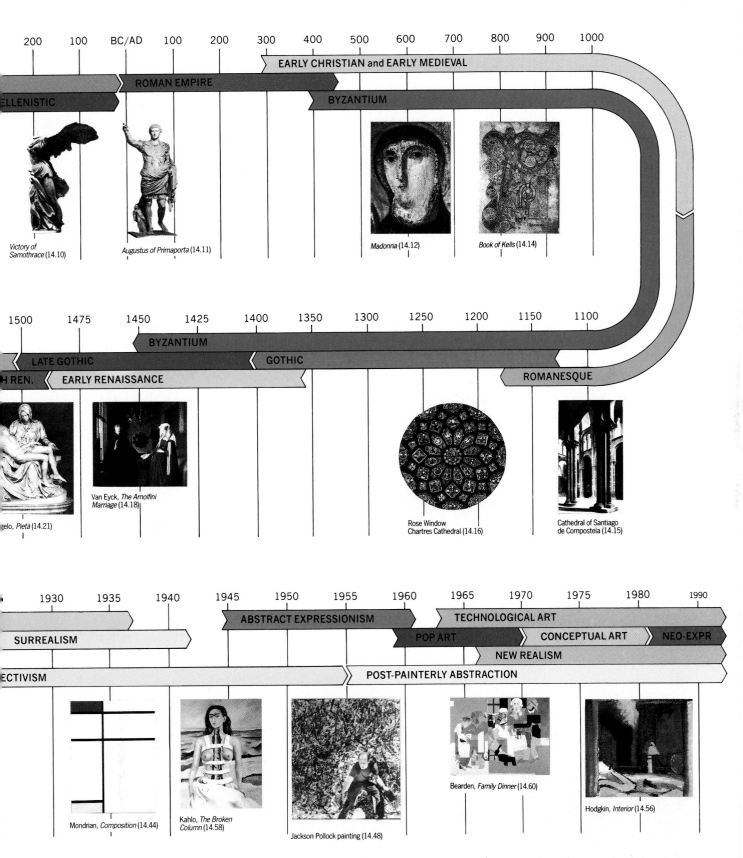

200   100   BC/AD   100   200   300   400   500   600   700   800   900   1000

EARLY CHRISTIAN and EARLY MEDIEVAL

ROMAN EMPIRE

BYZANTIUM

ELLENISTIC

Victory of
Samothrace (14.10)

Augustus of Primaporta (14.11)

Madonna (14.12)

Book of Kells (14.14)

1500   1475   1450   1425   1400   1350   1300   1250   1200   1150   1100

BYZANTIUM

LATE GOTHIC   GOTHIC

H REN.   EARLY RENAISSANCE

ROMANESQUE

gelo, Pietà (14.21)

Van Eyck, The Arnolfini
Marriage (14.18)

Rose Window
Chartres Cathedral (14.16)

Cathedral of Santiago
de Compostela (14.15)

1930   1935   1940   1945   1950   1955   1960   1965   1970   1975   1980   1990

ABSTRACT EXPRESSIONISM   TECHNOLOGICAL ART

SURREALISM   POP ART   CONCEPTUAL ART   NEO-EXPR

NEW REALISM

ECTIVISM   POST-PAINTERLY ABSTRACTION

Mondrian, Composition (14.44)

Kahlo, The Broken
Column (14.58)

Jackson Pollock painting (14.48)

Bearden, Family Dinner (14.60)

Hodgkin, Interior (14.56)

Differential timescales have been used, resulting in the relative compression of earlier periods. This apparent bias in favor of recency should be noted, although it is difficult to avoid: for if this Timeline represented all periods on the timescale used for the twentieth century, it would measure 315 feet (96 meters) in length.

417

THE BEGINNINGS OF WESTERN ART

PREHISTORIC

Very few traces remain of the lives of our earliest ancestors. We do know, however, that by 30,000 BC *Homo sapiens* were creating works we now regard as paintings and sculptures. Of the latter, the most famous is the tiny female figure found at Willendorf in Austria (**14.2**). Often referred to as the "Venus of Willendorf," she is only 4½ inches (11.5 cm) tall, small enough to fit comfortably in one's hand. Archeologists think she, like other similar figures from the same period, was probably a fertility image, judging from the exaggeration of her reproductive areas to the exclusion of facial features, or an image of the Creator as Mother. Somebody carved her of limestone and painted her red, just as the people painted their bodies with red ocher.

In addition to other small, stylized stone carvings of humans and animals, early peoples incised and painted remarkably realistic animals on the roofs and walls of caves. The most famous of the cave paintings were found in Lascaux, France (**14.1**), by children exploring an extensive cave beneath an uprooted tree. There are hundreds of paintings covering a series of chambers with large figures of bulls, deer, horses, bison, and ibexes. They were apparently created by many artists over many years, using fur, feathers, moss, sticks, or fingers to outline the creatures with pigments from natural minerals. These outlines were then colored in with powders perhaps blown through tubes of bone. Some of these cave paintings are so vividly wrought that archeologists at first thought they were fakes, but now their authenticity has been verified, and the ones at Lascaux have been dated to about 15,000 BC.

The Lascaux caves, like others in which prehistoric paintings have been discovered, were tortuous underground water channels up to 4000 feet

14.1 Main hall ("Hall of Bulls"), Lascaux, France, c. 15,000–10,000 BC.

It was in the Cyclades that the art objects most often found in the ruins of these civilizations seem to have originated. Like the figure shown in **14.3**, they were small stylized female figurines with folded arms, carved out of marble with hard obsidian blades and rubbed to a smooth surface. Remaining bits of paint suggest that they once had painted eyes and jewelry. The fact that they will not stand upright suggests that they were conceived as lying down; usually they have been found in tombs, perhaps as partners for the dead or as homage to the mother goddess. This translation of living, fully-round forms into abstracted, nearly flat geometric shapes did not begin to reappear in Western art until the late nineteenth century.

14.2 *Venus of Willendorf*, Lower Austria, c. 30,000–25,000 BC. Limestone, 4½ ins (11.5 cm) high. Natural History Museum, Vienna.

14.3 Cycladic figure from Amorgos, c. 2500–1100 BC. Marble, 30 ins (76.2 cm) high. Ashmolean Museum, Oxford.

(1300 m) long, with the painted areas far removed from the cave mouths where the people lived. They would have been very dark, illuminated only by small stone lamps, and very quiet, creating an atmosphere of other-worldly strangeness appropriate for the magical purposes for which some scholars think the paintings were created. Although we have no way of knowing for sure, it seems likely that the images were painted to insure success in the hunt, with their surprising representational accuracy a valuable aid in invoking the spirit of the animal ahead of time and ritually killing it. Those animals depicted as pregnant might have been magically encouraged to be fruitful.

AEGEAN

One of the earliest known Western civilizations was a seafaring culture centered in the Aegean Sea around Crete and islands to its north, known as the Cyclades.

NEAR EASTERN

The other earliest settled civilizations in the West were in Mesopotamia, on the plains between the Tigris and Euphrates rivers in what is now Iraq. The first of these organized urban communities were in Sumer, where each of many cities was protected by a local god or goddess, served and represented by human rulers. Much of the Sumerians' art was devoted to ritual religious themes, such as presentations of gifts to the gods. Some of the low-relief stone carvings and impressions made in clay or wax by cylindrical seals are lively and realistic. The statues placed around the inner walls in a temple devoted to Abu, god of vegetation (**14.4**), are more simply conceived as dignified, stylized cylindrical forms in an attitude of worship. The largest figure represents Abu. All are carved in rather soft gypsum marble, with painted hair and beards and inset eyes of black limestone or lapis lazuli against shells.

EGYPTIAN

In isolation from the Mesopotamian civilization, an elaborate culture was developing in Egypt that spanned about 2000 years. At first the arts of Egypt focused almost exclusively on the hereafter, particularly on insuring eternal life for deceased rulers. Great pyramids, such as those at Giza (**14.5**), were erected to house the mummies, statues, and

14.4 Statuettes from the Abu Temple, Tell Asmar, c. 2700–2600 BC. Marble, tallest figure 30 ins (76.2 cm) high. The Iraq Museum, Baghdad.

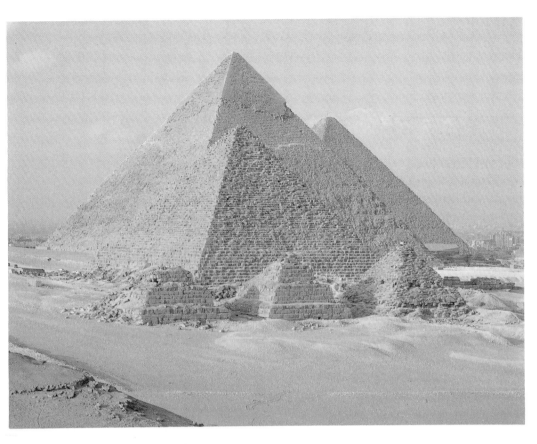

14.5 The Pyramids of Mycerinus (c. 2470 BC), Chefren (c. 2500 BC), and Cheops (c. 2530 BC), Giza, Egypt.

14.6 Portrait panel of Hesira, from Saqqara, c. 2700 BC. Wood, 4 ft 7½ ins (1.41 m) high. Egyptian Museum, Cairo.

belongings of kings. The pyramid form was intended as an image of the rays of the sun, a stairway on which the king could ascend to heaven. We still don't really know how these monumental structures were built, though many theories have been explored.

Egyptian paintings and sculptures (such as the block form of the Chancellor Senmut with Princess Nefrua as a child shown in Figure 2.20) often combined considerable artistic skill with rigid stylistic conventions. Sculptures were quite obviously rectangular; paintings and exquisite low reliefs of the human form (**14.6**) usually showed the head in profile, the torso in frontal position, and the legs in profile, leading to some anatomically impossible positioning. Such conventions were not designed to please mortals; they were ways of insuring that a statue would be a suitable dwelling place for the spirit, or that a painting gave as much information as possible. But as the New Kingdom evolved, with Egypt becoming the strongest entity in the Mediterranean area and Akhenaton declaring himself the son of a single god, the god of the sun, art became somewhat more earthly and less stylized. After Akhenaton's time, Egyptian art reverted back to earlier stylized conventions.

ART OF ANCIENT CULTURES

GREEK

From the sixth to second centuries BC, a remarkable civilization arose in Greece which is still regarded as one of the highest models for the arts. Even before this time, potters of the GEOMETRIC PERIOD were creating two-handled amphoras and other vessels of symmetrical beauty, worked with elaborate geometric patterns. The lovely wheelthrown *Dipylon Vase* (**14.7**), so named for the cemetery in Athens in which it was found, was of a type used to mark graves. Almost five feet (1.5 m) high, it had to be built in separate sections, which were then joined. In addition to the Greek fret pattern later used on buildings and bands of other geometrically

14.7 The Dipylon Vase, Attic Geometric amphora, 8th century BC. 4 ft 11 ins (1.5 m) high.
National Archeological Museum, Athens.

14.8 Kouros, c. 540–515 BC.
Marble, approx 6 ft 4 ins (1.92 m) high.
National Archeological Museum, Athens.

symmetric motifs, the amphora is decorated with a frieze of mourning human figures reduced to a visual shorthand.

The ARCHAIC PERIOD in Greece (approximately 700 to 480 BC) brought inquiry into the natural structure of the human body. The Kouros ("young male") statues (**14.8**) show great attention to anatomy, and the figures are fully freed from the block of marble from which they were carved, in contrast to the block-like Egyptian statues.

The Golden Age of Athens—the heart of the CLASSICAL PERIOD—lasted for only part of the fifth century BC, but its emphasis on rationality, idealized beauty of form, and avoidance of extraneous ornamentation has never been equaled. It was during this period that Pericles signaled his victory in Athens by rebuilding the Acropolis high above the city, with the *Parthenon* (**14.9** and 3.36) as its focal

14.9 The Acropolis, Athens, 448–405 BC. View from the West.

14.10 (right) *Victory of Samothrace*, c. 190 BC. Marble, 8 ft (2.44 m) high. Louvre, Paris.

point. In sculpture, artists abandoned the contrived Egyptian poses for more naturalistic ones, as in the *Spear Bearer* (2.21) and the *Warrior from Riace* (1.45). Both sculptures turn the body in a dynamic, spiral twist known as CONTRAPPOSTO in which the head and shoulders face a different way from the hips and legs.

After the elegant restraint of the Classical Period, the HELLENISTIC PERIOD was marked by greater emotionalism. During this period, dating from the death of Alexander the Great in 323 BC and spanning about 300 years, the power of the Greek city-states declined but Greek culture continued to spread and was adopted by the newly dominant Romans. One of the greatest works of this period was the life-filled, wind-blown *Victory of Samothrace* (**14.10**), a marble sculpture erected by the people of the little island of Samothrace to celebrate a victory at sea. The emotional drama of her form also characterizes the Hellenistic mosaic of *The Battle of Issus* (5.28). The more natural, informal style of the Hellenistic Period can also be sensed in the warm body of the *Venus de Milo* (2.75), and its predilection for "human interest" is reflected in the late Hellenistic bronze of the *Seated Boxer* (9.17).

MVNIF. PI. IX. P. M.
AN. XVIII

ROMAN

While the Greeks were developing a culture of ideas, the Romans were building a military empire that eventually controlled southern and western Europe and much of North Africa and the Near East. As people of varied cultural background, those living within the Roman Empire did not have a single artistic style, nor did the Romans themselves develop significantly new styles in art. In general, they copied the much-admired Greek art, to the point of using copies of Greek statues with sockets in their necks so that heads of Romans could be attached. Copies of Greek nude statues were also draped with Roman clothing, as in the statue of Augustus (**14.11**), which is thought to be based on the Greek *Spear Bearer* (2.21).

Many Roman sculptures were celebrations of the secular might of the emperors. Augustus' cuirass is covered with symbols of victory, and the equestrian statue of Marcus Aurelius (2.22) originally included the cringing figure of a captured barbarian leader beneath the horse's upraised hoof. As part of their empire-building, the Romans erected many public buildings, larger than those of Greece, on a scale facilitated by the introduction of concrete and space-spanning arches, vaults, and domes. It was the Romans who introduced non-functional architectural monuments, such as the Arch of Constantine (1.16) and Trajan's Column (2.132). Funerary art of the times included busts made from death masks and sarcophagi, such as the one featuring high reliefs of Dionysos and the Seasons (1.5), for honored corpses once the practice of cremation was abandoned.

EARLY CHRISTIAN AND BYZANTINE

In the first centuries after Christ's death, Christians were persecuted as threats to the state, so they kept what little sacred art they created secret and symbolic. Most of it consisted of burial pieces for those of the faith buried in the catacombs beneath Rome.

When the Emperor Constantine embraced Christianity in 313 as the official religion of the

14.11 *Augustus of Primaporta*, c. 20 BC. Marble, 6 ft 8 ins (2.03 m) high. The Vatican Museums, Rome.

Roman Empire and made Constantinople its second capital, Christian art began to flower. This was particularly so in the eastern half of the Empire as barbarian groups inundated the Western Empire in the fifth century. In the eastern BYZANTINE culture, which lasted 1000 years, all art was religious and created anonymously by the devout. ICONS, inspired paintings of Christ, the Virgin Mary, and the saints, were revered for their mystical wonder-working powers. The elongation of figures was stylistically distinctive (**14.12**). Elaborate mosaics (**14.13**), rendered in a stylized, spiritually expressive manner, covered the ceilings and walls of churches with Christian stories. The vast domed church of Hagia Sophia (2.39), built in Constantinople by the Emperor Justinian as the greatest of all Christian churches, was so large for its structure that it had to be rebuilt and buttressed after the dome collapsed.

14.12 *Madonna*, 6th–7th century AD. Detail, encaustic on wood. Santa Francesca Romana, Rome.

425

14.13 *Abraham's Hospitality and the Sacrifice of Isaac.*
Wall mosaic, San Vitale, Ravenna, Italy, c. AD 547.

500	c. 400–1453 Byzantine Empire c. 622–900 Islamic Empire	c. 500 Fall of Rome c. 570–632 Mohammad founder of Islam 652 Koran written down c. 700 porcelain invented in China	c. 6th–7th cent. *Madonna*, Rome, Italy (*14.12*) 532–37 Hagia Sophia, Istanbul (*2.39*) c. 547 *Sacrifice of Isaac*, Ravenna, Italy (*14.13*)
750	Feudalism in Europe to 900 c. 952–1056 Ottonian Empire	c. 750 "Beowulf" epic written c. 800 Charlemagne crowned Emperor of Western (Holy) Roman Empire c. 800–1000 growth of monasticism 868 first printed book in China	9th century *Book of Kells*, Ireland (*14.14*)
1000	c. 1050–1200 Romanesque period c. 1200–1400 Early Gothic	1096–1204 Crusades c. 1100 rise of universities in Spain, France, England c. 1200–50 Marco Polo travels to China and India	1077–1124 Cathedral of Santiago de Compostela, Spain (*14.15*) 1145–70 Chartres Cathedral, France (*12.16*) 1163–1250 Notre Dame, Paris (*12.18*) c. 1225 Beauvais Cathedral, France (*1.52*) 1243–8 Sainte-Chapelle, Paris (*2.96*)
1250	c. 1300 Beginning of Renaissance c. 1400–1500 Late Gothic	c. 1250 Arabic numerals introduced in Europe c. 1350 Black Death in Europe 1446–50 Gutenburg prints using movable type 1492 Columbus voyages to America	1280–5 Cimabue, *Madonna Enthroned with Angels*, Florence (*2.64*) 1305–6 Giotto, *The Lamentation*, Padua (*14.17*) 1339 Lorenzetti, *Allegory of Peace*, Siena (*5.8*) 1413–16 Limbourg Brothers, *Les Tres Riches Heures*, France (*2.142*) 1423 Da Fabriano, *Adoration of the Magi*, Florence (*2.143*)

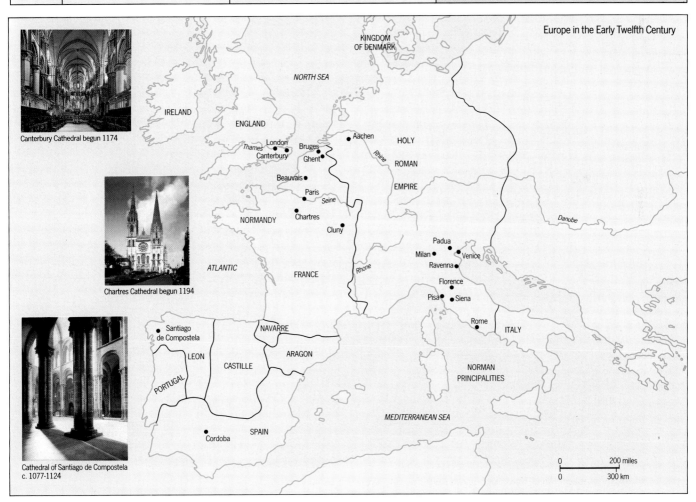

Canterbury Cathedral begun 1174

Chartres Cathedral begun 1194

Cathedral of Santiago de Compostela
c. 1077-1124

Europe in the Early Twelfth Century

14.14 Incarnation Initial from the *Book of Kells* (fol. 34), early 9th century AD.
Vellum, 13 × 10 ins (33 × 25 cm). Trinity College Library, Dublin.

MEDIEVAL ART

EARLY MEDIEVAL

Meanwhile, Western Europe was in the throes of the Dark Ages. Learning, spirituality, and art were kept alive in the monasteries and convents. A stunningly beautiful new development under these circumstances was the appearance of elaborate illuminated manuscripts. These unique, handmade copies of sacred texts, such as the Gospels, became especially ornamental in Ireland and the northern islands of Britain, where Christian fervor was allied with ancient traditions of interlaced and spiraling spiritual motifs. In the hands of the monks of the Iona community off the coast of Scotland, capital letters became extraordinarily ornate. In the *Book of Kells*, which they created, there are over 2000 illuminated capitals used at the beginning of Gospel passages. The one shown here (**14.14**) fills an entire page with intricate traceries surrounding the *Chi-Rho* monogram that begins St. Matthew's story of the birth of Christ.

14.15 Interior of the Cathedral of Santiago de Compostela, Spain, c. 1077–1124.

ROMANESQUE

In the middle of the eleventh century, Europe entered a new period of intense creative activity centered on the Christian Church. Life was still uncertain, and the Roman culture that had once dominated the area was still widely considered the height of the arts. Nevertheless, a new, distinctive aesthetic began to emerge. It was later called ROMANESQUE because of its supposed borrowings from classical Rome, but it had its own form, expressed primarily through architecture. The great longing for churches was answered with a sacred architecture characterized by rounded arches, thick walls and columns, and relief carvings in stone (3.31). The desire for repentance inculcated by the Church led many people to undertake long pilgrimages to certain churches, most notably the Romanesque Cathedral of Santiago de Compostela in Spain (**14.15**). These heavy structures admit only indirect lighting in most areas, lending Romanesque interiors a massive, blocky, almost fortress-like atmosphere.

GOTHIC

In the middle of the twelfth century, European art and architecture began to undergo an even more profound change. As burgeoning cities shifted the concentration of power from feudal rural areas, spirits seemed to lift, and with them soared the ethereal vertical heights of the new GOTHIC cathedrals. This way of building had a clear beginning in the directions given by Abbot Suger for the first Gothic cathedral: that space be used to symbolize the mystery of God, that God is mystically revealed in light, and that perfect harmony between parts is the

429

14.16 Rose Window, north transept, Chartres Cathedral, France, c. 1230. Stained glass, 42 ft 8 ins (13 m) diameter.

basis of beauty. The pointed arch, ribbed vault, and flying buttress allowed architects to replace the heavy appearance of Romanesque structures with more slender and vertical architectural details, such as those of Beauvais (1.52) and Chartres cathedrals (12.7). The new technology also allowed much larger windows, and these were often filled with intricate stained-glass designs and pictures of gemlike brilliance. They were created from cut pieces of colored glass, some of which were also painted for fine details, joined with lead strips, and reinforced with a framework of iron bands. The great rose window in Chartres Cathedral (14.16) is over 42 feet (13 m) in diameter; it offers an illuminated view of the Virgin Mary surrounded by angels, archangels, doves representing the Gospels and the Holy Spirit, and then outer circles of Old Testament figures.

In painting, artists began using the two-dimensional surface as a frame within which to create the illusion of three-dimensional depth. Although it was difficult to do so in the demanding medium of fresco, Giotto's *The Lamentation* (**14.17**) illustrates a revolutionary approach to the modeling of forms and the new effort to give figures an appearance of being alive and mobile, rather than frozen in static postures. These figures are also imbued with individualized human emotions, from the fierce grief of Mary to the sorrow of Mary Magdalene, to the philosophical acceptance of the two disciples to the right. Giotto was a Florentine artist whom many consider the originator of the movement that led to the Renaissance.

In contrast to Romanesque relief carvings, Gothic sculptures integrated into cathedrals were more three-dimensionally separate from their supports.

LATE GOTHIC

Although Gothic art appeared in countries throughout Europe, it waxed and waned at different times at different places, complicating our later efforts to piece together a coherent picture of art history. In north-western Europe, an increasingly expressive and naturalistic successor to the Gothic style lived on until about 1500. Painting was developed to new heights by artists of the Flemish

14.17 Giotto, *The Lamentation*, 1305–6.
Fresco, 7 ft 7 ins × 6 ft 7½ ins (2.31 × 2.02 m).
Arena Chapel, Padua, Italy.

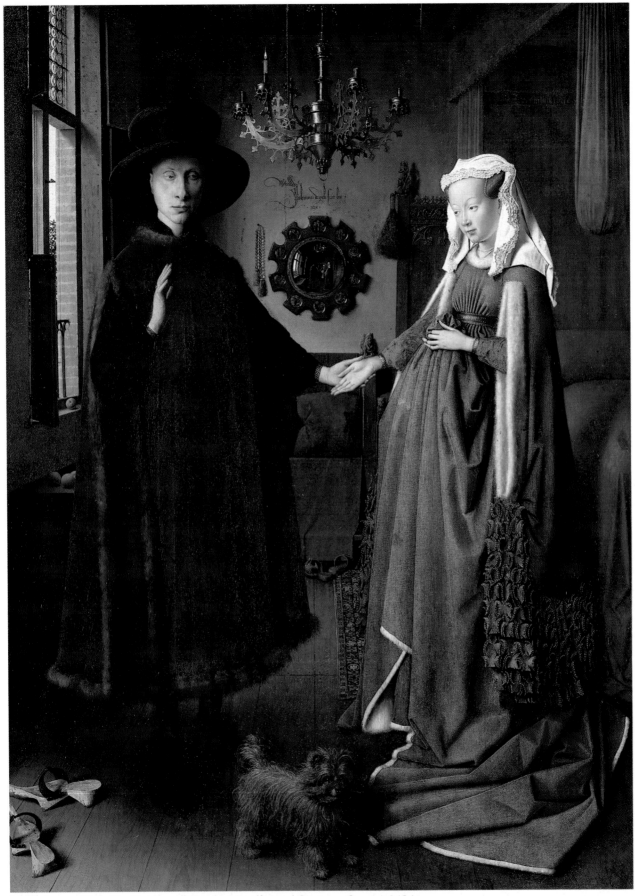

14.18 Jan van Eyck, *The Marriage of Giovanni Arnolfini and Giovanna Cenami*, 1434. Oil on oak panel, 32¼ × 23½ ins (81.8 × 59.7 cm). National Gallery, London.

school using the new medium of oil rather than tempera. The van Eyck brothers were early masters of the medium and used it to create the illusion of three-dimensional figures in deep space, with fine details and the luminous appearance possible only with skillful use of oils. Jan van Eyck's *The Marriage of Giovanni Arnolfini and Giovanna Cenami* (**14.18**) is studded with traditional symbols from the Gothic period—such as the dog indicating faithfulness in marriage, the single candle in the chandelier symbolizing Christ's sacred presence in the marriage ceremony, and the couple's shoes on the floor, reminders of God's commandment to Moses to take off his shoes when he was on holy ground. Yet the textures of metal, furs, fabrics, and wood are rendered with a realism never before achieved in any medium.

RENAISSANCE ART

EARLY RENAISSANCE IN ITALY

Meanwhile, in fifteenth-century Italy a major shift was underway from the metaphysics of the Middle Ages to a rebirth, or RENAISSANCE, of interest in the classical styles of ancient Greece and Rome. Classical sculptures and architecture were carefully studied for their principles of harmony and symmetry. To these were added a new understanding of perspective based on rediscovery of Euclidian geometry from classical Greece. The careful use of LINEAR PERSPECTIVE contributes to the sense of spaciousness in Fra Angelico's *Annunciation* (**14.19**), one of many frescos he painted for a Dominican convent in Florence. A gentle and conservative

14.19 Fra Angelico, *Annunciation*, c. 1440–5. Fresco San Marco, Florence, Italy.

14.20 Lorenzo Ghiberti, *Porta del Paradiso (Gates of Paradise)*,
1424–52. Gilt bronze, 17 ft (5.2 m) high. Baptistery, Florence, Italy.

monk, Fra Angelico retained many Gothic traits—such as bright pigmentation and the use of the flowery garden as a symbol of Mary's virginity—while incorporating some of the new devices such as perspective rendering and more realistic depiction of anatomy and fabric draping.

The work of the Florentine painter Sandro Botticelli, such as *The Birth of Venus* (1.46), likewise shows certain ties with Gothic traditions, such as a more two- than three-dimensional approach to figure drawing. But Botticelli's lyrical evocation of the idealized beauty of the human body and of harmonious configurations of forms is clearly innovative, with classical origins apparent in its style as well as its mythological subject matter.

The Early Renaissance also marked a rebirth of logic, though still in the service of the Church. In contrast to the devotional quality of Gothic arts, the Renaissance artist and art historian Lorenzo Ghiberti held that artists should be trained in grammar, geometry, philosophy, medicine, astronomy, perspective, history, anatomy, design theory, and arithmetic. Of his splendid gold-covered *Porta del Paradiso* ("Gates of Paradise") (**14.20**), paneled with ten scenes from the Old Testament, some incorporating scores of figures, he wrote that he "endeavored to imitate nature as much as possible, ... with buildings drawn to the same proportions as they would appear to the eye and so true that, if you stand far off, they appear to be in relief."[1] The doors are actually modeled in low relief, but the illusion is that of very deep space.

HIGH RENAISSANCE IN ITALY

During the brief period in Italy now known as the HIGH RENAISSANCE, roughly 1490 to 1520, a number of artists centered in Rome brought forth some of the greatest art the world has ever seen. This great outpouring was freed from the stylized conventions of earlier sacred art, and informed by but not held to classical traditions. The work of Michelangelo was passionately individualistic, glorifying the divine in the individual. After hundreds of years, people are still deeply moved by Michelangelo's *Pietà* (**14.21**), sculpted when he was only 24 years old. He regarded the human body as the prison of the soul, noble on the surface and divinely yearning within, and experienced sculpting as liberating a living form from inert stone. In addition to his anatomically and emotionally powerful sculptures, he also painted the vast Sistine Chapel ceiling (15.19), in an agonizingly awkward upward-looking position. Perhaps the extreme example of the Renaissance ideal of human freedom, Michelangelo refused to be enslaved by tradition or other people's standards, recognizing only his own divinely inspired genius and his longing for beauty as his guides.

Leonardo da Vinci applied his inventive genius to many fields, including art, and was thus the epitome of the "Renaissance man." His searching mind led him to engineering, mathematics, music, poetry, architecture, and natural science, as well as painting and sculpture. He continually studied animals, plants, human anatomy, the movement of water, and the play of light and shadow for a fuller understanding of the natural world. In art, his beautifully observed figure drawings are still consulted by artists as guides to the depiction of human anatomy. He used CHIAROSCURO effects not only to round his forms in space but also to enhance the emotional qualities of his paintings and guide the viewer's eye. In his compelling *The Virgin of the Rocks* (**14.22**), light glimmers on the flesh of the sacred figures and beckons in the mysterious distance.

14.21 Michelangelo Buonarroti, *Pietà*, 1499. Carrara marble, 5 ft 9 ins (1.75 m) high. St. Peter's, Rome.

1425–1640	Early Renaissance to Southern Baroque		
1425	Renaissance begins in Italy	1416–25 Brunelleschi reinvents linear perspective 1431 Joan of Arc burned at the stake 1434–94 de Medici dynasty in Florence c. 1450 printing press invented 1453 Turks enter Constantinople; end of Byzantine Empire	1425–52 Ghiberti, *Gates of Paradise*, Florence (*14.20*) 1440–5 Fra Angelico, *Annunciation*, Florence (*14.19*) 1460 Del Pollaiuolo, *Battle of Ten Nude Men*, Florence (*6.1*) c. 1482 Botticelli, *Birth of Venus*, Florence (*1.46*)
1485	c. 1490–1520 High Renaissance c. 1500–1600 Northern Renaissance c. 1525 Mannerism begins	Opening of European trade routes 1520–22 Magellan sails round the world 1543 Copernicus refutes geocentric view of universe	c. 1485 Da Vinci, *The Virgin of the Rocks*, Milan (*14.22*) 1495–8 Da Vinci, *The Last Supper*, Milan (*3.29*) 1498–9 Michelangelo, *Pietà*, Rome (*14.21*) 1501–4 Michelangelo, *David*, Florence (*9.2*) 1509–11 Raphael, *The School of Athens*, Rome (*14.23*) 1508–11 Michelangelo, Sistine Chapel ceiling, Rome (*15.20*) 1532 Correggio, *Danae*, Parma (*5.16*) 1550 Bronzino, *Portrait of a Young Man*, Florence (*5.2*) 1554 Cellini, *Perseus with the Head of Medusa*, Florence (*9.18*) 1592–94 Tintoretto, *The Last Supper*, Venice (*14.24*)
1595	Baroque period Colonial period in North America	1607–19 Kepler establishes planetary systems 1620 Puritans land in New England	1596 Caravaggio, *The Calling of St. Matthew*, Rome (*14.26*) 1656 Velázquez, *The Maids of Honor*, Spain (*14.27*) 1656 Bernini, Piazza of St. Peter's, Rome (*13.7*)

Villa Rotunda, Vicenza 1567-9

St. Peter's, Rome 1546-64

Milan
Vicenza
Verona
Padua
Venice
Avignon
Ravenna
Pisa
Florence
Rimini
Urbino
Siena
CORSICA
PAPAL STATES
ADRIATIC SEA
Rome
SARDINIA
Naples
TYRRHENIAN SEA
SICILY

Renaissance Italy

0   100 miles
0   150 km

14.22 Leonardo da Vinci, *The Virgin of the Rocks*, c. 1485.
Oil on panel, 6 ft 2⅝ ins × 3 ft 11¼ ins (1.89 × 1.2 m). Louvre, Paris.

14.23 Raphael, *The School of Athens*, 1509–11.
Fresco, 26 × 18 ft (7.9 × 5.5 m).
Stanza della Segnatura, Vatican Palace, Rome.

It was Leonardo who also developed SFUMATO modulations in oil painting to soften contours and create hazy atmospheric effects. Ever experimenting, he completed few works. His famous *Last Supper* (3.29) was done in tempera with a ground of pitch and mastic that he had invented—and which soon began to break down, requiring a series of restorations.

The artist whose work most clearly characterizes the High Renaissance was Raphael. In contrast to Michelangelo's passion and Leonardo's inventiveness, Raphael's work emphasizes classical harmony, reason, and idealism. His *The School of Athens* fresco (**14.23**) stands as a symbol of the humanistic High Renaissance appreciation of learning. The central figures are Plato and Aristotle, flanked by other ancient philosophers, mathematicians, scientists, and their students, including Pythagoras writing at the lower left and Euclid demonstrating a theorem at the lower right. This serenely balanced composition covers a 26-feet (8 m) span at the Vatican Palace in Rome. Raphael further developed the triangular composition associated with Leonardo, and it was thereafter used extensively in depictions of the Madonna and the Holy Family.

MANNERISM

In opposition to the humane balance and order of High Renaissance works such as *The School of Athens*, many Italian artists from 1525 to 1600 developed a more self-consciously sophisticated approach called MANNERISM by their detractors. Bronzino's work (5.2) is one example of the cool, sometimes almost sinister quality of elegance that some artists sought; Correggio (5.16) explored the refinements that technical perfection could lend to sensuality. A comparison of Tintoretto's version of *The Last Supper* (**14.24**) with that of Leonardo (3.29) reveals the great aesthetic distance between the Renaissance ideals of harmony and logic and the inventive theatricality of Tintoretto's Mannerism. As in his *Leda and the Swan* (3.10), bodies turn in

agitated gestures to tell a story of the infusion of the divine spirit into the bread and wine as if the narrative were being expertly enacted on a stage. In sculpture, Mannerism is most obviously exemplified by the sensuous work of Benvenuto Cellini (1.48 and 9.18).

NORTHERN RENAISSANCE

Beyond the Alps, the explosion of creativity in Italy at first had little effect on artists still following Late Gothic traditions, until 1500, when distinctively northern and Protestant versions of the new trends appeared briefly and vigorously in Germany. At one extreme was the dramatic intensity of Matthias Grünewald's work, such as *The Isenheim Altarpiece*, of which the agonizing central *Crucifixion* panel is

14.24 Jacopo Tintoretto, *The Last Supper*, 1592–4. Oil on canvas, 12 × 18 ft (3.65 × 5.5 m). San Giorgio Maggiore, Venice, Italy.

14.25 Matthias Grünewald, *The Crucifixion*, central panel of *The Isenheim Altarpiece*, c. 1510–15. Oil on panel, 8 ft 10 ins × 10 ft 1 in (2.69 × 3.07 m). Musée Unterlinden, Colmar, France.

shown here (**14.25**) and the exuberant *Resurrection* panel in Figure 2.112.

While only the individualistic aspects of the Italian Renaissance seem to come forth in Grünewald's work, Albrecht Dürer was so impressed by the disciplined, rational approach of the art he studied in Venice that he intentionally modeled himself as a humanistic scholar and wrote extensively to convince his compatriots of the value of Renaissance approaches to art. He was very influential because his skillful woodcuts (6.6) and engravings were widely distributed.

BAROQUE ART

SOUTHERN BAROQUE

Throughout Europe, the seventeenth century was a period in which the new middle classes joined the Church and nobility as patrons of the arts. Art became more realistic and emotional, speaking directly to viewers in sensuous, exuberant forms. In Catholic Italy, the tempestuous Caravaggio opened this BAROQUE period with his earthy focus on real people, an entirely new concept for religious paintings. In his *The Calling of St. Matthew* (**14.26**), he dresses Matthew and his companions in contemporary clothes and has them involved in a

14.26 Michelangelo Merisi da Caravaggio, *The Calling of St. Matthew*, 1596. Oil on canvas, 11 ft 1 in × 11 ft 5 ins (3.37 × 3.47 m). S Luigi dei Francesi, Rome.

game of chance when Christ appears, recognizing his spiritual beauty in the midst of familiar everyday life rather than in a formal, idealized setting.

The same unposed, naturalistic quality appears in the works of Velázquez, even when his subjects were the Spanish royal family. His famous *Las Meninas* (14.27) is not a formal family portrait, but a domestic scene of the young Princess Margarita with her attendants, with the king and queen's presence seemingly reflected in a mirror at the end of the room. Is Velázquez, who has painted himself before the canvas, looking at them? Does the mirror reflect part of the canvas instead? The artist's fascination with the effects of light is evident not only in these compositional ambiguities but also in the subtle variations of light and shadow throughout the work. Velázquez's highly skilled, suggestive brushwork led the later French Impressionists to regard him as the best of the painters of the past.

In sculpture, Bernini created ornate new forms for everything from fountains to building façades. His *The Ecstasy of St. Teresa* (1.36) reflects the actively emotional quality of the Baroque period, in contrast to the cool intellectualism of Mannerism. Swirling and diagonal lines create complex circular paths through the piece, in contrast to the serenity of classical draping, and Bernini dares to give St. Teresa a facial expression of supreme ecstasy whose sexual quality is hardly even ambiguous. Bernini's approach was soon copied by artists throughout Europe.

14.27 Diego Velázquez, *Las Meninas (The Maids of Honor)*, 1656.
Oil on canvas, 10 ft 5 ins × 9 ft (3.18 × 2.76 m). Prado, Madrid.

1500–1800	Northern Renaissance to Rococo		
1500	c.1500–1600 Northern Renaissance		c.1500 Bosch, *The Garden of Earthly Delights*, Brussels, Netherlands (*1.61*) 1508 Dürer, *Head of an Apostle*, Nuremburg, Germany (*2.12*) 1510 Bosch, *The Carrying of the Cross*, Ghent, Netherlands (*2.58*) 1510–15 Grünewald, *Isenheim Altarpiece*, Germany (*2.112, 14.25*) 1511 Dürer, *Saint Christopher*, Nuremburg, Germany (*6.6*) 1540 Hans Holbein, *Jane Small*, Basel, Switzerland (*2.61*) 1565 Bruegel, *Hunters in the Snow*, Antwerp, Netherlands (*2.47*)
		1517 Reformation begins 1521 Luther translates Bible into German, pub. 1534 1545–64 Catholic Counter Reformation 1566 iconclastic destruction in Netherlands Spread of Humanism, availability of books increases	
1600	Northern Baroque	1611 first authorised version of the Bible 1663 reorganization of the French Academy 1672 Bellori writes *Lives of Modern Artists*	c.1626 Rubens, *The Assumption of the Virgin*, Antwerp, Netherlands (*14.28*) c.1635 Rubens, *Landscape with Rainbow*, Antwerp, Netherlands (*1.23*) 1660 Claude Lorraine, *Campagna Landscape*, Lorraine (*4.14*) 1660 Rembrandt, *Self-Portrait*, Amsterdam, Holland (*1.64*) 1660–9 Rembrandt, *Sleeping Girl*, Amsterdam, Holland (*4.15*) 1665 Vermeer, *The Allegory of Painting*, Amsterdam, Holland (*1.2*) 1669–85 Palace of Versaille, France (*1.39*) 1675–1710 Wren, St. Paul's Cathedral, London (*14.29*)
1700	Rococo style	c.1710–95 Rise of Prussia 1789 French Revolution 1792 Paine *The Rights of Man*	1701 Rigaud, *Louis XIV*, France (*1.47*) 1743–1772 Neumann, Church of Vierzehnheiligen, Germany (*14.30*)

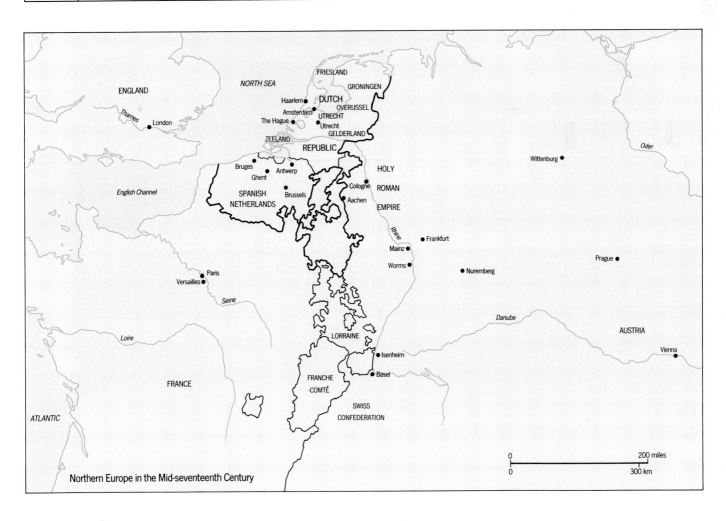

Northern Europe in the Mid-seventeenth Century

14.28 Peter Paul Rubens, *The Assumption of the Virgin*, c. 1626. Oil on panel, 49⅜ ×37⅛ ins (125.4 × 94.2 cm). The National Gallery of Art, Washington D.C. Samuel H. Kress Collection.

444

NORTHERN BAROQUE

The Baroque style in northern Europe found other forms. One of its greatest exponents was Peter Paul Rubens of Antwerp. His *The Assumption of the Virgin* (14.28) represents plump, rounded figures in an appreciative, joyful way, with flowing movement and warm colors. This was spirituality in the flesh. His typically large, swirling paintings are quite recognizable in style, even though Rubens employed a workshop of assistants to do much of the work on his 3000 signed paintings, a common practice at the time.

In Holland, where a Protestant culture drew its strength from a sober and prosperous middle class which rejected the influence of Rome, Rembrandt emerged as one of the greatest artists of all time.

14.29 Christopher Wren, St. Paul's Cathedral, London, 1675–1710.

Influenced by the work of Rubens—as well as that of many other artists, including those of non-European cultures—he made use of Baroque devices for leading the eye through undulating three-dimensional space. Highly spiritual, he brought the psychological impact of religious themes directly through to the viewer with subtlety and deep human understanding. His self-portraits (such as 1.64) and treatments of religious subjects, such as *The Three Crosses* (6.19–21), are the work of one who feels life profoundly, as well as of a master of the visual arts.

In architecture, the Baroque period was characterized by grand effects and exuberant, swelling forms. This tendency was combined with a certain classical restraint by Christopher Wren in his rebuilding of St. Paul's Cathedral (14.29) in London. He planned the structure from the bottom up, while it was under construction, and the clearly Baroque dome and towers are wedded to more classical lower levels inspired by the Italian Renaissance architect Palladio.

ROCOCO

In the late Baroque—or Rococo—period in central Europe (the first half of the eighteenth century), formal restraint was abandoned. In France, painters such as Antoine Watteau and Jean Honoré Fragonard (2.138) honored the whims of the aristocracy (led by Louis XIV, who called for a more lighthearted art) with dreamy scenes of carefree and beautiful people in a natural paradise. These visions were rendered with delicate, swirling lines and pastel colors in a style considered so frilly by the French revolutionaries who overthrew the aristocracy that they dubbed it "Rococo," a frivolous concoction of shells. Today the Rococo style is considered to have rather more substance—an intentional freeing of art from academic rules of composition in favor of exuberant, dancing lines and gentle coloring.

Architecture also became unabashedly ornate and fantastic. The most extraordinary of the German Rococo churches is Balthasar Neumann's pilgrimage church of Vierzehnheiligen (14.30). Everything seems to be in constant motion. There are few straight lines; curling motifs developed in France swirl endlessly, and the ceiling is treated to create a floating illusion of boundless space. The gaiety expressed here is a far cry from the heavy, still atmosphere of Romanesque churches or the soaring,

14.31 Jacques-Louis David, *The Oath of the Horatii*, 1784–5. Oil on canvas, approx. 14 × 11 ft (4.3 × 3.7 m). Louvre, Paris.

vertical thrusts of the Gothic cathedrals—yet all are conducive to certain kinds of spiritual experiences and appropriate for their times.

EIGHTEENTH-CENTURY ART

NEOCLASSICISM

In the swings of action and reaction that increasingly characterized art history, the late eighteenth century brought another return to the aesthetics of ancient Greece and Rome. As a reaction to Baroque and particularly Rococo styles and as an expression of the

14.30 Balthasar Neumann, Church of Vierzehnheiligen, near Staffelstein, Germany, 1743–72.

Enlightenment, artists likes Jean-Antoine Houdon sought a quiet, informal dignity (9.10). Archeologists' discoveries of classical cities such as Pompeii gave architects models to follow in their return to noble, restrained buildings. Winckelmann's highly influential *Thoughts on the Imitation of Greek Works of Art* (1755) held that "The only way to become great ... is by imitation of the ancients.... [Art] should aim at noble simplicity and calm grandeur."[2]

NEOCLASSICAL painters tried to re-create the style of classical sculptures, since little was known of ancient painting. Using his art to encourage a revolutionary patriotism and stoicism, Jacques-Louis David re-created a story of heroic self-sacrifice from Republican Rome in his *The Oath of the Horatii* (**14.31**). Its severity and clarity are clear departures from the works of the recent past.

447

1750–1950 Neoclassicism to Surrealism

1750	Neoclassicism, France	1775–83 American Revolution 1789 French Revolution	c.1779–80 Houdon, *Bust of a Young Girl*, France *(9.10)* 1784 David, *The Oath of the Horatii*, France *(14.31)*
1800	Romanticism, France and England	1804–14 Napoleonic Empire 1814 first steam engine 1815–50 industrialization of England 1837 invention of telegraph 1839 invention of photography (Daguerre) 1848 revolutionary uprisings in Europe	1808 Blake, *The Last Judgement*, England *(3.17)* 1818–19 Gericault, *The Raft of the Medusa*, France *(14.32)* 1842 Ingres, *Two Nudes*, France *(2.28)* 1845 Turner, *Looking out to Sea*, England *(5.20)*
1850	Realism c.1875–1900 Impressionism 1880–1900 Post-Impressionism	1859 Darwin *Origin of Species* 1861–1865 American Civil War 1876 Bell patents telephone 1894 Edison invents motion picture	1849 Courbet, *The Stone Breakers*, France *(14.33)* 1863 Manet, *Le Dejeuner sur l'herbe*, France *(14.34)* 1878 Degas, *Dancer with a Bouquet*, France *(2.55)* 1881 Renoir, *The Boating Party*, France *(3.26)* 1884–6 Seurat, *La Grande Jatte*, France *(14.37)* 1892 Monet, *Rouen Cathedral*, France *(14.35)* 1889 Van Gogh, *The Starry Night*, France *(1.35)* 1893 Gauguin, *The Spirit of the Dead Watching*, Tahiti *(1.63)* 1895–8 Cézanne, *Still-life with Apples*, France *(14.36)*
1900	c.1900–20 Expressionism Fauvism begins 1905 c.1907–14 Cubism Futurism begins 1910 c.1916–22 Dada Surrealism begins 1924	1903 Wright Brothers' first flight Rise of Women's Suffrage Movement 1914–18 World War I 1928 first sound movie produced 1939–45 World War II	1906 Derain, *The Pool of London*, France *(14.39)* 1907 Picasso, *Les Demoiselles d'Avignon*, France *(14.40)* 1911 Matisse, *The Red Studio*, *(2.111)* 1913 Boccioni, *Unique Forms of Continuity in Space*, Italy *(14.42)* 1917 Duchamp, *Fountain*, France *(14.45)* 1931 Dali, *The Persistence of Memory*, France *(14.46)* 1936–39 Wright, *Kaufman House*, Pennsylvania *(3.42)* 1939–40 Nervi, *Aircraft Hangar*, Ortbello, Italy *(12.31)*

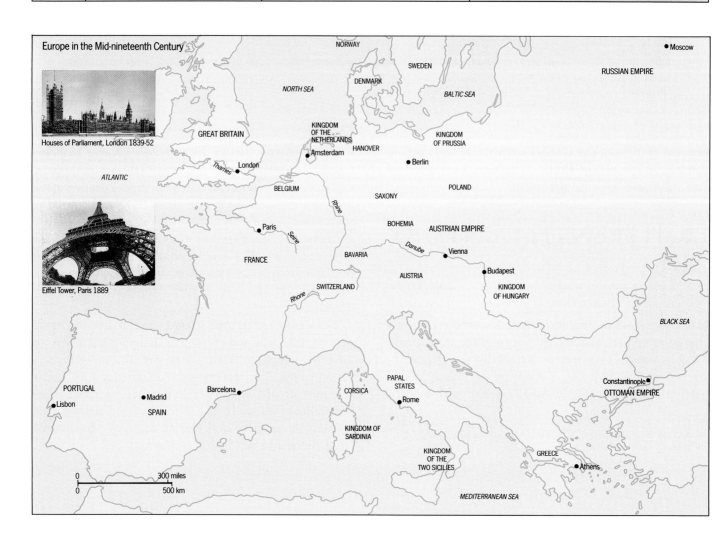

Europe in the Mid-nineteenth Century

Houses of Parliament, London 1839-52

Eiffel Tower, Paris 1889

ROMANTICISM

Throughout the history of Western art certain artists have focused more on emotion and imagination than on the logic and harmony of classicism. This perennial tendency surfaced in the ROMANTIC movement in the early decades of the nineteenth century, when it coexisted with Neoclassicism, championed by Ingres (2.28, 2.74). In contrast to the austere Neoclassical attempts to be impersonal, Romantic artists openly expressed their own feelings. In their landscape paintings, newly elevated to a position as significant as figure paintings, they portrayed the natural world as an extension of their own sensibilities, which ranged from the peacefulness of John Constable's rural scenes to the turbulence of Turner's seascapes (5.20). Turner discovered the emotional impact of pure color and pushed it to the point where it almost becomes the subject matter.

Théodore Gericault's *The Raft of the Medusa* (**14.32**) illustrates the emphasis on sensation and passion in content and dynamism in composition that characterized the French version of Romanticism. The huge painting depicts the 13-day ordeal of the few passengers who survived the sinking of a government ship. They were left adrift on a crude raft by the captain and crew. Emotions of despair, suffering, and hope are built into a strong double-triangle composition charged with energy.

The mystical prints and paintings of William Blake (3.17) carried something of the passionate emotional content of the Romantic movement, although Blake had his own unique visionary agenda. In architecture, Romanticism was expressed largely through nostalgia for Gothic structures.

14.32 Théodore Gericault, *The Raft of the Medusa*, 1818–19. Oil on canvas, 16 × 23 ft (4.9 × 7 m). Louvre, Paris.

14.33 Gustave Courbet, *The Stone Breakers*, 1849. Oil on canvas, 5 ft 3 ins × 8 ft 6 ins (1.6 × 2.59 m). Formerly Gemäldegalerie, Dresden (destroyed 1945).

NINETEENTH-CENTURY ART

REALISM

At odds with the idealized content of both Neoclassicism and Romanticism (for instance, Gericault's survivors are not gaunt and covered with sores), another approach to art began to appear as a recognizable movement in France from about 1850 to 1875. It was the work and theories of Gustave Courbet that led this rebellion against the "grand manner." In paintings such as *The Stone Breakers* (**14.33**), Courbet sought to present real people without artifice rather than idealized or heroic scenes drawn from the artist's imagination. It was his choice of subject matter—everyday contemporary life—as much as his attempt to portray it truthfully that represented a sharp break with the past. Courbet eschewed historical, mythological, or abstract subjects ("Show me an angel and I'll paint one"), insisting on painting only what he could see, exactly as he saw it, without artistic conventions. In his "Open Letter to a Group of Prospective Students" (1861), Courbet gave a clear definition of REALISM:

Painting is essentially a *concrete* art, and can consist only of the representation of things both *real* and *existing*. ... Imagination in art consists in finding the most complete expression for an existing thing, but never in imagining or creating this object itself. ... Beauty as given by nature is superior to all the conventions of the artist.[3]

IMPRESSIONISM

Realism was not considered good art by the academic juries who controlled most of the purchasing of art in France. They also rejected the work of Édouard Manet, whose *Le Déjeuner sur l'Herbe* (**14.34**) shocked even those who visited the counter-exhibition held in 1863 by many angry artists whose work had been refused by the official Salon. Manet used a classical composition borrowed, in heavy disguise, from Raphael, but in such a manner that we cannot figure out its meaning. In a complex way, he was denying the use of paintings to teach or arouse emotions; paintings, he asserted, can exist for the sheer beauty of colors, light, patterns, and the brushstrokes on the surface of the canvas.

Manet's NATURALISM was closely followed by a group of artists who were dubbed IMPRESSIONISTS. Some of them rejected not only story-telling and

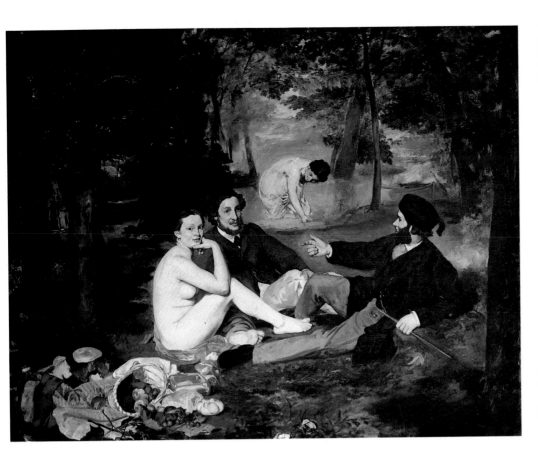

14.34 Édouard Manet, *Le Déjeuner sur l'Herbe (The Picnic)*, 1863. Oil on canvas, 6 ft 10 ins × 8 ft 8 ins (2.08 × 2.65 m). Louvre, Paris.

14.35 Claude Monet, *Rouen Cathedral*, 1892. Oil on canvas, 39¼ × 25⅞ ins (99.3 × 65.7 cm). The Metropolitan Museum of Art, New York. Theodore M. Davis Collection, 1915.

meaning but even realistic depiction of objects, seeking instead to capture the ephemeral impressions of light reflecting off surfaces under different atmospheric conditions. If anything, their dabs of unblended colors broke down images into montages of light, as in Monet's *Rouen Cathedral* (**14.35**). Whereas Realists often worked from photographs of everyday scenes, these Impressionists painted outside in order to observe and record the effects of natural lighting.

Others who are often grouped with the Impressionists—such as Degas (2.55, 4.10)—tried to capture the fleeting action or transient moments rather than focusing solely on the changing effect of light. Renoir (3.26) is also grouped with the Impressionists, but the style of his later works— luminous but blended use of color to describe lush, three-dimensional forms—varied considerably from the increasingly abstract brushstrokes of Monet. Renoir wrote:

> I had wrung impressionism dry, and I finally came to the conclusion that I knew neither how to paint nor how to draw. . . . Light plays too great a part outdoors; you have no time to work out the composition; you can't see what you are doing. . . .If the painter works directly from nature, he ultimately looks for nothing but momentary effects; he does not try to compose, and soon he gets monotonous.[4]

POST-IMPRESSIONISM

In some art historians' ways of categorizing styles, the late works of Degas and Renoir are included in a group of paintings known as POST-IMPRESSIONIST. In a narrower definition of this style, however, the major Post-Impressionists were Cézanne, Seurat, van Gogh, and Gauguin. What unites them is their movement beyond what they conceived as the limitations of Impressionism and their highly personal explorations of the art of painting. Van Gogh (1.35) distorted lines and forms to express essence; Gauguin (1.63) intentionally rejected a "civilized" style. In Cézanne, by contrast, there was a return to careful composition in an intense search for artistic perfection. But Cézanne did not return to the past; rather, he was perhaps the pioneering figure in modern painting. Rejecting both the messiness of Impressionism and the conventions of linear perspective used since the Renaissance to give the illusion of form and space, Cézanne tried to reinvent two-dimensional art from scratch. He built up spatial layers, geometric forms, and rhythms with colors, lines, and shapes alone (see 2.29), with careful attention to orderly relationships between forms across the picture plane. Even in his clearly representational works, such as *Still-Life with Apples* (**14.36**), he concentrated on meeting aesthetic

14.36 Paul Cézanne, *Still-Life with Apples*, 1895–8.
Oil on canvas, 27 × 36½ ins (68.6 × 92.7 cm).
Collection, The Museum of Modern Art, New York. Lillie P. Bliss Collection.

14.37 Georges Seurat, *A Sunday Afternoon on the Island of La Grande Jatte*, 1884–6. Oil on canvas, 6 ft 9 ins × 10 ft ⅜ ins (2.05 × 3.05 m). The Art Institute of Chicago. Helen Birch Bartlett Memorial Collection.

goals such as balance, intensity of color, and the *feeling* of depth, even if doing so meant distorting the outlines of objects.

Seurat's approach to painting was highly analytical. His POINTILLISTE technique of juxtaposing dots of unblended colors (to be blended optically)—as in his ground-breaking painting *A Sunday Afternoon on the Island of La Grande Jatte* (**14.37**)—is superficially similar to the unblended brushstrokes of the Impressionists. But his tiny vibrant dots of pigment are meticulously applied and calculated to define shapes rather than allow them to disintegrate under the effects of light. Under Seurat's systematic analysis, forms become precise, almost flat geometric shapes, carefully organized in space. Seurat's clearly delineated shapes and painstakingly applied dots of pigment contribute to a timeless sense of order that is in sharp contrast to the immediacy and spontaneity of Monet's paintings.

EXPRESSIONISM

As artists began departing from academic standards to do their own experimenting into the nature of reality and how it could be expressed in art, some inevitably turned their attention inward. Art used as a vehicle for the portrayal of inner psychological states has been called EXPRESSIONISM. This tendency was already evident in the late works of van Gogh (1.35), for whom trees and sky writhed in sympathetic resonance with his intense inner torments. The Norwegian Edvard Munch abandoned any attempt at objective reporting of external realities in his *The Scream* (**14.38**). The terror he feels inside becomes visible as wave upon wave of undulating colored bands, filling the environment. Prior to World War I, German artists in groups called *Die Brücke* ("The Bridge") and *Der Blaue Reiter* ("The Blue Rider") became Expressionists, usually

14.38 Edvard Munch, *The Scream*, 1893.
Oil, pastel, and casein on cardboard, 36 × 29 ins (91.4 × 73.6 cm). National Gallery, Oslo.

portraying states such as anxiety or anger rather than the hopeful sweetness and materialistic complacency they perceived in French Impressionism. German Expressionism encompassed many of the arts, including filmmaking, with works such as *The Cabinet of Doctor Caligari* (8.24).

FAUVISM

Meanwhile in France a group of artists led by Matisse held an exhibition in 1905 of works so revolutionary that the artists were called *les Fauves* ("the wild beasts"). They had abandoned any attempt at descriptive, naturalistic use of color and, in some cases, form. Instead they used these elements of design as ends in themselves or expressions of the essence of things, freed from strict associations with the observable world. André Derain's *The Pool of London* (**14.39**) illustrates the use of semi-realistic

forms with free choice of colors; Matisse's *The Red Studio* (2.111) uses color even more freely, with forms translated into flat shapes and painted with seemingly childlike abandon. Matisse had serious and orderly intentions, however. He rejected the "jerky surface" of Impressionist paintings, complaining:

> The splitting up of color brought the splitting up of form and contour. . . . Everything is reduced to a mere sensation of the retina, but one which destroys all tranquillity of surface and contour. Objects are differentiated only by the luminosity that is given them.[5]

By contrast, Matisse sought to create the sensations of space and form by using color purely and simply rather than in dabbed spots. Moreover, he felt that color, like other elements of design, should serve the expressive purposes of the artist. Matisse's seminal experiments in modern art continued, but the FAUVE group disbanded after three years.

14.39 André Derain, *The Pool of London*, 1906.
Oil on canvas, 25⅞ × 39 ins (65.7 × 99 cm). The Tate Gallery, London.

TWENTIETH CENTURY ART

CUBISM

The next significant steps in modern art were taken by Pablo Picasso and George Braque. Some of Picasso's early paintings, such as *The Old Guitarist* (2.110) were delicately representational. But in 1907 he abruptly switched directions. Heavily influenced by the geometric forms of Cézanne and the stylization of African sculpture, Picasso created in *Les Demoiselles d'Avignon* (**14.40**) a work considered so ugly that people tried to attack it physically when it was first shown in the United States. What he had begun to do in this work evolved into a movement in which a subject was fragmented into geometric planes that simultaneously revealed more than one side at once, as though the artist were walking around a three-dimensional form and reporting the view from many angles. The ancient Egyptians had stylistic conventions for doing somewhat the same thing, but under the angular analysis of Cubism, the subject sometimes becomes almost totally lost from view, as in Braque's *The Portuguese* (**14.41**).

Of this highly intellectual approach to art, Braque wrote, "The senses deform, the mind forms. Work to perfect the mind. There is no certitude but in what the mind conceives."[6] And Picasso asserted, "Nature and art, being two different things, cannot be the same thing. Through art we express our conception of what nature is not."[7]

14.40 Pablo Picasso, *Les Demoiselles d'Avignon*, Paris (begun May, reworked July 1907). Oil on canvas, 8 ft × 7 ft 8 ins (2.439 × 2.337 m). Collection, The Museum of Modern Art, New York. Acquired through the Lillie P. Bliss Bequest.

14.41 Georges Braque, *The Portuguese*, 1911.
Oil on canvas, 45⅞ × 31⅞ ins (116 × 81 cm). Kunstmuseum, Basel.

FUTURISM

In Italy, the sweeping changes of an industrializing civilization were answered by a call for revolution in the arts. In 1910 a group of artists set forth a passionate statement they called the *Manifesto of the Futurist Painters*. It contained these conclusions:

> Destroy the cult of the past, the obsession with the ancients, pedantry and academic formalism. . . .
> Elevate all attempts at originality, however daring, however violent. . . .
> Regard art critics as useless and dangerous. . . .
> Rebel against the tyranny of words: "Harmony" and "good taste". . . .
> Support and glory in our day-to-day world, a world which is going to be continually and splendidly transformed by victorious Science.[8]

14.42 Umberto Boccioni, *Unique Forms of Continuity in Space*, 1913. Bronze (cast 1931), 43⅞ × 34⅞ × 15¾ ins (111.2 × 88.5 × 40 cm). Collection, The Museum of Modern Art, New York. Acquired through the Lillie P. Bliss Bequest.

The principal aesthetic attempt of the FUTURISTS was to capture in art the vigor, speed, and militant pride they felt characterized modern life. In paintings, this meant portraying successive movements over time, as Duchamp had done in the "dynamic cubism" of *Nude Descending a Staircase* (2.137). In sculpture, Umberto Boccioni tried to express not form but action in works such as *Unique Forms of Continuity in Space* (**14.42**).

ABSTRACT AND NONOBJECTIVE ART

In the same year that Boccioni's *Unique Forms* was completed, the Russian-born painter Wassily Kandinsky created another of the abstract paintings he had been working on for several years: *Improvisation No. 30* (**14.43**). In the intellectual ferment that followed the freeing of art from meaning, naturalistic representation, and academic aesthetic standards, Kandinsky's piece reflected the penultimate stages of movement away from art that tries to represent forms from the outer world. In Kandinsky's painting, bare references to the phenomenal world are retained only to keep art from descending to mere pattern-making; he uses colors and barely recognizable forms (here, cannons and tall buildings) to lead the viewer into a world of nonmaterial spiritual realities.

Piet Mondrian used the process of ABSTRACTION to strip natural forms to their aesthetic essence, as in his abstract paintings of trees (1.25–27). But he—as well as generations of later twentieth-century artists—soon abandoned all references to natural forms, creating purely NONOBJECTIVE art. Works such as *Composition in Blue, Yellow, and Black* (**14.44**) and *Fox Trot A* (2.9) were so different from traditional paintings that Mondrian offered many written explanations of the theories behind nonobjective art. No longer were paintings self-evident; one needed an intellectual understanding of the artist's intention. Mondrian held that because paintings are created on a flat surface, they should honor that flatness rather than trying to give it the illusion of three-dimensionality. Furthermore, line and color are the essence of art, and to be seen most clearly they should be separated from forms to which each person brings personal associations. To display line and color nonobjectively, Mondrian chose the "universal" or "neutral" form of the rectangle.

14.43 Wassily Kandinsky, *Improvisation No. 30*, 1913. Oil on canvas, 3 ft 7¼ × 3 ft 7¼ ins (1.10 × 1.10 m). The Art Institute of Chicago, Arthur Jerome Eddy Memorial Collection.

14.44 Piet Mondrian, *Composition in Blue, Yellow, and Black*, 1936. Oil on canvas, 17 × 13 ins (43.2 × 33 cm). Kunstmuseum, Basel, Emannuel Hoffman Foundation.

DADA

In contrast with the sublime rationality of Mondrian's theories and paintings, a group of rebellious artists and authors in Zürich launched in 1916 an anti-rational, anti-aesthetic movement called DADA, babytalk which they claimed meant nothing. The members of this highly influential movement had decided that humans were so unjust to each other that they did not deserve art, so they set out to destroy it. The ironically humorous, intentionally uncensored output of the group included offbeat artforms with titles such as "rubbish constructions," "rayographs," "exquisite corpses,"

14.45 Marcel Duchamp, *Fountain*, 1917. Readymade, porcelain urinal on its back, inscribed on upper edge. Sidney Janis Gallery.

14.46 Salvador Dali, *The Persistence of Memory*, 1931. Oil on canvas, 9½ × 13 ins (24.1 × 33 cm). Collection, The Museum of Modern Art, New York. Given anonymously.

and "ready-made objects."

Marcel Duchamp's *The Fountain* (**14.45**) is one of the more infamous examples of Dadaist "art." It consists solely of a men's urinal, purchased from the Mott Works Company and presented lying on its back, otherwise unaltered except for the crude signature Duchamp painted on the front, "R. Mutt, 1917." This "work" defies not only logical analysis but also the traditional minimal expectation that art is something physically created by the artist. The anarchistic Duchamp claimed that it is simply the act of choice that defines the artist. In a tongue-in-cheek defence of the art of "R. Mutt," which was banned from an exhibition, an anonymous article apparently written by Duchamp insisted:

Now Mr. Mutt's fountain is not immoral, that is absurd, no more than a bathtub is immoral. It is a fixture that you see every day in plumber's show windows.

Whether Mr. Mutt with his own hands made the fountain or not has no importance. He CHOSE it. He took an ordinary article of life, placed it so that its useful significance disappeared under the new title and point of view—created a new thought for that object.[9]

SURREALISM

Many of the Dadaist artists became part of the next major twentieth-century movement: SURREALISM, in which the source of images is the subconscious. Rather than abandoning forms, surrealists render them with the illogic of dreams. Based on the theories of Freud, this approach spanned the period between World Wars I and II, for the most part, though surrealistic elements had appeared throughout the history of art and still do. One of the most famous Surrealist artists is Salvador Dali, whose 1928 movie *Un Chien Andalou* (8.25) was like a bad dream in itself. Expressed in a static painting rather than a time sequence, Surrealism often relies on unusual perspectives and symbols to express the apparently realistic but logically impossible contents of dreams. In Dali's *The Persistence of Memory* (**14.46**), there is a haunting sense of loneliness and of time become meaningless. Melting watches, lightstruck cliffs, and unrecognizable forms are meticulously described, as if in a vivid hallucination.

14.47 Andrew Wyeth, *Christina's World*, 1948. Tempera on gessoed panel, 32¼ × 47¾ ins (81.9 × 121.3 cm). Collection, The Museum of Modern Art, New York. Purchase.

TRADITIONAL REALISM

While all these modern art styles were cropping up, many artists continued to work in a variety of traditionally realistic, representational styles. The United States particularly had an historical fondness for realistic art, and even after industrialization brought the country into the forefront of international commerce many artists retained a distinctive appreciation for naturalistic representation of life in their homeland. The emerging artform of photography was dominated in the United States by those who wanted to remain true to their subjects, as well as their medium, such as Alfred Stieglitz (8.8), Dorothea Lange (8.9), and Ansel Adams (8.12). A number of painters who had been drawn to abstract movements in Europe returned to more realistic work, such as the perennially popular Andrew Wyeth. With meticulous tempera technique, he focuses on quietly meaningful rural scenes, such as the world of a small Maine island community as seen by a young woman with polio in *Christina's World* (**14.47**). The dreamlike content, symmetrical composition, and unusual point of view bespeak a modern approach to design, coupled with relatively representational imagery.

ABSTRACT EXPRESSIONISM

A parallel development at the opposite pole from traditional realism established New York as the leading center of modern art in the West. After World War II, the term ABSTRACT EXPRESSIONIST was applied to those of the New York school who rejected traditional painting styles and instead emphasized the spontaneously expressive gesture and all-over composition, with all areas of the canvas equally important. One of the major figures in this movement was Jackson Pollock. He engaged in what was known as ACTION PAINTING, throwing or dripping paint with whole-body motions onto a long sheet of canvas on the floor (14.48). Pollock did not feel that his movements were random; rather, his experience was that they were directed by the psychic forces within himself. To him, his paintings were a direct and fresh expression of the inner life which impels all artists. The frenetic, interlacing lines that he laid down have a restless energy that leads the viewer around and through, again and again, to no conclusion—perhaps an apt metaphor for the pace and meaninglessness of contemporary urban life. The subjective, "painterly" approach of expressing oneself through freely applied paint was also used by other mid-century New York artists, including Hans Hofmann (5.18), Willem de Kooning, and to a certain extent Mark Rothko (1.34), and is still present in the brushwork of James Brooks (5.4), among others.

POST-PAINTERLY ABSTRACTION

As the New York school evolved, many artists developed more controlled nonobjective styles that had in common the attempt to remove the evidence of their presence, allowing their work to stand by

14.48 Jackson Pollock painting. Photo by Hans Namuth.

14.49 Barnett Newman, *Vir Heroicus Sublimis*, 1950–1.
Oil on canvas, 7 ft 11⅜ ins × 17 ft 9¼ ins (2.422 × 5.136 m).
Collection, The Museum of Modern Art, New York. Gift of Mr. and
Mrs. Ben Heller.

itself as a stimulus to which the viewer can react. Barnett Newman explains these efforts in spiritual terms:

> The present painter is concerned not with his own feelings or with the mystery of his own personality but with the penetration into the world mystery. To that extent his art is concerned with the sublime. It is a religious art which through symbols will catch the basic truth of life.... The artist tries to wrest truth from the void.[10]

To engage the viewer in a direct experience of truth without using imagery, the Post-Painterly Abstractionists tended to focus on color and color relationships. The *Abstract Imagists* (or Chromatic Abstractionists) typically used open, relatively flat but fluid imagery created impersonally by pouring dyes onto unsized canvas, as in the work of Helen Frankenthaler (5.25). *Hard-edge* painters created flat, unvarying areas of pigment with immaculately sharp boundaries, sometimes with even nonobjective imagery reduced to a bare minimum. As Barnett Newman suggests by naming the hard-edged painting shown here (**14.49**) *Vir Heroicus Sublimis* ("heroic, elevated man"), such works may have a sublime, classical effect of ordered perfection and grandeur. But if you stare at his painting for a while, those fine stripes—which Newman called "zips" of light—may begin to create extra optical effects that

transcend the flatness of the colossal red field.

In fact, hard-edged paintings are called OP ART when they deliberately use the peculiarities of human vision to make people see things that have not actually been physically placed on the canvas. The artist steps back, allowing the experience of the work to take form in the perceptions of the viewer. Josef Albers, highly influential as a teacher as well as an artist, evoked optical color phenomena in his *Homage to the Squares* series (2.113). Some Op Art even creates illusions of color, space, and movement in black and white compositions, such as Bridget Riley's *Crest* (2.134) and Victor Vasarely's *Supernovae* (**14.50**).

POP ART

Another mid-century direction in modern art emerged in London and has encompassed some artists in the United States. This trend, called POP ART, uses objects and images from popular, commercial culture—from cartoons to beer cans—rather than the rarefied imagery of the fine arts. Some of the work is hostile toward contemporary throwaway culture; some presents it as having a rather zany aesthetic validity. As we have seen, Claes Oldenburg's monuments to the banal (such as his giant clothespin, 4.3) are humorously conceived. Some of Andy Warhol's famous pop creations, such as the well known painting of 200 Campbell's soup cans or his later self-portraits (6.31), reflect the repetitive visual patterns of the modern marketplace—a reminder of the aesthetic realities of modern life that one can interpret as one pleases. Roy Lichtenstein, one of the major early figures of the movement, exaggerated cheap printing techniques by rendering pop culture images with blown-up dot screens. He has carried this approach into the present with works such as *Mural with Blue Brushstroke* (**14.51**). It is his desire, he says, for his art to appear impersonal.

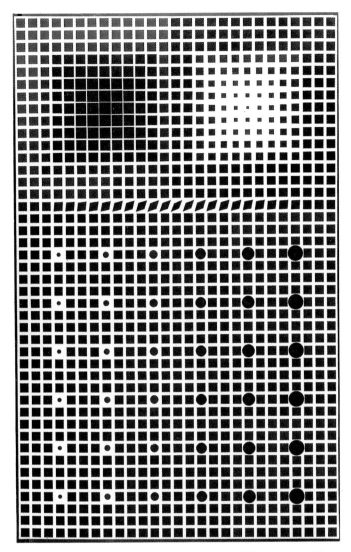

14.50 Victor Vasarely, *Supernovae*, 1959–61. Oil on canvas, 8 ft 1½ ins × 5 ft (2.42 × 1.52 m). Tate Gallery, London.

14.51 Roy Lichenstein, study for *Mural with Blue Brushstroke*, 1985. Cut-and-pasted paper, pen and ink, pencil, 34¼ × 17½ ins (87 × 44.5 cm). © The Equitable Life Assurance Society of the United States.

14.52 William Bailey, *Monte Migiana Still Life*, 1979. Oil on canvas, 4 ft 6 ins × 5 ft (1.37 × 1.52 m). The Pennsylvania Academy of Fine Arts.

NEW REALISM

Alongside the nonobjective and pop trends in modern art, a number of artists have continued or returned to more realistic treatments of actual objects. Their subjects have not necessarily been traditional ones, however. Many have explored the visual facts of industrialized life—the neon-lit shops, fast-food places, city streets, automobiles, depressed or overweight people. In recent years, this investigation has become *super-realistic* or PHOTOREALISTIC in the hands of artists such as Chuck Close (5.24) and Richard Estes (2.91). Some are finding beauty in close investigations of features of the environment such as

William Beckman's *Power Lines* (1.22) and Bill Martin's *Abalone Shells* (5.23). William Bailey (**14.52**) has turned from abstraction to figurative subjects in his painting, but with sensitivities developed from modern art, rather than traditional representative paintings. Using objects painted from memory and references to the actual objects, but without setting up a still-life, he works with aesthetic issues such as the meanings of groupings, intervals, tensions between the flatness of the picture plane and the illusion of space, and inferences of diagonals projecting into space. Bailey says, "I wanted a painting that was silent and unfolded slowly, that offered a contemplative situation."[11]

TECHNOLOGICAL ART

Although many named twentieth-century art movements have centered on painting styles, technological changes have brought changes in all the arts and have enabled the development of artforms that did not even exist in the past. As we have seen, there are new building materials and synthetic substitutes for traditional two- and three-dimensional media. In addition, industrial technologies have spilled over into art in an entirely new way. In the new arts of computer graphics (8.32, 8.33, 8.34) and laser shows (2.95), foreshadowed by the lovely light projections of Thomas Wilfred onto translucent screens (**14.53**), the hand of the artist at work has disappeared. Now it is a machine that directly creates the art, with the artist one step removed—building, programming, or operating the machine. Sometimes it is even the *observer* who seems to create the art, activating art-producing devices merely by being present in a certain space.

At one time, art and religion were closely linked in the West; now art and science are forming new alliances, and some very exciting contemporary art is coming out of the high-technology research laboratories, created by people whose skills and sensitivities encompass both science and art. Developments in fields such as fiberoptics and communications may in the future be used to create arts that stimulate the senses in ways yet unimagined.

14.53 Thomas Wilfred, from *Lumia Suite, Op. 158*, 1963–4. Third movement, elliptical. Lumia composition (Projected light on translucent screen). Three movements, lasting 12 minutes, repeated continuously with almost endless variations. Screen 6 ft × 8 ft (1.828 × 2.432 m). Collection, The Museum of Modern Art, New York. Commissioned by the Museum through Mrs. Simon Guggenheim Fund.

14.54 Guillermo Gomez-Pena and Coco Fusco making "ritual offerings" to welcome Columbus, performance piece at Mexican Museum, San Francisco, 1990. Courtesy of the artists.

INSTALLATIONS, PERFORMANCE ART, EARTHWORKS, CONCEPTUAL ART

Already the definition of art is being continually expanded: Art is whatever an artist declares to be art. Galleries and museums now display INSTALLATION PIECES, three-dimensional designed environments often set up only as temporary experiences, such as Stephen Antonakos's 24-feet-long (7.4 m) *Green Neon from Wall to Floor* (2.94). In PERFORMANCE ART, the work consists of an artist doing something, such as Charles Simonds building a miniature brick community for the Little People on his own nude body (13.21).

When performance and video art made their appearance in the 1970s, they were promoted as a way of ending the traditional emphasis on art as object, bringing art to viewers more directly as a sheer visual experience. It is now difficult to define the boundary between performance art, experimental theater, street theater, and "happenings." During the 1980s Guillermo Gomez-Pena organized a collective of Mexican and American artists—the Border Arts Workshop—to put on interdisciplinary pieces about cultural and psychological boundaries. They performed not only in galleries but also at checkpoints, in the streets of San Diego, and across the border, illegally sharing food and holding hands. Now Gomez-Pena is doing solo performance art with

14.55 Agnes Denes in a wheatfield she planted on Battery Park landfill, Manhattan, 1982.

ironic characters such as Warrior for Gringostroika, and "counter-Columbus" collaborations with artist and writer Coco Fusco to help re-evaluate Columbus's "discovery" of America (**14.54**). Although much contemporary performance art is purposely shocking, non-mainstream, Gomez-Pena asserts:

> The great challenge of incorporating politics into art is to do it in a way that pleases aesthetically. I don't believe performance artists should be marginal. In North America, marginality—the European myth of the artist as a marginal bohemian—is still very prevalent. I aspire to speak from the center, to be active in the making of culture. The same is true for gays, women, and artists of color, who can't afford to be marginalized anymore. Performance art is the one place where this can happen—where ritual can be reinvented, and where boundaries can be crossed.[12]

In EARTHWORKS it is the surface of the earth that becomes the sculptor's medium, for such massive alterations as Robert Smithson's *Spiral Jetty* (9.23). And in CONCEPTUAL ART, idea is more important than form, which may be as ephemeral as Geger and McMillins "*Surface Erosion*" (2.144), which was destroyed as soon as the high tide returned. In 1969, Sol LeWitt offered an explanation of conceptual art in his "Sentences on Conceptual Art":

> Ideas alone can be works of art; they are in a chain of development that may eventually find some form. All ideas may not be made physical. . . . If words are used and they proceed from ideas about art, then they are art and not literature.[13]

If there is form in conceptual art, it is usually ephemeral, recorded only in photographs. Agnes Denes planted an incongruous field of wheat on the Battery Park landfill in Manhattan during the summer of 1982, in the shadow of the World Trade Center (**14.55**). Her intent in this conceptual work was to evoke awareness of "the absurdity of it all"— of a world commodities trading system that is far removed from the realities of plants and hungry people. "Part of the basic concept," she said, was to "call people's attention to having to rethink their priorities."[14]

NEO-EXPRESSIONISM

In the continuing replay of earlier movements, with new twists, a major current redirection in painting is called NEO-EXPRESSIONISM. Its adherents around the world are using painting to express their own emotions, as the Abstract Expressionists did, but now with figurative imagery that is distorted by those emotions. Images are often derived from the mass media, and the emotional content is typically violent or anguished, charged with energy, as in Anselm Kiefer's *Athanor* (2.49). Howard Hodgkin's *Interior with Figures* (**14.56**) is a relatively quiet example, but even here the feelings expressed seem charged with sexual energy. Hodgkin tries to recapture the emotion of an experience through evocative objects, colors, and spatial effects. He says, "I want to include more because the more feeling and emotion you include in the painting, the more it will come out the other side to communicate with the viewer."[15]

THE CRAFT OBJECT

In the current redefining of the boundaries of art, one interesting direction is the merger of the fine and applied arts. Industrial design, for example, is benefiting from a sculptural approach, and handcrafts are being collected and shown as works of art. Exhibitions of applied design are of great popular interest, and new museums are arising that deal in applied disciplines alone. At the same time, a number of artists trained in traditional crafts are carrying their knowledge and skills into the creation of art for art's sake. The results are entirely new approaches to two- and three-dimensional design. Norma Minkowitz, for example (see box and figure **14.57**), has invented a technique that no one else in the world is yet using: She crochets three-dimensional forms, shellacs them to a hard state, and perhaps paints on their surfaces, thus creating see-through sculptures that are unlike any that can be developed through traditional sculptural media.

Many pieces bridge crafts and fine arts because although they may be built with craft techniques, they are nonfunctional, meant only to be experienced. Art quilts, for example, are often deliberately made too small to fit on any bed; they demand to be hung on a wall and responded to like a painting. As art critic Edward Lucie-Smith observes:

> Craft objects increasingly tend to be used in precisely the same way as paintings and sculptures in domestic and other interiors—as space modulators and as activators of particular environments, lending their own emotional coloring. We respect and value them as totems and touchstones as we do fine art.[16]

14.56 Howard Hodgkin, *Interior with Figures*, 1977–84. Oil on wood, 4 ft 6 ins × 5 ft (1.37 × 1.53 m). Saatchi Collection, London.

Norma Minkowitz

on

THE INTERFACE BETWEEN ART AND CRAFT

Norma Minkowitz's early work was in more-or-less-functional fiber arts, such as pillows in reverse appliqué revealing layer upon layer of fabric, and clothing that was just barely wearable, with great attention to texture and line and shape. Then in 1983 she crocheted around a shoe, removed the shoe, and discovered that she had created a transparent form. Since then she has been exploring the possibilities of these open crocheted sculptures, stiffened into hard but transparent forms which often make statements about containment. Minkowitz emphasizes that they are sculptures. At the same time, they have the intimacy of craft. She comments:

"This organic growth and shaping became possible from having a soft material become a hard material. It's very repetitious and time-consuming to create your own material, your own fiber, your own canvas. But through the medium of crochet the process becomes part of the content, and structure and surface are achieved at the same time. I am also motivated and excited by the intimate relationship that I have with the object I am creating, which is generally small and easy to hold on my lap. I sit in a quiet corner, alone with my thoughts and my work. At a time when many artists collaborate and have technicians to do part of their work (which is often monumental in size), I feel content with and more attracted to the oneness I feel with my work."

"The medium that I use is very important in my work, but yet the work isn't about the technique. I think in a successful art form there has to be a reason for the process used. The reason for my technique is that it becomes a really fragile but yet structured form which allows me to show an interior space. It's seeing within something, and the inside becomes ambiguous—Is it a shelter? Is it a trap? Is it someplace to be safe or someplace to be stifled or controlled? Many of my pieces show the feeling of being absorbed into the earth, bringing up universal themes of man's fear of death and dying and mortality. I try to impose meaning on my work because I feel that art is an extension of oneself and that, without a message or a meaningful reason for the choice of medium, it cannot be art."

"This piece (**14.57**) has a hand inside. Is the hand reaching out or is it being drawn down into this box, never to come out again? I could make the hand more obvious by darkening it, but I like having it be something that feels like it's there but yet it's not there. It almost has the feeling of a flower, a gentle flower. The floating red layer in the center was very hard to do because I had to crochet that part inside after

472

14.57 Norma Minkowitz, *Lotus*, 1989. Open crocheted sculpture, 15½ × 12 × 12 ins (39.4 × 30.5 × 30.5 cm). Photo by Bobby Hansson.

the shell was stiff; my knuckles kept bleeding because the stiffened fiber is very rough.''

''I think most artists, whether they are painters or sculptors or woodworkers or people working in fiber, are combining so many techniques and materials now that the line is very fine between what is craft and what is fine art. There is craftsmanship in a marble sculpture, and there is fine art in a fiber sculpture. It's no longer what material you are using—it's what you are saying with your work and what it means. If you see a beautiful wooden salad bowl, it's less of a statement in regard to expressive emotion and more of a statement about technique, craftsmanship, form, and function. But if you see something in fiber or wood that is purely sculptural and says something to you in a unique way, then it's an art form. If a piece motivates feelings and makes different people react in a different way, then the work is saying something intellectual and that's what makes it art. Art is something that is poetic; it reveals imagery that has not been done before and inspires a new way of seeing.''[17]

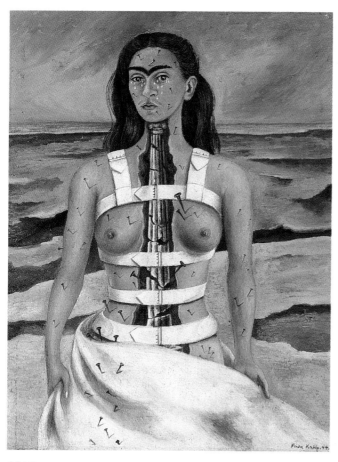

14.58 Frida Kahlo, *The Broken Column*, 1940. Mexico City, Museo Frida Kahlo, Collection Lola Olmedo.

RECOGNITION OF WOMEN'S ART

Simultaneously with the acceptance of craft pieces as art objects has come a growing appreciation of art created by women. Since women have long been devalued in most cultures, so has their art. In the past, relatively few women received art education or recognition as fine artists and their craft works have not been valued as art. One major art history textbook commonly used in the United States contained not a single woman artist in its first edition.

This situation is undergoing change. Art historians are now trying to unearth evidence of art by women from the past, and contemporary women artists are receiving more attention from the world of collectors, galleries, museums, and art critics.

As women's art gains recognition, some women are developing art explicitly about their personal experiences as women. One of the heroines of this movement is Frida Kahlo, who married Diego Rivera twice and died at the age of forty-four after a life of chronic pain. She had polio as a child, was further crippled by a terrible accident, suffered a miscarriage, and had her leg amputated shortly before her early death. Her own intense experiences are the main subject of her paintings, most of which are self-portraits. *The Broken Column* (**14.58**), for instance, explicitly reveals the cross of pain she carries from a broken spine. As other women are socially freed to discover their own identity, distinct from cultural roles prescribed for them, many are searching and creating art depicting previously taboo aspects of female life, such as menstrual blood and the vagina, and affirming and celebrating their sexuality.

RECOGNITION OF MULTI-CULTURAL ART

Another huge section of the world's population has long been ignored by the Western art establishment: the art of non-European people of color. Asian art was "discovered" hundreds of years ago by the dominant European and then the North American white cultures, but historical art by Africans and Native

14.59 Museo de Arte Contemporaneo de Monterrey, with Juan Soriano's *The Dove*, 1991. Courtesy Marco.

Americans was described as "primitive," and contemporary artists in Africa and Latin America were largely overlooked.

This situation is changing rapidly. In North America's multicultural society the art world is beginning to appreciate the contributions of non-European cultures, and there are now major museums and galleries devoted solely to the art of these previously neglected cultures. Others place multicultural art on a par with that of famous "white" artists, such as Mexico's new Museum of Contemporary Art in Monterrey (**14.59**). Despite economic difficulties, Latin American countries are developing partnerships between business, government, and the art world to train and show the work of their own artists and to research and preserve artifacts from their cultural heritage. Even world maps are being revised to show the true size of the neglected continents; the new Peters Projection reveals the immensity of Africa in contrast to the smallness of Europe.

There is a particular poignancy to the work of those whose cultural heritage and sense of self, as well as economic and social freedom, have been historically repressed. Sometimes the humanity of the oppressed is revealed in anger; sometimes it is as quietly moving as the montage paintings of the late Romare Bearden (**14.60**). Bearden said:

> I work out of a response and need to redefine the image of man in the terms of the Negro experience I know best. I cannot divorce myself from the inequities that are around me.[18]

14.60 Romare Bearden, *Family Dinner*, 1968. Collage on board, 30 × 40 ins (76.2 × 101.4 cm). ACA Galleries, New York.

Deborah Muirhead

on

ART AS ANCESTRAL EXPLORATION

Deborah Muirhead was born in Bessemer, Alabama in 1949 into an African-American family. She is now a respected East Coast artist and art professor whose dark, abstract paintings (**14.61**) combine formal aesthetic considerations with her own compelling interest in researching her roots. She has done extensive genealogical research in census records, county courthouses, and also in novels, poems, and texts on slave history, folklore, folk culture, and life in the agrarian South. She wonders:

"Who were these people in the eighteenth century? What did they believe in, and how much of their belief system survived? The cultural continuities from Africa began to merge with both Native American and Anglo beliefs to form a distinctly new culture.

As I began researching all of that my paintings got darker and darker. The genealogical research provided a correspondence to the paintings, a mystery, a kind of searching in the dark. I was so immersed in the research that I literally dreamed about these people. They were with me all the time, almost guiding me.

The dark paintings challenge the notion of darkness as void, for me, the dark paintings were full of richness and life. They were about history with all its tragic consequences for people. But they also were about life, and continuity.

I've been inspired by specific folklore legends, although I try not to illustrate. There is also a continuing legacy of the important effect of water in the lives of West Africans and then of African Americans. Water is traditionally one of the resting places of the ancestral world. The spirits reside in rivers, ponds, and streams. Africans of many tribal groups with this belief system came here and put down roots in this country, continuing belief in water's special spiritual significance. I was interested in the way that belief system combined with new religion which influenced many African Americans: Christianity, particularly Southern Baptist influence, in which there is total water immersion in baptism. The notion that you are a sinner, that you die in the water during total immersion, your sins are washed away, and you are reborn a new person free of your sins combined powerfully with the beliefs of

second or third generation African Americans in the spirit world in the water.

One of the things I've tried to do in this series of paintings is to create a surface that could resemble a watery surface, with undefinable objects, forms, or implements. They seem to arise mysteriously from all of this stuff that I'm thinking about and reading about and totally immersed in. I think in part they are farm implements and objects that might be devices of torture or fragments that might have some archaeological significance if you knew its context but now are just fragments with no known context.

Just after I visited the plantation where my people were slaves, the paintings became incredibly dark and opaque. There was almost no point in them in which you could find a light source. In the last year or two there have been more openings in the paintings. I want people to be moved by them—to find their haunting power. Some are moved by an overwhelming sense of tragedy, but you can move through that to something more significant, something about survival. I think because the dark surface also

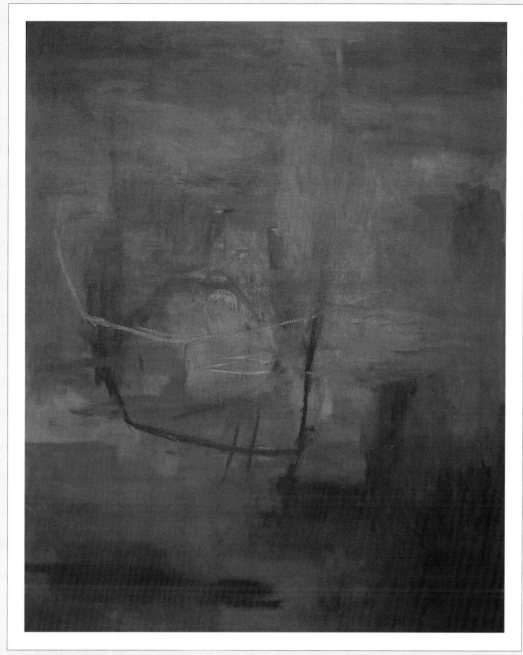

14.61 Deborah Muirhead, *Water World*
Voices from the Deep, 1991. Oil on canvas, 5 ft × 4 ft (1.52 × 1.22 m).
Courtesy of the artist.

resembles land or soil, it feeds a sense that life is always there, always coming back, always able to provide something.

I have all this ancestral research stuff swimming around in my head but the hard thing is to do a painting that is also about painting—that is about color, value, and chroma, and works formally, but not too formally, because if they do, then you've assembled the puzzle too neatly. I try to use as many colors as possible, and keep them really dark, working with the structure of low value and low intensity of color. People who spend a little bit longer time with them are amazed at what they begin to see. They are so elusive, like shadows on a landscape.

One of my former grad students said, 'I can smell these. These are like dirt.' It's the smell I love, in the spring after it rains. . . . So they're about a lot of things, and hopefully they're about paint, too.''[19]

1945–1990	Twentieth Century		
1945	1912–55 Abstract and Non-Objectivism Abstract Expressionism	1944 computer technology developed 1945 Atomic bomb dropped on Hiroshima, Japan 1946 xerography invented 1950–53 Korean War	1950s Jackson Pollock painting, New York (*14.48*) 1950–51 Newman, *Vir Heroicus Sublimus*, America (*14.49*) 1956 Rothko, *Green on Blue*, New York (*1.34*) 1956–73 Utzon, Sydney Opera House, Australia (*12.32*) 1958 Aalto, Church at Vuoksenniska, Finland (*12.35*) 1959–61 Vaserely, *Supernovae*, France (*14.50*)
1960	Minimal Art Op Art Pop Art	1961 Berlin Wall built, East/West Germany 1961–73 Vietnam War 1969 first manned moon landing	1963 Noguchi, *Red Cube*, New York (*1.40*) 1964 Riley, *Crest*, England (*2.134*) 1965 Hoffman, *Rhapsody*, New York (*5.18*) 1967 Oldenburg, *Clothespin*, New York (*4.3*) 1967 Warhol, *A Set of Six Self-Portraits*, New York (*6.31*) 1968–9 Close, *Frank*, America (*5.24*)
1970	Earthworks New Realism Installation and performance art Conceptual Art	1970 Greer *The Female Eunuch* 1973 first test-tube baby born in England 1978 personal computers become available	1970 Smithson, *Spiral Jetty*, Utah (*9.23*) 1971–8 Piano/Rogers, Pompidou Center, Paris (*12.38*) 1972 Heizer, *City Complex One*, Nevada (*2.25*) 1973 Hanson, *Woman with Suitcases*, America (*1.3*) 1975 Hicks, *Bas Relief Wall*, New York (*10.23*) 1976 Christo, *Running Fence*, California (*2.7*) 1977–84 Hodgkin, *Interior with Figures*, England (*14.56*) 1978 Estes, *Double Self-Portrait*, America (*2.91*) 1979 Bailey, *Monte Migiana Still-Life*, America (*14.52*)
1980	Neo-expressionism Technological Art	1982 first artificial heart implanted 1986 Chernobyl accident in Soviet Union 1989 fall of communist governments in Eastern Europe 1990 Germany reunited	1982 Denes, *Battery Park Wheatfield*, New York (*14.55*) 1983–4 Keifer, *Athanor*, Germany (*2.49*) 1989 Birnbaum, *Rio Video Wall*, Georgia (*8.32*) 1989 Nappi/Winkler, *Continuum I* (*8.34*) 1990 Gomez-Pena/Fusco, *Welcome Columbus*, San Francisco (*14.54*) 1990 Isozaki, Team Disney Building, Florida (*1.43*)

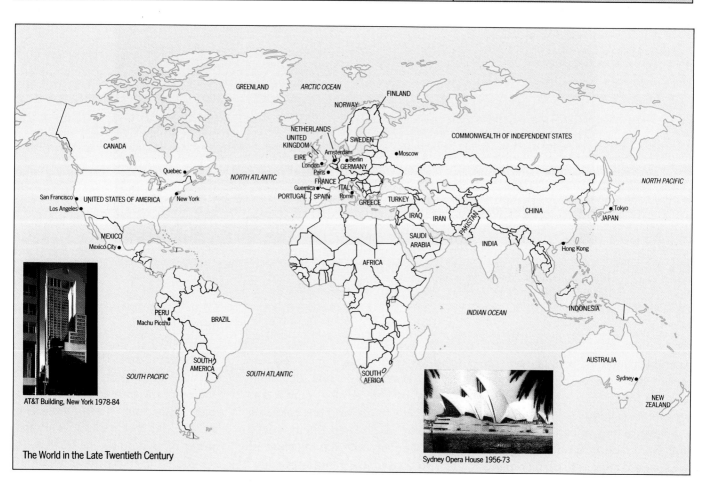

AT&T Building, New York 1978-84

The World in the Late Twentieth Century

Sydney Opera House 1956-73

RECOGNITION OF OUTSIDER ART

As these "discoveries" are breathing new life into the art world, perhaps the hottest trend is the embracing of OUTSIDER ART by galleries, museums, and collectors. In contrast to FOLK ART, in which relatively untrained artisans are working within a cultural tradition, outsider artists are those sheer individualists who are self-taught and are working totally outside of both community traditions and establishment ideas about what constitutes good art.

This nonconformist work is highly personal, spontaneously expressive, and often spiritual. The artist may begin by creating art as a private act, not for the eyes of others, and certainly not for sale. Bessie Harvey was a cleaning woman in a hospital, quietly following her inner spiritual calling to make sculptures of found wood for patients to help them heal, before people began noticing, loving, and collecting her work (**14.62**). Her inspirations come from vision and the spirits she senses in the wood:

> I talk to God for advice, not my neighbors. I talk to trees, weeds, and animals. I see things in dreams and when I close my eyes before sleep. I thought everyone was like that. When I meditate and close my eyes, faces and people begin to pass by—like watching a movie. Then one face stays. So I get up and try to draw it out or capture it in a piece of wood. All nature is crying out to tell us things.[20]

The first "insider" to laud such work was the Swiss painter Jean Dubuffet. At mid-century he collected a whole museum full of such pieces, which he termed "art brut" ("raw art"). In it lay true life, he felt; cultural conditioning had asphyxiated all other art:

> Simplifying, unifying, making uniform, the cultural machine, based on the elimination of flaws and scrap, on the principle of sifting in order to retain only the purest essence from its raw material, finally manages to sterilize all germination. For it is precisely from flaws and scrap that thought derives sustenance and renewal. A fixative of thought, the cultural machine has got lead in its wings.[21]

Dealers who have "discovered" outsider art are now swamping the outsider artists, snapping up cartloads of work, typically at prices that are only a fraction of their resale value in galleries. The

14.62 Bessie Harvey, *Tribal Spirits*, 1988. Mixed media, 45 × 26 × 20 ins (114.3 × 66 × 50.8 cm). Dallas Museum of Art, Metropolitan Life Foundation Purchase Grant.

exploitation of these sincere, eccentric artists is a growing scandal in the art world. Some have learned the hard way how to insist on honest pay for their efforts. Bessie Harvey asserts both her economic rights and the integrity of her own motivation as an artist:

> I'm not educated, but I'm not dumb. I've got a free spirit and I won't be under nobody's thumb. What they've taken from me they can have, but they can't have me. I'd rather be at peace with a biscuit and butter than to live in hell with steak and gravy.[22]

Jon Serl
inside
AN OUTSIDER'S MIND

Jon Serl (b. 1894) is one of the hottest discoveries of the collectors of outsider art, but he still lives as he has for decades, in a home-made 25-room ramshackle house in a small town in southern California, with chickens and dogs roaming through the dusty rooms. Until recently he kept to himself and didn't sell his paintings, but they are now shown in major galleries and museum collections. After years of a variety of jobs, including vaudeville theater as a female impersonator, Hollywood acting, dancing, and screenwriting, and vegetable gardening, he discovered his calling as an artist when he was fifty-five:

"I wanted a painting for a big wall in that house, but I didn't have any money, so I got a board and painted my own. I didn't think it was any good, but then a man who'd traveled around the world saw it and said, 'Where'd ya get that Rousseau?' And you see what happened? Man—pat him on the back and watch him purr. From that point on, painting took over my life. I don't own a radio or watch television—all I do is paint.

I paint all day, every day. The most difficult part of it is when you have to sign a painting and admit it's yours. Then you have to rake up everything in you and ask yourself: Is this what I wanted? I paint on wood now because when I was painting on canvas, I wound up putting a knife through most of my work. I no longer do that, but lately I've been burning quite a few.

[When I started painting] it was during the war. There was no art material available. Discarded soldier clothing boxes were used for panels—stains from berries and flower petals—even bark and roots gave color. I even used pulverized earth. I made my own charcoal—I still do! Later the town dump was the total source of supply. No used can of house paint was overlooked. Almost from the beginning, the fierce drive I feel from within demanded a constant search for supplies, so I could tell it while it was fresh. At times, the hillside mustard greens from my food plate had to be sacrificed for green stain needed on a canvas. Perhaps this seems drastic and fanatical, but there was no other way.

No one day is ever exactly like the day before. The position and intensity of the sun, the atmosphere, the green of trees, or color of distant buildings, dust, fog, and especially sudden rain storms all blend to offer a new and ever-changing canvas. And that is why the work I do is forever new.

If only a person will take time to observe. So much of our life is spent in sorrow and regret. All this is really waste, when with a bit more effort, all sorrow can be made a healthy happening. The world must be a gladsome place. At least, that is the way I see it.

Instead of listening to professors 'earn their keep' in schools or watching other painters copy each other into frustration, I looked as the caveman looked, to nature. 'Out there,' I found all answers to all things.

[I haven't had any art education.] Well, maybe in the fifth grade. The teacher said, 'One flower.' I bent it. She hit me on the hand with the ruler and said, 'Straight, straight.' I tore it up. Maybe that's when I became an artist.

I don't know why I've lived so long, because everyone in my family died young. Everybody's dead now and I wonder why I'm still living. I'm tired and I'm not glad to be alive because it's very hard. I'd like to be free and if it weren't for my paintings, I probably would've died long ago."[23]

14.63 Jon Serl, *Man and Papaya*, 1988. Oil on board, 48 × 32 ins (122 × 81.3 cm). Photograph courtesy of Jamison-Thomas Gallery.

15

APPRECIATING ART ON ALL LEVELS

Thus far we have looked at works of art from one perspective at a time—seeing, feeling, awareness of technical skill or design qualities, historical knowledge, or understanding of the content. When we have opportunities to see actual works of art, however, our appreciation is richest if we can bring all these levels into play. In this chapter we will take a more comprehensive look at five monumental works: a building, a painting, a piece of sculpture, a ceiling fresco, and a body of beadwork.

SHAKER ROUND STONE BARN

The round stone barn built in 1826 by the Shaker community in Hancock, Massachusetts (**15.1**)—is not yet well known beyond the north-eastern United States. When it was built, it was designed strictly for functionality and not for its aesthetic qualities. Nevertheless, looking at it today we can recognize it as a beautiful piece of architecture.

Often it is only with hindsight that the worth of particular artists or styles is valued. In the mid-nineteenth century, tastes of the mainstream society were for highly ornamental styles; people considered the extreme simplicity of Shaker design boring and tasteless. But the Shakers cared little for the opinions or possessions of the worldly. They were a Utopian sect who intentionally withdrew from the secular material world to devote themselves to a life of the spirit. Theirs was a unique experiment, for men, women, and children lived and worked together in celibacy as brothers and sisters. Following the dictum of their inspirational leader, Mother Ann Lee—"Put your hands to work, and your hearts to God"—they created 18 self-sufficient communities from Maine to Kentucky. In their hardworking, caring approach to meeting basic survival needs, they unselfconsciously created designs of great beauty by classical standards of harmony and proportion. Today furniture, baskets, and tools that the Shakers built are extremely valuable collectors' items.

15.1 Round Stone Dairy Barn, Hancock Shaker Village, Massachusetts, 1826.

The Anatomy of the

SHAKER ROUND BARN

with stone walls 21 ft. high, 270 ft. around, housing 52 cattle.

Cattle in lower ramp

upper ramp

Threshing and Wagons

Hay Mow

16'3"

Bracings 23'10"

15'

Cupola

Octagon center support

hay ladder

30" stone wall.

Windows (14 in all)

Bracings

wagon level and Threshing Floor

Wagon level

Hay storage *about 35' high and 55' diameter*

stone walls 30"

Cattle stables

HAY FLOORING

Cattle

16'

Manure Storage

Manure

About 90 ft. diameter

15.2 Round Stone Barn. Drawing by Eric Sloane.

The Shaker community in Hancock had a large herd of dairy cattle, and when the old barn burned down, Elder William Deming designed a new one that would allow many people to work at the same time without getting in each other's way (**15.2**). He based the design on a perfect circle, rather than the traditional rectangle, with room inside for eight to ten hay wagons unloading into a haymow that would hold 300 to 400 tons (30,481.5 to 40,642 kg) of hay. Earth was built into a gentle ramp so that the hay wagons could enter half-way up the height of the building and unload hay downward—easier than tossing it up—until the mow was half-full. An octagonal ventilation shaft ran up the center, ending in a cupola. Around the edges on the ground level were stanchions for 52 cows, easily fed by a person walking in a circle. At a later date, manure pits were dug beneath so that manure could be shoveled down through trapdoors behind the cows and collected for application to the fields. These pits undermined the foundations, however, resulting in cracks like the one visible in the old photograph (**15.3**). The barn was finally rebuilt in 1968 and is carefully maintained as a showpiece of ingenious functional design.

The aesthetic qualities of the barn's extreme functionality anticipated the Bauhaus principle that form should follow function. Everything the Shakers put their hands to was visually elegant, although they had no written theory of design and were guided instead by their own imaginative ergonomic solutions. Even hallways, with pegs to hang chairs on for convenience in sweeping beneath them, were places of beauty. Materials were presented honestly. Wood was used very sympathetically and rubbed to a soft glow that is all the more noticeable from the lack of unnecessary ornamentation.

15.3 Round Stone Barn photographed in 1932.

In the stone barn, stones were cut so carefully that the walls curve continually, with no bulges, while at the same time tapering in thickness from 3½ feet (106 cm) at the base to 2½ feet (76 cm) at the top. Stone and wood are beautifully mated, and no attempt is made to hide the structure. Structural innovations necessitated by the circular design include the splitting of the outer end of every other beam so that there is room for all of them to join at the middle but yet adequate support for the full circumference of the roof. The floor boards are likewise carefully cut in a radiating pattern. Window recesses in the deep stone walls are angled toward the interior to better spread the light. And from the outside, the great size of the barn is scaled down visually by its strongly horizontal form to fit among the other buildings. The proportions from circular stone base to 12-sided wooden third story to octagonal cupola seem just right. From any point in the Hancock community, the pale stone and white upper stories of the barn are a welcoming visual focal point.

And the structure does beckon one to step inside. Now, without cows and hay, the open interior is breathtaking (**15.4**). With its great central vertical thrust and the encirclement of light breaking through the deep walls, it has the atmosphere of a Gothic cathedral. People speak in hushed tones as if it were a sacred place. And perhaps it is. To the Shakers, there was no distinction between sacred and everyday. They dedicated every moment to God, making the work of their hands as much an act of devotion as their singing and prayers. Believing firmly that all things are imbued with the spirit, Mother Ann counseled unhurried but intense awareness in every task: "Do all your work as though you had a thousand years to live, and as you would if you knew you must die tomorrow."[1]

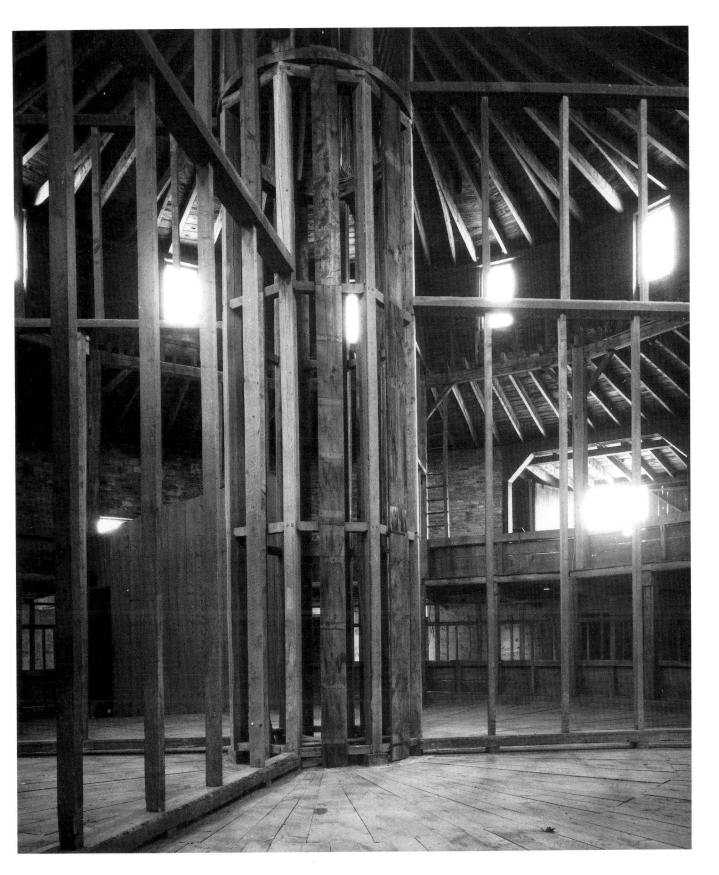

15.4 Interior of the Round Stone Barn.

PICASSO'S *GUERNICA*

By contrast with the relative obscurity of the Shaker barn, Pablo Picasso's *Guernica* (15.5) is thought to be the most looked-at painting of the twentieth century. It was commissioned by the Spanish Government in Exile during the Spanish Civil War, to be displayed in the 1937 Paris International Exhibition. At Picasso's request, it was then placed in the Museum of Modern Art in New York for safekeeping until "public liberties" were re-established in his homeland, Spain. In 1981, after Franco's fascist regime had ended, the painting was moved to the Prado in Madrid, where it is now somewhat hard to see behind security glass. It stands as a monument not only to the genius of the most prolific and influential artist of the twentieth century but also to human questioning of the sufferings caused by war.

The incident Picasso chose as his subject occurred less than a week before he began work on the painting. It was the bombing of Guernica, capital and symbolic heart of the Basque provinces. To break Basque resistance, Hitler's forces, who were supporting Franco's war against the Loyalist government, carried out one of the world's first experiments in saturation bombing of a civilian population. They dropped over 3000 incendiary bombs over a period of three hours and machine-gunned the people as they tried to flee. The world was aghast, and Picasso had his subject. But the way in which he presented it is symbolic of all wars, all repression. It is not at all a literal representation of the actual bombing of the city or its aftermath (15.6). The figures are highly allegorical, and the use of blacks, whites, and grays rather than more colorful hues erase any racial or nationalistic associations. The horror of Guernica becomes the horror of all war, an epic presentation that struck home in an age that thought itself too sophisticated for sentimentality.

Despite its evocation of the chaos of surprise attack, *Guernica* is held together by its triangular compositional devices. The major triangle runs from the open palm of the dead warrior at the lower left, up to the lamp held by the woman at upper center, down to the outstretched foot of the kneeling woman on the right. A secondary triangle on the left contains the head of the bull, facing away from the disaster, and the upturned head of the wailing woman with the dead baby hanging limp in her arms. There is also a bird on a table, with the same upward-turned imploring head as that of the mother. To the right, the outer triangle encompasses the agony of the burning woman—whose pose mirrors that of the woman with the dead baby—and the powerful questioning

15.5 Pablo Picasso, *Guernica*, 1937. Oil on canvas, 11 ft 5½ ins × 25 ft 5¼ ins (3.49 × 7.75 m). Prado, Madrid.

15.6 The city of Guernica after bombing by Nationalist forces, 1937.

form of the woman thrusting a light into the scene.

Within the central triangle, there is a jumble of fragmented parts. The body of the dead warrior stretches across the base of the triangle, visually sharing the right leg with the kneeling woman. In the center is the horse with the gaping wound, whom Picasso in a rare moment of explanation identified as the spirit of the people.

The strong diagonals send the eye zipping around through the painting, searching for understandable forms and clues. We note that most of the people are women and children; this is not an heroic battle scene but the aftermath of an assault on civilians. Above all the figures is a sun or ceiling lamp or an eye—or perhaps all of these—watching, and shedding some light on the scene.

What do these images mean? Picasso generally refused to explain his symbols, insisting that viewers respond through personal, subconscious associations and emotions rather than impersonal logic:

> This bull is a bull, this horse is a horse. ... It is necessary that the public, the spectators, see in the horse, the bull, symbols that they interpret as they understand them. These are animals. These are massacred animals. That is all, for me; let the public see what it wants to see.[2]

The painting rivets our attention and involves us by making us ask questions. It does not answer them. Is the bull, for example, a symbol of unthinking brutality, the detached and stupid presence of repression, pushing down all the human forces that are trying to rise? Is he the representative of humanity, affected by but yet isolated from what happens to each person? Is he the eternal power of Spain, reassuringly solid even in the midst of devastation? Or does he represent sheer force, power that is in itself neither good nor evil? The possibilities—and there are others—have intrigued viewers of the painting for decades, and whole books have been written about it.

Picasso himself approached *Guernica* with an

open, extremely flexible mind, continually changing its form. Quite aware of the historic significance of his attempts, he dated the scores of sketches in which he worked out the images and composed the powerful whole of the finished painting, leaving tracks for us to follow. From the very first compositional study (**15.7**), Picasso knew much of the basic structure. In this simplified visual note to himself, we can readily make out the woman with the lamp, the bull, and the horizontal shape of the dead soldier.

By the end of the first day, after five preliminary sketches, Picasso had worked out the composition study shown in Figure **15.8**. The woman with the lamp already has her distinctive cometlike shape. The fallen soldier is wearing a classical centurion's helmet; the spirit of the horse escapes through the wound in its side. At this point, the figures are fairly representational and drawn with curving lines, in contrast to their fragmented, straight-edged appearance in the final version, and there is a sense of three-dimensional space receding to the rear.

Picasso then introduced some new elements. A major group he added is the mother and the dead baby (**15.9**). Throwing her head back into a reverse scream makes her plight all the more hideous. The baby's eyes seem partially aware here; its blood oozes through the mother's fingers. By the final painting,

15.7 Pablo Picasso, First Composition Study for *Guernica*, 1937. Pencil on blue paper, 8¼ × 10⅝ ins (21 × 26.9 cm). Prado, Madrid.

15.8 Pablo Picasso, Composition Study for *Guernica*, dated May 1, 1937.
Pencil on gesso on wood, 25½ × 21⅛ ins (64.7 × 53.6 cm). Prado, Madrid.

15.9 Pablo Picasso, Study for *Guernica, Mother with Dead Child on Ladder*, dated May 9, 1937. Pencil on white paper, 9½ × 17⅞ ins (24.1 × 45.4 cm). Prado, Madrid.

the final composition. Three human corpses now lie on the ground, clenched fists rise heavenward, and the horse writhes into a new position.

In addition to the innovations in the sketches, Picasso continued to reassemble, add, and eliminate figures directly on the mural itself. Seven states preceding the final mural were photographed, giving us further insight into the evolution of the artist's thoughts. In the second state of the painting (**15.11**), the woman with the lamp is thrust into greater prominence than before: She is larger and brought forward by the flattening out of the crowded space of the picture. The flaming woman with upraised arms has appeared to fill the space at the far right. Triangles are everywhere elaborated. Perhaps the most striking—later abandoned—aspect of this state is the hopeful, defiant fist of the dead soldier, raised with a patch of Spanish turf against a luminous sun. This dramatic gesture is reduced to a subtle sign of hope that must be discovered in the final version: the small flower in the soldier's hand. And the sun dwarfs the light brought to the situation by the woman with the lamp, who seems to have been needed from the first as a call to the world to witness what has happened.

In the final mural, all those who are suffering are imploring upwards or looking to the left, while the eyes of the centurion have swiveled around to face us, staring blankly even in death. The other eyes that face us are those of the bull—and what do we read in them? Although the bull turns away from the violence, he is clearly involved with it on some level. And so are we. No one can see this huge mural, full of larger-than-life suffering figures, without being deeply affected by it. Most people walk toward it until it fills their peripheral vision and then stop, held back by the jagged points and the pain that is more felt than seen.

Even at a distance it is impossible to grasp the whole composition at once or to resolve the meaning of the whole. Its ambiguities, even on the most basic level (for instance, is this scene inside or outside?), keep us exploring and feeling our way through the work. It is quite likely that this painting will still be studied hundreds of years from now. Showing only the effects and not "the enemy," it stands as an incredibly powerful illumination of the suffering that we humans are capable of inflicting. In this compassionate awareness lies some hope for change.

the baby's eyes are mere empty half-moons and the blood is gone, making it the most peaceful figure in the general agony of the scene. Before Picasso worked out the fully extended reverse scream posture, he had experimented with bringing the mother and baby into the painting on bended knee at the right (**15.10**). At this point, Picasso also began to introduce the triangular shapes that play such an important role in

15.10 Pablo Picasso, Composition Study for *Guernica*, dated May 9, 1937.
Pencil on white paper, 9½ × 17⅞ ins (24.1 × 45.4 cm). Prado, Madrid.

15.11 Pablo Picasso, State II of *Guernica*, 1937.

15.12 Auguste Rodin, Sketch for *The Gates of Hell*, 1880. Pencil, ink wash, and white gouache. Musée Rodin, Paris.

RODIN'S *GATES OF HELL*

What may have been the greatest sculpture of the nineteenth century was never displayed until well into the twentieth. This work—*The Gates of Hell* by Auguste Rodin, who reinvigorated the art of sculpture at a time when most significant work was being done in painting—occupied the artist from 1880 to 1900 but was not cast in bronze until after his death in 1917. It had been commissioned for the proposed Museum of Decorative Arts in Paris, which was never built. Rodin welcomed the opportunity to prove his stature as a skilled and imaginative sculptor after charges that his earlier life-sized sculptures were so realistic that they must have been cast from live models. His proposal for the great door was a sculptural image of *The Inferno* from Dante's *Divine Comedy*, whose allegorical account of the soul's return to God had deeply moved Rodin. He peopled his portal with nearly 200 fluidly expressive bodies, all smaller than life. Some are modeled in such low relief that they disappear into the swirling inferno;

some reach out in full three-dimensionality toward the viewer. All bear witness to the profundity of Rodin's vision and his ability to use the human body to express the full drama of existence.

Historical precedents for the *Gates* included Ghiberti's Renaissance *Porta del Paradiso* (14.20), which Rodin had seen in Florence. Rodin started out with a similar concept. His first architectural sketches, such as the one shown in Figure **15.12**, divide the massive width of such a door into eight symmetrical panels. Yet even here, the organic forms they contain are starting to spill over their boundaries, until, in its final form, the straight lines of the architectural framework are mated to, and in places obscured by, the multitude of sensual figures.

15.13 Auguste Rodin, Terracotta study for *The Gates of Hell*. Musée Rodin, Paris.

Rodin soon abandoned any attempt at a literal, compartmentalized depiction of the levels of Hell described by Dante. An early terracotta study for the *Gates* (**15.13**) suggests its final form: a quasi-architectural framework with a cross at its center, topped by the seated figure later known as *The Thinker*. Rodin eventually executed *The Thinker* as an isolated sculpture; indeed, many of his sculptures first appeared in his preparations for *The Gates of Hell*. He worked with the malleability of clay, using live models moving freely as inspiration for gestures expressing their own inner lives. The figures and groupings thus developed were attached to a large wooden frame, on which clay was built up in relief. Plaster casts were then made of areas of the work, with the intention of using them as the basis for bronze lost-wax casts of the work. Only one of the casts that were ultimately made was done by the fine lost-wax process. Rodin actually dreamed of having the side jambs carved in marble, with the central panels cast in bronze.

Even the plaster casts themselves (**15.14**) reveal the extraordinary dynamism of Rodin's sculpture. Figures move far out and way back in space, creating areas of light and shadow that undulate continually through the piece. Extremely busy passages alternate with quieter ones, weaving another dimension into the visual rhythm of the piece. At the very top are the figures called *The Three Shades*. Like *The Thinker*, they were also cast and shown as a sculpture in themselves. They are actually the same figure cast three times and shown from three different angles. Their gestures keep directing the viewer's glance down into the turmoil below.

After absorbing an impression of the whole 18-feet (5.5 m) structure, viewers are inevitably drawn in to try to decipher individual forms blended into the writhing turmoil. Among the inhabitants of Hell—which Rodin conceived as a state of mind rather than a place in the hereafter—is Count Ugolino (**15.15**). He and his sons were historical figures who had been locked in a tower to starve. There is an ambiguous suggestion in Dante's account that Ugolino ate his sons' corpses in his hunger. The horror of their torment is expressed physically, with the aristocratic count reduced to the crawling stance of a beast. They are placed on the left panel at the viewer's eye level, making their agony inescapable.

Below the Ugolino group are the historical figures of Francesca da Rimini and her lover, Paolo, brother

15.14 Auguste Rodin, *The Gates of Hell*, fully assembled in plaster, photographed in 1917. Musée Rodin, Paris.

15.15 Plaster cast of *The Gates of Hell*. Detail of the lower section of the left door panel, with the Ugolino group and Paolo and Francesca.

of the man she had married for family political reasons. Her husband, who was deformed and ugly, killed the pair when he found them out. Rodin treats their forbidden love sympathetically, if tragically. In Rodin's Hell, it is humanity that torments itself with its frustrated longings and inability to find peace.

The only still figure in the work is that of *The Thinker*. Many observers consider him the self-portrait of the artist—one who separates himself enough from the endless motion of human strivings to see the whole picture, wondering why. All about

him bodies are struggling and climbing only to fall—even the angels (**15.16**). Within the maelstrom, some try to help and console each other; others are physically touching but isolated in their individual pain. As observers, we stand equal to the fallen, looking upward to the barrier one would have to cross to reach the level of the Thinker.

To complete this epic depiction of the human condition, Rodin had intended that his sculptures of Adam and Eve be placed on either side of the *Gates*, as suggested in one of his early sketches (**15.17**). This

15.16 Auguste Rodin, *The Gates of Hell*, detail. *The Thinker*, with portions of the door panels and tympanum. Bronze. Stanford University Museum of Art. Gift of B. Gerald Cantor Collections.

15.17 Auguste Rodin, Sketch for *The Gates of Hell*, with architectural setting, c. 1880–81. Pencil. Musée Rodin, Paris.

sketch also reveals his vision of the doors as a portal at the top of a flight of stairs, framed by an arch. If this were so, if the *Gates* had actually been installed architecturally as doors, imagine what it would feel like to walk up to and then through them, as if entering the world they describe. When the *Gates* are set up with the life-sized sculptures of Adam and Eve (**15.18**), a strongly triangular composition results from the obvious reading from Adam to the Three Shades to Eve, justifying the large scale of the Shades. And to enter Hell by passing reminders of the idea of original sin—one explanation for human suffering—extends the logic of the whole.

Keenly aware of the pain of human existence, Rodin himself died in poverty, neglected by a government that accepted his works in exchange for providing him with a place to live. Heating fuel was

15.18 Auguste Rodin, *The Gates of Hell*, with *Adam and Eve*, 1880–1917. Bronze (Coubertin Fondeur Cast No. 5), 251 × 158 × 33 ins (638 × 401 × 84 cm). Stanford University Museum of Art. Gift of B. Gerald Cantor Collections.

an overlooked detail, and Rodin died from the cold, while his sculptures were housed in a heated public museum. Desperate, he asked to be allowed to stay in a room in the museum, but his request was denied by the official in charge. Friends and authorities promised coal, but did not bring it.

Despite the difficulties of his own situation and the frequent rejections of his work by more conventional minds, Rodin was passionately fond of art—and of what it reveals to us of life.

Great works of art, which are the highest proof of human intelligence and sincerity, say all that can be said on man and on the world, and, besides, they teach that there is something more that cannot be known. ... We [artists] are misunderstood. Lines and colors are only to us the symbols of hidden realities. Our eyes plunge beneath the surface to the meaning of things, and when afterwards we reproduce the form, we endow it with the spiritual meaning which it covers. An artist worthy of the name should express all the truth of nature, not only the exterior truth, but also, and above all, the inner truth.[3]

MICHELANGELO'S SISTINE CHAPEL CEILING

The next piece of art that we will explore in depth in this chapter is earlier than the first three, but it is by no means less "evolved." The complexity of its conception and execution is staggering.

At the age of thirty-three, Michelangelo was commissioned by Pope Julius II to paint a fresco to decorate the ceiling of the Sistine Chapel in the Vatican, which was used for devotions and ceremonial purposes by the pope and those surrounding him, such as cardinals and archbishops. At the time, 1508, the ceiling was already painted to look like the blue heavens, studded with stars (**15.21**), with scenes from the lives of Jesus and Moses painted below the high windows and painted statues of the popes between the windows. Several years later, Raphael was commissioned to design tapestries which were hung in the place of the fictitious painted drapes near the floor. Michelangelo was reluctant to accept the ceiling commission, for he was embroiled in sculpting a tomb in which the same pope was to be buried eventually (a project which plagued him for the rest of his life, in continual wranglings with the authorities over funds and design). Furthermore, he considered himself a sculptor rather than a painter, and the difficulties he would face in painting the immense ceiling for the exaltation of its august visitors were staggering.

Michelangelo faced a vast curving surface 118 feet (38.5 m) long, broken by triangular arches over each window. He also had to create images that could be seen and make sense to people standing 70 feet (21 m) below on the floor. Fresco is a very demanding medium even on a vertical surface, and to work on the ceiling, Michelangelo had to perch on a scaffolding, apparently with his head continually thrown back and paint falling onto his face and beard. It was his first major attempt at fresco.

What he created under these extraordinarily difficult conditions is one of the world's greatest works of art. He painted it in two portions, during the winter of 1508 to 1509—when work stopped for lack of further funds, seemingly absorbed by the military operations of the Vatican—and then again from 1511 to 1512. He tried using assistants but soon gave up

15.19 Michelangelo Buonarroti, Sistine Chapel ceiling (before restoration), Vatican Palace, Rome, 1508–12.

and worked mostly alone in the Chapel, in pain and exhaustion, but apparently also driven by some kind of inner inspiration. We know from his letters that he dedicated himself as an artist to the service of religion and beauty, and that the two were not different in his mind. One of his sonnets explains:

15.20 Michelangelo Buonarroti, Sistine Chapel ceiling (after restoration), 1508–12. Detail of the ceiling showing the Intoxication of Noah to the Creation of Eve. © Nippon Television Network Corporation, Tokyo 1991.

Beauty was given at my birth to serve
As my vocation's faithful exemplar ...
To sense the Beauty which in secret moves
And raises each sound intellect to Heaven![4]

And in conversations recorded by a visiting Portuguese miniature painter, Michelangelo reportedly said in reference to Italian painting:

With discreet persons nothing so calls forth and fosters devotion as the difficulty of a perfection which is bound up in union with God. For good painting is nothing but a copy of the perfections of God and a recollection of His painting; it is a music and a melody which only intellect can understand, and that with great difficulty. And that is why painting of this kind is so rare that no man may attain it.[5]

15.21 G. Tognettis, reconstruction of the 15th-century Sistine Chapel before Michelangelo's frescoes. Vatican Museums, Vatican City.

Michelangelo's own surviving letters give us no clues as to what he was attempting aesthetically and theologically in the vast work. The pope had originally suggested that he paint the Twelve Apostles, with false painted architectural decorations about them, but Michelangelo argued that the Apostles wouldn't make good subjects because they were "too poor." He won, and the pope gave him a free hand. What evolved probably exceeded anybody's wildest expectations.

The sculptor-as-fresco-painter conceived the ceiling as an illusionary continuation of the architectural details of the building, within which over 300 figures tell the Christian story of the human situation. The panels in the crown of the vault contain the events recounted in Genesis, beginning over the altar with God's separating of the darkness and the light, proceeding through the stories of Adam and Eve, and ending with Noah, the flood, and Noah's drunkenness (**15.19**). The drama expresses God's creative power and humankind's unworthiness and need for divine salvation. Surrounding these panels are the nude *ignudi*, enigmatic nude male figures in a great array of poses. Michelangelo treated the curving sides of the vault as thrones for those who prophesied

the coming of Christ (the Prophets and Sibyls), with the real architectural triangles between them housing the ancestors of Christ. Between these concave triangles he painted illusionary "columns" of figures and stone ribs that seem to support the upward curve of the ceiling.

The scale of the figures changes continually, with God smaller than the Prophets and Sibyls along the sides, and with scale changes from one panel to the next through the center. Even our point of view switches from looking at God overhead to looking at God as if we were alongside, in witnessing the Creation and Fall of Adam and Eve. But rather than being disunified, these variations have the effect of a great symphonic work with many voices and recurring themes.

The major story carried through the center devotes three panels to God's creation of the world, three to the creation and fall of Adam and Eve, and three to the story of Noah, with the flood, Noah's sacrifice to God, and Noah's drunkenness. The first three portray the omnipotence of God, depicted as a gray-haired man who hovers and zooms above the spectator in the first three panels, bringing the sun and the moon into being with a gesture of his hand.

500

15.22 Michelangelo Buonarroti, Sistine Chapel ceiling, 1508–12, detail of *The Creation of Adam* with an overlay showing the "S" composition.

The next panel is the most famous portion of the whole ceiling: The Creation of Adam (**15.22**). It is said to be the first thing Michelangelo painted when he returned to it in 1511. The use of unfilled space draws our attention in contrast with all the busy details surrounding it, and the use of outstretched fingers that almost touch, but not quite, conveys an electrical sense of the infusion of the legendary first man with life. The actual biblical reference has God breathing life into Adam, but artistic license serves Michelangelo well here, for we can almost "see" the implied line as the spark of life jumps the gap between God and Adam. Compositionally, the panel is designed as a long horizontal "S," a device known as "the line of beauty" and used repeatedly by Michelangelo and other Renaissance artists in posing single figures and composing scenes.

The male prophets of the Old Testament alternate along the sides with female Sibyls, who were prophetesses from the "pagan" traditions of classical Greek and Roman culture. The Renaissance brought a resurgence of interest in these classical civilizations and attempts to embrace them within the fold of Christianity. To this end, oracles ascribed to the Sibyls prophesied the coming of Christ, and Michelangelo places them on equal footing with the Old Testament Prophets in this regard. Although they are supposed to be females, in Michelangelo's hands they become androgynous figures with the heavy musculature more characteristic of men. The Libyan Sibyl (**15.23**) is particularly famous as an idealized combination of the beauty of both sexes. Her exaggerated spiraling contrapposto pose and arched feet, like many of the great variations of poses in the ceiling, are thought to be precursors to the theatrics of Mannerist painting. On the other hand, some see Michelangelo as reaching backward in time to classical interest in depictions of the nude male body, accentuated by poses involving strain, thrust, and counterthrust.

The Prophet Jonah (**15.24**) seems flung backward from his perch above the altar, perhaps in awe of God, who hovers just above on the ceiling. Michelangelo's genius with foreshortening is particularly evident here, for we perceive the figure as leaning away in space even though architecturally this area curves forward. Notice, for instance, how Michelangelo has shortened Jonah's trunk and right thigh to help us "see" them as extending back from us in space. Notice also Michelangelo's strong use of complementary colors, with the green of the drape heightening the lively red glow of the skin.

Michelangelo's colors are currently the source of great controversy. For centuries the Sistine Chapel ceiling was so dulled by candle smoke and darkened varnish that people tended to assume that Michelangelo used muted, unsaturated colors. Many liked the ceiling that way. But there were clues that

15.23 Michelangelo Buonarroti, Sistine Chapel ceiling, 1508–12, detail of *The Libyan Sibyl*.

15.24 Michelangelo Buonarroti, Sistine Chapel ceiling, 1508–12, detail of *The Prophet Jonah*.

15.25 Michelangelo Buonarroti, Sistine Chapel ceiling, 1508–12, detail of a lunette before and after restoration.

these were not the original colors. For instance, one observer who saw the ceiling when it was new wrote about its unprecedented luminosity. Despite international protests, restorers began trying in 1980 to repair minute paint flaking and to remove the layers of old varnish without damaging the original fresco. They have found surprisingly bright and glowing colors beneath (**15.20**). The contrast is striking, as can be seen in comparing before-and-after-cleaning photos of one of the lunettes over the windows (**15.25**).

Restoration also reveals that Michelangelo worked almost exclusively in the pure Florentine *buon fresco* tradition, applying paint directly to a fresh layer of wet plaster, the *intonaco*. Rarely did he make corrections *a secco*, on dried plaster, a much less durable technique. He also apparently painted huge areas each day. Each of the lunettes, for example, was painted in only three days, with each day's work covering about 54 square feet (5 square meters). There is no evidence that he used a cartoon in these areas,

but rather he seems to have been painting directly and freely. He limited his palette to those colors that worked well in *buon fresco*, laying them side-by-side and often allowing the ground to show through for added brilliance.

Restoration is being documented by Nippon Television Network Corporation, which is also providing major funding for the restoration. The chairman, Yosaij Kobayashi explains:

> I have been asked countless times why a Japanese television company participated in the restoration of Michelangelo's frescoes in the Sistine Chapel. I always give the same answer. I believe that the works should be preserved as a legacy for mankind. . . . These newly restored works reveal a Michelangelo who is not simply a great artist, but also a great philosopher and a deeply religious man. When we think of all those who will see the completely restored frescoes in the Sistine Chapel, we are filled with pride and happiness. We are using every medium available to record this historic restoration project for the benefit of people around the world and for future generations.[6]

JOYCE SCOTT'S BEAD SCULPTURE

The final piece we will consider is *Ancha Melon* (**15.26**), a small beadwork sculpture by contemporary African-American artist, Joyce Scott. Is this a cute piece of kitschy racist folk art? Here is a black woman with an Aunt Jemima scarf on a watermelon head, smiling a watermelon-slice smile as she holds out something on a platter. But what is it on that platter? What's that hand gesturing over her head? To begin to make one's way into understanding Joyce Scott's complex art, one needs to hear from the artist herself:

> Risk is very important. And putting the spin on stereotypes is very important. Just when you think you know what this art is about, you don't—because that's what life is, for me, in many ways.[7]

To appreciate this artist's work requires delving into many areas—her family background, the historical experiences of Africans imported to the Americas as slaves, her performance art, her own statements about racism, sexism, cultural stereotyping, and her use of a crafts medium to create provocative, puzzling, compelling artistic messages.

Joyce Scott was born in 1948 in Baltimore, Maryland, into a family for whom art was not a separate, rarefied activity, but rather, a part of everyday life, a necessity in order to keep body and soul alive. Her great-grandfather was a shoemaker; his wife crocheted shoes from the bits of fleece left from shearing sheep and goats, with bullrushes woven into the soles to strengthen them. Her father's mother, Mamie Scott, made quilts into her nineties, piecing strips of cloth together in ways derived from West African traditions. Her paternal grandfather made decorated log canoes. On her mother's side, her grandfather Samuel Caldwell supported 14 children in the post-Civil-War South by moving from place to place to find work. In addition to sharecropping, horseraising, working on the railroad, and running moonshine, he was a blacksmith, and a basket-maker. He also made quilts to warm his family and to trade for grain and food. When Joyce was born, he made her a quilt from fabric pieces he had dyed with yellow ocher. His daughter, Joyce's Aunt Lucille, remembers living on only one meal a day, going to school hungry and not being able to concentrate on anything except the constant hunger.

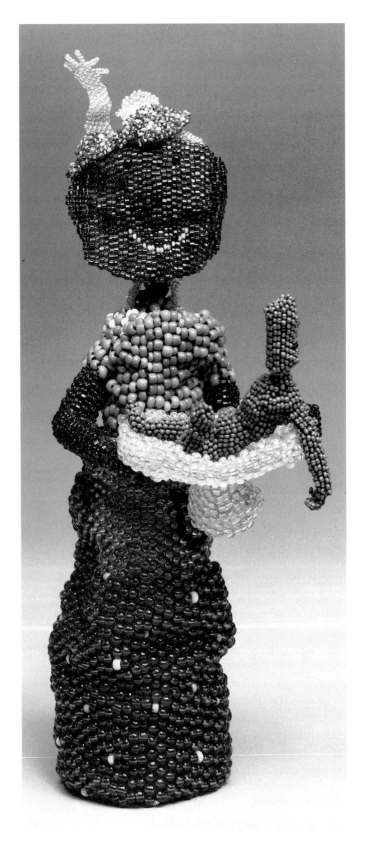

15.26 Joyce J. Scott, *Ancha Melon*, 1987. Beadwork and mixed media, 9½ × 5 × 3 ins (24 × 12.7 × 7.6 cm). Collection of Mr. and Mrs. Sanford M. Besser, Little Rock, Arkansas.

Joyce's mother Elizabeth Caldwell Talford Scott started quiltmaking when she was nine, and is now recognized as a major artist in the genre. Her quilts are always of her own design; she puts them together organically from irregular-shaped pieces, with stuffed, raised areas and rocks and other found objects elaborating the surface (**15.27**). The rocks are for strength and luck, she says, but she has to be careful that they are not interpreted negatively as witchcraft. Her best quilts all go into Joyce's hope chest. Joyce says they will probably never sell most of them because they are her heritage:

> I gain great strength from them. Being wrapped in these magic carpets that your relatives have made is being wrapped in personal stories. I believe that my mother has made a pact with the Sand Man. When I go on one of these special dream rides, under her tutelage, wrapped in her cloth arms, I'm taking a very special dream route. I wish other people could get that same kind of connection from their parents and know that art is beyond what it is popularly considered to be. It can be a life force. I think that's why people in other cultures integrate it into everyday use, because it is such a magnum force.[8]

When Joyce was a child, her mother had to take care of wealthier white families' children to help support her own family. Elizabeth assured Joyce that she was always thinking about her, even as she was consoling someone else's child, but the painful realities of economic inequality and racial prejudice brushed Joyce's heart nonetheless. A series of her beadworks entitled *No, Mommy, Me* deal explicitly with this theme. In *No, Mommy, Me II*, a front view (**15.28**) shows a solid, matronly black woman holding a very pink and healthy baby. This is only the external stereotype. Moving around the piece (**15.29**) reveals the nanny's own child crying on the floor, neatly dressed but bereft of attention when she needs it. The white baby is discovered to be only a flat cut-out, devoid of substance, and the nanny's face is small, vulnerable, and contorted in agony.

And what of *Ancha Melon*? The green figure in the bowl is the woman's own baby; she is "serving up the next generation to the stereotype," Joyce explains. What's that hand doing over her head?

> It's her clear conscience. She thinks, "I'm going to be collusive in this, because he'll be able to go to better schools." She'll send him to those schools and watch him be beaten because of integration and watch her people's own institutions dwindle because now we move into the other culture. She thinks, "He has to be hardened—he has to know what the real world is like." The clear conscience is how we all assuage our own fears.[9]

Watermelon was once very common in depictions of African-Americans—a visual cliché for cliched ideas about people as a group. Joyce uses the racist stereotype partly in humor, partly in outrage that her people were thus presented as being so lackadaisical that they wanted to do nothing but sit around eating watermelon, with mouths so large that they could put a whole slice in at once.

Because Joyce's pieces are painful to contemplate, once we begin to see what is going on, they cannot be seen as pleasing living room art objects. Even the necklaces tell complex stories about the human condition, rather than simply decorating the body. Joyce says:

> I believe that I have a real responsibility as an artist to keep some of those memories alive. Although the face may have changed, the problems are still the same. So I have to use my artwork as a way for people to keep remembering. As African-Americans in this country, we are very different from anybody else in this country, in the sense that we were the slave population. Even my mother and my cousin [from a sharecropping family, whose labor was exploited by the landowner, leaving them with nothing] were slaves—we were a different kind of slaves [from those in the pre-Civil-War South], but we were slaves. It's something that we probably shouldn't forget, because we are really liable to repeat it.[10]

This work is not just about prejudice against people of African background. Joyce says she uses black images because those are her "natural voice," but her pieces are about inhumanity and difficult issues among all peoples. She remarks:

> If I only look at it as a problem for African-Americans, I can assign blame and guilt to people other than myself and look only for very narrow solutions to the problem. But certainly all ethnic groups are involved. The *No, Mommy, Me* pieces are also about those hard choices that parents have to make about leaving the home and making money for the future. If the mother doesn't have a job, her child will be forced to have the same kind of lifestyle that she has. So her sacrifice of leaving home is the kind of sacrifice that hopefully will make the life of her child easier. Then one gets into the child's questions: "Would I rather be with you in a hovel than without you in a better apartment?"[11]

Even the use of beads carries multiple meanings. Joyce did not learn beadwork in art school; her mother had taught her how to sew, and adding beads to the thread was not a great technical leap. Joyce is extremely skillful in making them do whatever she wants them to do, and chose them partly for deliberate practical reasons:

15.27 Elizabeth T. Scott, *Lap Quilt*, 1989. Fabric, threads, beads, rocks, buttons, approx. 4 ft (1.22 m) diameter. Courtesy of the artist.

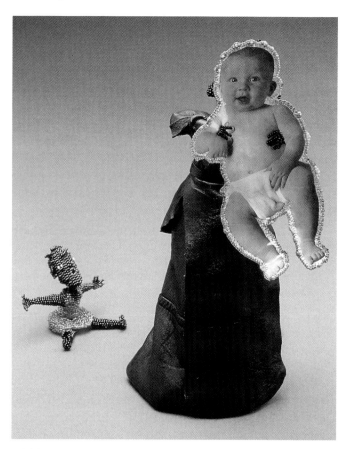

15.28 Joyce J. Scott, *No, Mommy, Me II*, View I, 1991. Beads, thread, wire, approx. 12 × 8 × 4 ins (30.5 × 20.3 × 10 cm). Courtesy of the artist.

I wanted something that wasn't toxic, that didn't take forever to dry, forever to cool, that you didn't have to cook, that you didn't have to wait for, that you didn't have to clean up for, that wasn't too hot to touch, that was immediate. It answered the same kind of art problems that any other material does—for instance, it can be opaque or transparent, reflective or absorbent. I wanted to be able to make something flat, manipulate it and make it sculptural, or make it serpentine. I wanted something that could be worn, something that could carry a message. Although beadwork is complete in itself, it is not so complete that it doesn't allow other materials or ideas to enter. So I can explore with it and integrate collage, assemblage, and other things, or I can do beadwork on its own.

Some people believe that working with the bead is working with the circle of life, the continuum. Certainly when you work with it for a while, you do set up a form, a body rhythm, a sort of meditation. I'm a very driven person, and I like to assault people. In a very safe way—I won't come and knock you down a flight of stairs, but I do interactive work on stage as performance art and in lectures. In the studio, I'm looking for something that's the opposite of that, lest I die from this assaultive behavior. For me, beadwork is very contemplative, very centering and calming.[12]

Then there's the spin, so common in Joyce's work. She also uses beads because their use has been highly developed in some indigenous and peasant cultures—African, Native American, Mexican, Russian, Czechoslovakian—but has not been respected in the past as "fine art." Joyce squarely challenges this limited notion of art. At first glance, her pieces might be taken for folk art, but these are utterly unique, sophisticated works of art.

Anyone who is unaware of Joyce's genius in slipping in barbs with the humor and the clichés would be enlightened by her performance art, which vigorously confronts stereotypes on all fronts. In these works she is a brilliant writer, performer, costume creator, and an excellent singer, with a keenly theatrical sense of timing. She speaks of the risk of exposing herself, but uses so many personae, so ironically, that one is never quite sure when she is speaking honestly, as "herself." In her performance piece "Generic Interference, Genetic Engineering" (**15.30**), Joyce initially engages the audience by playing the role of fast-talking "Gene 3000" as MC—"Master of Chromosomes"—complete with striped sunglasses and kewpie-doll genetic material. From this character we get future news of what genetic engineering might mean—such as elimination of such "abnormal" traits such as anger, individuality, pimples, and depression. Then Joyce speaks more or less in her own voice, using humor to question the disappearance of romance in sexuality. The next character Joyce embodies is a so-called feeble-minded Southern girl (15.32) who stands fixed at the foot of a ladder, speaking in a quiet, passive-aggressive voice about her forced sterilization. Then a Joyce-like character reappears to speak in rhyme about her concerns over genetic engineering.

15.29 Joyce J. Scott, *No, Mommy, Me II*, View 2, 1991. Beads, thread, wire, approx. 12 × 8 × 4 ins (30.5 × 20.3 × 10 cm). Courtesy of the artist.

15.30 Joyce J. Scott in *"Generic Interference, Genetic Engineering,"* performance piece. Courtesy of the artist.

15.31 Joyce J. Scott, *Evolution*, 1992. Beads, thread, wire, approx. 20 × 10 × 11 ins (50.8 × 25.4 × 28 cm). Courtesy of the artist.

15.32 Joyce J. Scott, another character in "Generic Interference, Genetic Engineering." Courtesy of the artist.

Even as she speaks informally about her art, Joyce continually takes on myriad different voices to poke fun at pretense and ignorance. She does not hesitate to apply her barbed wit to herself. She says seriously:

> My work is often small, but it's got to be able to catch you. I want you to be on the other side of the gallery and see this form that beckons you. But more than just a polite arousal—I want you to be uneasily drawn to it. Maybe you will have to reexamine some of the things you think.

Having said this, Joyce pulls the rug out from under herself:

> What I just said sounded like pure psycho-babble to me— that I expect you to go off with the answers to your life. "My God, I went to see one of Joyce Scott's exhibitions, and there was this glistening piece that beckoned to me—and from it I found the truth! I now can save the world."[13]

Nevertheless, Joyce's work does perennially challenge our assumptions. Joyce's "Evolution" (**15.31**) shows a white-skinned mother-of-the-world figure whose skin has been parted on the head, revealing an ancient African woman beneath. This piece refers to new genetic discoveries suggesting that the common ancestor of the entire human race is a 200,000-year-old African woman. Joyce says:

> If it's true that the mother of the human race is a 200,000-year-old African woman, then inside everyone, even if you're white, is your black mother. It's very difficult for people to hear that, because of the relationship of people of color with people of European stock. We've had so many horrendous problems between us. Your central self could be the same person you abuse. That makes us cousins, 50th or 60th cousins. There is absolutely no way I can't look at you and see me.
>
> If that's true, that means that we humans have to examine everything we do to each other. If we did that, there would be no hungry people in the street. The reason why I'm so knowledgeable is because I'm human. Everything that I've talked about, I'm sure I've done to someone. But I want to not keep doing it.[14]

When asked whether she feels one of the true values of art is to make social and political statements, Joyce replies:

> Oh, yes. I also think that is the route I've specifically chosen; I don't necessarily think it's right or true for everyone. It's important to me to use art in a manner that incites people to look and then carry something home— even if it's subliminal—that might make a change in them. My art is about change because this life is about change. To me, it isn't about being static. But through my art I cannot solve all our social problems. I can, hopefully, help get you, the viewer, to open your brain. I think that's what all artists do.[15]

NOTES

Chapter One

1 Quoted in Margaretta K. Mitchell, *Recollections: Ten Women of Photography*, Viking Press, New York, 1979, pp. 30, 32.
2 Quoted in Herbert Read, *A Concise History of Modern Sculpture*, Oxford University Press, New York, 1964, p. 14.
3 Conversation with Erik Satie, quoted in Carola Giedion-Weleker, *Brancusi*, Editions du Griffon, Neuchatel, Switzerland, 1959 (French edition), 31, p. 1.
4 Quoted by C. G. Guilbert, "Propos de Brancusi," *Prisme des Arts*, no. 12, 1957, p. 7, translated by Mary Pat Fisher.
5 Interview with Rick Bartow, June 20, 1989.
6 Quoted in Jack Coward and Juan Hamilton, with letters selected and annotated by Sarah Freenough, *Georgia O'Keeffe: Art and Letters*, National Gallery of Art, Washington D.C., 1987, pp. 202, 266, 242–3.
7 Pat Ward Williams, interviewed by Maurice Berger, "Speaking Out: Some Distance to Go," *Art in America*, September 1990, p. 83.
8 1918 writing quoted by Eleanor S. Greenhill, *Dictionary of Art*, Laurel/Dell, New York, 1974, p. 283.
9 From Klee's Jena lecture, 1924, quoted in Will Grohmann, *Paul Klee*, Harry N. Abrams, New York, 1954, p. 367.
10 Quoted in S. Rodman, *Conversations with Artists*, New York, 1957.
11 Letters 596 and 381 excerpted from W. H. Auden, ed., *Van Gogh: A Self-Portrait*, New York Graphic Society, Greenwich, Connecticut, 1961. Letters 504 and 507 excerpted from Alfred H. Barr, Jr., ed., *Vincent Van Gogh*, The Museum of Modern Art, New York, 1935.
12 Interview with Lisa Bradley, March, 1990.
13 Michael D. Eisner, as quoted in Beth Dunlop, "The Mouse Runs Up the Clock," *Elle Decor*, May 1991, p. 26.
14 Quoted in *National Geographic*, May 1985, p. 557.
15 Quoted in Robert Goldwater, *Paul Gauguin*, Abrams, New York, undated, p. 13.
16 Ibid.
17 Ibid., p. 118.
18 Ibid., p. 114.
19 Excerpted from *Paul Gauguin's Intimate Journals*, trans. by Van Wyck Brooks, Crown Publishers, New York, 1936, pp. 92–97.

Chapter Two

1 Quoted in Jonathan Fineberg, "Theater of the Real: Thoughts on Christo," *Art in America*, December, 1979, p. 96.
2 Barbara Hepworth: A Pictorial Autobiography, 1978 edition published by Moonraker Press, Bradford-on-Avon, Wiltshire, p. 27.
3 Henry Moore, "The Sculptor Speaks," article in *The Listener*, vol. XVIII, no. 449, 18th August 1937, pp. 338–40. Quoted in *Henry Moore on Sculpture*, ed. Philip James, Viking Press, New York, 1967, p. 62.
4 Henry Moore in H. Felix Man, *Eight European Artists*, Heinemann, London, 1954. Quoted in James, op. cit., p. 118.
5 Henry Moore in Donald Hall, "An Interview with Henry Moore," article in *Horizon, A Magazine of the Arts*, November 1960, vol. iii, no. 2, American Horizon, New York, 1960. Interview quoted without omissions in James, op. cit., p. 119.
6 Letters to Émile Bernard, Aix-en-Provence, July 25, 1904 and April 15, 1904, quoted in Robert Goldwater and Marco Treves, eds., *Artists on Art*, Pantheon Books, New York, third edition, 1958, pp. 364, 363.
7 Excerpted from Arshile Gorky, "Toward a Philosophy of Art," translated extracts from his letters in Armenian by Karlen Mooradian, reproduced in *Arshile Gorky: Drawings to Paintings*, Archer M. Huntington Art Gallery, The University of Texas at Austin, Austin, Texas, 1975, pp. 31–36.
8 Arshile Gorky (Vosdanik Adoian), interviewed by Malcolm Johnson, "Café Life in New York," *New York Sun*, August 22, 1941, as quoted in *Arshile Gorky: Drawings to Paintings*, The University of Texas at Austin, Austin, Texas, p. 67.
9 Helen Frankenthaler, as interviewed by Emile de Antonio, in *Painters Painting: The New York Art Scene 1940–70*, 1972, 116 minute video, Montauk, New York: Mystic Fire Video.
10 Al Held, personal communication, September 28, 1989.
11 Quoted in Barbara Rose, *Claes Oldenburg*, The Museum of Modern Art/New York Graphic Society, New York, 1970.
12 Personal communication, February 2, 1987.
13 Mark Rothko, quoted in Bonnie Clearwater, "How Rothko Looked at Rothko," *Art News*, November 1985, p. 102.
14 Wassily Kandinsky, *Concerning the Spiritual in Art*, trans. M. T. H. Sadler, Dover Publications edition, New York, 1977, p. 25.
15 Quoted in Isamu Noguchi, *The Isamu Noguchi Garden Museum*, Harry N. Abrams, New York, 1987, p. 98.
16 Quoted in Robert Goldwater and Marco Treves, eds., *Artists on Art*, op. cit., pp. 409–410.
17 Johann Wolfgang von Goethe, *Theory of Colors*, trans. Charles Lock Eastlake, The MIT Press, Cambridge, Mass., 1970, p. 317.
18 Josef Albers, *Search Versus Re-Search*, Trinity College Press, Hartford, Connecticut, 1969, p. 17.
19 Josef Albers, *Interaction of Color*, revised edition, Yale University Press, New Haven, Connecticut and London, 1975, pp. 1, 3, 5, 12, 34, 41, 42.
20 Quoted in Paul Gsell, *Art by Auguste Rodin*, translated by Romilly Fedden, Small, Maynard and Company, Boston, 1912, pp. 66–78.
21 Umberto Boccioni, Carlo Carrà, Luigi Russolo, Giacomo Balla, Gino Severini, "Futurist Painting: Technical Manifesto 1910," in Umbro Apollonio, ed., *The Documents of 20th Century Art: Futurist Manifestos*, Viking Press, New York, 1973 (English language translation copyright 1973 by Thames and Hudson Ltd., London), pp. 27–28.

Chapter Three

1 Quoted in John Dornberg, "One Way to Create Fine Art is to Take the Greatest Risks," *Smithsonian*, April 1985, p. 118.
2 Quoted in "The Courage to Desecrate Emptiness," *ARTnews* March 1986, p. 108.
3 Quoted in Wassily Kandinsky, *Concerning the Spiritual in Art*, trans. M. T. H. Sadler, Dover Publications, New York, 1977 (from *The Art of Spiritual Harmony*, Constable and Company Ltd., London, 1914).
4 Quoted in Frank Lloyd Wright, *An Organic Architecture: The Architecture of Democracy*, Lund Humphries, London, 1939, and in Edgar Kaufmann, Jr., ed., *An American Architecture*, Horizon Press, New York, 1955 (as quoted in *Frank Lloyd Wright: In the Realm of Ideas*, ed. Bruce Brooks Pfeiffer and Gerald Norland, Southern Illinois University Press, Carbondale, Illinois, 1988, pp. 32, 43.

Chapter Four

1 Personal communication, October 1986.

Chapter Five

1 Quoted in Martin Kemp and Margaret Walker, eds., *Leonardo on Painting*, Yale University Press, New Haven and London, 1989, pp. 15, 97, 98 and 162.
2 Diego Rivera, in Juan O'Gorman, *Diego Rivera: Fifty Years of His Work*, "Report on a Dissertation by Diego Rivera Concerning the Techniques of Encaustic and Fresco Painting," Department of Plastic Arts, National Institute of Fine Arts, Mexico City, undated, p. 269.
3 Helen Frankenthaler, as quoted by Barbara Rose, *Frankenthaler*, Harry N. Abrams, New York, 1970, p. 85.
4 Robert Rauschenberg, as interviewed by Emile de Antonio, in *Painters Painting: The New York Art Scene 1940–70*, 1972, Montauk, New York: Mystic Fire Video.

Chapter Six

1 Fritz Eichenberg, "Eulogy to the Woodblock," in *The Wood and the Graver: The Work of Fritz Eichenberg*, Clarkson N. Potter, Inc., New York, 1945, p. 178.
2 Personal communication, April 25, 1987.
3 Frank Boyden, interviewed June 20, 1989.
4 Interview with Janet Cummings Good, January 1992.

Chapter Seven

1 Interview with Peter Good, November, 1991.
2 Paul Rand, *Paul Rand: A Designer's Art*, Yale University Press, New Haven, Connecticut and London, 1985, pp. xiii, 7.
3 Quoted in Hermann Zapf, *Manuale Typographicum*, M.I.T. Press, Cambridge, Massachusetts and London, 1954 and 1970, p. 101.
4 William Morris, *The Ideal Book, Essays and Lectures on The Arts of the Book*, William S. Peterson, ed., University of California Press, Berkeley and Los Angeles, 1982, p. 73.

Chapter Eight

1 Quoted in Susan Weiley, "New Light on Color," *ARTnews*, October 1985, p. 88.
2 Excerpted from Nancy Newhall, ed., *The Daybooks of Edward Weston*, vol. 2, Horizon Press, New York, in collaboration with the George Eastman House, Rochester, 1966, pp. 13, 10, 18, 114, 206, 37.
3 Interview with Elizabeth Sunday, April 20, 1992.
4 William E. Parker, personal communication, April 7, 1992.

5 Susumu Endo, as quoted by Richard Thornton, "Space Transformations," Print magazine, January/February 1991, p. 91.
6 Stephen Dalton, At the Water's Edge: The Secret Life of a Lake and Stream, Century Hutchinson Ltd., London, 1989, p. 158.
7 David Hockney, quoted in David Sheff, "David Hockney: But is it art?" Publish, December 1991, p. 128.
8 Melvin L. Prueitt, Los Alamos National Laboratory, "Scientific Applications of Computer Graphics," The Visual Computer, 1986, vol. 2, p. 189.
9 Maureen Nappi, personal communication, February 26, 1990.
10 John Andrew Berton, Jr., "Film Theory for the Digital World: Connecting the Masters to the New Digital Cinema," Journal of the International Society for the Arts, Sciences, and Technology, Leonardo Supplemental Siggraph Issue 1990, pp. 6, 9.

Chapter Nine
1 Michelangelo Buonarroti, Rime, a cura di Enzo Noe Girardi Bari: Laterza, 1960, no. 151: 1–4, p. 82. As translated by Eugenio Garin in The Complete Work of Michelangelo, Reynal and Company/ William Morrow and Company, New York, undated, p. 525.
2 Excerpted from The Letters of Michelangelo, trans. E. H. Ramsden, vol. 1, Stanford University Press, Stanford, California, 1963, pp. 108, 110, 112, 148.
3 Henry Moore, as quoted by Tom Hopkinson, "How a Sculptor Works," Books and Art, London, November 1957, reprinted in Henry Moore on Sculpture, Philip James, ed., Viking Press, New York, 1967, p. 123.
4 Donna Forma, personal communication, October 11, 1989.
5 Interview with Linda Howard, April 26, 1992.
6 Excerpted from Charles Hope, ed., and Alessandro Nova, The Autobiography of Benvenuto Cellini, from the translation by John Addington Symonds, St. Martin's Press, New York, pp. 179–181.
7 Quoted in "Stankiewicz, Richard (Peter)", Current Biography Yearbook 1967, The H. W. Wilson Company, New York, 1967, p. 398.
8 Judy Pfaff, quoted in "Sculptors' Interviews," Art in America, November 1985, p. 131.
9 Michael Heizer, as quoted by Bertram Gabriel, "Works of Earth," Horizon January/February 1982, p. 48.
10 Robert Smithson conversation with Dennis Wheeler, quoted in Eugenie Tsai, Robert Smithson Unearthed, Columbia University Press, New York, 1991, p. 105.

Chapter Ten
1 Interview with Paula Winokur, April 21, 1992.
2 George Nakashima, essay in Derek Ostergard, George Nakashima: Full Circle, Weidenfeld and Nicolson, a Division of Wheatland Corporation, New York, 1989, pp. 104–5, 90–91, 109.
3 Maurice Marinot, as quoted in Robert A. Cohen, "Origins of the Studio Glass Movement," Glass Studio, no. 32, p. 37.
4 Susye Billy, as quoted by Ralph T. Coe, Lost and Found Traditions, University of Washington Press, Seattle, 1986, p. 232.
5 Sandra Sider, quoted in "New Works," Fiberarts, Summer 1991, p. 12.

Chapter Eleven
1 Eric Chan, quoted by Steven Holt in "The Art of Design," ARTnews, April 1990, p. 123.
2 Quoted in Jack Cocks, "The Man Who's Changing Clothes," Time, October 21, 1985, pp. 77–78.

Chapter Twelve
1 Richard Swibold, personal communication, January 4, 1990.
2 Ibid.
3 Quoted in Edgar Kaufmann, ed., Frank Lloyd Wright: An American Architecture, Horizon Press, New York, 1955, p. 106.
4 Excerpted from Hassan Fathy, Architecture for the Poor: An Experiment in Rural Egypt, University of Chicago Press, Chicago and London, 1973, pp. 9–11.
5 Le Corbusier, Plans, 12 February 1932, p. 40, as quoted in William J. R. Curtis, Modern Architecture Since 1900, Prentice-Hall, Inc., Englewood Cliffs, New Jersey 1987, p. 177.
6 Excerpted from R. Buckminster Fuller, "Conceptuality of Fundamental Structures," in Gyorgy Kepes, Structure in Art and in Science, George Braziller, New York, 1965, p. 68.
7 Alvar Aalto, "The Humanizing of Architecture," Technology Review, 1940. As quoted on p. 78 of Sketches, Alvar Aalto, ed. by Goran Schildt, trans. by Stuart Wrede, MIT Press, Cambridge, Massachusetts and London, 1985. Reprinted with permission from Technology Review, copyright 1940.
8 Alvar Aalto, "The Egg of the Fish and the Salmons," Architectural Design, vol. 49, no. 12, pp. 16–17. Originally published in Alvo Aalto: An Architectural Monograph. Reproduced here by permission of Academy Editions, London.
9 Quoted in Cathy Newman, "Pompidou Center, Rage of Paris," National Geographic, October 1980, p. 469.
10 The Aga Khan, as quoted by David Holmstrom, "Architecture with a Human Touch," The Christian Science Monitor, January 5, 1990, p. 16.

Chapter Thirteen
1 Quoted in ed., Bruce Brooks Pfeiffer and Gerald Nordland, Frank Lloyd Wright: In the Realm of Ideas, Southern Illinois University Press, Carbondale and Edwardsville, 1988, p. 24.
2 Patricia Johanson, quoted in Robin Cembalest, "The Ecological Art Explosion," ARTnews, Summer 1991, p. 99.
3 Lawrence Halprin, Cities, Reinhold Publishing Corporation, New York, 1963, p. 9.
4 Peter Schumann, Flyer from Bread and Puppet Theater, Glober, Vermont.
5 Elka Schumann, personal communication, October 25, 1989.

Chapter Fourteen
1 From the Commentaries of Lorenzo Ghiberti, quoted in Robert Goldwater and Marco Treves, eds., Artists on Art, op. cit., pp. 28–30.
2 Johann Joachim Winckelmann, Thoughts on the Imitation of Greek Works of Art, Dresden 1755, English translation 1765, quoted in Hugh Honour and John Fleming, The Visual Arts: A History, Prentice-Hall Inc., Englewood Cliffs, New Jersey, second edition, 1986, p. 496.

3 "Open Letter to a Group of Prospective Students," Paris, 1861, quoted in Goldwater and Treves, eds., Artists on Art, op. cit., p. 296.
4 Conversation with Ambroise Vollard, quoted in Goldwater and Treves, op. cit., p. 322.
5 Quoted in Faber Birren, History of Color in Painting, Reinhold Publishing, New York, 1965, p. 332.
6 "Reflections on Painting," Paris 1917, quoted in Goldwater and Treves, op. cit., p. 422.
7 An interview with Pablo Picasso, quoted in Goldwater and Treves, op. cit., p. 417.
8 Umberto Boccioni, Carla Carrà, Luigi Russolo, Giacomo Balla, Gino Severini, "Manifesto of the Futurist Painters 1910," in Umbro Apollonio, ed., The Documents of 20th Century Art: Futurist Manifestos, op. cit., p. 26, trans. Robert Brain.
9 Anonymous article in The Blind Man, published in May 1917 by Marcel Duchamp, Beatrice Wood, and H. P. Roche, quoted in Marcel Duchamp, ed. Anne D'Harnoncourt and Kynaston McShine, The Museum of Modern Art, New York, and Philadephia Museum of Art, 1973, p. 283.
10 Barnett Newman, as quoted in Thomas B. Hess, Barnett Newman, exhibition catalog, The Museum of Modern Art, New York, 1971, p. 38.
11 Personal communication, May 19, 1987.
12 Guillermo Gomez-Pena, as quoted by Margot Mifflin, "Performance Art—What is it and Where is it Going?", ARTnews, April 1992, p. 89.
13 Sol LeWitt, "Sentences on Conceptual Art," quoted in Lucy R. Lippard, Six Years: The Dematerialization of the Art Object, Praegar, New York, 1973, pp. 75–76.
14 Agnes Denes, as quoted in Margot Mifflin, op. cit., pp. 99–100.
15 Quoted in Judith Higgins, "In a Hot Country," ARTnews, November 1985, p. 65.
16 Quoted in Edward Lucie-Smith, "Craft Today: Historical Roots and Contemporary Perspectives," introductory essay for American Craft Today: Poetry of the Physical, American Craft Museum, New York, 1986, p. 37.
17 Norma Minkowitz, personal communication, October 23, 1989.
18 Romare Bearden, as quoted by John A. Williams, in M. Bunch Washington, The Art of Romare Bearden: The Prevalence of Ritual, Harry N. Abrams, New York, 1972, pp. 9, 11.
19 Interview with Deborah Muirhead, April 9, 1992.
20 Bessie Harvey, in interview July 1988, Alcoa, Tennessee, in "Spirit in the Wood/ Spirit in the Paint," curated by Sal Scalora, Artspace exhibit, New Haven, Connecticut, 1989.
21 Jean Dubuffet, quoted in Roger Cardinal, Outsider Art, Praeger, New York, 1972, p. 26.
22 Bessie Harvey, as interviewed by Eleanor E. Gaver, "Inside the Outsiders," Art and Antiques, Summer 1990, p. 85.
23 Jon Serl, as interviewed in Kristine McKenna, "Inside the Mind of an Artistic Outsider," Los Angeles Times, November 12, 1989, p. 86; Sullivan Gallery catalog for "The World of Jon Serl's Paintings," December 12, 1981—February 7, 1982; Dorrit Kirk Fitzgerald, "Four Viewpoints: Florence Arnold, Helen Lundberg, Jon Serl, and Beatrice Wood," Irvine Fine Arts Center.

Chapter Fifteen
1 Quoted in Edward Deming Andrews, *The People Called Shakers: A Search for the Perfect Society*, Dover Publications, New York, 1963, p. 24.
2 Quoted in Frank D. Russell, *Picasso's Guernica*, Allanheld and Schram, Montclair, New Jersey, 1980, p. 56.
3 Auguste Rodin, *Art*, Small, Maynard and Company, Boston, 1912, pp. 181, 178, translated from the French of Paul Gsell by Mrs. Romilly Fedden.
4 Michelangelo Buonarroti, sonnet "On Beauty," quoted in Robert Goldwater

and Marco Treves eds., *Artists on Art*, op. cit. pp. 59–60.
5 Michelangelo Buonarroti, "Conversations with Vittoria Colonna as recorded by Francisco de Hollanda," quoted in *Artists on Art*, op. cit., pp. 68–69.
6 Yosaij Kobayashi, "Michelangelo's Work: A Cultural Inheritance for Mankind," in Carolo Pietrangeli et al., *The Sistine Chapel: The Art, the History, and the Restoration*, Harmony Books/Nippon Television, New York, 1986, p. 266.
7 Interview with Joyce Scott, April 16, 1992.

8 Joyce Scott in "The Silver Needle: The Legacy of Elizabeth and Joyce Scott," Osiris Productions, 1990, video.
9 Interview with Joyce Scott, April 16, 1992.
10 Joyce Scott in *The Silver Needle*, op. cit.
11 Interview with Joyce Scott, April 16, 1992.
12 Ibid.
13 Ibid.
14 Ibid.
15 Joyce Scott, as interviewed by Terrie Sultan, for the Corcoran Gallery of Art, in the exhibition catalog for "Joyce Scott: I-con-no-body/I-con-o-graphy," September 14–November 17, 1991.

GLOSSARY

Where a definition includes a term that is itself defined elsewhere in the Glossary, that word is printed in small capitals.

A

ABSTRACT Referring to the essence rather than the surface of an object, often by stripping away all nonessential characteristics.

ABSTRACT EXPRESSIONISM The post-World War II movement centered in New York in which paint was freely applied to a large canvas, expressing the energy and feelings of the artist *nonobjectively*, usually with no emphasized FOCAL POINT.

ACRYLIC A water-based synthetic MEDIUM for painting, also called *acrylic emulsion*.

ACTION PAINTING A style of painting, most notably practised by Jackson Pollock, in which paint is dribbled and splashed onto the SUPPORT with broad gestural movements.

ACTUAL TEXTURE The true physical feeling of a form's surface.

ADDITIVE COLOR MIXING The combination of REFRACTED colors.

ADDITIVE SCULPTURE That which is created by a process of building up or combining materials.

ADZE A woodcarving tool with both chiselling blade and axlike handle.

AERIAL PERSPECTIVE The illusion—and illusionary device—that forms seen at a great distance are lower in VALUE contrast and less sharply defined than objects close to the viewer.

AERIAL VIEW A downward perspective on an image.

AESTHETIC Pertaining to a sense of the beautiful.

AESTHETIC DISTANCE The spatial relationship between the viewer and a work of art.

AESTHETICS Theories of what is beautiful.

AIRBRUSH A tool used for blowing a fine spray of paint onto a surface, to allow smooth gradations of VALUES and HUES.

ALLA PRIMA See DIRECT PAINTING.

ANALOGOUS COLORS Those lying near each other on the COLOR WHEEL, combined in a color scheme.

ANNEAL To heat metal to make it more malleable, to counteract the hardening typical as metal is worked.

ANTIQUE GLASS Sheets of glass that have been handblown as a cylinder, cut, and heated to flatten it; often characterized by bubbles and warps.

APPLIED ARTS Disciplines in which functional objects are created.

APSE In church architecture, the semi-circular end of the building.

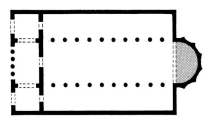

AQUATINT An INTAGLIO printmaking technique, producing grainy tones rather than lines, that uses acid to penetrate areas of a metal plate that are covered by porous powdered resin.

ARCH A curving or pointed structural device supporting an opening, doorway, or bridge.

ARCHAIC PERIOD In Greek arts, the 700 to 480 BC age during which interest in depicting the natural human body flourished.

ARMATURE An inner skeleton that supports a sculpture made of some malleable material.

ART BRUT "Raw art," Jean Dubuffet's term for OUTSIDER ART.

ARTISAN A person who is skilled at a certain CRAFT.

ASSEMBLAGE A combination of varying materials to create a three-dimensional work of art.

ASYMMETRICAL BALANCE Distribution of dissimilar visual weights in such a way that those on either side seem to offset each other, also called *informal balance*, in contrast to SYMMETRICAL or FORMAL balance.

ATMOSPHERIC PERSPECTIVE See AERIAL PERSPECTIVE.

AXIS An imaginary straight line passing centrally and/or longitudinally through a figure, form, or composition.

B

BALANCE The distribution of apparent visual weights through a composition. See ASYMMETRICAL BALANCE

BALLOON FRAME CONSTRUCTION Framing for a building in which relatively small pieces of wood are nailed together rather than heavy timbers connected by joinery.

BAROQUE Seventeenth-century artistic styles in Europe, characterized by swirling composition, sensuality, emotionality, and exuberant sculptural and architectural ornamentation.

BARREL VAULT A ceiling in the form of an unbroken tunnel.

BAS RELIEF See LOW RELIEF.

BEARING WALL CONSTRUCTION A support system in which the weight of ceiling and roof is borne by the entirety of the walls.

BINDER The material used in paint and some drawing MEDIA to bind the particles of PIGMENT together and enable them to stick to the SUPPORT.

BITMAP A matrix of pixels (dots in the computer's memory) of which an image may be composed in computer graphics.

BLIND EMBOSSING Pressing an uninked, cut plate of metal against paper to create a sculptured, uninked image.

BRACELET MODELING The use of oval lines disappearing over an edge to create the illusion of rounded form on a two-dimensional surface.

BUONO FRESCO "True fresco" in which paint is spread on wet plaster and becomes part of the wall surface itself as it dries.

BURIN A bevelled steel rod used for cutting lines in LINE ENGRAVINGS or WOOD ENGRAVINGS.

BURL A woody circular knob on the trunk of certain trees, prized for its whorled lines in woodworking.

BURNISH Rub to a shiny finish.

BUTTRESS An external supporting structure built against a wall to counteract the thrust of an arch or vault. See FLYING BUTTRESS.

BYZANTINE Referring to art of the Byzantine period in the eastern half of the Roman Empire, from AD 330 to the mid-fifteenth century. This art was primarily religious and characterized by STYLIZED elongated human forms and rich ornamentation.

C

CALLIGRAPHY The art of fine writing.

CAMERA OBSCURA A dark chamber in which the image of an object enters through a lens or small opening and is focused on a facing wall.

CANTILEVER A projection from a building or sculpture which is supported, anchored, or balanced at only one end.

CAPITAL The head of a column which bears the weight of the structure above.

CARTOON A full-sized drawing for a two-dimensional work, such as a FRESCO, which is transferred to the SUPPORT at the preparatory stage.

CASTING The creation of a three-dimensional form by pouring into prepared molds a molten or liquid material that will later harden.

CERAMICS The art of making objects of clay and FIRING them in a KILN.

CHALK Naturally deposited calcium carbonate, ground to a powder and reconstituted with a BINDER for use as a drawing MEDIUM.

CHARCOAL Charred vine or wood used in sticks as a soft drawing MEDIUM.

CHIAROSCURO The depiction in two-dimensional art of the effects of light and shadow, highly developed in RENAISSANCE paintings as a means of rendering the solidity of bodies.

CHROMA See SATURATION.

CINEMATOGRAPHY The artistic and technical skills involved in creating motion pictures.

CIRE PERDUE See LOST-WAX.

CLASSICAL The art and culture of ancient Greece and Rome.

CLASSICAL PERIOD Greek art from c. 500 to 323 BC, characterized by serene balance, harmony, idealized beauty, and lack of extraneous detail.

CLASSICISM Movements, periods, and impulses in Western art that prized qualities of harmony and formal restraint and claimed direct inspiration from CLASSICAL models. Traditionally contrasted with ROMANTICISM.

CLOSED FORM In sculpture, an unbroken volume with no projections or VOIDS.

COFFER A recessed panel, often repeated as a pattern, in a ceiling or vault.

COIL BUILDING A method of building a form of clay by rolling it into long ropes which are coiled in a spiraling pattern to raise the sides of the piece.

COLD COLOR (or "cool color") A hue traditionally thought to suggest low temperature and peacefulness, chiefly blues and greens.

COLLAGE A two-dimensional technique in which materials are glued to a flat surface.

COLOR WHEEL Relationships among HUES expressed in a circular two-dimensional model.

COMPLEMENTARY HUES Colors lying opposite each other on a COLOR WHEEL.

COMPOSITIONAL LINE A line that leads the eye through a work, unifying figures or parts of figures.

COMPRESSIVE STRENGTH In architecture, the amount of downward pressure a structural material can withstand without breaking.

COMPUTER GRAPHICS Various techniques of creating two-dimensional artworks by computer.

CONCEPTUAL ART Art which deals with ideas and experience rather than permanent form.

CONTÉ CRAYON A fine-textured non-greasy stick of powdered graphite and clay with red ochre, soot, or blackstone added for color, used as a drawing tool.

CONTENT The subject matter of a work of art and the emotions, ideas, symbols, stories, or spiritual connotations it suggests. Traditionally contrasted with FORM.

CONTOUR The outer edge of a three-dimensional form or the two-dimensional representation of this edge.

CONTRAPPOSTO In figurative works, counterpoised ASYMMETRICAL BALANCE between parts of the body, with most of the weight on one leg and an S-curve in the torso, first used by CLASSICAL Greek sculptors.

Graphite

Conté

Computer printer

Brush and ink

Pen and ink

CONTRAST Abrupt change, as when opposites are juxtaposed.

CONTROL To determine how an area will be seen or experienced.

COOL COLORS Those from the blue and green side of the COLOR WHEEL, thought to convey a feeling of coldness.

CORINTHIAN In classical Greek architecture, the lightest and most ornate order, with the appearance of outward-curling acanthus leaves on the capital.

CRAFTS Disciplines in which functional objects are made by hand.

CROP To delete unwanted peripheral parts of a design.

CROSS-HATCHING Crossed parallel lines used to create the illusion of form on a two-dimensional surface, by suggesting shadows and rounding in space.

CUBISM An early twentieth-century art movement dominated by Picasso and Braque, distinguished by its experiments with analyzing forms into planes seen from many sides at once and by liberation of art from representational depictions.

D

DADA An anti-rational, anti-AESTHETIC art movement begun in 1916.

DAGUERROTYPE An early photographic process invented by Louis Daguerre.

DECORATIVE LINE Line that embellishes a surface.

DEFENSIVE GRID Our ability to screen out unnecessary stimuli.

DESCRIPTIVE LINE Line that tells the physical nature of an object.

DIPTYCH A work consisting of two panels side by side, traditionally hinged to be opened and closed.

DIRECTIONAL Telling the eye which way to look.

DIRECT PAINTING Application of paint directly to a SUPPORT without UNDERLAYERS, in contrast with INDIRECT PAINTING. Also called *alla prima*.

DIVISIONISM See POINTILLISM.

DOME A hemispherical vault over a room or building.

DORIC In classical Greek architecture, the simplest order, with a heavy, fluted column, a dish-shaped capital, and no base.

DRY MEDIA A means of drawing such as graphite pencil, charcoal, pastel, conté crayon, or computer printer ribbon, in which the base that carries the PIGMENTS is not fluid. As shown in the drawing, each of these media creates a different line quality.

DRYPOINT An INTAGLIO printmaking technique, often used in combination with ETCHING, in which lines are scratched directly into the metal plate with a sharp-pointed tool.

DUCTILITY The capacity for being drawn out into wires or hammered into sheets, a varying property of metals. Gold and copper are noted for their especially high ductility.

DYNAMIC FORM A mass that appears to be in motion.

E

EARTHENWARE CERAMICS made from porous, coarse-textured clays such as terracotta.

EARTHWORK A large-scale sculpture in which the surface of the earth is the MEDIUM.

ECONOMY Use of as few means as possible to achieve a desired visual result.

EDGE A boundary where two areas treated differently meet.

ELEMENTS OF DESIGN The basic components of the visual arts: line, shape or form, space, texture, lighting, color, and perhaps time.

EMPHASIS Predominance of one area or element in a composition.

ENAMEL A colored glassy coating heat-fused to metal.

ENCAUSTIC A painting technique in which PIGMENT is mixed with a BINDER of hot wax.

ENGRAVING An INTAGLIO printmaking technique in which lines are cut on a metal or wood printing surface with a sharp tool.

ENTABLATURE The horizontal member atop a column, supporting what lies above.

ENTASIS A slightly convex curve given to the shaft of a column to correct the illusion of concavity produced by a perfectly straight shaft.

ENVIRONMENTAL DESIGN The art of manipulating outdoor areas for practical and aesthetic purposes, from landscaping to relationships among buildings in urban settings.

ERGONOMICS The study of the mechanics and proportions of the human body, with the aim of designing products with which the body can interact efficiently and comfortably.

ETCHING An INTAGLIO printmaking technique in which lines are produced by scratching away a protective covering of wax on a copper plate, which is then bathed in acid that bites channels where the metal has been exposed.

EXPRESSIONISM An art movement particularly strong in Germany prior to World War I, in which the artist reports inner feelings rather than outer realities.

EXPRESSIVE Giving form to emotions.

EXTERIOR CONTOUR The outside form of a three-dimensional piece.

EYE LEVEL LINE In LINEAR PERSPECTIVE drawings, the horizon line.

EYELINE The implied line along which the eyes of a human figure in a work of art seem to be looking.

F

FAÇADE The front or principal elevation of a building.

FANTASY Imagery existing only in the imagination.

FAT Referring to a painting medium, such as oil, that can be piled up in thick gobs and that dries slowly.

FAUVISM An art movement of the first decade of the twentieth century, using color boldly to express the inner qualities rather than superficial appearance of things.

FAX Technology by which a facsimile of text or line art is transferred electronically from one location to another via telephone connections.

FIGURATIVE Referring to artworks based on images of identifiable objects.

FIGURE-GROUND RELATIONSHIP In two-dimensional art, seeing images as having been applied over a background.

FIGURE-GROUND REVERSAL A two-dimensional work in which it is difficult to discern which is figure and which is ground, because they are visually interchangeable.

FINE ARTS The nonfunctional art disciplines, such as painting and sculpture.

FIRE To heat CERAMICS to make them durable.

FLYING BUTTRESS A BUTTRESS in the form of strut or segmented arch that transfers thrust to an outer support.

FOCAL PLANE SHUTTER A common type of camera in which there is a double curtain of shutters close to the film; when a flash is used, the film must be exposed at a relatively slow speed because the double shutters take some time to open and close.

FOCAL POINT The area of a composition to which the viewer's eye is most compellingly drawn.

FOLK ART Works created by aesthetically untrained artists working somewhat within a community tradition.

FORCED PERSPECTIVE The exaggerated illusion of deep space, often employed in setmaking for theatrical performances.

FOREGROUND In two-dimensional work, the area of a composition that appears closest to the viewer.

FORESHORTENING Contraction of the length and adjustment of the contours of a figure perpendicular to the viewer. This is done to counteract the perceptual distortion of proportions of objects receding from the viewer into the distance.

FORGE To hammer heated metal over an anvil to shape it.

FORM 1. The mass or volume of a three-dimensional work or the illusion of volume in a two-dimensional work. 2. The physical aspects of a work, as opposed to its emotional and intellectual CONTENT.

FORMAL BALANCE See SYMMETRICAL BALANCE.

FOUND OBJECT An object that is presented as a work of art or a part of one, but which was not originally intended as art; also called *objet trouvé*.

FRACTAL GEOMETRY Mathematical modeling of natural forms, often used in computer graphics.

FRAME CONSTRUCTION Building systems in which spaced horizontal and vertical members are interlocked to form a solid skeleton to which an outer skin is added.

FRESCO A wall painting technique in which PIGMENT in a water base is applied directly to fresh, still-damp plaster, into which it is absorbed.

FRONTAL Referring to sculpture designed to be seen only from the front.

FULL ROUND Referring to sculpture that exists in fully three-dimensional space, unattached to a backing.

FULL TONAL RANGE A term used chiefly in black and white photography to signify representation of all values in a single picture, from black through mid-grays to white.

FUTURISM A movement initiated in Italy in 1909 to sweep aside all artistic conventions and capture the qualities of modern industrialized life.

G

GEODESIC DOME A structural framework of small interlocking polygons forming a DOME.

GEOMETRIC Having mathematically regular contours, such as a circle, square, or rectangle.

GEOMETRIC PERIOD A stylistic phase of ancient Greek art between c. 800 and 700 BC characterized by abstraction of forms to geometric elements.

GESSO A fluid white coating of plaster, CHALK and SIZE used to prepare a painting surface so that it will accept paint readily and allow controlled brushstrokes.

GESTURAL A style of painting or drawing in which the artist's arm and hand movements are apparent in the finished piece.

GLAZE 1. A thinned, transparent layer of oil paint. 2. A mineral solution, applied to a CERAMIC piece, that vitrifies to a glossy and water-resistant coating when FIRED.

GOLDEN RECTANGLE A rectangle the lengths of whose sides correspond to GOLDEN SECTION proportions. Much used as a compositional and format-establishing device in Renaissance painting.

GOLDEN SECTION or MEAN In ancient Greek AESTHETIC theory, an ideal proportional relationship between parts, whereby the smaller is to the greater as the greater is to the whole. This ratio cannot be worked out mathematically, but is approximately 5:8, or 1:1.618.

GOTHIC A style of European art from the mid-twelfth to mid-fifteenth centuries, especially noted for its soaring vertical cathedrals, three-dimensional sculptures, and the sense of depth and emotion in two-dimensional paintings.

GOUACHE An opaque water-soluble painting MEDIUM bound with gum arabic, the lighter tones being mixed with Chinese white watercolor.

GRAPHIC DESIGN The arts involved in creating two-dimensional images for commercial purposes. Graphic designers often work with type as well as illustrations; the printed surface may range from paper to fabrics.

GRAPHITE A soft carbon used in drawing pencils.

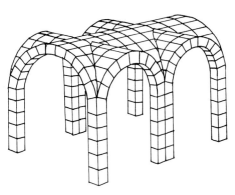

GROIN VAULT In architecture, two intersecting, identical BARREL VAULTS.

GROUND 1. See FIGURE-GROUND RELATIONSHIP. 2. The surface on which a two-dimensional work is developed.

H

HARD-EDGED A term used chiefly in referring to twentieth-century paintings in which clean, sharp edges are formed where areas of different colors meet.

HATCHING Fine, short parallel lines used in two-dimensional arts to create the effect of shadow on three-dimensional forms. See also CROSS-HATCHING.

HELLENISTIC PERIOD Greek art from 323 to 100 BC or later, characterized by greater dynamism, emotional drama, and naturalism than that of the CLASSICAL PERIOD.

HIGH CONTRAST Polarization of the normal ranges of VALUES towards the extremes of light and dark.

HIGHLIGHT A spot of highest (lightest) VALUE in a work—usually white.

HIGH RELIEF Sculpture in which figures emerge three-dimensionally from a flat surface to half or more than half of their natural depth.

HIGH RENAISSANCE The years between roughly 1490 and 1520 in Italy, productive of some of the world's greatest art, informed by but not bound to CLASSICAL traditions.

HIGH-TECH REVIVAL A late twentieth-century return to machine-like architectural structures.

HUE The property of a color that enables us to locate its position in the SPECTRUM or on the COLOR WHEEL and thus label it as "red" or "blue," etc. This is determined by its wavelength.

I

ICON A two-dimensional depiction of a sacred figure or figures, thought to work miracles, particularly characteristic of BYZANTINE sacred art.

ICONOGRAPHY Visual conventions and symbols used to portray ideas in a work of art.

IDEALIZED Referring to art in which REPRESENTATIONAL images conform more closely to ideal AESTHETIC standards than to real life.

IMPASTO Thickly applied paint—mainly oil or acrylic.

IMPLIED A line, shape, or form that is suggested to the eye but not actually present.

IMPRESSIONISM An art movement originating in late nineteenth-century France, in which the artist attempts to capture what the eye actually sees before the brain interprets the image. This may be a surface broken by fragmented lights or an ephemeral moment in time.

INDIRECT PAINTING Using a series of layers to produce a desired final effect, in contrast with DIRECT PAINTING.

INDUSTRIAL DESIGN The art of creating functional products that also have AESTHETIC appeal.

INSTALLATION PIECE A three-dimensional designed environment set up (often temporarily) as a work of art.

INTAGLIO A category of printmaking processes in which the desired image is cut into the surface of a plate, which is inked and then wiped, leaving ink only in the cut channels. Dampened paper is forced against the plate, picking up the ink.

INTENSITY See SATURATION.

INTERIOR CONTOUR The form of the inside of a three-dimensional piece.

INTERIOR DESIGN The art of decorating the insides of human environments.

INTERNATIONAL STYLE An architectural style, originating in Europe after World War I, characterized by rectangular forms, white walls, large windows, flat roofs, and the absence of ornament.

INTERPRETIVE COLOR Color chosen to represent an emotional atmosphere or idea rather than the visual reality of an object.

INTERPRETIVE VALUES Lights and darks used to convey an atmosphere or idea rather than a literal description of the actual VALUES of a real scene.

INTONACO In FRESCO technique, the final layer of plaster, to which paint is applied during the course of the day.

INVESTMENT A heat-resistant outer mold packed around a LOST-WAX CASTING.

INVESTMENT

IONIC In classical Greek architecture, an order characterized by fluted columns topped by scroll-like spirals.

K

KEYSTONE The central wedge-shaped piece of masonry in an arch, added last to lock the structure in place.

KILN A special oven or furnace for FIRING CERAMICS.

KINETIC SCULPTURE Three-dimensional work that moves.

L

LAMINATE To unite flat layers of the same or different materials, such as bonded plates of wood, paper, or plastics.

LATE GOTHIC Work produced in Europe toward the end of the GOTHIC period, characterized by increasing NATURALISM and expressiveness and by the fine details and luminosity of oil paintings.

LEAD CRYSTAL High-quality, exceptionally clear and colorless glass in which a large percentage of the formula is lead oxide.

LEAN Referring to a MEDIUM that forms a uniform thin film, such as TEMPERA, in contrast to a FAT medium.

LIGHT WELL A shaft that allows daylight to enter the interior of a building, or the optical illusion of a visual pool of light created by contrast with surrounding darker areas.

LIMITED PALETTE Highly selective use of only a few colors.

LINE ENGRAVING A PRINT made by cutting lines into a plate of metal, forcing ink into them, and printing the cut lines.

LINEAR PERSPECTIVE The illusion of deep space in a two-dimensional work through convergence of lines perpendicular to the PICTURE PLANE toward a VANISHING POINT in the distance.

LINOCUT A PRINT made by gouging away areas of a linoleum block that are not to be inked and printed.

LIQUID MEDIUM A fluid base used to carry pigments for painting or drawing, such as ink, oil, or acrylic emulsion.

LITHOGRAPHY A printmaking technique in which a flat stone or metal or plastic plate is drawn on with a greasy substance that retains ink when the wettened plate is inked for printing.

wettened stone
greasy image
paper

LOCAL COLOR The color usually associated with an object, as seen from nearby under normal daylight without shadows or reflections.

LOCAL VALUE The degree of light or darkness seen on an actual surface.

LOGO A graphic or typographic image that identifies a business or group.

LOST-WAX A CASTING process in which wax is used to coat the insides of molds and then melted away when the molds are assembled, leaving an empty space into which molten metal is poured; also called *cire perdue*.

LOW RELIEF Sculpture in which figures exist on almost the same PLANE as the background.

M

MALLEABILITY The capacity for being shaped by physical pressure, as in hand modeling or hammering.

MANNERISM An artistic style in Italy from approximately 1525 to 1600 in which artists developed a more subjective, emotional, theatrical approach than in the preceding HIGH RENAISSANCE period.

MAQUETTE A small model used for planning and guiding the creation of a sculpture.

MEDIUM (plural *media*) 1. The material or means of expression with which the artist works. 2. The liquid solvent, such as water or linseed oil, in which PIGMENT is suspended to make paint fluid and workable.

MEZZOTINT An INTAGLIO printmaking technique in which an overall burr is raised on the surface of the metal plate and then smoothed in places, creating various tones and textures.

MINIATURE A work of art done on a much smaller scale than the object being represented.

MIXED MEDIA Combined use of several different techniques—such as drawing, painting, and printmaking—in a single work of art.

MOBILE See KINETIC ART.

MODELING 1. In two-dimensional art, the depiction of three-dimensional form, usually through indications of light and shadow. 2. In sculpture, creating a form by manipulating a soft MEDIUM, such as clay.

MODULAR CONSTRUCTION A building system developed from preconstructed and perhaps preassembled parts.

MONOCHROMATIC Having a color scheme based on VALUES of a single HUE, perhaps with accents of another color or neutral colors.

MONOTYPE A printmaking process in which an image is painted directly onto a sheet of metal or glass and then transferred onto paper. The process can be repeated with some repainting of the plate, but this is basically a means of creating relatively few prints of an image.

MONTAGE 1. A composite two-dimensional image produced by assembling and pasting down cut or torn sections of photographs or drawings. 2. In cinematography, the composition of a sequence of short shots of related meaning.

MOSAIC Two-dimensional art created by attaching small pieces (TESSERAE) of ceramic tile, glass, pebbles, marble, or wood to a surface.

MOTIF A recurring pattern in a work of art.

MURAL A painting, usually large, done on a wall.

N

NAIVE ART That which is created by artists with no formal training.

NARRATIVE Referring to art with a storytelling quality.

NATURALISM A style of art that seeks to represent accurately and faithfully the actual appearance of things.

NAVE In church architecture, the central hall.

NEGATIVE SPACE Unfilled areas in the design.

NEO-CLASSICISM The late eighteenth- and early nineteenth-century return to CLASSICAL AESTHETICS in Europe.

NEO-EXPRESSIONISM A contemporary art movement in which painting is used to express the artist's feelings, projected as distorted images from the exterior world.

NONOBJECTIVE Referring to art that does not represent any known object.

NONREPRESENTATIONAL See NONOBJECTIVE.

NORTHERN RENAISSANCE Referring to German art from c. 1500, when the individualistic and rational aspects of the Italian RENAISSANCE were adopted and adapted to Northern styles.

O

OFFSET LITHOGRAPHY A commercial printmaking process in which the inking of illustrations and text is offset from the plate onto a rubber-covered cylinder that transfers them to paper so that the printed image reads the same way as the original, rather than being reversed.

ONE-POINT PERSPECTIVE In LINEAR PERSPECTIVE, the representation of parallel lines converging to a single point on the horizon, to create the illusion of deep space.

OP ART Paintings that produce visual phenomena in the perception of the viewer that do not actually exist on the canvas.

OPALESCENT GLASS Opaque glass used for art objects, with color oxides swirled through it as it is poured in a molten state into sheets.

OPEN FORM In sculpture, a volume broken by projections and/or VOIDS.

OPEN PALETTE Use of an unlimited range of colors in juxtaposition.

OPTICAL COLOR MIXTURES Those in which colors are mixed in the viewer's perception rather than in physically mixed pigments.

OUTSIDER ART Unique works created by untrained people who do not fit into any aesthetic tradition.

OVERLAPPING Hiding of part of one figure by another, a device used to suggest depth in space.

OVERPAINTING The final layers in an INDIRECT painting, such as GLAZES or SCUMBLING.

P

PASTEL A chalky stick of powdered PIGMENT, calcium carbonate filler, and BINDER, used as a drawing MEDIUM.

PATTERN An all-over design created by repetition of figures.

PEDIMENT In classical architecture, the triangular area at the front of a building; also a similarly-shaped area used decoratively over a window, door, or PORTICO.

PERFORMANCE ART Art in which the medium of expression is the artist's own body and its coverings.

PERSPECTIVE See AERIAL PERSPECTIVE; LINEAR PERSPECTIVE.

PHOTOCOPY A photographic reproduction of graphic material, in which a negative image is quickly taken and electronically transferred to paper as a positive.

PHOTOGRAM One of the precursors of modern photography, an image made by laying objects on light-sensitive paper and exposing it to sunlight, leaving the masked areas white while the rest of the paper turns dark.

PHOTOREALISM Art that is as REPRESENTATIONAL as a photograph, but created by other media; also called *super-realism*.

PICTURE PLANE The flat surface of a two-dimensional work, often conceived as a transparent window into three-dimensional space. See LINEAR PERSPECTIVE.

PIGMENT Powdered colored material used to give HUES to paints and inks.

PIXEL In computer graphics, one of many tiny points on the computer screen determined by intersections of *x* and *y* axis.

PLANE A flat surface.

PLANISH To hammer metal smooth.

PLANOGRAPHIC Referring to a printmaking technique in which images are transferred from a flat surface, as in LITHOGRAPHY.

POINTED ARCH An arch formed by the intersection of two curves of greater radius than that of the opening; an innovation introduced in GOTHIC architecture.

POINT OF VIEW The place from which a two-dimensional scene is reported.

POINTILLISM A technique of painting using dots of PRIMARY and SECONDARY HUES in close juxtaposition to make them mix in the viewer's perception. Also called *Divisionism*.

POP ART A movement beginning in the mid-twentieth century that uses objects and images from the commercial culture.

PORCELAIN CERAMICS made from the finest clays, which produce an extremely smooth, glossy surface when fired.

PORTICO A covered colonnade at the end of a building in classical architecture.

POSITIVE SPACE Filled areas in a design, or those intended to be seen as figures.

POST AND LINTEL An architectural construction system in which upright members support horizontal members, or lintels.

POST-IMPRESSIONISM Transcendence of the perceived limitations of IMPRESSIONISM by mid-nineteenth and early twentieth-century artists such as Cézanne, Seurat, Gauguin, and van Gogh.

POST-MODERNISM An architectural movement of the 1970s and 80s, countering the glass boxes of the INTERNATIONAL STYLE with more historically eclectic forms.

POST-PAINTERLY ABSTRACTION Various mid-twentieth-century styles of creating NONOBJECTIVE paintings that evoke certain responses in viewers, with the hand of the artist less obvious than in ABSTRACT EXPRESSIONISM.

PRIMARY COLORS The set of three basic HUES from which all other hues can be mixed; in REFRACTED colors, red, green, and blue; in REFLECTED colors, red, yellow, and blue.

PRIMARY CONTOURS The outer edges of a FORM.

PRINCIPLES OF DESIGN The organizing factors in the visual arts, including repetition, variety, CONTRAST, RHYTHM, BALANCE, compositional UNITY, EMPHASIS, ECONOMY, PROPORTION, and relationship to the environment.

PRINT An image made by transferring ink from a worked

surface onto a surface, usually paper, and usually in multiples.

PROPORTION Size relationships of parts to each other and to the whole.

PROSCENIUM 1. The part of a stage for theatrical production that projects in front of the curtain. 2. In ancient Greek theatre, the whole of the stage.

PROSCENIUM ARCH The arch that frames the stage, hiding its mechanics.

PUTTI (singular *putto*) Chubby nude male babies often depicted in Italian art from the fifteenth century onward.

Q

QUILTING Making blankets or other covers of two layers of fabric stitched together with padding in between, in which both the pieces of fabric and the pattern of stitching offer vehicles for aesthetic creativity.

R

RAISE In metalworking, to hammer a flat sheet over a stake to bring up the sides of a vessel and work them inward.

READ To see and assign meaning to aspects of a design.

REALISM The attempt in art to capture the appearance of life as it is, as opposed to STYLIZED or ROMANTICIZED portrayals. In mid-nineteenth-century France, the artistic movement of this name concentrated on subjects from everyday, and often working-class, life.

REDUCTION PRINT A color relief print in which portions of a single block are cut away in stages, with each stage overprinted in another color, rather than creating a series of registered blocks for the various colors.

REFLECTED COLORS HUES seen when light is reflected from a PIGMENTED surface.

REFRACTED COLORS HUES seen in light.

REINFORCED CONCRETE Concrete into which metal mesh or rods have been embedded so that the two interact to strengthen the structure.

RELIEFS 1. A sculptured work in which an image is developed outward

or inward from a two-dimensional surface. 2. A printmaking category in which areas that are not to be inked are carved away, leaving the image raised on the block.

RENAISSANCE A movement beginning in fifteenth-century Italy to recapture the harmony, symmetry, and rationality of CLASSICAL works, with an elaboration of LINEAR PERSPECTIVE.

REPOUSSÉ The working of a sheet of metal from the back to create designs in relief on the front.

REPRESENTATIONAL Referring to artworks that aim to present likenesses of known objects.

RESIST The waxy, acid-resistant substance used to coat the metal plate used for ETCHING, into which the lines of the image are drawn.

RETROUSSAGE The process of wiping ink from the surface of INTAGLIO plates, leaving ink only in the grooves of ETCHED or ENGRAVED lines, allowing white areas and sharp lines in the print.

RHYTHM The visual equivalent of notes and pauses in music, created by repetition, variety, and spacing in a design.

RIBBED VAULT In architecture, a masonry ceiling in which arched diagonal ribs form a framework that is filled with lighter stone.

ROCOCO The late BAROQUE period, particularly in France, southern Germany, and Austria, characterized by extremely ornate, curvilinear forms in architectural decoration and delicacy and looseness in painting.

ROMANESQUE A style of European art from about the eleventh century to the beginning of the GOTHIC period, most notable for its architecture of rounded arches, thick walls and columns, and stone relief carvings.

ROMANTICISM The tendency to emphasize emotion and imagination rather than logic, occurring at many

times in the history of Western art, including the first half of the nineteenth century. Traditionally contrasted with CLASSICISM.

ROUND ARCH An arch formed by a semicircle; an innovation introduced by Roman architecture and much used in ROMANESQUE architecture.

S

SANS SERIF Referring to a TYPEFACE that has no fine lines finishing the major strokes.

SATURATION The relative brightness or dullness of a color, also called *chroma* or *intensity*.

SCALE Relative size.

SCREEN PRINT See SILK SCREEN.

SCUMBLING In oil painting, putting one layer of opaque paint on top of another in such a way that the UNDERLAYERS partially show through.

SECONDARY COLORS HUES produced by combining two PRIMARY hues.

SECONDARY CONTOURS FORMS developed across the surface of a larger form.

SERIF In TYPOGRAPHY, the fine lines used to finish the heavier main strokes of letters; also used of a TYPEFACE that has this feature.

SERIGRAPH See SILK SCREEN.

SFUMATO Softly graded tones in an oil painting, giving a hazy atmospheric effect, highly developed in the work of Leonardo da Vinci.

SHADING Darkening of an area in a two-dimensional work to suggest curving of a three-dimensional form away from a light source.

SHAPE A flat, defined area.

SILK SCREEN A printmaking process in which ink is pressed through a fine screen in areas that are not masked by a stencil or other material; also called *serigraph*.
(see top of next page)

SILK SCREEN

SILVERPOINT A drawing MEDIUM in which a finely-pointed rod of silver encased in a holder is used to make marks on a slightly abrasive surface; the minute deposit of metal darkens by oxidation.

SIMULATED TEXTURE The illusion that an image would feel a certain way if touched, in contrast to the reality of its actual texture.

SIZE or SIZING A coating of glue or resin to make a surface such as canvas less porous so that paint will not sink into it.

SKENE In early Greek theatres, the building at the back of the performance area from which actors entered and exited, also used as a changing room and as a backdrop for the action.

SLAB BUILDING The process of building a form of clay by attaching flat shapes to each other.

SLIP A mixture of clay and water.

SOFT-EDGED In two-dimensional work, blending of hues where they meet, so that no hard line forms a boundary between them.

SPACE The area occupied, activated, or suggested by a work of art.

SPECTRUM See VISIBLE SPECTRUM.

STAINED GLASS Art glass colored with chemical colorants heated in a kiln with the glass base.

STATE One of the stages of an ETCHING, if printed separately.

STATIC FORM A mass that appears inert.

STILL-LIFE A two-dimensional representation of a group of inanimate objects such as fruit, flowers, and vessels.

STONEWARE CERAMICS made from clays that become very hard when FIRED at high temperatures.

STYLIZED Referring to distortion of REPRESENTATIONAL images in accordance with certain artistic conventions or to emphasize certain design qualities.

STYLOBATE In classical Greek architecture, the flat base on which a series of columns rests.

SUBTRACTIVE COLOR MIXING The combination of REFLECTED colors.

SUBTRACTIVE SCULPTURE That which is created by the process of carving away material to reveal the desired FORM.

SUPER-REALISM See PHOTOREALISM.

SUPPORT The solid material base on which a two-dimensional work of art is executed, such as canvas or panel in the case of a painting.

SURREALISM Art based on dreamlike images from the subconscious, appearing as a recognized movement beginning in the 1920s.

SYMMETRICAL BALANCE Distribution of equal forces around a central point or AXIS, also called *formal balance.*

SYNERGISTIC COLOR MIXING A system of OPTICAL COLOR MIXING in which new HUES are created in the spaces between colored figures.

SYNTHETIC MEDIA Liquid media in which industrially-created chemicals, such as acrylic emulsion, are used to carry the pigments.

T

TAPESTRY A heavy, handwoven textile with pictures woven into the surface of the fabric, usually used as a wall hanging.

TEMPERA A painting MEDIUM in which PIGMENTS are mixed in water with a glutinous material such as egg yolk, usually yielding a fast-drying, matte finish that cannot be blended.

TENSILE STRENGTH A measure of the ability of a material to be stretched without breaking.

TERTIARY COLORS HUES that are a mixture of a PRIMARY and a SECONDARY HUE lying next to each other on the COLOR WHEEL.

TESSERAE (singular *tessera*) The small cubes of colored glass, CERAMIC, or stone used in MOSAICS.

TEXTURE The surface quality of a form or the illusion that it would feel a certain way if touched.

THREE-DIMENSIONAL Having length, height, and width.

THREE-POINT PERSPECTIVE Two-dimensional spatial representations of three-dimensional forms showing their height as well as their width and depth, as seen from above or below.

THROWING See WHEEL THROWING.

TOKONOMA In a traditional Japanese home, an alcove devoted to contemplation of a single scroll painting, perhaps accompanied by a flower arrangement.

TONAL RANGE The degree to which a work (particularly a photograph) approaches the full range of VALUES from black through grays to white.

TRANSITION Abrupt or gradual change from one portion of a design to another.

TRIAD COLOR SCHEME The use of three HUES lying at equal distances from each other on the COLOR WHEEL.

TROMPE L'OEIL Work that "deceives the eye" into believing it sees something other than the reality of a surface, such as architectural forms on what is actually a flat wall or ceiling.

TRUSS In architecture, a framework of wood or metal beams, usually based on triangles, used to support a roof or bridge.

TWO-DIMENSIONAL Existing on a flat surface with only length and height but no depth in space.

TWO-POINT PERSPECTIVE In linear perspective drawings, the representation of a three-dimensional form viewed from an angle, so that the lines formed by its horizontal edges will appear to diminish to two different VANISHING POINTS on the horizon.

TYPEFACE One of many styles of letter design, in which the entire alphabet is rendered with certain repeating characteristics.

TYPOGRAPHY The art of designing, sizing, and combining letterforms on a printed page.

U

UKIYO-E Japanese representations of everyday life, usually WOODCUT PRINTS but also paintings.

UNDERPAINTING The initial layers of paint in INDIRECT PAINTING.

UNITY Visual coherence in a work of art; also used sometimes to refer to repetition of similar motifs in a design, in contrast to VARIETY.

UNSIZED Referring to canvas that has not been treated with a glaze or filler, leaving it porous to paint.

V

VALUE Degree of dark or light.

VALUE SCALE A graded representation of differences in VALUE.

VANISHING POINT The seen or implied spot in the distance where all lines perpendicular to the PICTURE PLANE would appear to meet if extended. In real life, a vanishing point can only be seen where one can look across a great distance; in art, if lines appear to converge rapidly to a vanishing point there will be an impression of great depth.

VARIETY Change rather than sameness in design elements.

VELLUM A fine parchment prepared from the skin of a calf, kid, or lamb.

VENEER A thin surface layer, such as a fine wood placed over other woods.

VIDEO A process of creating moving pictures by laying down images and sound as tracks on magnetic tape.

VIDEO RASTER GRAPHICS Computer-generated and -manipulated VIDEO images.

VIRTUAL REALITY Computer graphics in which the operator interacts with a scene as if existing within it.

VISIBLE SPECTRUM The color frequencies that humans can see; the distribution of colors produced when white light is dispersed, *e.g.* by a prism. There is a continuous change in wavelength from red, the longest wavelength, to violet, the shortest.

VISUAL WEIGHT The apparent heaviness of an area of design.

VOID In sculpture, a hole through a work.

VOUSSOIRS The wedge-shaped stones in an arch.

W

WALK-THROUGH Referring to large sculptures that the viewer can move through as well as around.

WARM COLORS Colors from the red and yellow side of the COLOR WHEEL, associated with heat.

WATERCOLOR A transparent water-soluble painting MEDIUM consisting of PIGMENTS bound with gum.

WHEEL-THROWING A method of creating forms of clay by centering a mass of clay on a circular slab and then pulling the sides up from it with the hands as this wheel is turned.

WOODCUT A PRINT made by carving away areas of a wood block and inking the remaining RELIEF surfaces.

WOOD ENGRAVING A PRINT made by cutting the end-grain of a piece of wood, capable of rendering finer lines than the lengthwise grain used for WOODCUTS.

WROUGHT IRON Iron that is shaped in a heated state with hand tools.

INDEX